The Story of Ancient History

THUCYDIDES

The Story of Ancient History

JAMES T. SHOTWELL

Columbia University Press
New York

The Story of Ancient History was published originally
as *The History of History, Volume I*.
Copyright © 1939 Columbia University Press, New York
Columbia Paperback Edition 1961
Manufactured in the United States of America

To
M., G., and H.

Preface

THE PRESENT volume is a belated product of a movement in the field of American historical criticism, which came of age in the decade preceding the World War, a movement toward the recasting of traditional perspectives in the light of original source materials. During the closing years of the nineteenth century scholars returning from Europe—or those trained under them—set about the task of remaking the teaching of history in our universities. The seminar method brought the student face to face with evidence, as libraries, filled with great collections of original documents, grew more and more adequate for historical research. The result was a profound change in the academic treatment of history. While the general public continued for a generation or so to enjoy what it had formerly enjoyed and gave up with reluctance cherished beliefs in the history of their own or other countries, universities and colleges vied with each other in the furtherance of what was known as the scientific method in history. Of this there were two outstanding evidences, the rewriting of college and high-school textbooks and the preparation of books of "Readings" of translated sections of original sources. Thus the study of history passed from a process of memorizing dates and events of little interest to the youthful student to the discipline of exercising caution in the examination of evidence and the exhilarating sense of direct contact with a living past.

Among the leaders in this historical renaissance in American education, none stood higher than Professor James Harvey Robinson. The outstanding difficulty for American students was the barrier of foreign languages, which only a select few regarded as anything more than a temporary acquisition of little use after the examinations in them were passed. As aids for the history classroom, therefore, Professor Robinson and his former colleagues, Professors Edward P. Cheyney and Dana Munro of the University of Pennsylvania, began the publication of a little series of cheap pamphlets entitled *Translations and Reprints from the Original Sources of European History*. For some years this miscellany held its own. Then Professor Robinson's college textbook on Western Europe opened a new era in history teaching, and along with it came his own and numerous other books of "Readings" in the sources, such as Professor Botsford and others had already compiled for ancient history.

It was in connection with this movement of the pre-War years that the author planned an extensive library of texts and studies, under the title *Records of Civilization: Sources and Studies*. The purpose of this collection was twofold: in the first place, to make accessible in English those sources of the history of Europe which are of prime importance for understanding the development of western civilization; in the second place, to indicate some of the more significant results of scholarship in the field covered. It was intended to supply, to those who could not read the documents in the original, the means for forming some idea of the problems of the historian. Arrangements had been completed for about twenty volumes, covering a considerable diversity of topics but bearing in one way or another upon the main purpose of the series, when with the entry of the United States into the War the Editor was called into Government service, which lasted through the Peace Conference. Work upon the series was therefore interrupted, with the result that only some seven volumes were published under his editorship. The series, however, was taken over by the Department of History of Columbia University under the editorship of Professor Austin P. Evans and now includes some forty volumes published or in preparation.

It was as an introduction to this source collection that most of the present volume was written. But, even in its first form as *An Introduction to the History of History* (published in 1922) it had already drifted far from its moorings. It was no longer a critical commentary to a book of extracts selected to give the reader an idea of what the ancient world thought about historians and what the historians thought about themselves. The commentary had grown into the body of the text, with only bibliographical references to the originals. Moreover it was no longer an introduction to mediaeval and modern historians, but an independent study of the origins and development of history in the ancient world. How this had come about was explained in the Preface to the *Introduction* in the following terms:

Nothing could have been farther from the original intention of the author than to write a history of antique historiography, which the book now in part resembles. But the absence of any satisfactory general survey covering the antique field led to enlargement in scope and critical comment until the work assumed the present form. It is freely recognized that the field covered belongs of right to the ancient historian, properly equipped not only with the classics and the languages of Western Asia but also with archaeology and its associated sciences. If any such had done the work, this volume would have remained the single chapter originally planned; so the classicist, who will undoubtedly detect in it the intrusion of an outsider, is at least partly to blame for the adventure, since it was the absence of a guide such as he might have offered which led to the preparation of this one.

However much of an adventure this is in itself, the circumstances under which the volume was made ready for the press have made it all the more perilous from the standpoint of scholarship. For it was prepared at odd moments, as occasion offered, in the midst of other work of an entirely different kind and involving heavy responsibilities. Part of it was written during European travel with only such books at hand as could be obtained in local libraries or could be carried along; part of it is drawn from fragments of old university lectures; and part was already prepared for a mere introduction to source selections. This will explain, if it does not excuse, some irregularities in treatment, and inadequacies in the bibliographical notes, as well as the use in most instances of available translations of extracts. Had there been any possibility of a separate and lengthy series of illustrative translations, as was originally planned, these extracts would not have appeared in the Introduction. Generally, however, a little examination will reveal something like a substitute for the bibliographies in the footnotes, or in a reference to some comprehensive manual which is the inevitable starting point for further work in any case.

For aid in the preparation of the volume in its original form the author is under lasting obligation to Professor Isabel McKenzie, formerly of Barnard College, now of the History Department of Hunter College, whose interest in the critical apparatus of the work has been extended to the present volume. In the preparation of the present text Robert E. Tschan, of Georgetown University, and J. W. Swain, Professor of Ancient History in the University of Illinois, have also co-operated, not only in the revision of the bibliographical references but also in checking the narrative with the output of recent scholarship. Professor Swain's contribution has been especially important. Throughout the volume the reader will find indications of various passages which have been added by him or substituted for those of the earlier text. The student of ancient history will undoubtedly regret that the plan of the present volume did not permit of further excursion into the field of scholarship for which he generously offered material. This volume, however, is not intended to replace the technical manuals which the research student of ancient historiography should use. Its purpose is to point out the way in which memory, poetry, and human interest fused into a lasting heritage for civilized man, passing from the vague beginnings of the primitive world into a disciplined criticism of the records of the past. The recasting and enlargement of the text has therefore been done not with the purpose of completing a survey of antique historiography, but with reference to the evolution of history in the centuries which followed—an evolution which reached its climax in the reconstruction of the past by the scholars of today.

JAMES T. SHOTWELL

Columbia University
  December 12, 1938

Contents

Part I: Introduction

I.	Definition and Scope of History	3
II.	The Interpretation of History	14
III.	Prehistory; Myth and Legend	36
IV.	Books and Writing	51
V.	The Measuring of Time	63
VI.	Egyptian Annals	74
VII.	Babylonian, Assyrian, and Persian Records	88

Part II: Jewish History

VIII.	The Old Testament as History	107
IX.	The Pentateuch	113
X.	The Remaining Historical Books of the Old Testament	124
XI.	The Formation of the Canon	136
XII.	Non-Biblical Literature; Josephus	142

Part III: Greek History

XIII.	From Homer to Herodotus	161
XIV.	Herodotus	177
XV.	Thucydides	193
XVI.	Rhetoric and Scholarship	214
XVII.	Polybius	230
XVIII.	Later Greek Historians	242

Part IV: Roman History

XIX.	History at Rome; Oratory and Poetry	255
XX.	Roman Annalists and Early Historians	270

Contents

XXI. Varro, Caesar, and Sallust 281
XXII. Livy 291
XXIII. Tacitus 301
XXIV. From Suetonius to Ammianus Marcellinus . . . 316

Part V: Christianity and History

XXV. The New Era 325
XXVI. Allegory and the Contribution of Origen . . . 336
XXVII. Chronology and Church History; Eusebius . . 347
XXVIII. The City of God 364
Index 381

Illustrations

Thucydides . . . . *Frontispiece*
Reproduced through the courtesy of the Earl of Leicester and the Oxford University Press

The Palermo Stone 78

The Story of the Deluge: Assyrian Clay Tablet (British Museum) 92
From Robert W. Rogers, translator and editor, "Cuneiform Parallels to the Old Testament"

Papyrus Rolls, Open for Reading and Closed (Showing Seals); Pen; Penholder with Inkwell 228
From Wilhelm Schubart, "Einführung in die Papyruskunde"

Part I
INTRODUCTION

CHAPTER I

Definition and Scope of History

UNTIL recently, history itself has lacked historians. There have been histories of almost everything else under the sun—of literature, philosophy, the arts and sciences, and, above all, of politics. But until the last few years—with the exception of a few works for students—the story of history has remained unwritten. Clio, though the oldest of the Muses, has been busy recording the past of others but has neglected her own, and apparently her readers have seldom inquired of her about it. For even yet the phrase "history of history" conveys but little meaning to most people's minds, seeming to suggest some superfluous academic problem for which a busy world should afford no time rather than what it really is, that part of the human story which one should master first if one would ever learn to judge the value of the rest.

The prime reason for this state of affairs is probably that which has just been hinted at. Clio was a Muse; history has generally been regarded as a branch of literature. Historians have been treated as masters of style or of creative imagination, to be ranked alongside poets or dramatists, rather than simply as historians, with an art and science of their own. Thucydides has been read for his Greek, Livy for his Latin. Carlyle ranks in book-lists with the word-painter Ruskin. Now and again historical criticisms of the "great masters" have appeared, and scholarly studies of limited fields. But so long as history could be viewed as primarily a part of literature its own history could not be written, for the recovery of the past is a science as well as an art.

The history of history, therefore, had to await the rise of scientific historical criticism before it attracted the attention of even historians themselves. That has meant, as a matter of course, that not many except the critics have been attracted by it. Masked under the unlovely title "Historiography," it has recently become a formal part of the discipline of historical seminars, but, with few exceptions, such manuals as there are have been mainly contributions to the apparatus of research. They have, therefore, lacked the allurements of style and often even of imaginative appeal which win readers for history, and few but the students have known of their existence.

And yet the history of history demands rather than invites attention. Art, science, and philosophy combined, history is the oldest and vastest of the interests of mankind. What was the past to Babylon or Rome? When and how was Time first discovered, and the shadowy past marked out by numbered years? What travelling Greeks first brought home that knowledge of the dim antiquities of Egypt and the East which made them critics of their own Homeric legends and so created history? What havoc was wrought in scientific inquiry by religious revelations and in revelations by scientific inquiry? By what miracle has the long-lost past been at last recovered in our own day, so that we are checking up Herodotus by his own antiquity, correcting the narrative of Livy or Tacitus by the very refuse deposited beneath the streets upon which they walked? This is more than romance or literature, though the romance is there to the full. For the history of history is the story of that deepening memory and scientific curiosity which is the measure of our social consciousness and of our intellectual life.

But we must first get our bearings, for the word "history" has two meanings.[1] It may mean either the record of events or events

---

[1] See Ernst Bernheim, *Lehrbuch der historischen Methode und der Geschichtsphilosophie* (6th ed., 1908), Chap. I. The German word *Geschichte*, meaning that which has happened (*was geschieht, was geschehen ist*), is even more misleading. R. Flint, *History of the Philosophy of History* (1894), page 5 called attention to the ambiguity of the term in English, but limits his distinction to the twofold one of objective and subjective history, as substantially in the text above. Bernheim insists (Chap. I, Sect. 5), upon introducing a third category—the knowledge or study of history, which is neither the events nor their artistic presentation but the science of research (*Geschichtswissenschaft*). There is a suggestive anthology of definitions in F. J. Teggart, *Prolegomena to History* (1916), Part III, Sect. 1. See also Johan Huizinga, "A Definition of the Concept of History," in R. Klibansky and H. J. Paton, eds., *Philosophy and History: Essays Presented to Ernst Cassirer* (1936), pp. 1-10.

Definition and Scope of History

themselves. We call Cromwell a "maker of history" although he never wrote a line of it. We even say that the historian merely records the history which kings and statesmen produce. History in such instances is obviously not the narrative but the thing that awaits narration. The same name is given to both the object of the study and to the study itself. The confusion is unfortunate. Sociology, we know, deals with society; biology with life; but history deals with history! It is like juggling with words.

Of the two meanings, the larger one is comparatively recent. The idea that events and people are historic by reason of any quality of their own, even if no one has studied or written upon them, did not occur to the ancients. To them history was the other thing—the inquiry and statement, not the thing to be studied or recorded. It was not until modern times that the phenomena themselves were termed history. The history of a people originally meant the research and narrative of a historian, not the evolution of the nation. It meant a work dealing with the subject, not the subject itself. And this is logically as well as historically the more accurate use of the word. Things are never historic in themselves. They can be perpetuated out of the dead past only in two ways: either as part of the ever-moving present— as institutions, art, science, etc., things timeless or universal; or in that imaginative reconstruction which it is the special office of the historian to provide.

This distinction must be insisted upon if we are to have any clear thinking upon the history of history. For, obviously, in this phrase we are using "history" only in its original and more limited meaning. We are dealing with historians, their methods, their tools, and their problems—not with the so-called "makers of history" except as materials for the historian, not with battles and constitutions and "historical" events in and for themselves, but only where the historian has treated them. And it is his treatment, rather than the events themselves, which mainly interests us.

A word first, however, upon history in the wider, looser sense of "what has happened." Does it include *all* that has happened? If so, it includes everything, for the whole universe, as modern science shows, is in process of eternal change. It extends beyond the phenomena of life into those of matter, for that vast story of evolution from amoeba and shellfish to man, of which we are learning to decipher the outlines from the pages of stratified rock, is but one incident in the whole. The rocks themselves have "happened," like the life whose traces they preserve. In short, if history includes *all* that has happened, it was under way not less when the first stars took their shape than it was when, about a century ago, science began to decipher and read it.

The deciphering of such history is, however, not the task of the historian but of the natural scientist. There is no harm, to be sure, in considering the analysis of matter as a branch of history when it reveals chemical action as essential to the occurrence of phenomena and the electron as probably responsible for chemical action. But this is not the historian's kind of history. Faced with such conceptions, he realizes that he must content himself with what is scarcely more than an infinitesimal fraction of the vast field of knowledge. And yet it is good for him to realize his place in that great fellowship which is today so busily at work upon the mystery of the processes of nature. For, once he has had the vision of the process itself, he can never face the old tasks in the same way. It transforms his perspective, gives him different sets of values, and reconstructs that synthesis of life and the world into which he fits the works of his own research. Although he realizes the partial nature of his outlook, yet it is not rendered invalid. On the contrary, it acquires a greater validity if it is fitted into the vaster scheme. The significance of his work grows rather than lessens in the light of the wider horizon. The perspectives of science are an inspiration for the historian, even while he recognizes that he can never master their original sources or trace their history. That is for the scientists to deal with. And, as the nature of their phenomena becomes clearer to them, they are becoming, themselves, more and more historical. The larger historical aspects of physics and chemistry, to which we have just alluded, are taken over by the astronomer, while "natural history" in the good old meaning of that term is the especial province of the geologist and biologist. Between them and historians the

Definition and Scope of History

connection is becoming direct and strong; and there is much to be said for the claim that, through both his work and his influence, the greatest of all historians was Darwin.

But if history in the objective sense is not *all* that has happened *how much* is it of what has happened? The answer to this has generally depended upon the point of view of individual historians. All are agreed, for instance, that the term "history" should be limited to substantially human affairs. And yet it cannot be narrowly so defined, for the body and mind of man belong to the animal world and have antecedents that reach far beyond the confines of humanity, while the natural environment of life—food, climate, shelter, etc.—are also part of the human story. When we try still further to limit the term to some single line of human activity, as for instance, politics, we shut out fields in which the expression of the human spirit has often been more significant, the fields of culture and ideas, of literature, art, engineering, education, science or philosophy. Why not, therefore, avoid trouble by admitting the whole field of the human past as history?

There seems to be just one qualification necessary: the data must be viewed as part of the process of social development, not as isolated facts. For historical facts are those which form a part of that great stream of interrelation which is Time.

This is still history in the objective sense, the field which the historian may call his own. But a careful reading of our definition shows that we have already passed over into a consideration of history in the truer meaning of the word—the performance of the historian, since it is the attitude assumed toward the fact which finally determines whether it is to be considered as historical or not. Now what, in a word, is this historical attitude? It consists, as we have already intimated, in seeing things in their relation to others, both in Space and in Time. Biography, for instance, becomes history when it considers the individual in his setting in society; it is not history in so far as it deals exclusively with a single life. It may deal with the hero as an isolated, solitary figure or as a type common to all times. In either case it lacks the historical point of view, for it is only by connecting the individual with his own society that he enters into that great general current of events which we call Time. The study of any farmer's life as a farmer's life, set in the unending routine of the seasons, is almost as timeless as the study of Shakespeare's mind. The New England farmer, on the other hand, and the Elizabethan Shakespeare enter the field of history because they are considered in their setting in society; and society is the reservoir of Time, the ever-changing, ever-enduring reflex of human events.

The same tests that apply to biography apply to antiquarian research. Because an event belongs to the past it is not necessarily historical. Indeed, in so far as the antiquarian isolates his material for our inspection, interested in it for its own sake, laying it out like the curator of a museum, he robs it of its historical character, for the facts of history do not exist by themselves any more than the lives of historical personages. They are parts of a process and acquire meaning only when seen in action. The antiquarian preserves the fragments of the great machinery of events, but the historian sets it to work again, however faintly the sound of its motion comes to him across the distant centuries.

History in the proper sense of the word began with the Greeks. They had already surpassed the world in the purely art creation of the epic, where the imagination, urging the laggard movement of events, restores the dynamism of the past which is the first condition of history. Then they turned from poetry to prose, and in sobriety and self-restraint began to criticize their own legends, to see if they were true. Before the sixth century B.C., so far as we know, no critical hand had attempted to sort out the data of the past, impelled by the will to disbelieve. This revolutionary mood, as happy in finding what had not happened as what had, marks the emergence of the scientific spirit into the great art of storytelling. History in the true sense is the combination of the two.

The word "history"[2] itself comes to us from these sixth-century Ionians and is the name they gave to their achievement. It meant not the telling of a tale, but the search for knowledge and the truth. It was to them much what philosophy was to the later Athenians or science to us. The historian was the critical inquirer. Herodotus was as much an investigator and an explorer as a

---

[2] Ionic ἱστορίη, Attic ἱστορία. (See below, p. 168.)

Definition and Scope of History

reciter of narrative, and his life-long investigation was "history" in his Ionian speech.[3] Yet Herodotus himself hints that the word may also be applied to the story which the research has made possible,[4] not to the guileless tale of the uncritical, to be sure, but to a narrative such as he and his soberly inquisitive fellows could tell. It was not until Aristotle,[5] and more especially Polybius,[6] that we have it definitely applied to the literary product instead of to the inquiry which precedes it. From Polybius to modern times, history (Latin, *historia*) has been literature. It is a strange but happy coincidence, that when the scientific investigator of today turns from literature to scholarship, from writing books to discovering facts, he is turning, not away from, but towards, the field of history, as the word was understood by those forerunners of Herodotus, to whom science was as yet but a dream and an aspiration.

This double aspect of history—the one no older than Ionia, the other reaching back to the dawn of Time—has apparently puzzled a good many who write about it. There are those who try to prove that history is either a science or an art, when, as a matter of fact, it is both. We shall recur to this in a later section, where we shall have to face the further question of the relation of art to science in general. But without entering into that problem yet, we may for the present, with a view to clarity, frankly divide our subject into two: the research which is science and the narration which is art.

The history of these two divisions runs in different channels and has always done so. History, the art, flourishes with the arts. It is mainly the creature of imagination and literary style. It depends upon expression, upon vivid painting, sympathy, grace and elegance, elevated sentiments or compelling power. The picture may be partial or incorrect, like Carlyle's description

---

[3] See the opening sentence, "This is the setting forth of the researches of Herodotus of Halicarnassus," etc.
[4] Book VII, Chap. 96.
[5] Aristotle, *Rhetoric*, Book IV, Chap. I, Sect. 8 (cf. note in edition by E. M. Cope and J. E. Sandys); *Poetics*, Chap. 9.
[6] Polybius, *Histories*. Book I, Chap. 30.

of revolutionary France; sympathies may warp the truth, as in Froude's *Henry VIII* or Macaulay's *History of England;* elegance of style may carry even Gibbon beyond the data in his sources, and the passionate eloquence of Michelet ride down the restrictions of sober fact. But in the art of history narration these are magnificent even if they are not true. Indeed the art in history seems to run, with most perverse intent, in the opposite direction to the science. Wherever the great masters of style have dominated, there one is likely to find less interest in criticizing sources than in securing effects. The historian's method of investigation often seems to weaken in proportion as his rhetoric improves. This is not always true, but it is sufficiently common to make the scientific historian eternally distrustful of the literary. The distrust in the long run has its sobering effect upon the literary historian, in spite of his contemptuous references to the researcher as a dry-as-dust who lacks insight, the first qualification of the historian. And from the standpoint of supreme historical achievement both criticisms are justified. The master of research is generally but a poor artist, and his uncolored picture of the past will never rank in literature beside the splendid distortions which glow in the pages of a Michelet or a Macaulay, simply because he lacks the human sympathy which vitalizes the historical imagination. The difficulty, however, in dealing with the art in history is that, being largely conditioned upon genius, it has no single, traceable line of development. Here the product of the age of Pericles remains unsurpassed still; the works of Herodotus and Thucydides standing, like the Parthenon itself, models for all time.

On the other hand, history the science has a development and a logical history of its own. Paralleling other scientific work, it has come to the front in our own age, so that it has not only gained recognition among historians as a distinct subject, but by the results of its obscure and patient labors it has recast for us almost the whole outline of our evolution. Impartial, almost unhuman in its cold impartiality, weighing documents, accumulating evidence, sorting out the false wherever detected no matter what venerable belief goes with it, it is piecing together with infinite care the broken mosaic of the past—not to teach us lessons

Definition and Scope of History

nor to entertain, but simply to fulfil the imperative demand of the scientific spirit—to find the truth and set it forth.

It is this scientific history—this modern fulfilment of the old Greek *historia*—which is responsible for the development of that group of auxiliary sciences (of which archaeology is the most notable) by means of which the scope of history has been extended so far beyond the written or oral records. The advance along this line, during the nineteenth and twentieth centuries, has been one of the greatest achievements of our age. The vast gulf which separates the history of Egypt by Professor Breasted from that by Herodotus gives but a partial measure of that achievement. By the mechanism now at his disposal, the scientific explorer can read more history from the rubbish heaps buried in the desert sand than the greatest traveller of antiquity could gather from the priests of Thebes.

This history of scientific history, from the Greeks to our time, is, therefore, the central thread of our story. But a proper historical treatment of it must not be limited narrowly to it alone. It includes as well the long pre-scientific and the subsequent unscientific achievements. All of these belong, more or less, to our subject. Indeed, in so far as they exhibit any clear sign of that sense of the interrelation of events which we have emphasized above, they are history, winning their place by their art if not by their science. One must not omit, for instance, the work of mediaeval monks, although they copied impossible events into solemn annals without a sense of the absurdity and although individually they are the last to deserve the title of artists. For they had, after all, a vision of the process of history, and one which was essentially artistic. The Christian Epic, into which they transcribed their prosy lines, was as genuine an art product as the Greek or Babylonian, although it was one which only the composite imagination of religious faith could achieve. The history of history must deal with such things—historically.

The same is true of the prescientific origins. These lie unnumbered centuries beyond that comparatively modern world of Hecataeus and Herodotus. They reach back, indeed, to the dawn of memory—when, as we suppose, some descendants of those shaggy simian brutes of the Tertiary forests and caves which were destined to produce humanity first learned, however dimly, to distinguish past from present. This means that the origins of history are as old as mankind. For the dawn of memory was the dawn of consciousness. No other acquisition, except that of speech, was so fateful for humanity. Memory—the thing which binds one's life together; which makes me *me* and you *you;* which enables us to recognize ourselves of yesterday in ourselves of today—that reproduction of the dead past thrilling once more with life and passion—that magic glass which holds the unfading reflection of what exists no more—what a miracle it is! Destroy memory and you destroy time so far as you and I are concerned. The days and the years may pass along, each with its burden of work or its boon of rest, but they pass from the nothingness of the future to the nothingness of the past like the falling of drops of rain upon the ocean. The past exists in the memory as the future in the imagination. Consciousness is itself but the structure built upon this tenuous bridge between the two eternities of the unknown, and history is the record of what has taken place therein. Memory, in short, reveals the world as a process, and so makes its data historical.

At first glance it might seem absurd to carry our origins back so far. We have been used to thinking of early history as a thing of poetry and romance, born of myth and embodied in epic. It demands a flight of the imagination to begin it not with rhythmic and glowing verse but almost with the dawn of speech. But the origins of history begin back yonder, with the very beginning of mankind, before the glaciers swept our valleys to the sea, instead of by the campfires of Aryan warriors or in the clamorous square of the ancient city. When men first learned to ask—or tell—in grunts and signs "what happened," history became inevitable. And from that dim, far-off event until the present, its data have included all that has flashed upon the consciousness of men so as to leave its reflection or burn in its scar. Its threads have been broken, tangled, and lost. Its pattern cannot be deciphered beyond a few thousand years, for, at first, the shuttle of Time tore as it wove the fabric of social life, and we can only guess by the rents and gashes what forces were at work upon it. What we do know, however, is that, although history itself in the true sense of the term did not start until midway down the process of social evolution when the social memory was already continuous, when deeds were inscribed on monuments, and when the critical spirit was at work—in short when civilization had begun—still the prehistoric history is of more than merely speculative interest; for civilization continued the pattern begun for it, and anthropology has shown us how absurd has been our interpretation of what civilized man has been thinking and doing, so long as we have ignored his uncivilized, ancestral training.

CHAPTER II

The Interpretation of History [1]

TWO great questions front all students of the social sciences: what happened? Why? History attempts to deal mainly with the first. It gathers the scattered traces of events and fills the archives of civilization with their records. Its science sifts the evidence and prepares the story. Its art recreates the image of what has been, and "old, unhappy, far-off things" become once more the heritage of the present. Though no magic touch can wholly restore the dead past, history satisfies in considerable part the curiosity which asks, "What happened?" But "Why?" What forces have been at work to move the latent energies of nations, to set going the march of events? What makes our revolutions or our tory reactions? Why did Rome fall, Christianity triumph, feudalism arise, the Inquisition flourish, monarchy become absolute and of divine right, Spain decline, England emerge, democracy awaken and grow potent? Why did these things happen when or where they did? Was it the direct intervention of an overruling Providence, for Whose purposes the largest battalions were always on the move? Or are the ways past finding out? Do the events themselves reveal a meaning?

These are not simply questions for philosophers. Children insist upon them most. He is a lucky storyteller whose Jack the Giant Killer or Robin Hood is not cut through, time and again, by unsatisfied curiosity as to *why* the beanstalk grew so high, *why* Jack wanted to climb, *why* Robin Hood lived under a greenwood tree. Many a parental Herodotus has been wrecked on just such grounds. The problem of the philosopher or the scientist

---

[1] This chapter is the reprint of an article in *The American Historical Review*, Vol. XVIII (July, 1913), No. 40. It was first given as a lecture in the University of Illinois in that year.

is the same as that brought forward by the child. The drama of history unrolls before our eyes in more sober form: our Robin Hood becomes a Garibaldi, our Jack the Giant Killer a Napoleon, but we still have to ask how fortune and genius so combined as to place southern Italy in the hands of the one, Europe at the feet of the other. Not only is the problem the same, but we answer it in the same way. Here, at once, we have a clue to the nature of interpretation. For any one knows that you answer the child's "Why?" by telling another story. Each story is, in short, an explanation, and each explanation a story. The schoolboy's excuse for being late is that he couldn't find his cap. He couldn't find his cap *because* he was playing in the barn. Each incident was a cause and each cause an incident in his biography. In like manner most of the reasons we assign for our acts merely state an event or a condition of affairs which is in itself a further page of history. At last, however, there comes a point where the philosopher and the child part company. History is more than events. It is the manifestation of life, and behind each event is some effort of mind and will, while within each circumstance exists some power to stimulate or to obstruct. Hence psychology and economics are called upon to explain the events themselves. The child is satisfied if you account for the career of Napoleon by a word "genius," but that merely opens the problem to the psychologist. The child in us all attributes the overthrow to the hollow squares of Waterloo, but the economist reminds us of the Continental System and of the Industrial Revolution which made Waterloo possible.

The process of interpreting history, therefore, involves getting as much as possible out of history, psychology, and economics—using economics in the widest possible sense as the affective material background of life. This does not get to final causes, to be sure. It leaves the universe still a riddle. Theologians and metaphysicians are the only ones who attempt to deal with final causes as with final ends. Certainly historians cannot follow them in such speculations. The infinite lies outside experience, and experience is the sphere of history. When we talk of the interpretation of history, therefore, we do not mean its setting in the universe, but a knowledge of its own inner relationships. We confine ourselves to humanity and the theatre of its activities. But within this realm of mystery man exists, acts, and thinks—or thinks he thinks, which is all the same for historians—and these thoughts and deeds remain mostly un-understood, even by the actors themselves. Here is mystery enough, mystery which is not in itself unknowable but merely unknown. The social sciences do not invade the field of religion; they have nothing to do with the ultimate; their problems are those of the City of Man, not of the City of God. So the interpretation of history can leave theology aside, except where theology attempts to become historical. Then it must face the same criticism as all other histories. If the City of God is conceived of as a creation of the processes of civilization, it becomes as much a theme for scientific analysis as the Roman Empire or the Balkan Confederacy. If theology substitutes itself for science, it must expect the same treatment as science. But our search for historic "causes" is merely a search for other things of the same kind—natural phenomena of some sort—which lie in direct and apparently inevitable connection. We interpret history by knowing more of it, bringing to bear our psychology and every other auxiliary to open up each intricate relationship between men, situations, and events.

This is our first great principle. What do we mean by the "meaning" of anything but more knowledge of it? In physics or chemistry we enlarge our ideas of phenomena by observing how they work, what their affinities are, how they combine or react. But all these properties are merely different aspects of the same thing, and our knowledge of it is the sum total of our analysis. Its meaning has changed, as our knowledge enlarges, from a lump of dirt to a compound of elements. No one asks what an element is, because no one can tell—except in terms of other elements. The interpretation, therefore, of physical phenomena is a description of them in terms of their own properties. The same thing is true of history, but instead of description we have narrative. For history differs from the natural sciences in this fundamental fact, that while they consider phenomena from the standpoint of Space, history deals with them from the standpoint of Time. Its data are in eternal change, moving in endless succession. Time has no

The Interpretation of History

static relationships, not so much as for a second. One moment merges into the next, and another has begun before the last is ended. The old Greeks already pointed out that one could never put his foot twice into the same waters of a running stream, and never has philosophy insisted more eloquently upon this fluid nature of Time than in the writings of Professor Bergson. But, whatever Time may be in the last analysis, it is clear that whereas physics states the meaning of the phenomena with which it deals in descriptions, history must phrase its interpretations in narrative, the narrative which runs with passing time.

Hence history and its interpretation are essentially one, if we mean by history all that has happened, including mind and matter in so far as they relate to action. Any other kind of interpretation is unscientific; it eludes analysis because it does not itself analyze, and hence it eludes proof. So theological dogma, which may or may not be true, and speculation in metaphysics are alike outside our problem. Indeed, when we come down to it, there is little difference between "What has happened?" and "Why?" The "Why?" only opens up another "What?" Take for example a problem in present history: "Why has the price of living gone up?" The same question might be asked another way: "What has happened to raise prices?" The change in the form of sentence does not solve anything, for who knows what has happened? But it puts us upon a more definite track toward our solution. We test history by history.

The earliest historical narrative is the myth. It is at the same time an explanation. It is no mere product of imagination, of the play of art with the wayward fancies of childlike men. Myths—real, genuine myths, not Homeric epics composed for sophisticated, critical audiences—are statements of "facts" to the believer. They are social outputs, built up out of experience and fitted to new experiences. The long canoes are swept to sea by the northeast hurricane, and year by year in the winter nights at the campfires of those who go by long canoes the story is repeated, over and over again, until the sea is left behind or a new race brings triremes with machinery in the inside. So long as the old society exists under the old conditions the myth perpetuates itself; but it also gathers into itself the reflex of the changing history. It therefore embodies the belief of the tribe, and this gives it an authority beyond the reach of any primitive higher criticism. Appealed to as the "wisdom of our fathers," as the universally accepted and therefore true—*quod semper quod ab omnibus*—it becomes a sort of creed for its people. More than a creed, it is as unquestioned as the world around and as life itself. The eagle of Prometheus or of the Zuñi myths is as much a part of the world to Greeks and Zuñis as the eagle seen yonder on the desert rim. The whole force of society is on the side of myth. The unbeliever is ostracized or put to death. What would have happened to the man who had dared to question the literal narrative of Genesis in the thirteenth century has happened in some form in every society. The Inquisition, we are told, was merely a refinement of lynch law. In any case, it would never have been effective without popular support. The heretics of all ages suffer because the faith they challenge is the treasured possession of their society, a heritage in which resides the mysterious efficacy of immemorial things.

Now it is a strange fact that most of our beliefs begin in prior belief. It does not sound logical, but it remains true that we get to believing a thing from believing it. Belief is the basic element in thought. It starts with consciousness itself. Once started, there develops a tendency—"a will"—to keep on. Indeed it is almost the strongest tendency in the social mind. Only long scientific training can keep an individual alert with doubt, or, in other words, keep him from merging his own beliefs in those of his fellows. This is the reason that myth has so long played so momentous a role in the history of the human intelligence—by far the largest of any one element in our whole history. Science was born but yesterday. Myths are millenniums old. And they are as young today as in the glacial period. Heroes and victims share the stage of the drama of history with those uncanny Powers that mock at effort or exalt the weak and trick with sudden turns the stately progress of society. Wherever the marvellous event is explained by causes more marvellous still, where the belief is heightened by basing it upon deeper mysteries, we are

The Interpretation of History 19

following the world-old method explaining by the inexplicable. Myths are unsatisfactory as explanations for various reasons, but the main one is that human events are subordinated to the supernatural in which they are set. This means that normal events of daily life generally pass unnoticed and attention is concentrated upon the unusual and the abnormal. It is in these that the divine or the diabolic intervenes. They are preëminently—as we still say of railway accidents—acts of God. So the myth neither tells a full story, with all the human data involved, nor directs to any natural sequence of events. Sickness and consequent catastrophe are not attributed to malarial mosquitoes—such as filled the temples of Aesculapius with suppliants and depleted Greece of citizens. All misfortune is due to broken taboos. When Roman armies are defeated the question is, "Who has sinned and how?" When death comes to the Australian bushman, there is always black magic to account for it. And pontiffs and medicine men elaborate the mythology which explains and justifies the taboos.

That is not to say that myths are the creations of priests. The creation is the work of the society itself. The priest merely elaborates. The initial belief resides in the nerves of primitive men, the fear of the uncanny, the vague apprehension which still chills us in the presence of calamity. Social suggestion is responsible for much of it—we tremble when we see the rigid fear on the faces of those beside us. When someone whispers in the dark, "Isn't it awful?" "it" suddenly thrills into being, like a ghost. Voltaire was wrong to attribute the origin of these beliefs of superstition to priestcraft. The priest merely took hold of the universal beliefs of his people and gave them form and consistency, as the minstrel wove them into poetry. The scruple about entering the dark wooded slopes beyond the village grainfields is enough to people it, for most of us, with all uncanny things. If you are the kind of person to have scruples about entering a wood by night, you are the kind to appreciate the possibilities of lurking danger in its shadows and moving presences in its thickets. So on a night when the moon is high and the wind is still you may hear the hounds and the wolf packs of the wild hunters—of Diana and Mars. It needs no priestly college to convince us of that. The wood and the wolves and our own nerves are enough. But the priestly college develops the things of night into the stuff of history, and centuries after the howling wolves have disappeared from the marshes around Rome the city cherishes, to the close of its history, the myth of its founding.

Men first tell stories. Then they think about them. So from mythology the ancients proceeded to philosophy. Now philosophy is a wide word. For some of us it means keen criticism of fundamental things. For others it seems a befuddled consideration of unrealities. But whatever it may be now, philosophy came into the antique world as science, critical analysis, and history was but another name for it. The "inquiry" of those Ionian *logographoi* who began to question Homer in the sixth century before Christ challenged and interpreted myth. So, all through its history, history has demanded of its students denial rather than acceptance, skepticism rather than belief, in order that the story of men and empires be more than myth. But the tendency to believe and accept is so strongly impressed upon us from immemorial social pressures that few have risen to the height of independent judgment which was the Greek ideal. Criticism, in the full sense of the word, is an interpretation. To reject a story means that one constructs another in its place. It establishes that certain things did not happen because certain other ones did. So the Greeks corrected myths, and in doing this made history more rational. Man came into the story more and the gods receded.

One may distinguish two phases of philosophic interpretation of history, that in which the philosophy is in reality a theology and that in which it is natural science. In the first phase we are still close to myth. Myth places the cause of events in mystery of some sort—deities, demons, the Fates or Fortune. Early philosophy proceeds upon these assumptions, which also penetrate most antique histories. Even Polybius, hard-headed, much-experienced man of the world, cannot quite attribute to natural causes the rise of Rome. Fortune, that wayward goddess of Caesar, had something to do with it—how much it would be hard to say. Livy had this myth-philosophy to the full; every disaster had its portent, every triumph its omen. This was the practical philosophy of all but the few calm thinkers whose skepticism passed into the second phase, which reached all the way from an open question as to whether or not the gods interfered in human affairs to the positive denial of their influence. The great source book for such interpretations of history is Cicero's *On the Nature of the Gods,* where one may find in the guise of a theological discussion a résumé of the various pagan philosophies of history. For the philosophies of history were more frankly philosophy than history; the question at issue was the intruding mystery rather than the circumstances of the intrusion, and one denied or affirmed mainly on *a priori* grounds. The denial was not historical criticism and the philosophy of doubt hardly more genuine historical interpretation than the philosophy of belief. Its conclusions more nearly *coincide* with the demands of scientific research; that is all. But mythology was not lightly to be got rid of, even among philosophers; as for the populace, it merely exchanged one myth for another, until finally it could take refuge in theology. The bold infidelity of a Lucretius was too modern for the age which was to give birth to Christianity, and the Voltaires of antiquity were submerged in a rising sea of faith.

Moreover there were two reasons why antique philosophy could not accomplish much. It lacked the instruments by which to penetrate into the two centres of its problem: psychology, to analyze the mind, and experimental laboratories, to analyze the setting of life or life itself. It had some knowledge of psychology, to be sure, and some experimental science, but relatively little; and it never realized the necessity for developing them. It sharpened the reason to an almost uncanny degree, and played, like a grown athlete, with ideas. But it followed the ideas into their ideal world and left this world unaccounted for. Above all, it knew practically nothing of economic and material elements in history. Even a Thucydides has no glimpse of the intimate connection between the forces of economics and of politics. History for him is made by *men,* not by grainfields and metals. It was not until the nineteenth century—just the other day—that economic factors in historical causation were emphasized as playing a role comparable to that of man himself. Thucydides did not realize how commercial and industrial competition could rouse the rivals of Athens to seek her overthrow. Polybius felt that Fortune was a weak excuse to offer for Rome's miraculous rise and fell back upon the peculiar excellence of her constitution. Both were rationalists of a high order, but they never extended their history—and therefore their interpretation—beyond politics. The gods tend to disappear, and mankind to take their place. But it is an incomplete mankind, rational beings moved by ideas and principles, not economic animals moved by blind wants and fettered by the basest limitations. In short, a political man is the farthest analysis one gets. But even Aristotle never knew how many things there were in politics besides politics. The extent of the interplay of material forces upon psychological lay outside his ken.

Upon the whole, then, there is almost nothing to learn from antique interpretations of history. They interest us because of their antiquity and their drift from the supernatural to the natural. But they did not achieve a method which would open up the natural and let us see its working. They are of no service to us in our own interpretations.

Christianity dropped all this rationalist tone of the Greeks and turned the keen edge of Greek philosophy to hew a structure so vast in design, so simple in outline, that the whole world could understand. History was but the realization of religion—not of various religions, but of one, the working out of one divine plan. It was a vast, supernatural process, more God's than man's. It was no longer a play of rival forces, the gods of Rome against those of Veii or the Baalim against Jahveh. But from all eternity the drama had been determined by the Wisdom that was infinite, and it was being wrought out by an almighty arm. Baal and Jupiter are creatures and puppets, like mere men. History has only one interpretation. Rome—city and empire—is the spoil of the barbarian, the antique world is going to pieces, all its long heritage of culture, its millenniums of progress, its arts and sciences are perishing in the vast, barbaric anarchy: why? There is one answer, sufficient, final—God wills it. No uncertain guesses as to the virtue of peoples, weights of battalions, resources of countries, pressures of populations, wasteful administrations,

Black Deaths, impoverished provinces. There is sin to be punished. The pagan temples of the ancient world, with their glories of art shining on every acropolis, are blasphemy and invite destruction. Philosophers and poets whose inspiration had once seemed divine now seem diabolic. Those who catch the vision of the new faith, shake off the old world as one shakes off a dream. Talk of revolutions! No doctrines of the rights of man have caught the imagination with such terrific force as these doctrines of the rights of God, which from Paul to Augustine were clothed with all the convincing logic of Hellenic genius and Roman realism. It is hard for us Christians to realize the amount of religion which Christianity injected into the world; not merely among the credulous populace, on the religious *qui vive,* but among thinking men. It saturated philosophy with dogma and turned speculation from nature to the supernatural.

The earliest Christians cherished the belief that the world was soon to end and lived under the shadow of the day of doom. As time went on, this millennial hope seemed to grow fainter; but in reality it merely took a more rigid form. It became the structural heart of the new theology. The pageant of history, which had seemed so gloriously wonderful, so inspiring to a Polybius back in the old heroic days, was now a worn and sorry thing. It had no glory nor even any meaning except in the light of the new dispensation. On the other hand the new *patria,* the *Civitas Dei,* transcending all earthly splendor, was absorbing not merely the present and the future, but the past as well. For all the tragic lines of war and suffering were now converging. All the aimless struggling was now to show its hidden purpose. In Christianity, the story of nations, of politics, economics, art, war, law—in short of civilization—culminated, and ceased!

Such was the thought which underlay all Christian apologetic theology from the first. But it received its classic statement in the *City of God* by Augustine, written when the city of Rome had fallen, and—if it were not for the heretics and the barbarians— the claims of theology seemed almost realizable. For a thousand years and more it was the unquestioned interpretation of the meaning of history, easily adaptable to any circumstance because it covered all. It still is found wherever pure theology satisfies historical curiosity. That includes—or has included—not merely theologians but most other people, for, however slight has been the interest in theology, it has been greater than the interest in scientific history, at least until recent times. Religion has supplied the framework of our thought and the picture of our evolution. The most influential historians of Europe have been the parish priests. In every hamlet, however remote, for the lowly as for those of high degree, they have repeated the story week after week, century after century. Greek writers and thinkers, mediaeval minstrels and modern journalists can hardly match the influence of those priests upon the mind of the mass of men. The tale itself was an unrivalled epic, dark with the supreme central tragedy upon which Christendom itself rested, rising to the keenest voicing of the hopes of life. Its very element was miracle. No fairy story could rival its devious turns, while at the same time the theme swept over the whole path of history—so far as they knew or cared. It was the story of a chosen people, of divine governance from Creation to the founding of their own church, guarded in a sacred book and interpreted from a sacred tongue.

Slowly, however, the setting of the Church had changed. The vision of the day of judgment died away almost altogether. Men who dared to dream apocalypses—like Joachim of Flora—or their followers were judged heretics by a church which had planted itself in *saeculo* and surrounded itself with all the pomp and circumstance of temporal power. There was still a lingering echo of the older faith, heard most often in the solemn service for the dead. So long as the universe was Ptolemaic—the world of Dante and of Milton—the heavy chord of *dies irae* would cut in upon the growing interest in the world itself. But once the crystalline sphere was shattered by Copernicus and Galileo, and the infinite spaces were strewn with stars like our own, the old idea of a world to "shrivel like a parched scroll" had to be revised and readjusted, and with it the simple conception of the divine purpose, centred upon the centre of things, and working by direct intervention through constant miracle. There was no sudden revolution; the old ideals were too firmly fixed for that.

The Interpretation of History 25

Moreover, science began to challenge the theological history of the universe before it challenged the theological history of man himself. But when geology began to bring in evidence of the age of our residence and physics achieved the incredible feat of weighing the forces and determining the conditions which held the worlds together, then the details of the scheme of Augustine had to be recast as well. From Augustine to Bossuet one may trace an almost unbroken line of theological interpretations. But some, at least, of the generation which listened to Bossuet were also to watch Bolingbroke and Voltaire whetting the weapons of rationalistic attack.

Now what is the weakness of the theological interpretation of history? It is of the same character as that we have seen in the myth. The interpretation is outside history altogether. Grant all that theology claims, that Rome fell and England arose, that America was discovered, or was so long undiscovered, because "God wills it." That does not enlarge our knowledge of the process. It satisfies only those who believe in absolutely unqualified Calvinism—and they are becoming few and far between. If man is a free agent, even to a limited degree, he can find the meaning of his history in the history itself—the only meaning which is of any value as a guide to conduct or as throwing light upon his actions. Intelligent inquiry has free scope within a universe of ever-widening boundaries, where nature, and not supernature, presents its sober phenomena for patient study.

This patient study, however, had not yet been done when the eighteenth-century deists attacked the theological scheme, and their philosophy shares to some extent the weakness of the antique, in its ignorance of data. Natural law took the place of an intervening Providence; history was a process worked out by the forces of nature moving uniformly, restless but continuous, unchecked, inevitable. The process comprised all mankind; no chosen people, implying injustice to those not chosen; no miracles disturbing the regularity of nature. This was an advance toward future understanding because it concentrated attention upon nature and the method of evolution, yet in itself it cast but little light upon the problem, for it did not explain details. One sees its failure most where it risked hypotheses with most assurance, in its treatment of religion. It would not do for philosophers to admit that religion—at least of the old, historic type—was itself one of the laws of nature, implanted in humanity from the beginning. Consequently it was for them a creation of priestcraft. No dismissal of its claims could be more emphatic. Yet the old theologies have since proved that they have at least as many natural rights in society as the criticism of them, and now, with our new knowledge of primitive life, dominated by religion as we see it to be, we cast aside the rationalist conception as a distortion of history almost as misleading as those of the mythology it tried to dispose of.

But the work of Voltaire and his school in disrupting the old authority of Church and Bible—bitterly denounced and blackly maligned as it has been—is now recognized by all thinking minds, at least by all leaders of thought, to have been an essential service in the emancipation of the human intellect. The old sense of authority could never afterwards, as before, block the free path of inquiry; and the Era of Enlightenment, as it was fondly termed, did enlighten the path which history was to take if it was to know itself. The anticlerical bias of Hume and Gibbon is perhaps all that the casual reader perceives in them. But where among all previous historians does one find an attitude so genuinely historical? Moreover, in Hume we have the foundations of psychology and a criticism of causality which was of the first importance. It would be tempting to linger over these pioneers of the scientific spirit, who saw but could not realize the possibilities of naturalism. Their own achievement, however, was so faulty in just this matter of interpretation, that it was not difficult for the reaction of the early nineteenth century to poke holes in their theories, and so discredit—for the time being—their entire outlook.

Before Voltaire had learned in England the main lines of his philosophy, a German-Scottish boy had been born in Königsberg, in Prussia, who was destined to exercise as high if not as extended a sovereignty over the intellect of the nineteenth century. Immanuel Kant was, however, of a different type. He fought no ringing fights with the old order. He simply created a new realm in metaphysics, where one could take refuge and have the world as his own. The *idea* dominates. Space and time, the *a priori* forms of all phenomena, lie within us. Mathematics is vindicated because the mind can really master relationships, and the reason emerges from its critique to grapple with the final problem of metaphysics. This at first sight has little to do with interpreting history, but it proved to have a great deal to do with it. The dominance of ideas became a fundamental doctrine among those who speculated concerning causation in history, and metaphysics all but replaced theology as an interpreter.

One sees this already in the work of the historian's historian of the nineteenth century, Leopold von Ranke. To him each age and country is explicable only if one approaches it from the standpoint of its own *Zeitgeist*. But the spirit of a time is more than the temporal environment in which events are set. It is a determining factor, clothed with the creative potency of mind. Ranke did not develop this philosophic background of history, he accepted it and worked from, rather than toward, it. His *Zeitgeist* was a thing for historians to portray, not to speculate about. History should concern itself with the preservation of phenomena as they had actually existed in their own time and place. It should recover the lost data of the past, not as detached specimens such as the antiquary places in his museum, but transplanted like living organisms for the preservation of the life as well as of the organs. Now, where should one look for the vital forces of history other than in the mind of the actors? So, if the historic imagination can restore events, not simply as they seem to us, but as they seemed to those who watched them taking place, we shall understand them in so far as history can contribute to their understanding. In any case, this is the field of the historian. If he injects his own theories into the operation, he merely falsifies what he has already got. Let the past stand forth once more, interpreted by itself, and we have the truth—incomplete, to be sure, but as perfect as we shall ever be able to attain. For, note the point, in that past, the dominating thing was the *Zeitgeist* itself—a thing at once to be worked out and working out, a programme and a creative force. Why, therefore, should one turn aside to other devices to explain history, since it explained itself if once presented in its own light?

Ranke developed the implications of his theory no further than to ensure a reproduction of a living past, as perfect as with the sources at his disposal and the political instincts of his time it was possible to secure. But this high combination of science and art had its counterpart in the philosophy of Hegel. At first sight nothing could be more absurd than the comparison of these two men, the one concrete, definite, searching for minute details, maintaining his own objectivity by insisting upon the subjectivity of the materials he handles, the other theoretic, unhistorical, creating worlds from his inner consciousness, presenting as a scheme of historical interpretation a programme of ideals, unattained and, for all we know, unattainable. It would be difficult to imagine a philosophy of history more unhistorical than this of Hegel. Yet he but emphasized the Idea which Ranke implicitly accepted.

Hegel was a sort of philosophic Augustine, tracing through history the development of the realm of the Spirit. The City of God is still the central theme, but the crude expectations of a miraculous advent are replaced by the conception of a slow realization of its spiritual power, rising through successive stages of civilization. So he traces, in broad philosophic outlines, the history of this revelation of the Spirit, from its dawn in the Orient, through its developing childhood in Asia, its Egyptian period of awakening, its liberation in Greece, its maturity in the Roman balance of the individual and the State, until finally Christianity, especially in the German world, carries the spirit life to its highest expression. In this process the Absolute reveals itself—that Absolute which had mocked the deists with its isolation and unconcern. And it reveals itself in the Idea which Kantian critique had placed in the forefront of reality and endowed with the creative force of an *élan vital*. So theology, skepticism, and metaphysics combined to explain the world and its history—as the working out of an ideal scheme.

As a series of successive ideals, the Hegelian scheme may offer some suggestions to those who wish to characterize the complex phenomena of an age or an empire in a single phrase. But it is no statement of any actual process. The ideals which it presents remain ideals, not realities. History written to fit the Hegelian metaphysics would be almost as vigorous a distortion as that which Orosius wrote to fit Augustinian theology. The history of practical Christianity, for instance, is vastly different from the history of its ideals. It is an open question whether the ideal could ever be deduced from the practice, and not less questionable whether we are any nearer realization than at the start. There has been little evidence in outward signs of any such determinant change in the nature of politics or in the stern enforcement of economic laws during the history of western Europe. We find ourselves repeating in many ways experiences of Rome and Greece—pagan experiences. Society is only partly religious and only slightly self-conscious. How, then, can it be merely the manifestation of a religious ideal? Surely other forces than ideals or ideas must be at work. The weakness of Hegel's interpretation of history is the history. He interprets it without knowing what it is. His interest was in the other side of his scheme, the Absolute which was revealing itself therein. The scheme was, indeed, a sort of afterthought. But before historians directed any sufficient criticism against his unhistoricity, skepticism in philosophy had already attacked his Absolute. It was the materialistic Feuerbach, with his thoroughgoing avowal that man is the creature of his appetite and not of his mind (*Der Mensch ist was er ist*), who furnished the transition to a new and absolutely radical line of historical interpretation—the materialistic and the economic.

Materialism has a bad name, partly earned, partly thrust upon it. But whatever one may think of its cruder dogmatic aspects, the fact remains that interpretation of history owes at least as much to it as to all the speculations which had preceded it. For it supplied one half of the data—the material half! Neither theology nor metaphysics had ever really got down to earth. They had proceeded upon the theory that the determination of history is from *above* and from *within* mankind and had been so absorbed with working out their scheme from these premises that the possibility of determination from *around* did not occur to them, until the physical and biological sciences and the new problems of economics pressed it upon their attention. To the old philosophies, this world was at best a theatre for divine or psychic forces; it contributed no part of the drama but the setting. Now came the claim that the environment itself entered into the play and that it even determined the character of the production. It was a claim based upon a study of the details from a new standpoint, that of the commonplace, of business, and of the affairs of daily life. The farmer's work depends upon his soil, the miner's upon the pumps which open up the lower levels. Cities grow where the forces of production concentrate, by harbors or coal fields. A study of plains, river valleys, or mountain ranges tends to show that societies match their environment; therefore the environment moulds them to itself. So the nature of the struggle for existence, out of which emerges intelligence, is determined by the material conditions under which it is waged.

This is innocent enough. One might have expected that philosophers would have welcomed the emphasis which the new thinkers placed upon the missing half of their speculations. For there was no getting around the fact that the influences of environment upon society had been largely or altogether ignored before the scientific era forced the world upon our view. But no. The dogmatic habits had got too firmly fixed. If one granted that the material environment might determine the character of the drama of history, why should it not determine whether there should be any drama at all or not? There were extremists on both sides, and it was battle royal—Realism and Nominalism over again. One was to be either a Hegelian, booted and spurred, sworn, cavalierlike, to the defense of the divine right of the Idea, or a regicide materialist with a Calvinistic creed of irreligion! The total result was that their opinion of each other brought *both* into ill repute. Philosophies of history became at least as discredited as the materialism they attacked.

Now the materialistic interpretation of history does not necessarily imply that there is nothing but materialism in the process, any more than theology implies that there is nothing but spirit. It will be news to some that such was the point of view of the most famous advocate of the materialistic interpretation of history, H. T. Buckle. His *History of Civilization in England* (1857-1861) was the first attempt to work out the influences of the material world upon the formation of societies. Every one has heard of how he developed, through a wealth of illustration, the supreme importance of food, soil, and the general aspect of nature. But few apparently have actually read what he says, or they would find that he assigns to these three factors an ever-lessening function as civilization advances, that he postulates mind as much as matter and, with almost Hegelian vision, indicates its ultimate control. He distinctly states that "the advance of European civilization is characterized by a diminishing influence of physical laws and an increasing influence of mental laws," and that "the measure of civilization is the triumph of the mind over external agents." If Buckle had presented his scheme politely, right side up, as it were, it could hardly have had a sermon preached at it! But he prefaced it with his opinion of theologians and historians—and few, apparently, have ever got beyond the preface. It was not encouraging reading for historians—a class of men who, in his opinion, are so marked out by "indolence of thought" or "natural incapacity" that they are fit for nothing better than writing monastic annals. There was, of course, a storm of aggrieved protest. But now that the controversy has cleared away, we can see that, in spite of his too confident formulation of laws, the work of Buckle remains as that of a worthy pioneer in a great, unworked field of science.

Ten years before Buckle published his *History of Civilization*, Karl Marx had already formulated the "economic theory of history." Accepting with reservations Feuerbach's materialist attack upon Hegel, Marx was led to the conclusion that the motive causes of history are to be found in the conditions of material existence. Already in 1845 he wrote, of the "young Hegelians," that to separate history from natural science and industry was like separating the soul from the body, and "finding the birthplace of history, not in the gross material production on earth, but in the misty cloud formation of heaven." [2] In his *Misère de la*

[2] *Die heilige Familie* (1845), p. 238.

philosophie (1847) he lays down the principle that social relationships largely depend upon modes of production, and therefore the principles, ideas, and categories which are thus evolved are no more eternal than the relations they express but are historical and transitory products. From these grounds, Marx went on to socialism, which bases its militant philosophy upon this interpretation of history. But the truth or falsity of socialism does not affect the theory of history. In the famous manifesto of the Communist party (1848) the theory was applied to show how the Commercial and Industrial Revolutions, with the attendant growth of capital, had replaced feudal by modern conditions. This, like all history written to fit a theory, is inadequate history, although much nearer reality than Hegel ever got, because it dealt more with actualities. But we are not concerned here with Marx's own history writing any more than with his socialism. What we want to get at is the standpoint for interpretation. Marx himself, in the preface to the first edition of *Capital,* says that his standpoint is one "from which the evolution of the economic formation of society is viewed as a process of natural history." This sounds like the merest commonplace. Human history is thrown in line with that of the rest of nature. The scope is widened to include every factor, and the greatest one is that which deals with the maintenance of life and the attainment of comfort. So far so good. But Marx had not been a pupil of Hegel for nothing. He, too, went on to absolutes, simply turning Hegel's Absolute upside down. With him "the ideal is nothing else than the material world reflected by the human mind." [3] The world is the thing, not the idea. So he goes on to make man, the modifier of nature with growing control over it, only a function of it—a tool of the tool, just when he has mastered it by new inventions.

But strange as it may seem, Marx's scheme, like Buckle's, culminates in mind, not in matter. The first part is purely economic. The industrial proletarians—"the workers," as socialism fondly terms them—are, like capitalism, the product of economic forces. The factory not only binds the shackles upon the wage slaves of today, it even fills the swarming *ergastula* of city slums

[3] Preface to the second edition of *Capital.*

by the stimulation of child labor. So the process continues until the proletariat, as a last result of its economic situation, acquires a common consciousness. Then what happens? The future is not to be as the past. Consciousness means intelligence, and as soon as the proletariat *understands,* it can burst shackles, master economics, and so control, instead of blindly obeying, the movement of its creative energy. Whether socialism would achieve the object of its faith and hope is not for us to consider, but the point remains, that in the ultimate analysis even the economic interpretation of history ends uneconomically. It ends in directing intelligence, in ideals of justice, of social and moral order.

Where are we? We have passed in review the mythological, theological, philosophical, materialistic, and economic interpretations of history, and have found that none of these, stated in its extreme form, meets the situation. Pure theology or metaphysics omits or distorts the history it is supposed to explain; history is not its proper business. Materialism and economics, while more promising because more earthly, cannot be pressed beyond a certain point. Life itself escapes their analysis. The conclusion is this: that we have two main elements in our problem which must be brought together—the psychic on the one hand, the material on the other. Not until psychology and the natural and economic sciences shall have been turned upon the problem, working in coöperation as allies, not as rivals, will history be able to give an intelligent account of itself. They will need more data than we have at present. The only economics which can promise scientific results is that based upon the statistical method, for, in spite of Bergson, brilliant guesses can hardly satisfy unless they are verified. The natural sciences are only beginning to show the intimate relation of life to its environment, and psychology has hardly begun the study of the group. But one sees already a growing appreciation of common interests, a desire on the part of economists to know the nature of the mechanism of the universe whose working they attempt to describe, an inquiry from the biologist as to the validity of uneugenic social reform.

Now the interpretation of history lies here with these coöperative workers upon the mystery of life and of its environment and their interplay. That does not mean that history is to be explained from the outside. More economics means more history—if it is good economics. Marx, for instance, attempted to state both facts and processes of industrial history, Malthus of population, Ricardo of wages, etc. Both facts and processes are the stuff of history. The statement of a process may be glorified into a "law," but a "law" merely means a general fact of history. It holds good under certain conditions, which are either historical or purely imaginary, and it is only in the latter case that it lies outside the field of history. It is the same with psychology as with economics. Psychology supplies an analysis of action, and action is history. Explanation is more knowledge of the same thing. All inductive study of society is historical.

The interpretations of history are historical in another sense. Looking back over the way we have come, from Greek philosophers to modern economists and psychologists, one can see in every case that the interpretation was but the reflex of the local environment, the expression of the dominant interest of the time. History became critical in that meeting place of East and West, the Ionian coast of Asia Minor, where divergent civilizations were opened up for contrast with each new arrival from the south and west and where travellers destroyed credulity. In the same way, as we have traced it, the isolated landed society of the Middle Ages, with its absence of business and its simple relationships, could rest complacent with an Augustinian world view. Nothing else demanded explanation. When business produced a Florence and Florence a Machiavelli, we have a gleam of newer things, just as Voltaire and Hume mirrored the influences of Galileo and the voyages to China. With the nineteenth century the situation became more complicated, and yet one can see the interpretation of history merely projecting into the past—or drawing out of it—the meaning of each present major interest. Kant and Hegel fitted into the era of ideologues and nationalist romanticists, and their implications were developed under the reaction following the French Revolution. Buckle drew his inspiration from the trend of science which produced—in the same year—the *Origin of Species*. Marx was the interpreter of the Industrial Revolution.

But this does not mean that interpretations of history are nothing more than the injection into it of successive prejudices. It means progressive clarification. Each new theory that forces itself upon the attention of historians brings up new data for their consideration and so widens the field of investigation. The greater knowledge of our world today reveals the smallness of our knowledge of the past, and from every side scholars are hastening to make the content of history more worthy of comparison with the content of science. From this point of view, therefore, interpretation, instead of assuming the position of a final judge of conduct or an absolute law, becomes only a suggestive stimulus for further research.

We have, therefore, an historical interpretation of interpretations themselves. It accepts two main factors, material and psychical, not concerning itself about the ultimate reality of either. It is not its business to consider ultimate realities, though it may be grateful for any light upon the subject. Less ambitious than theological, philosophical, or even economic theories, it views itself as part of the very process which it attempts to understand. If it has no ecstatic glimpses of finality, it shares at least to the full the exhilaration of the scientific quest. It risks no premature fate in the delusive security of an inner consciousness. When you ask it "Why?" it answers "What?"

CHAPTER III

Prehistory; Myth and Legend

ALTHOUGH the origins of history are as old as humanity, the history of history reaches back to no such dim antiquity. There was storytelling by the campfires of the cave men, before the ice sheets had receded or the continents had taken their shape, when the Thames emptied into the Rhine and the British Channel was the valley of the Seine. But no trace remains of the tales that were told. Anthropology may surmise something of their content from the study of savages today, but the history we reconstruct from the chipped stones and burial mounds of our prehistoric ancestors is our own, not theirs. It is a closing chapter, not the opening, of the history of history.

The term "prehistoric history" is, therefore, new. Once, not so very long ago, prehistory meant what it seems to say; it implied in a general way that there were ages of peoples, prior to those known to us, which were devoid of history. One did not generally stop to inquire whether they themselves were devoid of it or whether it was ourselves who were devoid of whatever history they may have had. In either case the main point was clear; the term was a general negative. Its application, on the other hand, was definite; it referred to what lay beyond the Old Testament, Herodotus, and a few other texts from the classics. For what lay beyond them was an unreal world of myth and legend, vague in outline, irrecoverable.

In our own day all this has changed. Archaeology, pushing the frontiers of knowledge into that seemingly impenetrable past, has enlarged the field of history, both by the recovery of texts written over a thousand years before the oldest texts of the Bible and by its own modern story of still more remote antiquities. Since this latter is the more comprehensive,—and the more important, it,

Prehistory; Myth and Legend

rather than the work of any hieroglyphic or cuneiform writer, is commonly taken as the measure of the field of history and its farther limits as the boundaries between the historical and the prehistorical. Taken strictly, this would mean that those boundaries would shift with every new discovery of archaeology, and, as the result would be unending confusion, it is customary now to regard the whole field in which the archaeologist can find any recorded texts as lying within the field of history. The test for the distinction between history and prehistory is therefore the existence—or persistence—of inscriptions, since upon them depend the possibilities of history. Even where the inscriptions are not yet deciphered, the fact of their existence makes the field potential history. The implements are at hand by which, some day, the past from which they came shall be known, and if, at present, we have not learned to use them, the confident movement of modern scholarship includes them in the field of history along with those already mastered.[1] The distinction between history and prehistory has in it a certain flavor of anticipation as well as of achievement and does not always meet the facts of the case. Where this anticipation involves too great a strain upon one's faith, it is at times disregarded; but upon the whole it is as good a distinction as has been found, and the archaeologist is justifying it by works.

The term "prehistoric" is therefore to be used, not so much for the preknown past—since much inside the field of history remains unknown and on the other hand much beyond it is known—as for the preinscriptional or preliterary past. This, at first sight, may seem a very inadequate test, since inscriptions furnish even the literary archaeologist with only a meagre portion of the sources from which he pieces together his story. But in reality it is as nearly decisive as anything can be. It marks the line between

---

[1] In a sense, the meaning has not changed so much as might seem; for when the field of history did not reach beyond the Bible and Herodotus, the hieroglyphs were unread and the key to them supposedly lost for all time. So the oldest texts limited the field of history. One may say, however, that the term "prehistory" is used upon the whole with something of the vagueness of the term "history." Different writers use it differently. Sometimes it seems to mean the history of peoples devoid of civilization, in particular of those in the Stone Age, preceding the ages of metals.

the possibilities of narratives about definite persons and the vague movements of peoples—in short, the line between the particular and the general. But more than this, writing alone, among all the sources of history, preserves events. Monuments furnish only hints and implications of them. The stone circles of Stonehenge indicate that once a numerous tribe concentrated its energy upon a great achievement. But we do not know what tribe it was or what motive, religious or monumental, led to this concentration of energy. All we have is the achievement. Even drawings, unless they have some word or sign attached, do not perpetuate definite events. The bison drawn by the palaeolithic cave men may be symbols from the realm of magic or memories of the hunt; there is no way of knowing which. The hieroglyph, which is half picture, half writing, can arrange its succession of symbols so that by the addition of many, side by side, a sort of moving-picture narrative is told. But only writing, that mobile medium, responsive to changing fact, can record motives or deal with action; and these are the proper themes of history.[2]

The field of prehistory is joined with that of history by archaeology, which works with impartial zeal in both, though with different methods. In the prehistoric field, since the documents are lacking, it can only verify its conclusions by the comparison of the remains of the culture of unknown peoples with the output of similar cultures today. This is the *comparative method* of anthropology which has thus been called into service to enable us to recover the unrecorded past before history began. Tasmanian savages a generation ago or African Bushmen today illustrate

[2] The mention of the moving picture suggests that, if the test for the distinction between prehistory and history is the use of writing, we may be at another boundary mark today. Writing is, after all, but a poor makeshift. When one compares the best of writings with what they attempt to record, one sees that this instrument of ours for the reproduction of reality is almost palaeolithic in its crudity. It loses even the color and tone of living speech, as speech, in turn, reproduces but part of the psychic and physical complex with which it deals. We can, at best, sort out a few facts from the moving mass of events and dress them up in the imperfections of our rhetoric, to survive as fading simulacra in the busy forum of the world. Some day the media in which we work today to preserve the past will be seen in all their inadequacy and crudity when new implements for mirroring thought, expression, and movement will have been acquired. Then we, too, may be numbered among the prehistoric.

the life and society of the men of the old stone age in Europe. Where bone implements are added to the primitive equipment and tools of the hunt become more efficient, the Eskimo may furnish a clue not only to the mode of life but even to the mental outlook. Thus, through varying grades of culture, the comparative method may test the sources of archaeology by the data of anthropology.

This is not the place to enter into a critical description of such a method; but it may not be out of place, as we pass along, to repeat the warning which anthropologists have frequently issued, that there is no more treacherous method in the scientific world today than this use of analogies, which at first sight seems so easy. One should be trained in the method of anthropology before using it, just as one should be trained in the use of historical sources before writing history.[3] In the first place, the things compared must be really comparable. This sounds like an absurdly elementary principle, and yet a vast amount of anthropological history has been written in disregard of it. Institutions from different tribes, which bear an external resemblance, have been torn from their setting, massed together and made the basis of sweeping generalizations as to the general scheme of social evolutions, and the data of the prehistoric world have then been interpreted in the light of inferences from these conclusions. Such schemes are not history, but speculation. Some of them may even yet be verified by fact and turn out to be true; but the historian should not mistake their character. If his training in the historical method has amounted to anything, he should not lose sight of the fact that phenomena are never quite the same outside of their environment, for the environment is part of them. The significance of an institution depends not so much upon its existence or form as upon its use.

However, within broad limits and used with due caution, the

[3] For examples of the comparative method as applied by the earlier anthropologists, accompanied by a thoroughgoing criticism by John Dewey, see W. I. Thomas, *Source Book for Social Origins* (1909), Part II: "Mental Life and Education." A long bibliography is appended to the section. The numerous works of Franz Boas, as well as those of his former students, furnish both direction and example in sound methods in anthropology.

comparative method may furnish an anthropological history of the prehistoric world. It can suggest manners and customs and even—which alone concerns us here—a glimpse of the mental outlook of peoples who have kept no history of their own, for, in a general way, the reactions of all men in similar circumstances are alike. The tales they tell in Mexico resemble those of ancient Babylon. Heroes perform almost the same feats through the entire semisavage world, varied only by the local conditions, and the mysteries of Olympian councils are disclosed in recognizable terms.

Now, upon the whole, it is the case that tales are retold only when they are worth telling. The test as to whether they are worth telling or not is whether they are listened to. This furnishes us with a clue as to their general character, for men do not gather willingly to hear about commonplace things of daily routine, which, so far as possible, have been turned over to the women. Just as the men have taken to themselves the careers of adventure, of war and the chase, they wish to make their tales adventures of the mind. This means that the universal content of all early tales is myth.[4] For myth alone can supply enough of the element of surprise, of the strange and mysterious. In the world of luck and miracle, with its constant possibility of dramatic turns, the dramatis personae are only supernatural. The explanation of this lies in the tendency of the savage to "animize" his world. Dawn and clouds, fire, running water, dark caves or groves, animals, queer things or people, whatever strikes his fancy and remains un-understood, is likely to become a "presence," an uncanny something that lies in that fearsome realm where things are lucky or unlucky in their own right, sacred or accursed, acting irresponsibly or, in any case, beyond the normal line of mere

---

[4] The term myth is used here in the definite sense of the tale involving supernatural elements. It is also used in English loosely to include all legendary material. The instances cited in the Oxford dictionary furnish a commentary upon the unformed state of thinking in this field. The classic chapters on mythology in E. B. Tylor, *Primitive Culture*, although published in 1871, are still worth reading in this connection. Since those pioneering days, however, anthropology has supplied whole libraries of material.

human conduct. The world is so full of these uncanny things that the story of even daily life among primitive peoples is bound to contain enough myth to condemn it utterly in a rationalistic society. And yet it may be mainly true—true to the experiences of its authors and perpetuators.

The commonest theme of such myths is that which gives the savage mind its greatest adventure, the myth of the origin of things. All people have their versions of Genesis. The curiosity which prompts one to keep asking how the story ends is not less keen in inquiring how it began. Where different people have lived much alike, the explanations of their similar worlds are strikingly similar. One can match not a few of the elements in the Hebrew book of origins by the myths of the savage world. But this is too varied and too unhistorical a problem for us to pursue in detail here.

The world of myth is one of miracle, where gods and even heroes are transformed before one's eyes, where, as in a land of dreams, animals talk, invisible presences are heard along the winds, trees imprison, and earth engulfs. So unreal do these seem to the civilized man that he thinks of them as the conscious effort of invention, a product of that poetic capacity which he takes for granted in early peoples. But, however strongly the fancy plays in simple minds, the myth is seldom, if ever, the creation of individual, conscious effort—the result of a single expedition of the questing intelligence. It is rather the booty of the tribe, the heritage from immemorial quests. The shaman or priest may mould mythologies and transform them, as the epic poet may develop original incidents in his legend, but the range of his creative imagination is anything but bold and free in the sense in which Plato thought of its freedom. For instance, when Homer makes Athene take the form of a swallow he is not inventing as Kipling may have done in his *Jungle Books*. Athene, or some such goddess, had been transforming herself for untold centuries before Homer embodied the miraculous incident in his narrative.[5]

---

[5] A more definite contrast might be cited in the descent of Athene from Olympus (*Iliad*, Book IV, lines 75 *sqq.*), and Milton's description of Satan's fall. Homer's picture is based upon the fall of stars. "Even as the son of Kronos the crooked

In fact, what strikes the student of mythologies most is the poverty, rather than the richness, of the primitive imagination. Imagination must use the materials of experience to build its creations, however fantastically it may combine them, and as the range of experience of early man is much narrower than that of the civilized, the myths, which register these creations, run in relatively narrow grooves. There are common themes which one finds repeated with almost identical details in the most widely scattered tribes—not only in the myths of origin but of such events as wars in heaven and floods on earth and universal heroes who slay dragons, fight giants, and rescue the weak by prowess and miracle. Anthropologists formerly sought to trace these back to some common source and viewed them as evidence of a common origin of the varying cultures which preserved them. But now it is seen that no such history need exist. The war of the gods in which the beneficent deities of light and life overthrow the dragon-like forces of evil and chaos was a theme native to many other places besides the Nile and the Euphrates. Myths like those of Marduk and Horus were independent of each other; for the sun-god represented the triumph of order and settled life, when the earliest farmers began to tame the wastes, drain the swamps, and plough the fields. In short, the history of the gods was but a reflection of the activities of the society which produced them. In this sense they are a sort of perverted, divine reflection of history, preserving in a distorting but vivid medium some portions of the general story of a people. "Myth is the history of its authors, not of its subjects; it records the lives, not of superhuman heroes but of poetic nations."[6]

This social origin and authorship of myth, while it does not preclude the possibility of individual creations and modifications now and then, enables one to understand two things which would otherwise puzzle one in dealing with the primitive mind. In the first place, that realm of mystery is not entirely mysterious. It

---

counsellor sendeth a star, a portent for mariners or a wide host of men, bright shining, and therefrom are scattered sparks in multitude, even in such guise sped Pallas Athene to earth..." Such portents furnished the inevitability of the simile.

[6] E. B. Tylor, *Primitive Culture* (3d ed., 2 vols., 1891), I, 416.

Prehistory; Myth and Legend

is as much a part of nature as the rest. This means that the savage is conscious of crossing no barriers as he turns from the real to the imaginary. In the second place, the social belief in the tale brings to its explanations somewhat the force of a suggestion of nature itself, and so they impose themselves upon the mind with the sense of things final and inevitable.

At once, this brings us upon a fact more vital for the history of history than all the content of the myths—the tendency to believe. It is well to interest oneself in the fate of the gods, but it is impious to inquire too much of them. This religious attitude of acceptance is largely responsible for the absurdities which the myths contain, since it is not fitting to apply the canons of common-sense criticism to them. But its significance extends far beyond the boundaries of myth and prehistory. It is still, in spite of the growth of criticism and of science, the ordinary attitude of the ordinary man. The first impulse upon hearing any tale is to accept it as true,[7] unless it in itself contradicts what has already been believed or seems to imply such a contradiction. Credulity is a natural attitude of mind; criticism is one of the most difficult acquisitions of culture. The importance of this fact will furnish some of the main themes in the history which follows.

The credulity of the primitive, however, has more excuse than ours, for he has a different appreciation of fact. We draw distinctions between the real, the probable, and the possible, between things that are in their own right and things whose existence depends upon that of others. This borderland of possibility we place outside the realm of fact, not losing sight of the condition upon which it rests. The savage stresses the fact and tends to forget the condition. The unhappy anthropologist who offers to do something for a native "if he can" finds himself regarded as having broken his word if he does not fulfil his promise, even if the conditions remain unfulfilled. When we apply such an attitude

---

[7] Dr. Paul Radin has furnished me with an unusually interesting instance of this. During his researches among the Winnebagos he asked a half-breed, who affected disdain for most of the Indian beliefs, if he thought there were any truth in a medicine man's graphic and detailed story of his former incarnations. The puzzled reply was that he didn't know but thought there might be something in it, "for otherwise why did the shaman say so?"

of mind to problems of mythology it explains largely the positive character of the creations of what we call the primitive imagination.[8]

Under such circumstances, the myth develops a life of its own. The conditional elements in it drop away; uncertainties become fact by the mere force of statement. Its origins are lost sight of. Hera may once have been the air and Demeter a sheaf of wheat, but somehow in the course of divine events, by common human consent, they became deities and lived henceforth the life divine. To us moderns it was a purely imaginary existence, but the myth acquires its authority upon the very opposite assumption. And when temples are erected to the deities, art and literature find in them their inspiration, when states trust to their protection and individuals turn to them for salvation, both imagination and memory are left far behind; the myth becomes a real and potent element in the facts of history and life.

And yet it is the divine or supernatural element in the myth which is its own best preservative. Whatever lies within the sphere of religion is protected, the world over, by a vast and unrelenting primitive law, which we call the taboo. Everything connected with worship, from magic to mysticism, is sacred, and whatever is sacred cannot be treated like ordinary things. It contains something of the power, diabolic or divine,[9] which moves by supernature and mystery to afflict or bless those who come in contact with it. Sacrilege needs no legal penalties in societies where religion really rules; it enforces its own punishment through the terrors of the psychic world. So, just as the fetishes and altars used in worship are surcharged with this sacredness which ensures their protection, the myths which embody the story of the gods are preserved by their own religious quality. To know the story of the god, and especially to know his true name, is of the greatest importance to the worshippers, since in the story and the name lies some mysterious suggestion of potency. So the shaman and his priestly successors, as those best fitted to deal with such sacred

---

[8] The simple-minded novel reader in the modern world has much the same attitude. The conditions of the story are forgotten.

[9] Sacredness is a general term and has the power to curse as well as to bless.

Prehistory; Myth and Legend

things, tend to become the keepers of the mystic tale along with the other objects of cult. In the early world such specialization is more or less informal and by no means rigid; but the tendency to intrust the myths to theological care is already evident long before the development of hierarchies.

We are not interested here in the later fate of the myths as parts of theological systems, for there they lose all but a faint echo of their historical sources, if such existed, and become at last a rather artificial element of religions which grow away from them—as the modern world has grown away from the more incongruous stories of the Old Testament and the more miraculous legends of the saints and martyrs of the Middle Ages. Ritual,[10] in which the baldest, most compact statements and representations are reduced to epigrammatic and poetic terseness, preserves a last suggestion of the ancient origins, by reason of its direct connection with the altar and the rite—sometimes even after the religion in which it is set has ceased to understand its meaning—as in the well-known case of the Arval priests at Rome, reciting in archaic speech what had become little more than a magical charm.[11] And yet, in such faint and unintelligible ways, the traces of past ages lasted on—less history for the worshippers who listened to the mummery than for the modern historian to whom they are no longer sacred utterances, and who is therefore free to trace their human origins.[12]

---

[10] Ritual, whether in word or act, must be performed with absolute accuracy. Any error is sure to bring the wrath of the gods upon all concerned and the vengeance of society upon the blunderer. Anthropology supplies many instances of the infliction of severe punishment for carelessness or mistake.

[11] The magical or priestly formula sometimes repeats the potent words of the gods in some ancient myth, of which the formula is the only fragment preserved. A good example is given in A. Erman, *Life in Ancient Egypt* (tr., 1894), p. 353. A charm for burns was obviously taken from a call of Isis, the mistress of magic, for the aid of Horus: "My son Horus, it burns on the mountain, no water is there, I am not there, fetch water from the bank of the river to put out the fire." In this connection it might be recalled that the recital of the names of the gods, with all their attributes, in incantation or prayer, involved a certain amount of mythological lore.

[12] The persistence of even a mere divine name may furnish the clue to great events; the images of the gods, the robes and sacrificial implements of the priests may preserve archaic traces which open up lost pages of history. We do not have to go outside Jewish and Christian rituals to see the persistence of similar suggestions of the past. The whole calendar of sacred festivals is a reminder of sacred

But there is a human, as well as a divine, side to the myth, and as the divine tends to drop away or change except where embodied in ritual and preserved by priests, the human side develops, mainly by way of poets, into that antetype of history—the legend. The gods still come and go; they hold their councils as of old, and they seem to outrange the feeble will of man; but in reality the human beings are the heroes, upon whom the interest of the tale and the sympathy of the listener are concentrated, and even the gods dispense with their divinity wherever the interests of the story demand it.

It is not possible definitely to mark off the myth from the legend, for myths enter into all early narratives. And yet it may clarify our survey if we regard as legend those stories which carry the human theme uppermost. The legendary, therefore, lies between the mythical and the historical. As we have just seen, myth penetrates it and long furnishes the dramatic element, the sudden turns, the swift surprises, the justice that tracks the feet of crime, the fate that stands behind and mocks—and pulls the strings. Thus, often, as in Homer, the legend seems to be largely a repository for myth, in spite of all its worldly interests. Indeed the poet, far from being a bold innovator carrying the social outlook frankly away from the myth, is really a conservator of what is otherwise outworn. The ancient tale acquires in his eyes a kind of sanctity which is the secular parallel of its sacredness in religion.

In the naïve creations of the early epics this emphasis upon the gods is taken for granted; but once the poets start upon their proper work of conscious creation in the realm of imagination, their true attitude toward myth becomes apparent. There has been only one great poet of the uncompromising, scientific mind, Lucretius. Even to our own day the mythology of the world has survived in its poetry. Nor is this all to be dismissed as the play of pure fancy. In an age of faith, Dante or Milton can impress

---

history; J. T. Shotwell, "The Discovery of Time," in *The Journal of Philosophy*, Vol. XII (1915), No. 10. Religion has proved to be the greatest reservoir of past usages; but its service to history is that of a social archivist rather than that of a social historian.

their schemes of cosmology upon the world with at least as much success as the theologians. Even in Goethe's day the philosophy of life lost nothing by being deliberately expressed along the lines of old folk myths, and the cruder imaginations could find more than symbol in the story of Faust. Poetry, in short, may have furnished a bridge from myth to history, but its connection with the farther shore has never been broken, and although the inquisitive thought of the civilized world has moved across it to the conquest of reality, it still retains its ancient character.

Legends, therefore, so long as they are preserved by the poets, mark but a single stage of the advance toward history. Poetry, as Thucydides pointed out, is a most imperfect medium for fact. Its ideal is of another kind. Beauty or power, emotional stress and thrill are its aims, and to achieve these it properly forsakes dull, calculable reality. Its mythical elements are the least misleading, for its human heroes are given imaginary roles; their exploits are set in the world of romance, and from of old the world of romance has been, some way or other, the world of the unreal. Homeric warriors, for instance, use the bronze weapons of an age already growing distant in the days when the poems were recited. Then the bard exaggerates or distorts his story to please his listeners; which means that each society in which it is recited impresses changes upon it. So, although much of the early past has been handed down to us in epic, in ballad, and in the poetically turned legends of folk lore, these artistic creations belong rather to the history of literature than that of history proper.

And yet the early poet, like the priest, knew the tribal lore. He was held in high regard, not as a mere entertainer like the travelling minstrel of a later day, but as a sage who knew the ways of gods to men, and who could draw enough lessons from the past to satisfy any barbarously moralizing Ciceros or Carlyles. He may have lacked history in the true sense of the word, but he at least knew that philosophy which teaches by experience. For the most important part of his tale came to him by tradition, in contrast to the part he himself invented. The first qualification of the bard was memory rather than imagination. Imagination filled in the gaps, but the past supplied the theme.

Legendary history is preserved by this oral tradition. There is, naturally, no other way to preserve it among preliterate or illiterate peoples. But the extent of it and its relative reliability are a source of unfailing wonder to the student of history. For unlettered societies, when left to themselves, with no modern devices to fall back upon, make up for the absence of reading by an almost incredible extension of the power of memory. It is not the bard alone who can recite his story; tradition becomes to a large degree a social heritage, and nothing is more remarkable than the way in which a tribe or a clan will repeat its legends, generation after generation. Hour after hour, almost day after day, the primitive storyteller can recite not merely the deeds of gods and men, but the exact words of the ancient myths. Indeed this is, perhaps, one of the main reasons for the form of poetry in which it is cast, for rhythm and metre swing the memory along, while prose seems to snap the cord. So among early peoples the *whole* record of the past tends to be embodied in poetry—more or less—from bald lists of names in genealogies arranged for a singsong chant to inspiring epic and stirring ballad. The role of memory is now lessening. We trust to books and put our memories with them on the shelf. But we can still testify to the acuteness of the primitive methods. When we try to memorize even a few names in a row, we unconsciously fall back upon the devices of our bardic forerunners and, if we can, commit them to memory in a singsong.[13]

When we turn to examine the content of these early, legendary traditions where they are accessible, we find them, like the myths, perpetuating all kinds of things. It is impossible to delay here over any detailed examinations of them. Their study belongs to the field of folk lore, a field in which scientific methods have as yet made but little progress.[14] But history may sometimes find

---

[13] This is not advanced as a general theory for the origins of poetry. There is virtue in rhythm besides its aid to memory, as the dance sufficiently indicates. Ritual also plays its role. But the rhythmic element in mere prosy lists hints at its utility there as well.

[14] At the close of the eighteenth century Herder pointed out the importance of folk lore in the crude, natural poetry preserved by historic peoples down to the present. The work of the brothers Grimm and of the whole romanticist movement greatly enriched this popular literature. But the romanticists overburdened it with

Prehistory; Myth and Legend

in it at least a general guidance in matters otherwise unrecoverable. The incidental mention of natural objects helps to throw light upon the character of the civilization which produced the legend. For instance, the tales of early Rome point to a farming community. In like manner, the very absence of mention is sometimes just as significant. None of these same early Roman legends points to the sea. The story of Aeneas's wanderings came in after Greek civilization had penetrated Italy. It was obviously manufactured after the Romans knew about Greece and appreciated Homer enough to wish to trace their ancestry to the fields of Troy. We know that this was the case because there are no primitive traditions that correspond to it. It was invented to suit the occasion by men of a later age.[15]

There are, however, various types of legend: the folk tale that no one made, that was born in no one brain, but, like Topsy in *Uncle Tom's Cabin,* met a social demand, ready-made; the heroic legend invented long after the events with which it deals, a romance produced to glorify a monarch, a nation, or a noble house, like the tales of early wars or genealogies that reached back to the gods and so flattered their happy recipient with divine ancestry; and, finally, the aetiological legend which evoked some alleged fact of history to explain how something came to be the

---

the trappings of their imaginations and made it unreal either as representing primitive or modern ideas. Historical criticism, which had seen the legends of Homer and regal Rome destroyed, was, therefore, unwilling to grant even proper recognition to folk lore as a serious occupation. Finally at the opening of the twentieth century, the comparative method, rescued in turn from its cruder uses, has enabled the historian to proceed upon cautious and promising principles for the appraisal of the value of traditions.

[15] The myths of the historic nations, especially those of Greece and Rome and, to a less extent, of the north of Europe have been published in such a variety of forms and have entered into literature to such an extent as to make any short survey of the field well-nigh impossible. Beginning with *Handbücher* and dictionaries of classical antiquities, the student may pass a busy life in merely keeping up with the available works dealing with the subject. One thing only need be said here, and that is that since the comparative method was first applied, by Max Müller, to the elucidation of the myths of Greece and Rome—basing it upon philology, on the one hand, for the names of the gods, and upon natural phenomena (sky, sun, earth, etc., for their origin)—the study has made long progress. The anthropological archaeologists forcibly invaded the field in the twentieth century, and, although their first attempts at interpreting were somewhat too confident and a bit careless, they have made over almost our whole conception of the religious outlook of the antique world.

way it was, why a certain spot was sacred or a certain ceremony was performed. The folk tale may be roughly compared to the fiction of our own day; but the heroic and aetiological legends did for primitive society what much historical writing does for more advanced societies—they lauded and magnified men or institutions which were held in popular esteem, and they explained the present by invoking its origins in the past.[16] Frequently these legends contained a considerable element of truth, but the difficulty of deciding which kind of legend one is dealing with and whether it is primitive or artificial makes the task of the scholar who would learn true history from them an extremely delicate and treacherous one. For even the genuine folk tales come to us worked over by successive generations until they are often so obscured that with the combined resources of archaeology, anthropology, and history one can but guess at their value and true meaning.

Looking over the field of myth and legend as a whole, we see that we are everywhere outside the boundary of genuine history. History may incorporate portions of their substance, but it differs from them in both means and end. It is not a thing of poetry but of prose; it needs sobriety and commonplaceness of expression, just as it needs rigid outlines, if the fancy which runs wild in legend is to be checked and the narrative made worthy of the credence of inquiring men. Then, that narrative must be intrusted to something more reliable than memory—even social memory at its best. And finally it must be kept definite in outline and positive in dates. So history must pass by way of written records out of the realm of taboo and folk lore, which priests and poets perpetuate. The vague or rambling tradition must become a straightforward narrative, taking into account the steadily passing years. There are, therefore, outside myth and epic, two indispensable bases for history: writing and mathematics; the one to record what time would otherwise indifferently blot out, the other to measure time itself in calendars and chronology.

[16] For a fuller discussion of this point see J. W. Swain, "What Is History?" in *Journal of Philosophy*, Vol. XX (1923), Nos. 11, 12, and 13, esp. pp. 282 *sqq.*

CHAPTER IV

Books and Writing

WRITING ranks next to speech itself as the implement and embodiment of thought. Yet its evolution has been exceedingly slow and is still most imperfect. Even today, if we take the world as a whole, a majority of men and women must learn by word of mouth alone whatever they are to know, since the magic of the alphabet and of its combinations on the printed page is still beyond their grasp. Yet the Australian blacks, the lowest of existing mankind, can read crude markings on twigs made by distant tribes; the Bushmen of South Africa—of low grade among the Africans—can draw their pictures of the hunt almost to match the hieroglyphs of Egypt. From message sticks to picture writing the gulf seems wide, and the next step—from picture writing to an alphabet—seems small in comparison. But on the contrary, while the cave dwellers of Europe, ten to twenty thousand years ago, could draw the bison and the reindeer with a skill to match the artist of today, such simple things as letters are the invention of those comparatively recent times when merchant ships from Tyre and Sidon were already exploiting the markets of the Mediterranean. As for the extensive use of writing, in literature, records, or journalism, it occupied no such place in the cultures of antiquity—even of Greece at its best—as it does today.

One reason for this is obvious—the lack of paper. We have been taught in our history manuals the revolutionary effects of the invention of the printing press upon the history of western thought, but paper is just as important as the press. Imagine what it would be like if our libraries were stacked with chiselled slabs of stone or tablets of baked clay, if our newspapers were sun-dried bricks. When papyrus, the paper of the ancient world, came to be used in Egypt, the writing changed, lost its slow, old pictures, and became much like ours; and instead of a few walls or steles covered with hieroglyphs, there were libraries filled with manuscripts. Stone, as a medium for writing, has a double disadvantage; it is not only hard to manipulate, it is practically immovable. One has to go to it to read. The inscription is part of a monument instead of a thing in itself, like the writing on a piece of papyrus. Babylonia never suffered from this handicap as Egypt did; owing to lack of stone it wrote on clay, inferior to papyrus but usable. It is hard to draw pictures or to write with a round hand on clay, so the Babylonian bricks and cylinders were scratched with straight little wedgelike marks. And the weight of brick or cylinder was such as to force the scribe to write with almost microscopic fineness.

It takes but a moment's thought to realize how the medium for preserving literature conditions its scope and its place in society. What is written depends in a great degree upon what it is written on. It is well, therefore, before surveying the early records of history, to examine hurriedly the manner and method of the composition, the more so, as historiography seldom deigns to cast its eye on so purely material a basis for its existence.[1]

Stone and clay, the first two media of Egypt and Babylonia, were, as we have seen, definitely limited in their possibilities. There was need of a lighter, thinner substance, suitable for carrying around yet strong enough not to break easily with general use. Egypt ultimately had recourse to the use of papyrus, Babylonia more to that of leather. But there was a primitive substitute for both of these which we must not forget. Leaves of trees sometimes furnish such a medium in tropical countries, particularly the tough-fibred palm leaf, of use especially in India. The hieroglyphs preserve traces of its use in Egypt as well. In temperate climates where even this fragile writing surface is not at hand, wood furnished the commonest substitute. Our barbarian ancestors in northern Europe, improving a little on the twigs, which the

---

[1] The literature on this interesting background of history mainly goes back to the capital work of Th. Birt, *Das antike Buchwesen* (1882).

earliest savages notched for messages or memoranda, inscribed their runic markings on rudely cut branches of trees.

A new era in literature was made possible by the use of the metallic saw. When boards became common, they offered a good and ready medium and were in general use throughout the antique world, wherever lumber was plentiful. Small, square, or oblong boards were especially in demand as tablets for notetaking or memoranda; as such they were used by schoolchildren far back in ancient Egypt. But, although also serving at times for recording literature, they were more generally used in Greece and Rome for matters of business and for correspondence, being lighter and cheaper than lead or other metallic tablets, which were also used, and cheaper than leather. In such cases it was customary to fold two tablets together,[2] and the interior cover was commonly covered with wax. Boards were also used, however, for formal inscriptions, the most famous being the white tablet, known as the album, upon which the Pontifex Maximus inscribed the events of the year and which was displayed at the Regia, the origin of the official annals of Rome. In early Greece they were used to write down the works of the poets, which a still earlier age had committed to memory. Tradition has it that Greek tyrants, presumably copying the example of the library of Assurbanipal of the seventh century, gathered libraries and employed scholars to edit the classical texts. But the scholarly activity could not achieve much when it would require two hundred wooden tablets to arrange and handle the two Homeric epics. It is clear that wood, like stone or brick, serves only for the preliminary and casual phases of the history of writing.

The antique world could never have developed the classical literatures in all their variety and freedom of scope, had there

---

[2] These tablets were also sometimes of lead or other metals. The two folded together were known as the diptych. Often it was ornamented on the outer covers. Used widely for correspondence, diptychs were also sent around by consuls and other officials upon assuming office, to apprise their friends of the dignity and title. The Christian church, adopting this use, kept diptychs with the names of clergy, saints, and martyrs at their altars. The relation of these with mediaeval annals is of much interest in this connection.

been nothing better to write upon. Two substances saved the situation, papyrus and leather. Of these two, the latter played little part in the Mediterranean world during classical antiquity. In the Orient, leather had always been in use, and in the fourth century of the Christian era that form of it known as parchment came to be used in the West for books and documents which were to be preserved. But the *paper* of Greek and Roman times was papyrus.

As far back as the fourth millennium B.C., Egyptians knew how to cut through the stem of the papyrus reed, and, pasting two thin slips of its stringy marrow back-to-back, crossways on, secured a tough and satisfactory writing surface. As we have already pointed out, the scribe could write upon it with a flowing hand, which eliminated much of the toilsome picture writing of the genuine hieroglyph upon the stone. But yet, so impressive were the monumental inscriptions, so rigid the strength of Egyptian traditions, that the home of the papyrus did not produce that last essential to writing—the alphabet.

By the twelfth century B.C., the business men of the market ports of Phoenicia, keen-witted as their Hellenic neighbors of a later day, seem to have realized the usefulness of Egyptian papyrus, for Egyptian records show that they imported it to their cities at least as early as the middle of that century.[3] The use of papyrus elsewhere seems to have spread rather slowly. In western Asia it did not displace the widespread use of leather to any great extent. The Hebrew scriptures, for instance, were written on rolls of leather, not on papyrus. The Greeks, too, were surprisingly slow to adopt it. Already by the middle of the sixth century B.C., they were familiar with the material, which they named "biblos" ($βύβλος$ or $βίβλος$) from the Phoenician city which traded in it. Herodotus, however, in the fifth century decribes the papyrus growing in Egypt without mentioning its use as paper and so has left an open conjecture as to what he had in mind when he

[3] J. H. Breasted, *Ancient Records of Egypt* (5 vols., 1906-1907), IV, 284. It seems likely that they also manufactured a paper from other reeds, perhaps from some grown nearer home. This may explain the treatment by Herodotus.

Books and Writing

referred to $\beta \acute{v} \beta \lambda o \varsigma$.[4] As a matter of fact, the Greeks were always hampered by the scarcity of papyrus, which they had to import. This partly accounts for the extent to which their literature was cast in form for oral delivery rather than for private reading. Papyrus began to appear at the time of the great lyric poets, and to it is probably due the preservation of the works of Sappho, Alcaeus, and Anacreon. Written prose dates from the end of the sixth century. Herodotus first composed his history for public recitation. Indeed, Thucydides was apparently the first Greek to write a long book primarily for readers rather than for listeners.

Scholarship as we know it, research based upon written texts, was naturally slow to develop under these conditions. Thucydides, like Herodotus, conducted his investigations largely by word-of-mouth inquiry. There was apparently no great library at Athens, even under Pericles. The first public library in that city was not erected until the reign of Hadrian. It was in the land of the papyrus itself that the first great Greek library flourished. The date of the founding of the libraries of Alexandria is not quite certain, but the first was probably founded by Ptolemy Philadelphus in the middle of the third century B.C., probably in imitation of the celebrated library of Assurbanipal in the seventh century or of the temple libraries of Egypt under the Pharaohs. Later there were celebrated libraries at Pergamum and Ephesus, and Augustus founded one at Rome. Under the Empire there were good libraries in all important cities. Thus, thanks to papyrus, scholars were able to familiarize themselves freely with the works of their predecessors.

The influence of these libraries of Alexandria, and of their librarians, upon the literature and thought of antiquity was very great. Even the seemingly trivial needs of the shelf-room classification had most important results; for, in order to arrange their writings readily, they cut them up. The average strip of papyrus

---

[4] From Biblos comes our word Bible. The paper itself, before it was written upon, was called $\chi \acute{a} \rho \tau \eta \varsigma$ or *charta*, which also suggests a changed history. A length of papyrus was termed $\tau \acute{o} \mu o \varsigma$ or *tomus*, from the fact that it was "cut off," or, in Latin, a *volumen*, from the fact that it was wound up. The Latin word *liber* refers to the whole book and is identical with *volumen*.

which could be easily filed away and in which one could readily find references was from twenty to thirty feet long. The roll was therefore cut off to about this length. Since the older authors, those prior to the age of Alexandrian savants, had not composed their works with reference to any such bibliographical needs, the scholars deftly divided them into sections, "tomes" or books, to suit their needs. So the text of Herodotus was divided into nine sections, each set apart under the symbol of a Muse. Thucydides' history was similarly broken up into eight books. After the scholars had thus recast the literature already written, the authors of more recent antiquity wrote with an eye to dividing their own texts so that the rolls would be of proper length and the pigeon-holes on the library walls would easily take them in. In this way the expedients of the ancient librarians affected the classics.

All the antique, classical literature was produced under these conditions. Yet, until the recent discoveries of archaeology, not a classical text has reached us in its original form of papyrus roll. In fact papyrus itself disappears from common use, and its place is taken by parchment.[5] The reason for this is not altogether clear. There was a decline in the output of the papyrus plant itself, and then it disappeared from the Nile delta altogether. From the fourth century of our era the papyrus roll was replaced by an entirely different form of book, the parchment codex.

The name parchment comes from the city of Pergamum, on the coast of Asia Minor. There, in the second century B.C., a Greek tyrant, Eumenes II (197–159), made his capital of a state that had been built out of the Macedonian Empire. On the crest of a lofty hill, which dominated the city, he placed a palace, a temple, and a library that was one of the wonders of the world.[6] Legend, as recorded by the antiquarian Varro,[7] had it that the rival tyrant in Egypt, Ptolemy VI, refused to send papyrus and

---

[5] Papyrus paper was still used to some extent through the first part of the Middle Ages. For instance, it was used at the papal court until the eleventh century. But parchment was much more durable. The ancients regarded a papyrus two or three centuries old as rare.

[6] J. W. Clark, *The Care of Books* (2d ed., 1902), pp. 8 *sqq.*

[7] Pliny, *Naturalis historia*, Book XIII, Chap. 11. Jerome repeats the story, with slight variation, *Ep. VII ad Chromatium* (Th. Birt, *Das antike Buchwesen*, pp. 50 *sqq.*).

that, as a substitute, Eumenes invented parchment. The story, though still frequently quoted, does not hold; for the use of leather as writing material is as old as that of papyrus, or older; it was common throughout Asia, and was referred to already by Herodotus. But the name of Pergamum, attached to the sheets of leather (*pergamena charta*) seems to indicate a new process of tanning and preparation, and a centre of the trade at Pergamum.

For some five hundred years after the founding of the Pergamum library, papyrus still remained the common medium of writing. Finally, in the fourth century of our era it was superseded by the parchment, no longer wound into long rolls, but cut like the leaves of a modern book and fastened together in somewhat the same form as the tablets of wood had been, in what was called a codex.[8] Into these codices the works of antiquity were transcribed from the worn papyrus rolls by Christian scribes. What was not so transcribed was lost, for, as we have said above, no papyrus text survived. The fate of the classical literatures, and of much history, depended upon the smaller pages of the new form of book.

The parchment codex was not only more durable than the papyrus roll, it was more practicable. It enabled the Christians to have the entire Bible in one, easily handled volume. The earliest codices still preserved are the Bibles, the Vaticanus and the Sinaiticus, both of the fourth century. The ease with which the vellum or parchment could be washed or scraped to clean off its past writing and the surface used again for more pressing needs, also recommended it especially to the mediaeval scribes, since writing materials were so very scarce. Such palimpsests [9] still bore traces of their former use and in this manner the half-obliterated original was often preserved, when a feebler texture like papyrus would not have retained it. The papyrus leaves could be cleaned by a sponge, but were not strong enough to be used a second time for lasting documents. The practice of scraping the wax tables is also referred to by Cicero and must have been common, whatever the material used, so long as it was difficult to procure. The

---

[8] The word *caudex* or *codex* first meant the tree trunk.
[9] From the Greek πάλιν, *again*, and ψάω, *scrape*.

mediaeval palimpsests show by the fragmentary character of the original texts they preserve that the scribes supplied themselves with material from any old volumes that happened to be at hand without any care as to what had to be obliterated to make room for their own writing. Fragmentary as they are, however, these old texts, treated chemically and read critically by modern scholars, have restored many a precious passage of the lost literatures of antiquity. It is one of the ironies of history that books of devotion, used for centuries in the service of the Church which denounced the vanities of pagan thought and practice, kept for the modern humanist those very texts of myth or history which otherwise would have passed into complete oblivion.

The use of the codex persisted through the Middle Ages, and gave the suggestion for the modern book. Fortunately, during the century preceding the invention of printing by movable types, another substance began to be sufficiently common to cope with the increasing demand for writing materials. Paper was originally invented in China but was brought into Europe through the Mohammedan cultures of the Near East and Spain. As early as the twelfth century, sheets of it drifted into Christendom through those two open doors, the Moorish and the Italian trade, but it was not until the latter part of the fourteenth century that paper became the general medium for writing. It still remained comparatively rare—and generally good—until the invention of a machine at the close of the eighteenth century enabled manufacturers to make more than the one sheet at a time produced by the old hand process, even now in use in rare papers, bank notes, and the like. But with the vast and rapid increase in the output of paper in our own day comes an attendant danger to contemporary history, of which historians and librarians have warned repeatedly in vain. For the paper made today is the most fragile stuff to which any civilization has ever intrusted the keeping of its records. All but a tiny fraction of the vast output of our printing presses is crumbling and discolored waste a few years after it is printed upon. We are writing not upon sand but upon dust heaps. The thought is a sobering one to anyone who looks back, even in so short and superficial a survey as this, over the fate of other civilizations and the slight and fragmentary traces they have left.

We have mentioned, in passing, that the form of writing has to some extent depended upon the materials used. But writing has a history of its own, a history of so great importance to the historian that the study of the history of handwriting is a science in itself, palaeography. Even after the alphabet supplants hieroglyphics and so becomes the mere barren framework of words, its style changes with different cultures, and only those can read it who have made it a special study. For it requires constant familiarity with the crabbed and compressed text, with the forms of abbreviations and devices for shortening the interminable labor of transcription, to decipher the ancient manuscripts. Into this field, fundamental as it is to historical research, it is impossible to enter here. Fortunately the student of history today is able to travel far toward his goal, even in mediaeval and ancient history, without having to decipher manuscripts for himself. For, especially during the last hundred years, generations of scholars have been at work preparing the texts, and others have been equally busy criticizing them, so that the day is almost past when the historian has to make his pilgrimage from archive to archive to compare and copy the major texts of his sources and so be his own palaeographer.[10] The discipline involved is one which may always be indulged in to advantage, but the results to be obtained are growing steadily less, as the great collections of sources, edited by the most eminent of scholars, fill the shelves of our libraries at home.

All writing is in a sense historical, in that its purpose is to record something. So far we have been treating it almost as though it were an end in itself, but it is only a means for doing something else, such as stimulating thought or action. When we turn from the

[10] The development of the various devices for photographing, especially that of the photostating (since 1920), should be mentioned here. This is a field which archivists and librarians have shared with historians. A Joint Committee on Materials for Research, under the chairmanship of Professor Robert Binkley, has been reporting to the Social Science Research Council and the Council of Learned Societies for a number of years, but they regard their study as still in its initial stages. Progress in invention may, and probably will, change the very nature of all historical records in the not distant future.

means to the end, we are brought face to face with the origins of history.

The earliest markings were largely aids to memory, such as are in use throughout the savage world—scratches on sticks or leaves or bark of trees, runic signs, wampum belts, ensuring that both parties to an agreement remember alike, or spreading news, or recording it. One of the most important of such devices is the indication of rights of property by symbols denoting ownership. Thus the Maoris of New Zealand marked their lands by wisps of grass on boundary trees. Trespassers knew that the inclosed spaces were taboo to all but the owner, by reason of curses, of which the wisp of grass was but the symbol. A much more definite symbol of ownership would naturally be the representation of the proprietor's name, or that of his tribe. The common use of this was possibly long impeded by the fear that an enemy might secure such a name-picture for evil magic, for if he secures your name and anything of yours, he can have power over you. In spite of such fear, which must have hindered not only literature but the development of private property, the use of totem signs is common to indicate the name of a tribe or clan.

The earliest inscriptions, out of which grow the records of history, were, like these, mere monograms of names. They were, of course, the monograms of royal names, stamped on Egyptian stone or Babylonian brick, much as the letter boxes of England bear the symbol G. R. to indicate the reigning king. Such monograms, chiselled into the rock over five thousand years ago, retain for us the name of the reputed founder of the first dynasty of Egypt. Recovered only a few years ago, they prove to us that Menes of Memphis, that shadow figure which headed the long list of shadow kings and was already legend by the days of Herodotus, was a real man. The first inscriptions of Babylonia are similarly royal names and titles. They are historical records only by courtesy. Imagine the history of Anglo-Saxon England based upon nothing but the Alfred jewel or a historian of the distant future reconstructing the history of the Victorian era from a few stray stones on which the full titles of the empress queen were engraved! In time, however, the titles expand, indicating conquests by including new dignities and enumerating the lands over which the monarch rules. As the years go on, the titles grow more specific and detailed, and now and then in the boastful phrases of an epitaph (which had been carefully prepared during the lifetime of the king), we have almost a summary of the main events of the reign. This, for instance, is as far as the records of the old Babylonian kingdom seem to have gone.

As we have seen, the narrative grows out of the simple inscription almost unconsciously. Indeed it exists to some extent in the titles themselves, since the graphic hieroglyph tells the story as it depicts the results. The lord of the upper Nile smites the cowering inhabitants, the conqueror of Syria carries away the Semitic victims in chains. But the narrative also develops, alongside the public inscriptions, in tombs and temples; in tombs for the gods to read, in temples for the priests. Here, at last, we are on the verge of history; the temple record is the origin of annals. We are not beyond the verge, however, for these bald narratives are not histories, in the strictest sense. History is retrospective; these are mere lists of contemporary happenings. As the calendar developed, the events were entered year by year, giving us annals. But still that did not make them history. They were a sort of primitive journalism or official record, marking the present, not the past. The annalist writes down what is happening or what has just taken place. He enters on the temple lists the death of a priest or a king when it occurs, or he registers conquests under the royal command of the conqueror himself. It is only because the present is eternally becoming the past that these notes of contemporary events take on the character of history—as today's evening papers will be history tomorrow.

But the annal is also potentially historical. The past, not the present, gives it its value and interest. Moreover, the step from the annal to the chronicle is a short one. Prefix a few genealogies or the legendary deeds of the sovereign's divine ancestors and the narrative becomes historical. Where such a narrative follows a rigid scheme of years, as in the annals, we term it a chronicle. To the reader of the narrative there is little difference, and the two terms are used loosely and interchangeably throughout the history of history. Moreover a pure annal, containing nothing except mention of contemporary events, would be hard to find. Even the official annals of Rome, inscribed by the pontiffs with the yearly exploits of the citizens or prodigies of the gods, contained portions of the earlier years rewritten from later sources.

The subject matter of the annal or chronicle was therefore a miscellany, woven out of religion, war, catastrophes, legendary exploits, or mere business items. Genealogies, for instance, which patriarchal illiteracy perpetuated in the singsong verses, were more safely embalmed in writing. These were especially valued by noble houses, who, in imitation of royalty, were sure to reach the gods at the other end. Needless to say, while they afford many a hint to the student of today, they were not more reliable than those prepared for some of our fellow citizens at present.

Since the annalists were generally the priests they early kept temple records, mainly from a business instinct. Donations from pharaohs or kings were sure to be entered, and along with these developed lists of priests and priestesses in long succession. But, most important of all, they noted the festivals of the gods, and in watching the recurring seasons with the changing moon and the lucky and unlucky days, they *began to measure Time*. This, along with the discovery of writing itself, was the most decisive forward step in the history of history—perhaps hardly less in the history of civilization. We must turn aside to consider it in some detail.

CHAPTER V

The Measuring of Time

TIME is the basis of history, as space is of geography or matter of the physical sciences. Until some method of keeping accurate track of it was discovered, the data of history were like an uncharted land or an unanalyzed substance. To us with our almanacs this seems like the simplest matter of observation and arithmetic, merely a counting of days, weeks, months, and years. But when history began there were no almanacs or calendars to consult. Weeks were unknown, months were observed only from the superstitious fears and beliefs attached to the changing moon, and the revolving years were too vast and vague to be measured off with any accuracy. There are really only two measures of time of which the primitive mind is fully conscious: the day (and one day is like another); and the season (and the seasons vary). A little thought shows that whole new sciences had to be evolved before the dates could be set along the margin of our annals—the sciences which make possible astronomy and, through it, a settled calendar for events that recur and a fixed chronology for those which happen but once.[1]

Anthropologists point out that the greatest social revolution of primitive mankind came about when men, settling on the soil instead of wandering, and so accumulating goods which involved foresight, began to calculate for a future. From that dim sensing of futurity in which civilization dawned, the whole evolution of society has been conditioned by some reckoning of the passing of time. The calendars upon our walls make this now so simple and familiar that the fact escapes our attention. But it takes considerably more thought than most people are ever likely to devote

[1] See J. T. Shotwell, "The Discovery of Time," in *The Journal of Philosophy*, Vol. XII (1915), Nos. 8, 10, 12.

to it, to realize that the calendar itself is an invention rather than a discovery, an art creation, magnificent in its mathematical perfection but a product of human ingenuity all the same and not the mere revelation of some laws of nature.

Yet the artificial character of our calendar can be seen very easily. Some of our time divisions are artificial on the face of them, the divisions of the day and the massing of days into weeks. We could do without seconds or even minutes without much inconvenience and do so most of the time. Even hours vary greatly. The twelve-hour unit comes to us from Babylon through Ionian Greece—twelve being like our ten, the unit of measurement for anything. We might as well have had a decimal instead of a duodecimal system; it all depends on the arithmetical tables one used. But one should not put too much stress on the hour as a division of the day, for, in general, it is only the point of time, within the hour or at its beginning or close, of which we are keenly conscious—especially the time for commencing or quitting work. It is the same with weeks. There were none in the Greek calendar. The weeks, like the hours, come apparently from Babylon. They mark off seven days, because seven was a sacred number. Habits and religious beliefs have settled this cycle upon our minds with the weight of centuries; the rhythmic Sunday pause in our busy weekday industries impresses itself upon the imagination so that poetically inclined people attributed to nature itself a restful note upon the sacred day. But this is merely our tribute to social convention and taboo. Every day is a sun-day. Weeks are a fiction based upon superstition but perpetuated for their social value. Even now, however, there are many people who pay no attention to them; in the mills of modern industry, on railways or ships, where work continues without ceasing, the weeks are practically unrecognizable. But days, months, and years are different. Here nature seems itself to mark an interval. The turning of the earth on its axis, of the moon around the earth, and the earth around the sun, seem to furnish real units. It was undoubtedly these which first gave men a mathematical idea of time. But when we come to apply the lesson, it is not so easy.

The calendar began in registering these celestial phenomena.

The Measuring of Time

The first chronometer was the universe itself; its ever-recurring movements struck off the days, months, and years as our clocks strike off the hours. The days and years are thus in reality on a par with the minutes and the hours, only they are the product of a larger clock. Unfortunately, however, the clocks of the universe do not run together. The days do not fit the years and the months fit neither one. The exact solar year is not even 365¼ days, awkward as that multiple would be; it is 365 days, 5 hours, 48 minutes, 46 seconds! We have frankly given up trying to keep track of months that really go by the changes of the moon—a cycle that has no relation to our night or day. Yet this was the unit for twenty or thirty centuries in that home of astronomy, Babylon. When we pause a moment to consider these things, we begin to realize what baffling mathematics lies behind our calendars and almanacs. For there are the stars, too, to keep track of, with their revolutions and conjunctions, coming and going at all sorts of intervals, planets zigzagging across the heavens in crazy patterns, out of touch with everything, and yet somehow forming, apparently with the sun and moon, a final unit, composing a universe. What a tangled problem for Babylonian and Egyptian astronomers to work out! No Chaldaean shepherds, "killing time" in pastoral loneliness and innocence, were ever able to evolve the science of astronomy. That venerable myth still lingers in respectable books; but astronomy was the product of learned priests, those first scientists and intellectual leaders, who developed it, through astrology, for the service of religion.

The calendar developed everywhere as a cycle of religious feasts. It was the gods, not men, by whom or for whom the days were first marked out. The times for hunting and fishing, for sowing and reaping, the phases of the moon, the summer and the winter solstice, and the like, to which the attention of primitive men was so forcibly directed, early became associated with some idea of miraculous power. The times themselves became "lucky" or "unlucky"—an idea still so common that we never stop to ask what it means.[2] There was an uncanny power let loose in the

---

[2] See Hutton Webster, *Rest Days, a Study in Early Law and Morality* (1916), for an exhaustive survey of time taboos.

world when the moon still hung visible in the sky by day, or under the blazing mid-summer sun. The primitive man cannot exactly tell whether the power is in the moon or the sun or the day itself; but on that day he knows that it is there. So when animism produces its gods and demons these days are consecrated to them. The time for reaping is sacred to the god of the harvest, and so forth. The old scruples take a more definite turn. A part of the time becomes the property of the gods. It is henceforth a violation of divine law to work or transact business on the days thus set apart. Holidays were at first genuinely holy days, and the calendar grew up around them. It was necessary to find some way by which the festival day, the *dies nefastus*, on which business was sacrilege,[8] should not be violated. It was taboo; to violate it was not only wrong but dangerous. The power of an inherent curse, which is essential in the early idea of the sacred, protected the day and assured it social recognition. Accordingly it had to be kept track of in order to ensure that the proper ceremonies should be celebrated upon it. Hence the elaboration of that succession of religious feasts and fasts which still persists in our church calendar. The idea would not naturally occur to one that the lists of saints' days and holy days which preface our liturgies are the historic remnants of the first marking of time. But in the practically universal superstitions about planting crops, gathering herbs, or doing almost anything in the dark or the full of the moon we have a trace of something infinitely older than any sacred date in the prayer book—a trace of that first vague fear of the unusual or uncanny, out of which theologies, as well as calendars, were born.

Once grant that days differ in their virtues, that some are good for one thing, some for another, and it is of the utmost importance to know which is which. In Hesiod's *Works and Days* we have the programme outlined for the farmer of the earliest age of historic Greece. In the so-called Calendar of Numa we have the priestly reckoning for ancient Rome. But in Egypt and especially in Babylon, where the sky is so clear that, as the report ran in Rome,

---

[8] The Romans, characteristically viewing things from the practical point of view, had the terms inverted: the *dies fasti* were those on which business was permitted.

The Measuring of Time

even the stars cast shadows, the mechanism of the heavens first produced an adequate system.

Babylon bears the proud title of Mother of Astronomy. It was a title already admitted by Greeks and Romans, to whom the words "Chaldaean" and "astronomer" (or rather astrologer) were practically synonymous. Modern scholars agree as to the justness of the claim; but the careful study of newly found inscriptions places the scientific achievements of Babylonia and Assyria not at the opening, but at the close, of their long history. However much the priests of those distant centuries watched the heavens for portents and omens, their observations were not sufficiently systematic to enable them to measure the recurring periods of sun, moon, and stars with that accuracy necessary for an unvarying calendar, until after at least two thousand years of priestly lore. The Semites clung with the conservatism of superstition to the phases of the moon. Although they had grown civilized—and civilization must arrange its work according to the sun, because nature does so, bringing the recurring duties of the seasons—these old desert dwellers, and their neighbors who learned from them, never broke away from the lunar month and the lunar year.

No one knows when or how this reckoning was first adopted; but a study of primitive peoples the world over today shows that the moon, not the sun, is generally the earliest guide toward the calendar. Wherever agriculture is not much developed, the moon dominates, owing both to its uncanny associations and to the shortness of its cycle. The origins of the lunar calendar of Babylonia, therefore, apparently lie beyond all the long story of its civilization. The records themselves carry us back, however, to the middle of the third millennium, when we find a Babylonian year of twelve lunar months, making up 354 days, with a thirteenth month thrown in once in a while—making that year 384 days—to bring the religious festivals and the business world right again. There was no absolute certainty as to which years should be lengthened and which should be left the normal length; the matter was in the hands of the priests. This unwieldy calendar spread throughout western Asia, wherever the cuneiform script carried the message of Babylonian culture. It was adopted by the

Jews and—apart from other fragments of it embedded in our calendar—we still have a positive reminder of its difficulties in our festival of Easter.

But so much observation of the moon ultimately produced an astronomical cycle of great importance, that of the moon with reference to the sun. It was discovered that in nineteen years the moon returned almost to its original position with reference to the sun,[4] a period destined to be used for chronology by the Greeks. This discovery, however, was not made until the eighth and seventh centuries B.C., in that period when the study of the universe began to assume more calculable form, and astrology—still rooted in religion, but verging toward science—rose to supersede the crude old fantasies of the earlier and barbarous priestcraft. Then we come upon a strange and happy interworking of calendar and chronology. To foretell an eclipse or a conjunction of the stars, it was necessary to know the period of time which had elapsed between such eclipses or conjunctions in the past. So, looking forward to forecast the future, the astrologer found himself obliged to consult the records of the past, and the more he sought for accuracy in his calendar the more he needed it in the royal or priestly annals which supplied him with the data upon which he had to build. In short, mathematics began to emerge from the position of a mere tool of superstition, in which the luck of numbers combined with that of the stars in a jumble of folly, and to assume its proper role as the basis of definite knowledge.

This was an epoch in the history of thought, an epoch of fundamental importance for history, for from that time to the present the years have been numbered in regular, unbroken succession. The list of the kings of Assyria whose dates are thus fixed and accurate began in the year 747 B.C., the first year of a somewhat insignificant monarch, Nabonassar. This list was used by the great astronomers of Alexandria, who finally worked out the problem of calendar and chronology as far as they were solved in antiquity, and it has been preserved in what is called the Canon of Ptolemy. Through these savants the Babylonian-Assyrian year

---

[4] The time between eclipses was seen to be 18 years, 11 days, or 223 lunations ("Saros").

The Measuring of Time

was translated into the "fixed" year of Egypt, *i.e.*, 365¼ days; and to the "Era of Nabonassar" were added those of the Persian and Alexandrian empires, and finally the list of Roman emperors, down to the year 160 of our era. So that from 747 B.C. until the present, the years have been kept track of in continuous, if varied, reckoning. But the Canon of Ptolemy was used by astronomers, not by antique historians.[5]

The mention of Alexandria naturally suggests the contribution of Egypt. But it was not Egyptian so much as Greek science which made the name of Alexandria so illustrious in antiquity, and the great astronomers who worked there found little in the long centuries of Egyptian culture to help them in their study of astronomy or chronology. This seems strangely paradoxical when in modern histories of ancient Egypt one reads of the great achievements of its science and, above all, that it bears an even prouder title than Babylon as the land which produced the solar year. The date when that event took place is a matter of dispute among Egyptologists. Formerly those who followed Professors Eduard Meyer and J. H. Breasted reckoned that if the calendar year of 365 days was introduced at a time when it fitted the solar year day for day, the nineteenth of July,[6] 4241 B.C., would be the first day of the first year of the new calendar.[7] Shortly before his death Professor Breasted advanced the date to 4236, while other competent Egyptologists date it only from the twenty-eighth century B.C., the approximate age of the pyramids. What long and puzzling computation, what tables of priestly science and records were at the disposal of those who inaugurated it no

[5] The importance of the "Era of Nabonassar" for chronologists was first seen by Panodorus, the creator of the Alexandrian school of chronologers, at the beginning of the fifth century A.D. See H. Gelzer, *Sextus Julius Africanus und die byzantinische Chronologie* (1898), Part II, p. 227, which traces the development of the Canon of Ptolemy through Syncellus into Byzantine chronology and so opens up the connection with the Middle Ages.

[6] The day when the star Sirius rose at dawn, at the opening of the Nile floods.

[7] This date was reached by calculating back from a known date in the third century of our era, when a Latin writer, Censorinus, tells us that the solar year of Egypt was two months behind the calendar year. As the calendar year was about a quarter of a day short in length, it had been gaining on the solar year that much yearly, so that in 1460 years (4 × 365) it would gain a whole year. Thus, the two had coincided about 140 A.D. (of which fact further evidence exists) and again at 1460-year intervals.

one can tell. When one compares this solar year, only a little over six hours wrong, with the grossly inaccurate lunar year of 354 or 355 days in use in the rest of the world throughout most of antique history, it seems at first to indicate something like a Hellenic rationalism at work in Egypt as long before the Greeks as we are after them. But this impression of Egyptian superiority is hardly borne out by fuller study. For, not only did Egypt fail to make good its early promise in astronomy,[8] but by failing to rectify the error of a quarter of a day, its calendar year came to have no real correspondence with the solar year.

In the science of chronology the Egyptians made no such contribution as might be expected from the promise of their early texts. The years were numbered, not in a straight and continuous succession, but according to striking events, campaigns, the years of the Pharaoh's reign, or (especially) the levy of taxes. When the state was thoroughly organized, the treasury officials "numbered" the royal possessions every two years, and the regnal years were known as "Year of the First Numbering," "Year after the First Numbering," "Year of the Second Numbering," etc. Whatever knowledge the priests may have had of the period involved in the long succession of Egyptian dynasties—and Hecataeus and Herodotus show that they had some—it was left for the twentieth century A.D. to disentangle the problem for the world at large, and much is still to do.

The Babylonians and Assyrians had the practice of *naming* rather than *numbering* their years. There was some priestly or royal functionary whose duty it was to proclaim what event or man should give the name to the year. It was to be the year of the magistracy of so-and-so, or the year when a battle was fought or a city taken. There is a touch of casual history in this, but it is too haphazard to be of much use. For, in the first place, one never knew until the functionary made up his mind—perhaps toward the end of the year—what the year really was! Combine that with a lunar calendar, and one can see that there is work for the Babylonian scholar as he struggles with the problem of Sumerian date lists, which contain the names of the years, as

---

[8] It even failed to note eclipses.

The Measuring of Time

recorded by the Babylonian scribes. Neither Greeks nor Romans worked out by themselves any adequate reckoning of time. The lunar year was the basis, and with all their ingenuity, they could not make it work. In Greece it was easily seen that the 354 days did not exactly fit the twelve lunations of the year, being short by 8.8 hours. So (if the old accounts are correct) they put in a month every second solar year, which brought the total up to about 7½ days more than the right amount. In order to compensate for this inaccuracy, the intercalation was then omitted every eighth year. This *octaëteris* or luni-solar cycle of eight years was in itself not rigorously exact and was not systematically carried out. In 432 B.C. the astronomer Meton proposed the nineteen-year luni-solar cycle, of which we have spoken above. It was not adopted, however, until the second half of the fourth century. Once adopted, it was naturally destined to play a very important role in later classical and ecclesiastical chronology. The astronomical cycle is really slightly less than nineteen years, however, and further corrections were necessary. In fact so long as the motions of the moon remained the basis of reckoning, the calendar was sure to be imperfect.

The Romans began with a lunar calendar, but, since they regarded odd numbers as the lucky ones, they made the year 355 instead of 354 days. Then, every second year, they added a month of 22 and 23 days alternately, inserting it between the 23d and 24th of February, so that the mean length was 366¼ days. To get rid of the extra day they had recourse to a clumsy device—perhaps based upon the old Greek eight-year cycle—ordering that every third period of eight years should have three instead of four intercalary months, and that they should be of 22 days each. This made the year 365¼ days. But the pontiffs were left discretion in adjusting the calendar to the needs of astronomy, and they seem to have adjusted it (in some cases at least) rather to the needs of their friends—having long years when those were in office whom they wished to favor, and short ones when their enemies were in power! In any case, the calendar fell into such confusion in the last years of the republic that it was out by three months, judging by the solar year. The decree of Julius Caesar was the result, fixing the year at 365 days with an extra day in every fourth year. The ancients have attributed the reform to the intercourse with the savants of Alexandria, but there is also some ground for connecting it with a simple old-fashioned solar year of Italian farmers, of which we have fragmentary but definite traces even in the official calendar and which, in its turn, may have been affected by the farming calendar of the Greeks. If this be true, we have a single line from Hesiod to Caesar.

The first reformed year began on the first of January, 46 B.C. (708 A. U. C.). The months took their place in it,[9] and then Christianity brought in the weeks from Judaea—and Babylon. The year remained, as we have seen, a fraction of a day too short, and there was no absolute agreement yet as to when it should begin. But these were matters never settled until the sixteenth, and even the eighteenth, century of our era.

We need to know this much of the origins of the calendar in order to complete our survey of antique chronology. In both Greece and Rome—after the fashion of Babylon and Egypt—the year bore the name of the ruling magistrates. In Rome it was named after the consuls, in Athens after the first archon, in Sparta after the first ephor, etc. As it was found necessary for practical purposes to keep lists of these, we pass from the calendar not only to chronology but to the crudest of annals.[10] Thucydides, for instance, had only the Athenian lists of archons, the Spartan lists of ephors, and the lists of the priestesses of Hera in the temple of Argos to rely upon, in addition to the festivals.[11] The cycle of

---

[9] Julius Caesar's months were to be of alternate length, the odd numbers being 31, the even numbers 30 (except February). That would have made a simple year to reckon with. But when the eighth month (the fifth in the old year) was named after Augustus, his vanity was gratified by adding a day to it to make it as long as that of Julius. Then, in order to avoid having three months of 31 days together, September and November were reduced to 30, and 31 were given to October and December.

[10] The vagueness of an idea of extent of time in Greek history can be seen by the fact that "generations" were used to help reckon time and this was roughly put at 33 years, although the period varies. In Herodotus one comes upon a system of 23 years.

[11] The only continuous list of the Attic archons which has come down to us is a copy preserved in the history of Diodorus, but a growing body of inscriptions

The Measuring of Time 73

the Olympiad, the four-year period based upon the celebration of the Olympic games, by which later ages reckoned Greek history, was never used officially by the city states, and really was not taken over by historians and chronographers until about the end of the third century B.C. The credit for its introduction seems to belong to Timaeus (c. 350 B.C.), an indefatigable antiquarian and historian whose unphilosophical cast of mind apparently left him free to indulge a singularly un-Hellenic taste for dates. But it was a geographer rather than a historian who finally attacked the problem of chronology in a critical spirit. Eratosthenes, who flourished about 276 to 194 B.C., and who, as librarian of the Alexandrian library, was equipped with the science of the East as well as with his native Hellenic genius, fixed the dates of the great epochs of Greek history in what was destined to be the accepted chronology of antique as well as of Christian historians. Into this we cannot go further at present.[12] Nor need we do so for this chapter of our history of history. The crude old reckoning of Rome, from the fabled founding of the city, 753 B.C., and the Olympiads remained, for later classical antiquity, the two eras in general use.

Looking over this chapter of our intellectual evolution, one is impressed with the slowness of its progress. The ancient world could come to its full maturity without any clear idea of the passing years, with even no accurate knowledge of what a year should be. Yet does not such vagueness correspond with our own experience? The past is all one to us, yesterday as dead as the centuries of Egypt. Only by the magic of memory can we even recall its faded color or catch an echo of its silenced voices. How that memory has become a social and undying heritage, a heritage that hallows its own possessions, is the theme of the following chapters on the history of history.

---

supplements it now and enables the modern scholar to recover more than the ancients knew themselves.

[12] Apollodorus of Athens, applying the conclusions of Eratosthenes, drew up a metrical *Chronica* in four books, dedicated to Attalus of Pergamum, which became the popular handbook on the subject. Both this and the works of Eratosthenes are lost, but fragments were preserved by the Christian chronologers, Julius Africanus, Eusebius, Jerome, and Georgius Syncellus, and so this still is a primary base for the old Greek chronology.

CHAPTER VI

Egyptian Annals

THE historians of ancient Egypt and Babylonia are not ancient Egyptians or Babylonians but modern archaeologists. Their achievement—one of the greatest in all the history of scholarship—piecing together the annals of centuries which often left no conscious record of their own, has obscured the poorness of the sources out of which the history of the earliest civilizations is made. In reality, the written history of the first nations of the ancient world was a very slight affair. In all that vast spoil of the East which now lies in our museums, there is a surprisingly small amount of genuine historical record.

It is possible, of course, to make too confident statements about the scope of a subject of which our knowledge depends almost entirely upon chance. For it is chance which has preserved what has been preserved of the material of this early history. The statement is true of all history but is especially applicable where thousands of years and changing civilizations have in turn devastated and used again the material of earlier ages. Moreover, the permanence of such a record does not depend upon its importance —as is the case, more or less, with traditions. It is due rather to the durability of the substance upon which the record is inscribed and the chance that the inscription lies undisturbed. Mortgages for garden plots, baked into the clay of Babylon, have survived long after the plot was desert sand and Babylon itself a heap of ruins. Sometimes chance plays strange tricks, preserving frail papyri or parchment while stone disappears. A building inscription was placed upon a huge stone stele by Sesostris I, in his temple at Heliopolis, nearly two thousand years before Christ. "The great block itself has since perished utterly; but the practice-copy made by a scribe, who was whiling away an idle hour in the

Egyptian Annals

sunny temple court, has survived, and the fragile roll of leather upon which he was thus exercising his pen has transmitted to us what the massive stone could not preserve."[1] The stone had been there five hundred years before the copy was made; but now stele and temple have alike disappeared. The student of history can never know how much of what was set down in distant ages has been blotted out in a similar manner. Archaeology, it must not be forgotten, is a science of ruins.

By taking the sources as we have them, the striking fact remains that history, the one branch of literature which one might expect to find develop first, seeing that it carries on tradition and that its poetic counterpart is the epic, nevertheless is hardly to be found at all in these early cultures, except where a mythic content contributes the interest of marvels and wonders—a world flood or something of the sort. In all the inscriptions of ancient Egypt there is no work that can be termed a "history of Egypt." There are some annals that are expansions of the lists of royal names; and there are boastful notices of contemporary pharaohs, but of the idea of a history of the successive ages of Egyptian civilization there is not a trace.

One reason which has been advanced for this absence of history in ancient Egypt is that the pharaoh of the time was so intent upon his own greatness that his courtiers did not venture to exalt the deeds of his ancestors for fear of belittling his own. The path to royal favor lay rather in covering the walls of monuments with inscriptions describing what the present pharaoh had done or could do. In any case, no successor of even great monarchs of the eighteenth dynasty ever deigned to record their exploits in the form of history. The court scribes busied themselves with the more profitable enterprise of depicting the events or scenes of their own day. In the literature of ancient Egypt, history, as we understand it, is absent.

Mention of "the scribes" recalls the high esteem in which their work was held. It was the profession for ambitious men, who might rise even to princely state by means of it. Scribes kept the accounts of either government or nobles, for everything in the

[1] J. H. Breasted, *Ancient Records of Egypt*, I, 4-5.

large establishments was recorded by these busy forerunners of the modern lawyers or trust companies. "Nothing was done under the Egyptian government without documents; lists and protocols were indispensable even in the simplest matters of business. The mania for writing ... is not characteristic of the later period only; doubtless under the Old and the Middle Empire the scribes wrote as diligently as under the New Empire."[2] In the case of legal texts we have almost the whole modern machinery. "The documents were then given into the care of the chief librarian of the department they concerned, and he placed them in large vases and catalogued them carefully...."[3] and so had them readily available for reference, in case the lord called for them. But so completely was this bureaucracy under the thumb of the ruler that it does not furnish a starting point for that criticism which is the beginning of historical knowledge. The old writings were sometimes appealed to in the practice of government, as when the founder of the twelfth dynasty, in deciding upon the boundaries of the provinces, fell back upon "what was written in the books and what he found in the old writings" "because he so loved the truth."[4] But the love of the truth for its own sake, in the unpractical fields of scientific research, was left for a later age.

There is something mediaeval in the attitude of later Egypt toward her own past, a sense of dimness, a failure to grasp its reality even with reference to such abiding things as religion. This was accentuated by the change which came over hieroglyphics, rendering the old writing hard to understand. Under the circumstances they did what other people have always done under the same circumstances; their learned men, mostly priests, sought in allegory an explanation of the texts, and having found that key to the past had less need of another.

Egyptians may have done little with history but they treasured

[2] A. Erman, *Life in Ancient Egypt*, pp. 52, 112. Cf. J. H. Breasted, *A History of Egypt* (2d ed., 1909), Chaps. V, XI, XIII.

[3] A. Erman, *Life in Ancient Egypt*, p. 114. The largest and finest of all the papyri, the Harris papyrus, is an enumeration of the benefactions of Ramses III to gods and men during his reign. It is 133 feet long, containing 117 columns, usually of 12 or 13 lines. Cf. J. H. Breasted, *Ancient Records of Egypt*, IV, 87-88.

[4] From R. Lepsius, *Denkmäler aus Aegypten und Aethiopien*, Sect. II, Vol. IV, Plate 124, quoted in A. Erman, *Life in Ancient Egypt*, p. 91.

Egyptian Annals

myth and legend. In the twentieth century B.C. we already meet with the prototype of Sinbad the sailor. Tales of wonder wrought by ancient wise men and magicians were as effective then as now in whiling away hours of leisure, when history would be too forbidding a discipline There were also myths of origin; stories of the gods, how they came from the Holy Land in the south country. But as the centuries passed, the myths got strangely mixed. For instance, the misreading of an inscription on the tomb of an early king at Abydos led to a popular belief that Osiris himself was buried there, and thus started a new cult. We shall find such local name myths again in the origins of the Old Testament. But there is no need to follow them here into the tangle of Egyptian religious conceptions.

If Egypt did not produce "history" in our sense of the word, it at least possessed the framework for it in the lists of royal names, which were displayed in magnificent profusion, along with the reigning monarch's monogram or portrait. Three such tablets, of Abydos, Sakkara, and Karnak, may be mentioned for light they throw on Egyptian chronology. In the first, Seti I, of the nineteenth dynasty (about 1300 B.C.), accompanied by his son Ramses II, has before him seventy-five of his predecessors; in the second, Ramses II has some forty-seven names on the list before him; while in the third, Thothmes or Thutmose III of the eighteenth dynasty is adoring sixty-one. Modern research has verified the accuracy of the two former lists, by comparison with the monuments. No wonder the priests who kept such lists were able to make a lasting impression upon the Greek travellers who were to come at a later date to learn from them the folly of tracing one's descent from the gods in the sixteenth generation.[5] The fact that Egypt was itself a museum, preserving a sort of monumental history of the kings, must also have impressed the mind with an enduring sense of the past; but religion rather than

---

[5] See below, pp. 172-173. Sometimes the names were not safe in the care of a jealous descendant. Queen Hatshepsut, "an Egyptian Catherine II," had the name of her brother, who preceded her, erased from his monument. A. Erman, *Life in Ancient Egypt*, p. 43. Thothmes III, in turn, had her obelisk walled up. See J. H. Breasted, *A History of Egypt*, pp. 282-283.

history profited from such curiosity as the spectacle produced. The weight of authority was in the hand of time.

The earliest historical record which has come down to us, however, is a development from just such lists of names. It is the famous Palermo stone, so-called from the fact that it is in the museum at Palermo—a small stone, of black diorite, one of the hardest of stones, only about seventeen inches high, nine and a half wide, and two and a half thick. On this stone, somewhat less than two thousand years before the oldest parts of the Old Testament were written, Egyptian scribes copied the names and recorded the known facts of the reigns of five dynasties before their time. The stone itself, as is apparent from its general appearance and from the character of the text, is but a small fragment, broken from a larger slab. Egyptologists, calculating from the spaces of reigns and their arrangement, have supposed that the original slab was about seven feet long and two feet high; but this is mere conjecture.

The date when the annals were inscribed upon the stone can be set with confidence towards the end of the fifth dynasty, which ruled in Egypt, according to a widely accepted reckoning, from 2750 to 2625 B.C. The preserved portions of the stone cover only the first three reigns of that dynasty.[6]

---

[6] Besides the portion at Palermo, there is a slightly smaller fragment at Cairo. Although known to Egyptologists for some forty years, no careful studies of the Palermo stone were made before the twentieth century. The first reference to it was made in 1866 by E. de Rougé in his *Recherches sur les monuments qu'on peut attribuer aux six premières dynasties de Manéthon* (p. 145), using a print that had been sent him. The stone was then in a private collection, but in 1877 it passed into the possession of the Museum of Palermo, where it was seen by several Egyptologists in the subsequent years, without realizing its significance. Finally, a study of it, accompanied by plates of the text, was published in 1896, by A. Pellegrini, in the *Archivio storico siciliano* (new series, XX, 297-316). Working from this, the eminent French Egyptologist, E. Naville, interpreted the document as a "sort of calendar containing donations made by a certain number of kings of ancient Egypt and the indication of the feasts to be celebrated" ("Les Plus Anciens Monuments égyptiens," in G. Maspero's *Recueil de travaux relatifs à la philologie et à l'archéologie égyptiennes et assyriennes*, XXI (1899), 112 sq.) In 1899, however, Naville visited Palermo and collated the text, publishing the results —with plates—in 1903, in the same series (Vol. XXV, or Vol. IX of the new series). There his conclusion was that it was a fragment of religious annals, probably drawn up by the priests of Heliopolis, "of which the chronology, at least

THE PALERMO STONE

A picture of this fragment from ancient Egypt appears as an illustration in this volume. Its claim to such a place is unquestioned, for it contains the earliest of all known annals in the history of history. Fortunately, however, the illustration in this case is much more than a mere picture, for it offers as well the text of the original. At first glance this may not seem of very great interest to those who cannot read the hieroglyphs, and their interest is not likely to be quickened when they learn that even Egyptologists do not quite agree as to the meaning of parts of the text. But a very little study of the original, in the light of the clues offered below, will enable any one, even if he has never read a hieroglyph before, to puzzle out the way in which it was written and even understand some sections of the text. There can be few more interesting puzzles for the student of history.

At the top of the stone there is a simple row of oblong spaces, with relatively few signs in them. The lower section of each of these furnishes the clue to their meaning, for it contains the sign for the king of lower Egypt, a figure wearing the red crown and holding one of the royal insignia, the flail. Consequently, each symbol in the space above must be the name of a king. This row, therefore, is the list of the names of early kings of lower Egypt, of whose reigns apparently nothing had come down to the scribes of the fifth dynasty but the royal names themselves. In any case, no events are recorded. It should be noted here that these, like all Egyptian hieroglyphs, are to be read from right to left.

With the second row or series, however, one comes upon entirely different data. The dividing lines, curling over at the top,

---

in the first part, appears to depend upon the periods or cycles which do not correspond with the reigns of the kings" (p. 81). Meanwhile an even more detailed study had been undertaken by the German scholars H. Schäfer, L. Borchardt and K. Sethe, the general conclusions of which appeared in 1902 under the title "Ein Bruchstück altägyptischer Annalen," in the *Abhandlungen der königlichen preussischen Akademie der Wissenschaften, Philosophische und historische Classe* for 1902, with excellent photographic plates of the original. J. H. Breasted's translation, in *Ancient Records of Egypt*, I, 51-72, is based mainly upon Schäfer's text. A photographic plate of the front face of the stone is also given in Breasted's *History of Egypt*, facing p. 46. See also the discussion of the stone in A. Weigall, *A History of the Pharaohs* (1925), I, 2 *sqq*.

The present text is drawn from Breasted's and Schäfer's, rearranged somewhat for purposes of clarity.

are themselves the hieroglyphic signs of palms, signifying years. If one looks carefully one can see a short cross-mark on each one, about three quarters of the way up the stem, which definitely establishes their meaning.[7] But in a few instances the line is also run straight up, through the intervening long parallel space, the series above. These long straight lines are taken to indicate the close of reigns, and are accompanied by some specific reckoning, as may very well be seen by glancing a moment at the spaces on each side of the first one. On the right of it one can easily distinguish six new moons, one above the other, which mean six months, and a circle representing the sun and seven strokes, which indicate seven days. On the other side of the vertical line one sees four months and thirteen days—the symbol for ten being the two strokes joined at the top instead of crossed as in Roman counting. Consequently, here is obviously some detail as to the time when the reign ceased. The name of the king is given in the long horizontal space above the yearly records, although only two such are visible on this side of the fragment, one at the extreme right above the third row, and the other at the left above the fourth row.

The measurements in the little square below each yearly record are supposed to register the height of the Nile flood. The forearm represents a cubit, the other indications stand for hands and finger-lengths.

The general character of the material here preserved is of great interest, however one may regard the details, for on this little block of stone one can see how history grows out of the thin data of the earliest lists. At first there are only rows of unknown kings, mere names, and even these of strange archaic sound.[8] It is supposed that the lost portion may have contained the kings of upper Egypt or a list of the gods. Then, in the second line we come upon the story of a reign of the first dynasty, giving the events year by year.

[7] This was not apparent in Pellegrini's plates, but is clearly brought out in those of Schäfer and Naville.
[8] The first line reads: -pu; Seka; Khayn; Teyew; Thesh; etc. It should be recalled that the text is read from right to left. The vocalization is that adopted by Breasted; the Egyptian alphabet noted only the consonants.

Egyptian Annals

This first of all annals reads as follows:

Year 1 Fourth month; thirteenth day.[9] Union of the two lands. Circuit of the wall.
Six cubits [the height of the Nile].
2 Worship of Horus.[10] Festival of Desher.
3 Birth of two children to the King of Lower Egypt.
Four cubits, one palm.
4 Worship of Horus; [undeciphered].
5 [Plan] of the House, "Mighty of the Gods." Feast of Sokar.
Five cubits, five palms, one finger.
6 Worship of Horus. Birth of the goddess Yamet.
Five cubits, one palm.
7 Appearance [or coronation] of the King of Upper Egypt.
Birth of Min.
Five cubits.
8 Worship of Horus.
Birth of Anubis.
Six cubits, one palm.
9 First appearance of the Festival of Zet.
Four cubits, one span.
10 [Destroyed.] [11]

These are still mainly the data of religion—festivals of the gods and scraps of divine history. The chief human activity is the building of temples. In the fourth line, however, we come upon the second dynasty, and the items recorded steadily grow more secular. We even come upon the regular system of the numbering of the land and its resources, which may be viewed, if one so wishes, as the earliest trace of economic history.[12] It is not until

---

[9] Date of the king's accession. On this day the new king ascends the throne. Note the upright line dividing the reigns. The new king's name was apparently farther to the left, and is lost.

[10] Celebrated every two years.

[11] Proceeding upon the assumption that the king's name was placed over the middle years of his reign, and that it would itself spread over six others, Schäfer (p. 187) reckons that since this king's name is not yet reached in the ten years here shown, he must have reigned at least sixteen years more; and the stone extended at least that far to the left. Similarly the king whose name occurs at the extreme right of the next line must have already reigned as long as the period shown here (13 years + 5 for the name, or 18 in all).

[12] In the third space from the right of the fourth line. It reads "Worship of Horus. Fourth numbering. Four cubits, two fingers." Since this numbering took place every other year, and this is the fourth numbering for this king, the reign probably began seven years earlier.

the third dynasty, however, on the last line of the fragment, that the annal becomes at all detailed. The story depicted in the three years here preserved runs as follows:

Building of the 100-cubit dewatowe ships of meru wood, and of 60 sixteen [oared?] barges of the king. Hacking up of the land of the negro. Bringing of 7,000 living prisoners, and 200,000 large and small cattle. Building of the wall of the Southland and Northland [called] "Houses of Snefru." Bringing of 40 ships filled with cedar wood.[13]

Making 35 houses ... of 122 cattle. Building of a 100-cubit dewatowe ship of cedar wood and two 100-cubit ships of meru wood. Seventh occurrence of the numbering.

Five cubits, one palm, one finger.

Erection of "Exalted is the white crown of Snefru upon the Southern Gate" [and] "Exalted is the red crown of Snefru upon the Northern Gate."[14] Making the doors of the king's palace of cedar wood.

Two cubits, two palms, two and three-fourths fingers.

The inscriptions on the reverse continue the story, through part of the fourth dynasty and of the three first reigns of the fifth dynasty. The detail is much richer here, but the condition of this face of the stone is so bad as to render decipherment very difficult, and the mere fact that the material is richer on each reign limits the scribe to fewer reigns. As a result interest in these sections of the annals hardly extends beyond Egyptologists, and further comment may be omitted here.

So slight a chronicle, even if it be the first, seems hardly worth delaying over, were it not that we have the original text before us, and that its very slightness tempts one to linger. There must have been many such simple textual products as this in the possession of the priests of Egypt; but it is hardly to be wondered at that it needed the best of stone to preserve them, for there is little enough in the text itself to enforce immortality. More human interest attaches to the records of single reigns, in which the royal scribe has every incentive to tell a striking story, and dress it up in all the detail of actuality. Such records are less "historic" than

---

[13] An expedition by sea to Lebanon.
[14] The names of two gates or parts of the palace of Snefru. See J. H. Breasted, *Ancient Records of Egypt*, I, 66 *n.c.*

Egyptian Annals

the dry-as-dust chronicle we have just been examining, but they are at least of livelier interest for the modern reader.

There are a large number of these. They form the bulk of the great collection of Professor Breasted's *Ancient Records of Egypt*. It will suffice to take as an example the most notable of these, the "annals" of the great monarch of the imperial period, Thothmes or Thutmose III. As the Palermo stone is the first, this is "the longest and most important historical inscription in Egypt." [15] It was written under the king's command on the walls of "the corridor which surrounds the granite holy of holies of the great Karnak temple of Amon" [16] and describes some seventeen campaigns which he carried on, year after year, as he maintained the sovereignty of Egypt over western Asia. The most noteworthy of these was that in which the king met and defeated the forces of Syria at Armageddon, or Megiddo; and so detailed is the account of this exploit that modern historians are able to reconstruct the strategy according to the map and to follow the story day by day. The description of the battle itself, which has just a touch of something Homeric in it, is as follows: [17]

Then the tents of His Majesty were pitched, and orders were sent out to the whole army, saying, Arm yourselves, get your weapons ready, for we shall set out to do battle with the miserable enemy at daybreak. The king sat in his tent, the officers made their preparations, and the rations of the servants were provided. The military sentries went about crying, Be firm of heart, Be firm of heart. Keep watch, keep watch. Keep watch over the life of the king in his tent. And a report was brought to His Majesty that the country was quiet, and that the foot soldiers of the south and north were ready. On the twenty-first day of the first month of the season Shemu (March-April) of the twenty-third year of the reign of His Majesty, and the day of the festival of the new moon, which was also the anniversary of the king's coronation, at dawn, behold, the order was given to set the whole army in motion. His Majesty set out in his chariot of silver-gold, and he had girded on himself the weapons of battle, like Horus the Slayer, the lord of might, and

---

[15] J. H. Breasted, *Ancient Records of Egypt*, II, 163 *sqq*. It is 223 lines long.
[16] *Ibid.*, note.
[17] Translation of E. A. W. Budge, *The Literature of the Ancient Egyptians* (1914), pp. 104-5. See also J. H. Breasted, *Ancient Records of Egypt*, II, 184, Sect. 430.

he was like unto Menthu [the War-god] of Thebes, and Amen his father gave strength to his arms. The southern half of the army was stationed on a hill to the south of the stream Kīnā, and the northern half lay to the south-west of Megiddo. His Majesty was between them, and Amen was protecting him and giving strength to his body. His Majesty at the head of his army attacked his enemies, and broke their line, and when they saw that he was overwhelming them they broke and fled to Megiddo in a panic, leaving their horses and their gold and silver chariots on the field. [The fugitives] were pulled up by the people over the walls into the city; now they let down their clothes by which to pull them up. If the soldiers of His Majesty had not devoted themselves to securing loot of the enemy, they would have been able to capture the city of Megiddo at the moment when the vile foes from Kadesh and the vile foes from this city were being dragged up hurriedly over the walls into this city; for the terror of His Majesty had entered into them, and their arms dropped helplessly, and the serpent on his crown overthrew them.

The scribe who thus graphically describes the flight to Meggido evidently repeats a royal regret at the delay of the Egyptians to plunder the enemy, for he devotes the whole of the next section to a description of the spoil. Indeed, as Breasted remarks, he is being a priest, really more interested in the booty than in the strategy, because the booty fell largely to the temples. Hence the annals as set forth "are little more than an introduction to lists of feasts and offerings,"[18] which cover adjoining walls of the temple.[19] Fortunately, however, he preserves the source of his narrative, showing that it was taken from the daily record kept by the secretaries of Thutmose III, a copy of which, made on a roll of leather, was preserved in the temple of Amon.[20] The temple inscription was, therefore, an excerpt from a sort of royal journal, arranged and chosen "as a record for the future,"[21] a conscious effort at current history in the grand style, in keeping with the theme and place. Whatever the daily journal of the king amounted

---

[18] J. H. Breasted, *Ancient Records of Egypt*, II, 166.
[19] *Ibid.*, p. 218.
[20] *Ibid.*, Sects. 391, 392, 433. Sect. 392, "Now all that his majesty did to this city [Megiddo], to that wretched foe and his wretched army was recorded on each day by its name, under the title of [title not deciphered]. [Then it was] recorded upon a roll of leather in the temple of Amon to this day."
[21] *Ibid.*, Sect. 568; cf. Sect. 392.

to, the official in charge of it was no mean dignitary; by a strange chance one of them has left in the epitaph on his tomb by Thebes an indication that it was he—Thaneni by name—who followed Thutmose on his campaigns and wrote the original record, to which the inscription refers.[22]

It is unnecessary here to delay long over annals of this kind. Detailed study of them belongs to the history of Egypt rather than to such a survey as this. Although here and there one comes upon notable passages, particularly in the descriptive sections that deal with the administration of the realm, we are not yet, strictly speaking, dealing with historical literature, but with semi-religious, semi-biographical epitaphs, intended, like the monuments on which they were inscribed, to preserve the glory of the present for the future, not to rescue a past from oblivion. Their existence, however, made the latter possible so long as the hieroglyphs could be read; and Herodotus shows us how the scribes and priests could profit from living in such pictured archives as their temples had become, as well as from the treasures in their keeping. So, to some extent, they kept the long perspective open.

Finally, in the early third century B.C. when the history of Egypt was already ancient, a priest and scribe set down in Greek the lists of pharaohs, through all the centuries. Manetho, this one Egyptian historian of Egypt of whom we know, was no mean scholar. He shows, by comparison with the monuments now discovered, that he had at his disposal relatively accurate and adequate data for a suggestive outline without a rival in any antique narrative for the length of time it covers. Unfortunately, we can judge of his work only by the fragments which it suited Josephus, the Jewish historian, to preserve and by the epitomes used by the Christian chroniclers, Julius Africanus and Eusebius. Judged by

---

[22] The inscription runs as follows (J. H. Breasted, *Ancient Records of Egypt*, II, 165): "I followed the Good God, Sovereign of Truth, King of Upper and Lower Egypt, Menkheperre (Thutmose III); I beheld the victories of the king which he won in every country. He brought the chiefs of Zahi as living prisoners to Egypt; he captured all their cities; he cut down their groves; no country remained.... I recorded the victories which he won in every land, putting (them) into writing according to the facts."

the latter, which is hardly fair, he seems to have made it his chief aim to secure correct lists of the pharaohs, coming like a careful mathematician to add up the items in the long lists now practically closed. In doing this he left a device, which Egyptologists still find of use; he divided the names into groups or dynasties, the familiar divisions of today. What we have in the Christian chronologies is apparently rather a reflection of their interest in Egyptian history than of that of Manetho. The same is true of Josephus; but fortunately it suited his purpose in his defense of Jewish historiography to quote from Manetho sufficiently to give us an idea—though only one—of the extent to which the work measures up to the standards of history. It is best to quote the opening section of Josephus' reference, in which he adduces Manetho to prove that the Hyksos were the Hebrews: [23]

Manetho was a man who was by race an Egyptian, but had made himself master of the Greek learning, as is very evident; for he wrote the history of his own country in the Greek tongue, translating it, as he himself says, out of their sacred records: he also finds great fault with Herodotus for having given through ignorance false accounts of Egyptian affairs. Now this Manetho, in the second book of his Egyptian history, writes concerning us in the following manner. I shall set down his very words, as if I were producing the very man himself as a witness.

"There was a king of ours whose name was Timaus, in whose reign it came to pass, I know not why, that God was displeased with us, and there came unexpectedly men of ignoble birth out of the eastern parts, who had boldness enough to make an expedition into our country, and easily subdued it by force without a battle. And when they had got our rulers under their power, they afterwards savagely burnt down our cities, and demolished the temples of the gods, and used all the inhabitants in a most hostile manner, for they slew some, and led the children and wives of others into slavery. At length they made one of themselves king, whose name was Salatis. And he lived at Memphis,[24] and made both upper and lower Egypt pay tribute, and left garrisons in places that were most suitable for them. And he made the eastern parts especially strong, as he foresaw that the Assyrians, who had then the greatest power, would covet their kingdom, and invade them. And

---

[23] Josephus, *Against Apion*, Book I, Sect. 14.
[24] See Josephus, *The Wars of the Jews*, Book I, Chap. 9, Sect. 4.

as he found in the nome of Sais a city very fit for his purpose (which lay east of the arm of the Nile near Bubastis, and with regard to a theological notion was called Auaris), he rebuilt it, and made it very strong by the walls he built round it, and by a numerous garrison of two hundred and forty thousand armed men whom he put into it to keep it. There Salatis went every summer, partly to gather in his corn, and pay his soldiers their wages, and partly to train his armed men and so to awe foreigners. When he had reigned nineteen years he died. After him reigned another, whose name was Beon, for forty-four years. After him reigned another, called Apachnas, thirty-six years and seven months. After him Apophis reigned sixty-one years, and then Janias fifty years and one month. After all these reigned Assis forty-nine years and two months. And these six were the first rulers among them who were very desirous to pluck up Egypt by the roots. Their whole nation was called Hycsos, that is shepherd-kings; for Hyc according to the sacred dialect denotes a king, as does Sos a shepherd and shepherds in the ordinary dialect, and of these is compounded Hycsos. But some say that these people were Arabians."

From this extract, which contains the greater part of the text preserved by Josephus, one can judge the character of the Egyptian history of Manetho. It seems to have been a respectable performance, a work of wide scholarship, extending over a comparative study of the rich materials that lay open to the men of the Hellenic age; the kind of history one might welcome to the reference shelves of the great library at Alexandria. But whatever the content, the enterprise was apparently less Egyptian than Hellenic.

In conclusion, it may be remarked that if the text of Manetho is as good as this sample in the part that deals with the history of the Hyksos, it probably reached still greater excellence in the more purely Egyptian theme of the great days of the Empire, for which ample materials were at hand. The critic of Herodotus may therefore fairly claim the title of the one historian of Egypt.

Such, in short, is the history of history of Egypt. The student will find much of interest as he turns to that vast descriptive literature which modern scholars have now deciphered. But there are no signs of anything comparable to their own work; no mastery of time perspectives and source criticism such as is now demanded of every one who attempts to recast the ancient story.

CHAPTER VII

Babylonian, Assyrian, and Persian Records

THE art of writing in cuneiform—making wedge-shaped marks in clay by means of a reed—was developed as early as the fourth millennium B.C. by the people who lived in the mud flats and among the reedy marshes of the lower Euphrates. They were not Semites, like the nomads of the desert to the west, but "Sumerians," a strange Asiatic people, living mainly in towns and engaged already in business or in truck farming where dikes secured that most fertile soil. History, in that part of the world, dawns for us—since the rise of modern archaeology—with the scratches of those early scribes, noting the sales of a merchant, the title to a plot of land or some such item of current business, or a religious text. For not only has time preserved many a hardened lump of clay, which served them for book and paper, but also the art of writing itself was never lost, through all the changing civilizations which followed on the soil of Babylonia. Indeed it remained one of the fundamentals in Mesopotamian culture, an essential in the transaction of business and of government. From the days when Hammurabi dictated his dispatches and had his laws inscribed, to the closing of the Persian era, the little lumps of clay, baked and sealed, were as important instruments in carrying on affairs as the armies of the kings or the goods of the merchants. And if the devices of literacy helped to hold the Mesopotamian world together, they also united the centuries. Libraries preserved the tablets by scores and hundreds, and scholars copied the classical ones or those their royal patrons were interested in. In short, from a time so remote that it was almost as far away to the Persians as to us, through three millenniums at least, the people of Babylonia-Assyria kept producing and studying the data of history; yet the thing itself they never produced.[1]

The history of history in Babylonia is very similar to that in Egypt, so similar that we do not need to delay long over the details. But there is an added significance to the failure of Babylonia; for it *did* develop the two elements which are the essentials of historical production: a curiosity about the origin of things which resulted in a mythical literature that has been of lasting importance in religion, and a care for the texts of the past, which is the first step toward historical criticism. Had criticism supervened, we should have had genuine history. But criticism presupposes skepticism, and in Babylon as in Egypt, religion—or superstition—block the way to science.

The myths of Babylon have a personal interest for us, not so much on account of what they contain as on account of their subsequent history. Preserved and transformed by the Jews, they became the basis of our own story of the origin of things; and when the originals were found and deciphered, only a little over half a century ago, the controversies which they aroused passed the frontiers of either science or religion, as the very foundations of biblical faith seemed shaken. Here, however, we have no theological problems to solve and must limit ourselves to considering them in their own time and setting, although it must be admitted that, were it not for their later use, we should hardly be tempted to do so, seeing that we passed by in silence the Pyramid texts of Egypt, which have a content intrinsically not less significant. But the coming of Osiris, however much it contributed to that process of intricate and subtle syncretism which tinged with wistful hope and moral purpose the Greco-Roman world in early Christian days, did not enter into the fabric of Jewish belief as did the Babylonian stories of Creation and the Flood, and so its conscious influence in western thought is not to be compared with theirs.

The myth of Creation as preserved on seven tablets, is long and involved, with much repetition; but the parts of interest for

[1] Berossos had Greek antecedents.

comparison with the story in Genesis are only a few lines. It
begins with the creation of the gods themselves.

> When above the heaven was not named,
> And beneath the earth bore no name,
> And the primeval Apsu, who begat them,
> And Mummu and Tiamat, the mother of them all,—
> Their waters were mingled together,
> And no field was formed, no marsh seen,
> When no one of the gods had been called into being,
> And none bore a name, and no destinies [were fixed],
> Then were created the gods in the midst of [heaven].[2]

Then comes a struggle between Tiamat, dragon of darkness and
disorder, and the champion of the parent god Anshar, who was
Ea when the tale was told in Eridu, Marduk when it was told in
Babylon. The text rises to fine epic quality as it describes the hero
advancing to the combat.

> He made ready the bow, appointed it as his weapon,
> He seized a spear, he fastened ...
> He raised the club, in his right hand he grasped it,
> The bow and the quiver he hung at his side.
> He put the lightning in front of him,
> With flaming fire he filled his body.[3]

It was only after Tiamat's body was cut, so that one half made
heaven and the other half the earth, that Marduk determined to
create plants and animals, and man.[4]

When Marduk heard the word of the gods,
His heart moved him and he devised a cunning plan.
He opened his mouth and unto Ea he spoke,
That which he had conceived in his heart, he made known unto him:
"My blood will I take and bone will I *fashion,*
I shall make man that man may ...
I shall create man who shall inhabit *the earth,*
Let the worship of the gods be established, let *their* shrines be built.

There is also the legend of a certain Adapa—or perhaps
Adamu [5]—who is cautioned by his father Ea not to eat or drink

---
[2] R. W. Rogers, *Cuneiform Parallels to the Old Testament* (1912), p. 3.
[3] *Ibid.,* p. 26.
[4] *Ibid.,* Sixth tablet, lines 1-8, p. 36.
[5] *Ibid.,* pp. 67 *sq.*

of the food the gods will provide him, and by obeying—not by disobeying—he misses eternal life. This Adam is not a first man; in the Babylonian myth, he is a god who breaks the wings of the south wind. It is a pretty story, even in the form in which we have it.

But the great myth-epic of Babylonia was that of Gilgamesh and the Flood. It is "the most beautiful, most impressive, and most extensive poem which has been preserved to us of the literature of the ancient Babylonians." The text we have was written on twelve large, closely written tablets, some of which are badly broken; it was copied for a royal Assyrian library, that of Assurbanipal (668–626 B.C.), from some old Babylonian sources, such as have been in part preserved as well from the first Babylonian dynasty, of about 2000 B.C. Gilgamesh was the ruler of one of the city-states, Erech or Uruk, who wandered to that mysterious country beyond the western sea, where he learned from the lips of Noah himself,—whose Babylonian name was Ut-napishtim—the story of the Flood. The epic which preserves this tale is a strange mixture of sublime Oriental poetry, rich with imagery, swift and powerful in narration, with sections of commonplace details as to the measurements of the ark and of the business routine of its management. The more prosy account in Genesis is here embedded in a poem that rivals the Hellenic or Germanic epics. Evidently a real event that drifted over into the realm of legend and romance.

The myths of Babylonia reflect, though dimly, real conditions and events, but they lack the secular tone of the Homeric epics. They belong with religion rather than with the preliminary processes of history. Myths of origin or of half-fabulous heroes have in them the data of history; but they can seldom reveal their historical qualities to the people who produce them, for that requires an attitude of unbelief on the part of the listener, sufficient to enable him to apply the ruthless surgery of criticism. And the age that applies such methods to discover the truth must know how to use the scalpel or it simply kills the whole process, so that myth and fact alike disappear. It was not until the present that readers of the ancient texts could so discriminate between fact and superstition in the early tales of Babylonia; the scholars of later Babylonian ages took them as they were.

Babylonian scholarship did produce another set of sources, however, which brings one to the very threshold of historical literature. No civilization ever produced more codification of documents. The code of Hammurabi was but one of several, and recent discoveries carry the procedure back to Sumerian beginnings. The data of religion, as well as those of law, were codified; vast literatures of omens and charms grew up for the conduct of life in that borderland of luck and morals which was the field of Babylonian magic and religion. Mathematics and a study of the stars finally brought the content to the verge of science, through astrology, and so left a doubly deep impress upon the ancient world. But the interest in this work of codifying and passing along the ancient lore was in the application for the future, as the codifying of laws was for the present. The interest in the past was not destined to produce as notable a contribution, mere lists of names and dates rising at last to the dignity of chronicles.

The earliest records are lists of the names of kings. These are of great importance for the archaeologist, and two such lists, know as the Babylonian King Lists A and B, copied out in the late Babylonian period, show how these could persist in their mud tablets for centuries, to be available for the scholars of the last age of Babylon; similar Sumerian lists have also been discovered, enabling comparison. This shows that long before the days when Hammurabi was inscribing his code, scribes were also ensuring an accurate statement of the succession of rulers. Date-lists were also kept, in order to place the years, the Babylonian way, by events or names.

When we turn from these meagre lists to inscriptions recording events, we find, as in Egypt, that the notable ones deal with current affairs, for the most part glorifying a single monarch. A common device is to present the narrative either as coming from the king himself or from a god—a sure mark of authenticity combined thriftily with devotion! The chronicle grows out of these naturally, but the growth in Babylonia was slight enough. Thin

THE STORY OF THE DELUGE: ASSYRIAN CLAY TABLET

Babylonian, Assyrian, and Persian Records

dynastic narratives have been found, which carry a continuous story from reign to reign—or would if the fragments were less fragmentary. There are some that go back to recite the exploits of Sargon I, the Semitic Charlemagne of this literature, whose legendary figure loomed large through later ages, and of Naram-Sin, his son. But after all, we have only a few lines at best.

The contribution of Assyria to historiography is closely linked with that of early Babylonia. Like the meagre lists of Babylonia, we find here lists of those officers whose names gave the name to the year, arranged in an Eponym Canon.[6] On some of these, as on the calendar tablets of the mediaeval monasteries, they jotted down short notes of events in the year, especially military expeditions, which were to Assyria what temple-building was to Babylonia. But from the crude beginnings such as we might expect of warring hillsmen who had taken over a great heritage, they made progress in historiography to the point of producing it as literature. From the earliest known royal annals, dating from the 14th century B.C., the record grew to embrace not only the king's exploits in war or in the chase, but the arts of peace which prospered under him as well. This fuller narrative was made possible by the use of the clay cylinder or prism upon which several columns of crowded characters might be scratched. For example, four of them, recovered from the ruins of a temple in Assur, describe the first five years of the reign of Tiglath-Peleser I, about 1100 B.C., in such detail that the translation fills twenty pages.[7]

The annals of the great Assyrian monarchs were not, however, confined to cylinders, but were inscribed on stone and on the walls or floors of rooms. Thus open to the constant scrutiny of the king whom they glorified or of the members of his court, these records of great exploits or achievements could hardly bear upon their face the pale light of disinterested truth. That critical unbelief which marked the temper of the Greeks found little encouragement in the precincts of the Assyrian palaces; for it must not be forgotten that the annals of the Assyrian kings were

[6] See above, Chap. IV.
[7] D. D. Luckenbill, *Ancient Records of Assyria and Babylonia* (1926), I, 72-91.

written close to the events which they described and that the participants were the interested readers. Upon accession to the throne, each king began publishing his annals and adding to them as time went on. A comparison of the several versions of the annals of a king which this method of compilation produced would be in itself a valuable exercise in source criticism for any qualified student of the text;[8] yet it is doubtful if there is any other part of the history of history in which the nontechnical student is more baffled by the lack of archaeological equipment than in this field of the shifting Mesopotamian cultures. A recent appraisal goes so far as to claim that "in a very real sense true history begins with the Assyrians";[9] but judged on the basis of the purpose of scientific history—to seek the truth and tell it without fear or favor—the Assyrian royal annals left much to be desired. As literature they provide passages that are both graphic and detailed, and they leave us living pictures of Sennacherib, Tiglath-Peleser, Shalmaneser, and Esarhaddon, who are now as real to us as the figures of classical history. But as trustworthy narratives they are still in the borderland of heroic legend.

It remains only to note the attempt made under the last of the great Assyrian kings, Assurbanipal (668–626 B.C.), to improve upon his predecessors and to give to his inscriptions something of the character of history. The king himself was not only a famous conqueror but a patron of learning, and found time from his wars to bring together a vast library; some 20,000 tablets remain to show the activity of his scribes, who copied the great

[8] In the later versions events are magnified, the exploits of the king greater and more spectacular, and the share of others in his achievements less important. The earliest account of Shalmaneser III's battle at Qarqara (854) announces that 14,000 of the enemy were slain; subsequent versions raise the figure to 20,500, then to 25,000, and finally to 29,000. On one occasion Sargon boasted of capturing 1,235 sheep; a later edition of his annals made the number 100,235. The worst offender of all in this regard was the celebrated Assurbanipal. In three separate annals, published during the early years of his reign, he spoke of a minor campaign conducted by the "governor" of a certain province; twenty years later another version of the royal annals informs us that the king himself conducted the expedition. And even this is not all. Before the end of his life Assurbanipal was quite shamelessly claiming as his own his father Esarhaddon's conquest of Egypt! See A. T. E. Olmstead, *Assyrian Historiography* (1916), pp. 22, 41, 54, 55.

[9] A. T. E. Olmstead, *History of Assyria* (1923), p. 577. See also D. D. Luckenbill, *Ancient Records of Assyria and Babylonia*, I, 25-26.

cuneiform heritage.[10] His own inscriptions forsake the terse phrases of the older style for an essay in history in the grand style, the finest product Assyria could yield. But the substance remains much the same, and the attempt to rearrange events in some topical order instead of following the strict chronological sequence leads to confusion and loses more than it gains.

In spite of all their boastful assertions of power, a persistent minor note runs through most of the royal annals. For, however sure the king may be of his control of the world of his own day, he is uneasy about the future. It is to safeguard that, that "memorial stones" are inscribed for the coming generations. Yet even the inscriptions may not be safe at the hands of one's descendants. The thought is disquieting, and the kings either plead with or threaten those who are to come after. There have been few more ruthless criminals in the world's history than Ashur-nasir-pal III, the Assyrian Tamerlane, who reigned from 885 to 860 B.C.; and few annals from the monuments equal his account of his conquests, which established the Assyrian power in western Asia. But his grasp upon the future is feeble enough.

... O thou future prince among the kings, my sons ... thou shalt not blot out my name which is inscribed (hereon), but thy own name thou shalt inscribe beside my name.[11]

But the records of the Assyrian kings were hardly safe if left to the kindly offices of their successors. Curses were more effective, as Shakespeare, too, thought; and so the chronicle would close with a good round formula, the power of which must have been considerable in the land of omens and augural science. The curse of Ashur-nasir-pal presents so realistic a picture of what may happen to royal records that it may be quoted at length:

Whosoever shall not act according to the word of this, my memorial stone, and shall alter the words of my inscription, or shall destroy this

---

[10] E. Meyer, *Geschichte des Altertums* (3d ed., 1910-1913), Vol. I, Sects. 315-16; R. W. Rogers, *History of Babylonia and Assyria* (2 vols., 1915), II, 427 *sqq.;* H. R. Hall, *Ancient History of the Near East* (1913), p. 500. To it we owe the preservation of such sources for Babylonian history as the Sargon chronicle, etc.
[11] E. A. W. Budge and L. W. King, *The Annals of the Kings of Assyria* (1902), I, 165. See the similar plea of Tiglath-Peleser I, *ibid.*, I, 104. Such formulae are common in the inscriptions.

image or conceal it, or shall smear it with grease or bury it in the earth, or burn it in the fire, or cast it into the water, or place it so that beasts may tread on it or cattle pass over it, or prevent men from beholding and reading the words of my inscription, or shall do violence to my memorial stone so that none may behold it; or, because of these curses shall send a foe ... or a prisoner or any living creature and cause him to take it, and he shall deface it or scrape it or change it into a foreign tongue, or he shall turn his mind ... to alter the words—whether he be scribe or soothsayer or any other man— ... and he shall say "I know him not! Surely during his own rule men slew him and overthrew his image and destroyed it and altered the words of his mouth," ... may Ashur, the great lord, the god of Assyria, the lord of destinies, curse his destiny, and may he alter his deeds and utter an evil curse that the foundation of his kingdom may be rooted up.[12]

With such an appeal to the guardianship of the gods and the fears of men one might leave the record to the keeping of history. It was all one could do. Yet it was not enough. The history of the Assyrians was soon lost. Already by the time of Xenophon, no one could tell the true meaning of the nameless mounds in which lay embedded all that was left of the splendor of Nineveh.[13] The Greeks knew something of Babylon, but almost nothing of Assyria.[14]

More significant from the standpoint of history itself were the synchronistic chronicles which Assyrian scholars prepared to give parallel events in Babylon and Assyria. A tablet of this kind of history, copied long afterwards from an inscription of an earlier king, gives an account of the relations between Assyria and Babylon for several centuries. Its reference to treaties and boundaries have led to the surmise that it was compiled from official archives. Although a work of learned research it was, however, inaccurate to such a point that it even made mistakes in the order of the kings. Moreover the closing words show that nationalism is no mere creation of modern times. The historian ends with the pious

---

[12] *Ibid.*, I, 249 *sqq.*
[13] *Anabasis*, Book III, Chap. 4, Sects. 1-10. He marched past in 401 B.C.
[14] It is striking that the case is somewhat reversed now; we know the history of Assyria better than that of more ancient Babylonia. As E. Meyer remarks, in his work, *Geschichte des Altertums*, Vol. I, Sects. 315-316, the sudden destruction of Nineveh was fortunate, for the remains were at once buried and so preserved, while Babylon was repeatedly despoiled.

Babylonian, Assyrian, and Persian Records

hope that some day a ruler of Assyria may completely subdue the Babylonians, and adds, "Whoever takes it, may he listen to all that is written, the majesty of the land of Ashur may he worship continually; as for Sumer and Akkad, their sins may he expose to all the regions of the world." [15]

The future, however, to which this appeal was addressed, had other things in store. It was Nineveh which was to be destroyed by Babylon in 612 B.C. The new kingdom, known to us as the Second Babylonian or Chaldaean Empire, lasted for less than a century; but it produced annals written in the traditional vein. Finally, however, a chronicle of late Assyrian history was written which "marks the highest achievement of cuneiform historiography." [16] The date of its composition is unknown, because the only tablet we have, written in 500 B.C., was copied from a much earlier one. It covers the years 745 to 668; but, as it is marked number one, the suggestion has been made that it may very well have carried the narrative down to the fall of Nineveh. Olmstead comments upon it as follows:

> The author is remarkably fair, with no apparent prejudice for or against any of the nations or persons named. The events chosen are naturally almost exclusively of a military or political nature, but within these limits he seems to have chosen wisely. In general he confines himself to those events which have an immediate bearing on Babylonian history, but at times, as, for example, in his narration of the Egyptian expeditions, he shows a rather surprising range of interest. If we miss the picturesque language which adds so much to the literary value of the Assyrian annals, this can hardly be counted an objection by a generation of historians which has so subordinated the art of historical writing to the scientific discovery of historical facts. In its sobriety of presentation and its coldly impartial statement of fact, it may almost be called modern.[17]

It was but natural that the Chaldaean kings should look backward to the earlier Babylonian Empire. They were thus led to investigate their own ancient history. Among these researchers was King Nabonidus (556–539 B.C.), who was himself, if not

---

[15] A. T. Olmstead, *Assyrian Historiography*, p. 31.
[16] J. W. Swain in communicated notes.
[17] *Assyrian Historiography*, pp. 61-62.

a royal historian, at least an archaeologist. While the Persians under Cyrus were gathering in the nations along the north and making ready to strike at the old centre of civilization there, the king of Babylonia was excavating the remains of its distant past as he sunk the foundations for his own new temples through the debris of the city where they stood. Although his son Belshazzar, to whom the administration of the realm fell, could see the handwriting on the wall, Nabonidus was not interested in war, but was recording with a scholar's enthusiasm such facts as that he had unearthed a foundation stone of Naram-Sin "which no king before me had seen for 3200 years." The scribes of Nabonidus also searched the libraries to place in their proper places in the lists the kings whose inscriptions he found and to calculate the stretch of years before their time. But gods and men share honors alike in this careful though undiscriminating survey of what were already ancient times in Babylonia.

The Chaldaeans were succeeded by the Persians, whose king, Cyrus, captured Babylon in 538. The Persian kings continued the regal tradition of Babylonia-Assyria, and one of the greatest records in the world is that which, on the almost inaccessible precipice of Behistun, recites the deeds and exalts the glory of Darius the Great to the untenanted desert! But though the desert roads are unfrequented now, this Gibraltarlike rock stands facing the one great highway between central Asia and Mesopotamia, and there, where the traffic between East and West would pass, on the bare face of the cliff, three hundred feet above the roadway, were sculptured the figures of Darius and the "rebels" he overthrew and the long inscription describing the events of his reign.[18]

The inscription was destined to do more than Darius could have

---

[18] Professor A. V. W. Jackson, who visited Behistun in 1903, thus describes it in *Persia, Past and Present* (1906), p. 187: "With all I had read about Behistun, with all I had heard about it, and with all I had thought about it beforehand, I had not the faintest conception of the Gibraltar-like impressiveness of this rugged crag until I came into its Titan presence and felt the grandeur of its sombre shadow and towering frame. Snow and clouds capped its peaks at the time, and birds innumerable were soaring around it aloft or hovering near the place where the inscriptions were hewn into the rock. There, as I looked upward, I could see, more than three hundred feet above the ground, the bas-relief of the great King Darius."

imagined, for by means of it the key was found which unlocked cuneiform to modern scholars. The text had been recorded in Persian, Elamite, and Babylonian, and when, in 1833–1837 (and again in 1844), Sir Henry Rawlinson, then a young officer in the Indian service, at the risk of his life clambered down the rock and copied the inscription, he was able (later) to translate it as well. In such dramatic fashion, did the Behistun inscription become the Rosetta stone of the cuneiform texts.[19]

The inscription of Darius is divided into some fifty or sixty sections, each devoted to a different subject and each beginning "Thus saith Darius the king." The first ten give the genealogy of Darius and a description of the provinces of his empire. With the tenth section the history begins, and it may be quoted to give an idea of how the succeeding ones run:

(Thus) saith Darius, the king: This is what was done by me after I became king. He who was named Cambyses, the son of Cyrus, one of our race, was king here before me. That Cambyses had a brother, Smerdis by name, of the same mother and the same father as Cambyses. Afterwards Cambyses slew this Smerdis. When Cambyses slew Smerdis, it was not known unto people that Smerdis was slain. Thereupon Cambyses went into Egypt. When Cambyses had departed into Egypt, the people became hostile, and the lie multiplied in the land, even in Persia, as in Media, and in the other provinces.[20]

The inscription closes with an appeal to posterity, similar to those of the other regal chronicles described above:

If thou seest this inscription beside these sculptures and destroyest them not, but guardest them as thou livest, then shall Auramazda be thy friend and thy race shalt thou perpetuate, and thou shalt live a long life and whatsoever thou desirest to do shall Auramazda cause to prosper.[21]

---

[19] See the fine volume, with notable illustrations, *The Sculptures and Inscription of Darius the Great on the Rock of Behistun,* published anonymously by the British Museum (1907). The authors are L. W. King and R. C. Thompson, who prepared a new copy by careful work on the spot. See also R. W. Rogers, *History of Babylonia and Assyria,* I, 80.
[20] L. W. King and R. C. Thompson, *The Sculptures ... on the Rock of Behistun,* Persian text, pp. 6-7.
[21] *Ibid.,* Elamite text, p. 149.

But if not, then the curse of Auramazda is invoked on the evildoer. Fortunately the curse has not been tested by the vandal; the texts are too inaccessible. Other Persian kings likewise prepared and set up annals of their reigns: these annals are, of course, valuable to the modern historian, but as they merely imitate—though they never equal—the great annals of Assyria, they are not of importance to our study of the development of history.

Like Egypt, though, the Empires of Asia were touched into new life when the Greeks invaded them, either as travellers or as beneficiaries of the Macedonian conquest. The earliest of these wanderers whose record of his impressions we possess was no less a personage than Herodotus, the "Father of History" himself.[22] But the story of Assyria-Babylonia accepted in the ancient world was largely drawn from that of Ctesias of Cnidus, who lived from 415 to 398 B.C. as personal physician to the King of Persia, Artaxerxes Mnemon. His *Persica* was a *magnum opus* of twenty-three books, the first three of which dealt with the ancient kingdoms, the fourth with their overthrow by the Medes, and the remaining nineteen with Persian history. This uncritical mixture of invention and credulity, utterly unreliable, has not even the merit of a romance, since it imposed itself as history upon the sober chronographers of Alexandria.[23]

[22] As Herodotus reproduced Hecataeus in part, we have some trace of the investigations of Hecataeus as well.
[23] Professor Swain comments as follows: "Though he enjoyed excellent opportunities, his history was a wretched piece of work. His superficial mind made it possible for him to live years at the Persian court and yet know less about Persia than Herodotus had learned in a few months of travel. Indeed, he probably got most of his material for the early books from the Greek *Persica* of the fifth century. His books dealing with Artaxerxes II may have contained some accurate information, but the historical worth of the rest was virtually nil. It was from him that the Greeks and Romans learned of Ninus the first king of Assyria—really a mythical person, eponym of Nineveh—and Semiramis his wife, the reputed founder of Babylon. Even the myths he told about them were probably Ionian rather than oriental. Nevertheless, Ctesias' work was widely popular throughout ancient times; it was read by such men as Plato and Isocrates in his own day, by historians such as Diodorus and Nicholas of Damascus shortly before the time of Christ, and by Photius in Byzantine times; and its information regarding Assyrians, Medes, and Persians, was taken at second or third hand by Eusebius and other Christian chroniclers, who passed it on to the Middle Ages. Ninus, for example, was almost as important as Adam—or his counterparts—in some of these late histories. Moreover, this book greatly influenced the writers of the Alexander romances, which did so much to inflame the imaginations of later conquerors; and

Berossos, a Babylonian priest of Bel, who wrote his three books, *Babylonica* or *Chaldaica*, about 280 B.C., was better equipped to open up to the Hellenic world the mysteries of his homeland. He could know the sources in the original. The text is lost, but such extracts as have been preserved enable us to form a very fair idea of it.[24] There were these different parts: first a mythical, legendary section dealing with the period from Creation to the Flood; then a thin list of names of kings from the Flood to Nabonassar with no account of their deeds; and a closing section of detailed narrative of the more recent history. The whole work was prefaced with a description of the country, apparently in the manner of Herodotus.[25] The myth with which his narrative begins, that of the gift of the arts of civilization to man by a seamonster Oannes, is taken by modern historians to contain a possible dim reflection of a tradition that the Sumerians, that earliest of all people of Babylonia, came from India by way of the Persian Gulf.[26] On the chance that it may be so, and that it is, therefore, the farthest echo of historical fact that has reached our ears from beyond the frontiers of knowledge, we may quote the grotesque narrative as Eusebius has preserved it:

---

perhaps it helped to inflame the imagination of Alexander himself. Ctesias, like Xenophon, may therefore be reckoned among those historians who have made history by writing it; and he certainly illustrates the truth, which we shall have occasion to comment upon many times in the course of the present study, that the importance of a history is not always dependent upon the accuracy of the history it contains."

[24] The extracts, as in the case of Manetho, were preserved by Josephus (*Against Apion*, Book I, Sects. 19 *sqq.*), and by Eusebius (at the opening of his *Chronicorum liber primus*, quoting Alexander Polyhistor, an antiquarian of the time of Sulla). Texts and translation by I. P. Cory in *Ancient Fragments of Phoenician, Chaldaean, Egyptian ... and Other Writers* (2d ed., 1832).

[25] Eusebius (*Chronicorum liber primus*, Chap. 2) summarizes this as follows: "And first, he says, that the land of the Babylonians lies on the river Tigris and that the Euphrates flows through the midst of it, and the land brings forth of itself, wheat, barley, lentils, millet, and sesame. And in the swamps and reeds of the river were certain edible roots called gong, which have the strength of barley-bread. Dates and apples and all kinds of other fruits grow there too, and there are fishes and fowls and birds of fields and swamps. The land has also arid and barren territories (the Arabian); and opposite the land of Arabia, it is mountainous and fruitful. But in Babylon an enormous mass of strange people was settled, in the land of the Chaldaeans, and they lived in licentiousness, like the unreasoning animals and the wild cattle."

[26] See H. R. Hall, *Ancient History of the Near East*, p. 174 *n*.

In the first years, so he [Berossos] says, there appeared from the Red Sea, even there in the midst of the territory of the Babylonians, a terrible monster, whose name was Oannes.... And of this animal he says that it was in daily intercourse with men, never touching food; and it taught men writing and the manifold arts, the building of cities and the founding of temples; also the giving of law and the terms of boundaries and divisions. Also it is said to have taught men the harvest of wheat and fruit; and indeed everything which is of use to the life of organized society was delivered by him to man. And since that time nothing more has been invented by anyone.[27]

And at sunset the monster Oannes plunged again into the sea, and passed the night on the high sea. So that it led a double life to a certain extent. And later other similar monsters appeared which he says he treats of in the book of the kings. And Oannes, he says, has written the following account of the creation and the commonwealth and bestowed speech and aptness to the arts upon man.[28]

That Berossos could turn from such luxuriant Oriental myths as this to a mere list of names in his historical section argues well for his sense of scholarship if not for his critical ability. For obviously he was following his sources closely, a fact which recent investigations tend to corroborate. But his antique editor took another point of view. The inference he drew was that one who knew so little in one section must be an unreliable witness in another! The comment of Eusebius shows what temptation to give a little more than full measure lay in the path of the antique historian! [29]

It would be only fair to Berossos to quote, in contrast to these legendary and chronological sections, something from the later part, where he is on firmer historical ground. Josephus gives us a long enough excerpt of this to show that here it rose to something of the dignity of genuine history.[30] There is a description of Babylon in its last splendor, with the "hanging gardens" and the

---

[27] Note this magnificent statement of the static, conservative idea.
[28] Eusebius, *Chronicorum liber primus*, Chap. 2.
[29] *Ibid.:* "If they [the Chaldaeans] had only told of deeds and works accomplished by the long succession of rulers in these thousands of years, corresponding to the vast extent of time, one might properly hesitate whether there were not some truth in the matter after all. But since they have merely assigned to the rule of those ten men so many myriads of years, who is there who should not regard such indiscriminate accounts as myths."
[30] Josephus, *Against Apion*, Book I, Sects. 19-20.

other feats of engineering, and a criticism of the mistakes of Greek historians who held to the myth of the founding of Babylon by Semiramis. But this is about all we have; in view of the relatively small fragment of the whole history which has been preserved, we are hardly justified in delaying further over it. And with Berossos we quit Babylonia.

Part II

JEWISH HISTORY

CHAPTER VIII

The Old Testament as History

WHEN we turn from these poor and thin records of the great empires of the East to the history of that little branch of the Semites which clung to the perilous post on the land-bridge between the Euphrates and the Nile, the Hebrews of Palestine, we are struck at once with the comparative wealth of its national annals. In contrast with the product of Egypt or Babylonia, the Bible stands out as an epoch-making achievement. A composite work of many centuries, filled with much that the historian rejects, it yet embodies the first historical work of genuinely national importance which has come down to us.[1] Modern criticism has robbed it of its unique distinction as a special revelation of Jehovah, denied the historicity of its account of the Creation, and destroyed the claim of the legends of the patriarchs to be regarded as authentic; the great name of Moses disappears as the author of the Pentateuch, and that of David from the book of Psalms; the story of Joseph becomes a romance, the Decalogue a statement of late prophetic ideals; the old familiar books dissolve into their component parts, written at different times and by different hands. In short, a national record, of varying value and varying historical reliability, has replaced the Bible of the churches, of stately uniform text and unvarying authority. Nevertheless, it is possible to claim that, judged as historical material, the Old Testament stands higher today than

[1] The treatment of the historical records of the Jews is here taken up from the standpoint of the completed output, the Bible as we now have it. This is mainly for the sake of clarity. A more historical treatment would be to begin with the elements as they existed in the earliest days and bring the story down, as it really happened, instead of going backwards, analyzing the completed text. The volume by Julius Bewer (in "Records of Civilization"), *The Literature of the Old Testament in Its Historical Development,* should be at hand to develop, and perhaps to correct, the points touched upon in these pages.

when its text was protected with the sanctions of religion. For it was not until its exceptional and sacred character was denied that it could be appraised by the standards of history and its value as a repository of national, if not of world, story be fairly appreciated. So long as the distinction existed which exalted the Jewish scriptures as sacred inspiration above the rest of the world's literature, the historicity of the Old Testament had to be accepted on a different basis from that of other narratives. Sacred and profane history are by nature incomparable; for the author of the one is God, of the other, man. Now, no higher tribute could be paid to the historical worth of the Old Testament than the statement that, when considered upon the profane basis of human authorship, it still remains one of the greatest products in the history of history, a record of national tradition, outlook, and aspiration, produced by a poor, harassed, semibarbarous people torn by feud and swept by conquest, which yet retains the undying charm of genuine art and the universal appeal of human interest. That is not to say that, viewed from the standpoint of modern history, it is a remarkable performance, for while it embodies some passages of great power and lasting beauty, the narrative is often awkward, self-contradictory, clogged with genealogies, and overloaded with minute and tiresome ceremonial instructions. The historian, however, should not judge it from the modern standpoint. He should not compare Genesis with Ranke, but with the products of Egypt and Assyria. Judged in the light of its own time the literature of the Jews is unique in scope as in power. It is the social expression of a people moving up from barbarism to civilization; and if its pastoral tales reveal here and there the savage Bedouin and its courtly chronicle is touched with the exaggerations of hero myths, if its priestly reforms and prophetic morals are allowed to obscure the currents of more worldly politics, all of these elements but mirror a changing outlook of different ages in the evolution of one of the most highly gifted peoples of the ancient world.

The trouble has been that this mass of literary remains has been taken for something other than what it was. The rabbis came to view its last editorial revision as the authoritative and divine

The Old Testament as History

statement of the whole world's story, and the theologians of succeeding centuries accepted their outlook with unquestioning faith. In short, the Bible became more and more unhistorical as it became more and more sacred. Higher criticism, viewing the texts historically, at last reveals their setting in their own time and place, and presents them as a national product instead of a record of creation in the words of the Creator. For the former it is adequate; for the latter no doctrinal apologies could save it from the shafts of ridicule.

The most important service, however, which higher criticism has rendered the Old Testament, is that it has allowed us to distinguish between the validity of different parts, to detect the naïve folk tale in which Jahveh and the patriarchs meet at old hill-sanctuaries and the late priestly narrative reconstructing the whole in terms of the temple at Jerusalem. The finer passages are no longer involved in the fate of the rest. It is therefore possible to appreciate the genuine achievements of the chief historians of Israel for the first time.[2]

The Bible, as the name implies, is a collection of books.[3] It is not a single, consistent whole, but a miscellany. The first step in understanding it is to realize that it comprises the literary heritage of a nation,—all that has survived, or nearly so, of an antiquity of many centuries. It includes legends from the camps of nomads, borrowings from Babylon, Egypt, and Persia, annals of royal courts, laws, poems, and prophecies. It preserves these, not in their original form, but in fragments recast or reset to suit the purpose of a later day, for, down to the very close of Jewish history the process of editing and reëditing this huge, conglomerate mass went on. Moreover, as the editors were theologians rather than historians, the result was as bad for history as it had been

---

[2] The analysis of the text which is given here was based upon a survey of biblical criticism as it stood at the time these chapters were written. While it is believed that recent discoveries have not shaken the conclusions here stated, it may be said that, in general, they have tended to give support to the more conservative historical outlook as over against conclusions drawn solely from internal evidence.

[3] Βίβλος was the inner bark of the papyrus, hence applied to the paper made from it. From this it was applied to the book made of the paper. Βιβλία (bible) is the plural of βιβλίον, a diminutive of βίβλος. See above, Chap. III.

accounted good for theology, and the historian today has to undo most of this work to reach the various layers of sources upon which they built the Bible as we know it—sources which represent the real heritage of the ancient days. One must dig for these beneath the present text, just as one digs the soil of ancient cities for the streets and walls of former times. For the literary and the material monuments of a people share a somewhat similar fate. The Bible of today stands like some modern Athens or Rome upon the fragments of its former elements. The legends and laws of the early time are buried deep beneath the structure of later ages. More than once they have been burned over by conquest and civil feud, and, when restored, built up to suit new plans and different purposes. Today, however, the historian can lay bare the various strata, recover the ancient landmarks, and from their remains reconstruct in imagination each successive stage of the story. So, like the archaeologist, who sees not merely the city of the present or of its classic splendor, but the cities of every era in the long, eventful past, the student of higher criticism can now trace the process of the formation of the Bible from the crude, primitive beginnings—the tenements of barbarian thought—to the period when its contents were laid out in the blocks of books as we have them now, faced with the marble of unchangeable text, and around them all were flung the sacred walls of canonicity. The walls are now breached; and the exploring scientist can wander at will through the historic texts, unhampered by any superstitious fears. We shall follow him—hurriedly.

There was once a historian of our southern states who prepared himself for his life's work in the highly controversial period of the Civil War by taking a doctorate in mediaeval history. In an alien field, where his personal feelings could not warp his judgment, he learned the scientific temper. Something of his discipline is incumbent upon every student of the Bible. Let us imagine, for instance, that instead of the Jewish scriptures we are talking of those of the Greeks. Suppose that the heritage of Hellas had been preserved to us in the form of a Bible. What would be the character of the book? We should begin, perhaps, with a few passages from Hesiod on the birth of the gods and the dawn of civilization mingled with

The Old Testament as History

fragments of the *Iliad* and both set into long excerpts from Herodotus. The dialogues of Plato might be given by Homeric heroes and the text of the great dramatists (instead of the prophets) be preserved, interspersed one with another and clogged with the uninspired and uninspiring comments of Alexandrian savants. Then imagine that the sense of their authority was so much obscured as centuries passed, that philosophers—for philosophers were to Greece what theologians were to Israel—came to believe that the large part of this composite work of history and philosophy had been first written down by Solon as the deliverance of the oracle of Zeus at Dodona. Then, finally, imagine that the text became stereotyped and sacred, even the words taboo, and became the heritage of alien peoples who knew nothing more of Greek history than what this compilation contained. Such, with some little exaggeration, would be a Hellenic Bible after the fashion of the Bible of the Jews. If the comparison be a little overdrawn there is no danger but that we shall make sufficient mental reservations to prevent us from carrying it too far. Upon the whole, so far as form and structure go, the analogy holds remarkably well.

The Jews divided their scriptures into three main parts: the Law or Torah, the Prophets, and a miscellany loosely termed the "Writings." The Law is better known to Christians by the name given it by the Jews of Alexandria when they translated it into Greek, the Pentateuch [4]—or five books—or by the more definite title of the "Five Books of Moses," an attribution which rests on late Jewish tradition.[5] It is with these books that we have mainly to deal, for they furnish most of the fundamental historical problems of the Old Testament; but the finest narrative lies rather in the second group, which included as well as the books of prophecies, the four histories, Joshua, Judges, Samuel, and

[4] They are also responsible for the names of the separate books, Genesis, Exodus, Deuteronomy, Leviticus. Numbers (*Numeri*) comes from the Latin. It is customary now to group with these five books Joshua, which is closely connected both in form and matter. This makes a Hexateuch instead of a Pentateuch.

[5] This attribution of the Pentateuch to Moses is probably found in II Chronicles 23:18, 25:4, 35:12; Ezra 3:2, 6:18; Nehemiah 13:1; Daniel 9:11, 13. It is found in Philo (fl. at the time of Christ), and in Josephus (first century A.D.). It also occurs in the New Testament.

Kings.[6] The third division, the "Writings" or "Scriptures," of which the Psalms, Job, and Proverbs are typical, also contained some of the later histories—Chronicles, Ezra and Nehemiah,[7] and the amazing book of Daniel.

To the first of these groups we now turn.

[6] The "Prophets" included the three major prophets, Israel, Jeremiah, and Ezekiel, and the "Twelve" (*i.e.* minor prophets), whose prophecies formed one book.
[7] The full list of the "Scriptures" is: Ruth, Psalms, Job, Proverbs, Ecclesiastes, Song of Songs, Lamentations, Esther, Daniel, Ezra, Nehemiah, Chronicles.

CHAPTER IX

The Pentateuch

THE Pentateuch—or, to include Joshua, which really belongs with it, the Hexateuch—is composed of four main sources, dating from about the ninth century to about the fourth. Only two of these, the two oldest, are properly historical, but the other two, while chiefly taken up with laws and ritual, have so recast the text of the earlier ones that all four must be considered in a survey of Hebrew historiography.

The earliest text, which runs through Genesis to Kings, is a repository of prehistoric legend. There had been legends of the patriarchs of the Israelites, passed down by tradition from the dimmest antiquity. They were just like those of any other primitive people, tribal legends of reputed ancestors and heroes, intermingled with myths of tribal religion. Anthropology can match them with similar stories from all over the world. They were kept alive, apparently—or at least some of them were—by recital at local shrines and holy places, of which the land was full. Every village had its altar for sacrifices to its divinities and often a feast hall for the festivities which followed. There were sacred groves and hilltop sanctuaries, haunted rocks and piles of stones; and around each clung some legend of the olden time, some story of a hero who had once been there. If one reads the narratives of the patriarchs, even in the form in which we have them in Genesis now, one is struck with the continual punctuation of the stories by the erection of altars and the dedication of holy places. Wherever an oath is sworn, a sacrifice offered, or a vision seen, the stones are piled up for an altar, which in most cases "remains even unto this day."[1] Often across successive editings one catches the touch

---

[1] For such instances, cf. Genesis 12:7, 8, 13:4, 18; 16:7-14; 21:12-21, 31; 22:14; 23:1, 19, 20; 24:62; 25:9, 10; 26:25, 32; 28:17-19; 31:13, 46-49; 32:30; 33:20; 35:14, 15, 20; 48:9; 49:30; 50:3.

of genuine local color in these incidents, and it does not take much analysis to discover in them the remnants of myths or legends of origin, like those which in the Middle Ages attributed so many foundations of churches and monasteries to the apostles.[2]

Such stories—at least among primitive peoples—are not to be attributed to conscious invention. They grow up of themselves. One might almost say that they are believed before they are told. The process of their fabrication is a purely social matter and is as much alive today as it was before Moses. How many colonial houses have had a visit from George Washington, or have become in some way associated with him? One person supposes heroic incidents *may* have happened here, another thinks they *must* and a third thinks they *did*. If there are skeptics, they are soon frowned down, because the world wishes the story. So Abraham built an altar in Schechem,[3] Isaac dug the well of Shebah,[4] Jacob piled boundary stones at Gal'ed—or Gilead,[5] while, above all, two sacred mountains, Horeb and Sinai,[6] were rivals for the vaster prestige of being the scene of the lawgiving Moses.

These legends not only dignified the locality by a connection with the patriarchs and their divinities; they also enriched the patriarchal tradition itself with a wealth of local detail. The material was therefore at hand for a great national saga, which should weave the incidents together in harmony with the major theme of the origins of the nation itself, looking back from settled agricultural life to that of nomadic herdsmen from the fringe of the desert and beyond. Such national legends must be large enough in scope to include all the tribes who hold themselves akin

[2] C. F. Kent, *Student's Old Testament* (5 vols., 1904-1914), I, 8-12, classifies the legends under the headings: 1. Biographical; clan and family legends, with the family as the central theme, held in the memory of wandering tribes for four or five centuries. 2. Institutional, *e.g.* explanatory of the origin of Sabbath or Passover. 3. Of sacred places, giving the origin of their names. 4. Of origin of proper names, *e.g.* Abraham from ab-hamon, the father of a multitude. 5. Entertaining stories, *e.g.* the journey of Abraham's servant for Rebekah. These latter were great favorites. The most stimulating work of recent times on these subjects, bringing great wealth of anthropological lore to illustrate the setting of Jewish legend and cult, is Sir J. G. Frazer's *Folk Lore in the Old Testament* (3 vols., 1918).

[3] Genesis 12:6, 7.

[4] Genesis 26:33, "Wherefore the name of the city is Beer-Sheba unto this day."

[5] Popularly believed to be the etymology.

[6] The mountain is Sinai in the accounts of P and probably J; Horeb in E and D.

The Pentateuch

and bold enough to face the further question with which every mythology deals in some form or other, the origin not only of the tribesmen but of the world itself. Beyond the Nibelungen of this Semitic migration, therefore, there reached out memories of premigration legends—the story of a flood in the old homeland east of the desert, the land of Shinar, or Sumeria, and of a garden of Eden where the first man learned the secrets of the gods. The patriarchal legends were thus prefaced with Babylonian creation and flood myths.

These primitive materials were worked over into more or less consistent stories by various hands, and finally, about the year 900 B.C., they were pulled together by a genuine master of narrative whose text still furnishes most of the naïve and picturesque parts of the Old Testament from Genesis to Kings.[7] Since the distinctive note and unifying thread of the story, undoubtedly following the trend of the earlier models, is not so much the fortunes of the tribesmen as the way in which those fortunes depended upon the favor of the tribal god whose name is Jahveh,[8] the unknown author—or rather reviser—is known to scholars by the simple epithet, "the Jahvist" or, since there were several Jahvists, as "the great Jahvist."[9] The latter epithet would be justified, even had there been no need of contrast, for the Hebrew Herodotus tells his ancient folk tale with epic force and presents the materials, however crude, as they came to him. Although his own conception of God rises to heights of genuine sublimity, such as those passages where the splendor of Jahveh passes before the bowed figure of Moses in the cleft of the mountains—a spectacle which calls forth a lyric outburst worthy of the Psalms[10] —yet he begins by repeating the naïve account of Adam and Eve in the garden of Eden and God walking there in the cool of the day, of the curse on snakes and men, of giants and demigods, and of the flood. He does not balk at any semisavage tale such as

[7] Except Ruth, which is a product of the Persian or Greek period.
[8] The emphasis, as will appear later, is upon the name.
[9] Or following German orthography, just "J" for short. The narrative by him is generally so indicated, merely by the letter.
[10] Exodus 33:12-23 and 34:6-9.

that of Hagar turned off into the wilderness to die, the lying cunning of Jacob toward his father and brother, etc. Obviously these tales came down to him sanctioned by too universal acceptance to be discarded, although belonging to a lower grade of culture and morals than those of his own day. Like Herodotus, five centuries later, he left the ancient stories embedded in his own narrative; but, unlike Herodotus, he offered no suggestion that the fables he retold were unworthy of credence.

Within about a century after the work of the great Jahvist, a new compilation of the stories of the patriarchs appeared. The source of the Jahvist had been Judaea in southern Palestine; this was from the northern kingdom of Israel. It was to a large degree parallel with the Jahvist but with variations and different local touches. Its main distinction, however, is that throughout the narrative of the patriarchs it does not use the name Jahveh at all, but refers all the supernatural element in it to Elohim, a word difficult to translate, since, like so much of the language of religion, under the guise of primitive vocabulary it carries the conception of Divinity on to higher planes. Elohim, the plural of Eloah, means supernatural powers or Power.[11] Mythologically it is connected with such spirits as one may find at hilltop altars or see if one sleeps in lonely places, local or household gods of a people just emerging from fetishism. This second of the prime narratives of the Old Testament is therefore known to biblical criticism as the Elohist account.[12] According to it, "the god of Abraham, Isaac and Jacob" was really unknown to them, since they did not know his name and not to know the name of a god in primitive mythology is not to know the god himself.[13] In other words, the nomadic period, with its barbarous morals and low-

---

[11] Cf. the Latin *numina,* some of which develop later into *dei.*
[12] More often simply as "E." It is also well to recall that "J," Jahvist, is now used often by scholars to signify Judaistic, and "E," Ephraimistic, from their sources.
[13] The sacred character of the name is insisted upon wherever religion is invested with the power of curse or blessing. Anthropology supplies evidence of the universality of this belief. The formulas of blessing or benediction by the sacred name have lost most of their primitive meaning, but the oath still retains the power of the curse.

grade theology, is represented as a pre-Jahvistic age. The god who eats his supper by the tent door and cannot even throw Jacob in a wrestling match except by a foul is not Jahveh as J lightly assumes, for Jahveh is a more exalted deity. The ancestors of Israel, according to this narrative, worshipped local deities or their own protecting genii in about the same way as the rest of the primitive world. It is therefore in the interests of a higher conception of Jahveh that his name is omitted from the story of the crude beginnings of the age of migration. According to the Elohist, Jahveh first definitely appears in the national history after the period of nomadic life, at the second great era in Hebrew history—that of the conquest and settlement. It is at that dramatic point where Moses hears the oracle from the burning bush, commissioning him to lead the Israelites out of Egypt.[14] In response to the insistence of Moses, the god Elohim at last reveals his name, in cryptic, oracular fashion: "I am going to be what I am going to be." Thus Jahveh enters definitely into the story of the Elohist, which from this point on runs along much like that of the Jahvist. It differs, however, in two or three important particulars. In the first place it presents a higher conception of the deity, who does not show himself bodily to men but reveals himself only in visions or by a voice from the unseen. He dwells in the heavens, which only a ladder of dreams can reach, and—a fact of prime importance—uses as the medium of communication a special class of men, devoted to his service, gifted with second sight and the power of miracle. This latter element, that of the miraculous, thus enters into the story to a marked degree, more so than in the naïve account of J. For instance, the waters of the Red Sea are driven back by a high wind according to J; they are made to divide miraculously at the touch of Moses' wand, according to E. This enhancement of miracle, introduced to exalt the dignity and the claims of Jahveh, served its purpose throughout all succeeding centuries. So long as miracle was regarded as the special mark of divinity the more miracle the Bible could boast the more authentic it seemed. Now, however, in an age of science, when miracles are disowned on general principles, the

[14] Exodus 3.

romantic additions to the primitive tale contributed by the narrative of E merely lowers its value as history. One is confronted with a situation similar to that of mediaeval saint legends, where the miracles multiply the farther one goes from the original source, and multiply almost according to formula.

If the account of J is more reliable than E in its treatment of incident—that is, more nearly a reflection of primitive myth—the same is true of the treatment of morals. E toned down the cruel and crude stories of the olden time, which J had allowed to stand as tradition had preserved them. A higher moral standard in the present was demanding a more edifying past. Under such circumstances E, which apparently began as an independent and parallel compilation, drawn from similar—or the same—sources as J, became the basis for a revision of the whole mass of legend. For, like the Jahvists, the Elohists worked closely with the prophets of their day, and their text came to reflect definitely the great reform of the prophets Amos and Hosea, in which the national religion was recast almost as completely as when Christianity broke away from it some seven or eight centuries later. The tribal deity—chiefly a war god—who had replaced the local divinities through the ardent propaganda of the Jahvist prophets, now was conceived of in terms of pure moral conduct. His true worship was not sacrifice but upright living. Nothing could be more foreign than this to the ideas of the olden time. Then Jahveh had been the fierce, unforgiving god of taboo and ceremonial; now he was transformed into a god of love and righteousness. This reconstruction of religion involved a reconstruction of history, a reconstruction so sweeping as to be termed by some modern scholars the first attempt at higher criticism. The old tribal story was recast to make the role of Jahveh more consistent with the newer ethics [15] and, incidentally, more credible. The men who wrote the decalogue—for the Elohists were responsible for the ten commandments—did not hesitate at what would now be accounted changing the records in order to permit them to insert it as divine command.

Sometime in the seventh century a Judaean author joined J and

[15] For instance, the condemnation of the worship of Jahveh in the form of a bull.

E into a single narrative known as JE—a rather careless weaving of the two strands, not eliminating contradictions and repetitions. Evidently this bungling performance was forced upon the editor by the vitality of the various versions, but he rather increased than lessened his difficulties by adding further variants from still other sources. Unsatisfactory as his compilation is from the standpoint of a finished artistic production, the biblical critic is often grateful that it is as poor as it is; for the trace of the different strands, which we have just been examining, might otherwise have been obliterated. Had Judaea produced a Thucydides for the perpetuation of its national history, capable of rising to the full height of his theme and recasting the fragmentary and uncouth materials into the mould of art, the history of the world would now be poorer instead of richer, for the sources would have been lost.

But the process of Pentateuch authorship was not complete with the final edition of JE. In the second half of the seventh century a new element was introduced, preserved mainly in the book of Deuteronomy, and so known to biblical scholars simply as the Deuteronomist—or D for short. Although not narrative in the sense of J or E, this body of religious precept was responsible for a yet bolder attempt than E to upset much of the accepted text in order to swing the whole in line with its exalted outlook. That the outlook was really exalted—the finest in the Old Testament—any one will admit who reads the fifth to the eleventh chapters of Deuteronomy and then compares them with the rest of the world's literature before the climax of antique civilization.[16] In order, however, to realize this high ethical religion it was necessary to discredit the crude heathenism which still persisted at those local shrines where J had gathered so much of its narrative —the very shrines which were set up by the patriarchs themselves. D insisted that Jahveh could be sacrificed to in one place only—the temple at Jerusalem.[17] Local altars tend to a localiza-

[16] "The core of D is CC. 5-11; 12-26; 28." G. F. Moore, *The Literature of the Old Testament* (1913), pp. 58-59.

[17] E had denied that the cult at high places of the early period had been a real cult of Jahveh. The Deuteronomic reformers now went much farther. They denied

tion of the deity—as they still do—so they must go, and the priests who attended them must become priests of Jahveh in his one and only temple.[18]

The reformers had to find the justification for such a sweeping innovation, which tore up the customs of village life by the roots, in oracles of Jahveh from the olden time, and since these were lacking, they were obliged to invent them to meet the emergency. Most of the invention naturally was attributed to the greatest figure of the Hebrew legends—Moses. The ancient texts (especially E) had already made him the mouthpiece of Jahveh at a sacred mountain; D elaborated his deliverances with new divine instructions. This is the main change made by D. It is more law than history, but the history had to accommodate itself to the law; and D is responsible for the transformation of the figure of Moses from that of a prophet and seer to that of the greatest lawgiver of antiquity, a transformation which was completed by the next and last of the four main contributions to the Pentateuch.[19]

The last contribution to the Pentateuch was written either

---

that this hilltop and village worship could ever be legitimate in the religion of Jahveh.

[18] Deuteronomy 18:6, 7. The move proved impossible on account of the vested rights of the Jerusalem priesthood. A degradation of these priests to levites resulted and was justified by Ezekiel.

This helps to date D with certainty. Hosea does not show any belief in the special sacredness of the temple. This doctrine does not come before the latter part of the seventh century. But Hosea's influence upon D's conception of God is obvious. Language and style also point to the seventh century.

[19] The book of Deuteronomy came to light in the eighteenth year of the reign of Josiah. The story is told in II Kings 22. While repairing the temple, under orders of Josiah, Hilkiah, the high priest, found it. "And Hilkiah the high priest said unto Shaphan the scribe, I have found the book of the law in the house of the Lord. And Hilkiah gave the book to Shaphan, and he read it.... And Shaphan the scribe read it before the king. And it came to pass, when the king had heard the words of the book of the law, that he rent his clothes. And the king commanded ... saying: Go ye, inquire of the Lord for me, and for the people ... concerning the words of this book that is found." So they consulted a "prophetess" who instructed them to follow it. Then (Chap. 23) the reform was inaugurated, the local altars broken, the groves cut down, and all the sacred places polluted with dead men's bones or otherwise profaned. Not the least significant incident from the standpoint of historiography is the consultation of the "prophetess" to learn of the validity of the law.

The Pentateuch

during the exile at Babylon or during the Persian period which followed.[20] It is known as the Priestly History, or P for short,[21] for it reviews the whole history of J and E from the standpoint of the priesthood of the temple. This is, perhaps, the most important of all the contributions so far as the present text of the Bible is concerned, for it furnishes the general framework of history, as we have it now.

That framework is very remarkable. We are far removed in it from the naïve, gossipy narratives of the olden time. Five hundred years or so had elapsed since the Jahvist wove together his material—already hoary with age when he found it. In those five centuries we may almost be said to pass from a Froissart or Gregory of Tours, credulous, simple-minded, but a born raconteur, to a Hegel, with a philosophy of history. P arranges the phenomena of the past according to a theory, a theory very similar in general outline to that of Hegel. He finds the meaning of history in successive self-revelations by Jahveh. With this principle as a guide, the author groups the main incidents of history around four great figures and into four great epochs—those of Adam, Noah, Abraham, and Moses. Upon these figures all the different lines are made to converge, the first three as ancestral heroes, the last as the especial mouthpiece of Jahveh. Lines of genealogy—P is responsible for this dismal element in the text—serve both to link the chief personages and to indicate the passage of time.[22] One must not credit P with the imagination necessary for the invention of so impressive a scheme, for the data already suggested it. Legends tend to concentrate upon a few heroic figures and to culminate in dramatic epochs. But

[20] It is generally thought to be the book of the Law (Torah) which Ezra brought back with him to Judaea when sent to Jerusalem by the Persian Artaxerxes in 458 B.C. But the text does not bear the mark of the theological interests of the period of Nehemiah—the especial prohibitions of mixed marriages.

[21] A better title is "The Book of Origins" (H. Ewald, *The History of Israel*, 8 vols., tr. 1869-1886, I, 74 *sqq.*).

[22] The difficulties in this problem were easily met by giving fabulous ages to the generations of which few names were known. On the genealogies, see note on Nehemiah below, p. 132, *n.* 26. P carries the genealogies from Creation to Abraham as follows: the generations of Adam, Genesis 5; of Noah, 6:9; of the sons of Noah, 10; of Shem, 11:10; of Terah, 11:27.

what had been a natural development of the story became under the hand of P artificial, doctrinal, and unreal.[23] All history led up to the establishment of the temple, all the fortunes of Israel depended upon the observance of the taboos codified under Moses. The prescriptions for the temple worship are asserted to have been given already at Sinai, anticipating the temple itself by many centuries.[24] The prerogatives of the priests—with their levite temple servants and national tithes for their support—are safeguarded by miracle and exalted to dominate the nation to an incredible extent. In short, P is less a historian than an apologist and theologian. Yet it was his account which gave the tone to the completed scriptures, for, sometime in the fifth or fourth centuries B.C., a final edition fitted the composite JED into the narrative of P and so gave us the text of the first five books of the Bible.[25]

We must close this section of our survey by a glance back at its opening—the story of Creation. The first chapter of Genesis comes from P—an account written almost in the days of Herodotus. In any case it was not until his time that the second chapter (from J) was added to the first. Herodotus, too, was interested in the origin of things, so much so that he made a special journey to the Phoenicians to verify an Egyptian account of the beginnings of human society, where "Hercules" played somewhat the role of Jahveh. If ever the historian is justified in speculating on what might have been, he may surely be allowed the privilege of conducting the Father of History the few miles inland to Jerusalem, to discuss the matter with the author of Genesis! It is doubtful if the intellectual heritage of succeeding ages would

---

[23] A comparison of the first chapter of Genesis (by P) with the second (by J) will show how far removed the last contribution is from the first, not only in matter but also in style. In the one, creation comes from the fiat of a god who remains aloof from His universe; in the other He breathes into the dust to make man live and then associates with him as a companion. The style of P is here suitable to his theme, for the lack of detail which makes the rest of his story bald and dry was here most appropriate. Later on his inferiority is more apparent.

[24] All sacrifice except by the priesthood is illegitimate, hence P does not admit that the patriarchs ever sacrificed.

[25] This is a simplification of the actual process, for the separate J and E continued to circulate after JE was made, and there are other elements in the composition not covered here.

have been much changed by such a meeting, for Herodotus could not have guessed that the mixture of myth and tribal legend which the Jewish historian was editing would have been taken at rather more than its face value by the whole of western civilization for almost two millenniums, as the explanation—*the* genesis —of the entire world; and the Jew could have understood just as little the rational temper of his Greek confrere, or the importance of his inquiry. But in the days when religion and history began once more to be studied by the comparative method, such as Herodotus tried to use, and the priests of Egypt and Babylon to be interrogated, this time in their own tongue, nothing could match in interest, for the critic of the Bible, such an imaginary conversation recorded by the hand of Herodotus.

CHAPTER X

The Remaining Historical Books of the Old Testament

THE main sources of the Pentateuch run on into the books which follow. The old collections of traditions, J and E or similar narratives, tangle themselves together; Deuteronomist historians use them to preach their lesson that disaster is always due to sin and especially to the anger of Jahveh, then priestly hands insert at likely points in the narrative sections—largely imaginative—which exalt the role of the priesthood. Then comes the work of the author-editors, who throw the miscellany into approximately the present form, a work which was not completed until later. Since we have already seen this composite process of authorship worked out in some detail in connection with the Pentateuch, we shall pass in more hurried review over these remaining books.

Joshua is so intimately connected with the five preceding books that it is now customary to treat it along with them, the six forming the Hexateuch. It carries over into the conquest the same elements we have seen in the Pentateuchs or continuations of them. The book falls rather clearly into two main parts: the first twelve chapters dealing with the conquest, the next ten with the division of the land, while an appendix of two final chapters gives a valedictory warning of Joshua after the fashion of that of Moses.[1] Of these, the second section, that describing the allotment of the tribes, is obviously an invention emanating from the same kind of priestly imagination of a late day as the P (Book of Origins) of the Pentateuch, but the imagination in this case became somewhat too businesslike when it asserted that forty-

---

[1] In Deuteronomy 33:1-8. Of course there are interpolations within these sections.

eight cities, some of them the best in the country, belonged by right of original assignment to priests and levites. We need not delay long over that kind of "history." [2] The story of the conquest is told by a Deuteronomic moralizer,[3] who used the two older sources, continuations of J and E, to suit his taste. Now, these earlier narratives did not agree as to how the Hebrews conquered Canaan, for the one (J) made it a movement of scattered war bands, who settled in the open country, being unable to take the walled towns, while the other (E) had a great tale of how they destroyed the Canaanites root and branch, in a vast migration, somewhat the way the Saxon invaders were credited in the old histories of England with the destruction of the Britons. The taste of the Deuteronomic editor—whose edition was taken over by the author of Joshua—was for this latter source, with its story of miracles and slaughter. This accounts for such tales as the crossing of the Jordan, which repeats all the wonders, with which legend had surrounded the reputed crossing of the Red Sea—waters piled up and a march through in priestly procession.[4] It also accounts for the story of the falling of the walls of Jericho at the sound of trumpets, although traces of the fact that the city was taken by storm in the ordinary way are still to be detected in the narrative. The book of Joshua frankly excluded the plain facts of history in favor of heroic legend. Strangely enough, however, the substance of the unheroic narrative (J) was preserved in another place. The opening chapter of Judges and the first five verses of the second chapter sum up the story of the conquest as it probably happened.[5] There the truth crops out that the advance of the Israelites was a slow, intermittent movement, and that it left the fortified cities practically untouched, making inevitable that racial blend and intercourse against which the prophets of Jahveh were to protest so vehemently. One can see, in the light of their national fanaticism, how

[2] Although some of it rests on older material, especially E.
[3] One, that is, thoroughly associated with the spirit and style of the writers of Deuteronomy.
[4] The infertility of the myth-making faculty becomes apparent here. Folklorists are familiar with this limitation of the imagination to a few staple exploits, which repeat themselves indefinitely. The legends of the saints are mostly alike.
[5] Subsequent events of Hebrew history agree with it.

natural it would be for writers, saturated in the doctrines of these prophets, to believe in the exaggerated rather than the true account of the war upon the native population. That is perhaps the explanation for the portions of relatively poor history in the book of Joshua.

The book of Judges begins, as we have seen, with the fragments which might have been used as a basis for the opening of Joshua. The proper narrative of the "judges" begins at the close of this short review of the conquest and the death of Joshua.[6] The keynote to the book is struck at once.[7] The Israelites are continually forgetting Jahveh or violating his taboos; his anger is aroused and he turns them over to spoilers;[8] then "judges"—war-chieftains and petty rulers—rise to throw off the yoke; again the people sin and again are given up to tyrants; again a "judge" arises to smite the oppressor and to rule for a generation; again comes anarchy and again a deliverer, etc. It is an eternal round. Such history is suspect on the face of it. It is even more so when one looks at the chronology, for the periods of disaster and deliverance run regularly for twenty, forty, or eighty years, or approximately so. When we recall that this chronology runs through Samuel and Kings, that the reigns of David and Solomon are each given as forty years, which was reckoned as the average length of a generation in the Old Testament, we see here a schematic arrangement of history quite too regular and symmetrical to be true. Each moral lesson is framed in a generation. We do not have to look far to see the principles upon which the whole is constructed. The Deuteronomist interpreted tribal wars and the anarchy of Bedouinlike people as part of the providential scheme of Jahveh, and it is a significant fact that whenever a theologian—of any religion—has attempted to use history to justify the ways of God to man, he has the history rearranged so that its artificial character may convince the reader that it was actually planned![9] As for the exact time allowed each judgeship, the chronology apparently was fixed so as to try to fill in the four

---

[6] Judges 2:6. Verses 6, 8, 9 are literal repetitions from the last chapter of Joshua.
[7] Judges 2:11-23.
[8] Judges 2:14, 15.
[9] We come upon this especially in the work of the Christian historians.

hundred and eighty years which, according to I Kings 6:1, lay between the exodus and the building of the temple, although the attempt is not quite successful.

But if the main part of the book of Judges [10] was cast into this form by a Deuteronomist writer in the sixth century, the material which he used is genuine, old, legendary stuff, tales of heroes and semisavage men, often unvarnished, with all their vindictive cruelty and cunning, their boastful exaggeration, both of prowess and of slaughter. The very savagery of these stories is in their favor; they bear the mark of their time and reflect, through all their bombast, the wild age when, as the narrative plaintively repeats, "there was no king in Israel." It was surely a triumph for the compiler of this material to reduce it, even partially, to be food for sermons. Fortunately he was still enough of a savage himself not to rub out all the savagery of his ancestors.

When we come to the narrative of the founding of the kingdom,[11] our sources work out in a remarkable way. The originals become both more reliable and fuller. Contemporary accounts from those who knew intimately the ins and outs of camp and court have been preserved almost untouched by subsequent editing. There is no such artistic manipulation of events as we have just seen in Judges, by seventh- or sixth-century reformers. They left almost untouched the great story of David, because they could not have improved upon it in any case. Through a period of national expansion and successful war, the worship of the national god, Jahveh, was not likely to meet with serious rivalry from the local deities of earth and the fertility gods—the Baals —which in time of peace were continually drawing the attention of the farmers. The building of the temple at Jerusalem was the logical conclusion of the war period begun by Saul's battle with the Philistines; the war god was enthroned on the citadel. Conse-

---

[10] To the end of the sixteenth chapter.
[11] The stories of Eli and Samuel really belong with those of the Judges. Even in the form in which we have it now, this connection is emphasized by the address, which Samuel delivers in I Samuel 12 and which forms a fitting literary close to the Judges, similar to the addresses of Moses and Joshua. This at least seems to fit one stratum of sources.

quently the later prophets and priests of Jahveh had relatively little to change in the sources which carried the narrative of J up to its fitting and triumphant conclusion, and we have fairly contemporary and unspoiled narratives.

Here, therefore, at last we come upon the best product of Hebrew historiography. The storytelling art of J[12] is no longer working over the naïve old tales of Genesis, but deals with well-known men and recent events, and in the tale of the houses of Saul and David we have something which will rank with the best the world can offer. Few figures from antiquity stand out more clearly, in all their complex humanity, than that of David. We have him in all his weakness as well as his strength; no shocked moralizer got rid of his sons at the expense of his character. Legend, which always surrounds great men even when alive, added something, so that subsequent ages endow him with extravagant gifts of poetry as they did his son with equally extravagant gifts of wisdom, but his personality and the story of his reign remain on the solid basis of history.

This detailed, reliable history runs through the two books of Samuel into the first two chapters of the first book of Kings. But from the reign of Solomon a vastly different type of narrative takes its place. The events of four centuries are chronicled in the same amount of space as was devoted to the lifetime of David alone, and even this meagre outline is blurred by the Deuteronomic editors. For the history of the period from Solomon to the Babylonian captivity is cast in the same mould as that which we have already seen in Judges. Disaster is due to neglect in the worship of Jahveh, and more especially to the persistence of the old worship in high places in spite of the claims of the temple at Jerusalem to be Jahveh's sole abode. The result of this line of interpretation of history, carried to the extreme, is that we have less a history of kings than a commentary upon Jahveh-worship,

---

[12] The source of Samuel is so much in the spirit of the J of the Pentateuch and Joshua, that the same symbol is used for it; but that does not necessarily imply the same authorship or even that the text in Samuel is a continuation of the J of the older part. But whatever their relationship, the conception and style are so similar as to justify the symbol for both.

for the author pays little attention to the importance of the reigns he catalogues except as they can be made to illustrate the theological point he is making. For instance, Omri, who founded a great dynasty in the Northern Kingdom, is dismissed in one verse,[13] although Assyrian inscriptions recognize his greatness to the extent of calling the Kingdom of Israel Beth-Omri.[14] Since this founder of the city of Samaria, however, permitted the old worship of the golden calves, he was obviously not an edifying figure for a history which was intended to prove that such heathenish rites spelled disaster. In such cavalier fashion the book of "the Kings" treats the successive reigns of both Judah and Israel. Historians have seldom resisted the temptation to draw a moral from history, but here the history itself was drawn into a moral, until it distorted the whole perspective.[15] The fact that even today only biblical scholars are able to recover the correct perspective is sufficient comment upon the poor quality of these last chapters of Hebrew national history, and the critics have received most of their hints from elsewhere—cuneiform inscriptions and a study of the prophets.

From time to time, however, through this mangled chronicle, a remark is inserted which excites the interest of the historian. The reign of Solomon is cut short with the remark: "And the rest of the acts of Solomon, and all that he did, and his wisdom, are they not written in the book of the acts of Solomon?"[16] Similarly at the close of the account of Jeroboam and Rehoboam: "And the rest of the acts of Jeroboam, how he warred and how he reigned, behold, they are written in the book of the Chronicles of the Kings of Israel."[17] ... "Now the rest of the acts of Rehoboam, and all that he did, are they not written in the book of the Chronicles of the Kings of Judah?"[18] The formula occurs practically without fail at the end of the narrative of every

---

[13] I Kings 16:24.

[14] On the translation of this see R. W. Rogers, *Cuneiform Parallels to the Old Testament*, p. 304 *n.* 2.

[15] See G. F. Moore, *The Literature of the Old Testament*, p. 103: "Some one has said that history is philosophy teaching by example; for the author of Kings history was prophecy teaching by example."

[16] I Kings 11:41.   [17] *Ibid.*, 14:19.   [18] *Ibid.*, 14:29.

reign.[19] This means that, in the eyes of the author, his work was less a history than a commentary. It also shows us that from the days of Solomon, there were royal annals, like those of Assyria, which were kept in the capital, and that after the separation of the ten tribes under Jeroboam, each kingdom kept its record. The Bible does not preserve these for us; it preserves only as much as suited the priestly and prophetic writers intent upon making history a handmaid to religion.[20]

This royal chronicle (referred to but not reproduced in the Bible) marks the end of the age of tradition and brings us, at last, into that of written records. The separate tribes had been welded into a nation, and while the different settlements undoubtedly still preserved their ancient stories, the breaking-up of their isolation made the traditions complex, hard to remember, and more or less trivial and irrelevant. The great feats of Saul and David were bound to overshadow the less notable past. So when the Hebrew system of writing came in, as it did for the first time under the kingdom, history developed at the court of Solomon in apparently somewhat the same official way as in the courts of the late Babylonian kings. The legend was giving way to annals, romance yielding to businesslike records, a change which has taken place in every country at the moment when it begins to acquire what it calls civilization.

There remains only one other Hebrew history—that which runs through the books of Chronicles,[21] Ezra, and Nehemiah. This is a single work, written by one hand, probably after 300 B.C. It is a summary of the whole history given in the preceding books, at least so far as immediately concerned the kingdom of Judah and Jerusalem. Its author uses the "Book of the Kings of Judah and Israel" and the "Book of the Kings of Israel" and other such sources which have since been lost.[22] He was evidently a learned

---

[19] See also I Kings 15:23, 31; 16:5, 14, 27; II Kings 8:23; 10:34; 12:19; 13:8, 12; 14:15, 18, 28; 15:6, 11; 16:19; 20:20; 21:17, 25; 23:28; 24:5, etc.

[20] Other sources were used as well as these annals. There are traces of tradition, and especially there are the heroic legends of the prophets Elijah and Elisha.

[21] The name *Chronicon* was Jerome's rendering of the Hebrew title.

[22] From this period dates the development of that type of literature which the Hebrews call Midrashim, stories with a moral purpose built around historical events

Historical Books of the Old Testament

priest of the temple at Jerusalem, intent upon its preëminence and especially interested in its liturgy. His exaggerations of the glory of the Davidic Kingdom are especially noticeable, but for that matter the work is generally unhistorical in viewpoint and is not important as history until we leave the book of Chronicles and come to Ezra.

The two books of Ezra and Nehemiah are really one and bear the title Ezra in the Jewish Bible. This contains the history of the Jews from the Persian release to the coming of Alexander. Its main interest for us, however, lies less in its value as source material to the modern historian than in the unique personal memoirs of Nehemiah and Ezra which have been embedded in the narrative. In spite of the fact that they were sadly mutilated in the process of fitting them in, these two documents remain unique in Hebrew and perhaps in antique historiography. The memoirs of Nehemiah are especially fine. The restorer of Jerusalem gives no petty copy of the vainglorious boasting of Assyrian kings when they recited their great deeds. Instead, he seems to have kept a remarkably sane appreciation of the proportion of things. His sense of the importance of what he is doing does not conceal the fact that he is dealing with petty tribal neighbors, who could end it all if he would stray over to one of their villages.[23] Homely detail lifts the story into that realm of realism which only really great writers can risk entering without loss of authority.[24] The result is one of the most graphic pictures in the Bible, sketched in a few words. Take, for instance, the building of the wall: "They which builded on the wall and they that bare burdens ... everyone with one of his hands wrought in the work and with the other held a weapon.... And he that sounded the trumpet was by me.... So we labored in the work, and half of

---

or characters. The taste for these grew; there are hundreds of them in the Talmud, dating mostly from the early Christian centuries.

[23] One possible piece of exaggeration seems to be the statement that the walls were completed in fifty-two days. Josephus, relying on other sources, says it took two years and four months (*Antiquities of the Jews*, Book XI, Chap. 5, Sect. 8). But a preliminary wall may have been built, or the text may have been corrupted.

[24] His interest in economic matters is especially noteworthy. See Nehemiah 5 and the laws codified in Leviticus 25:35-55.

them held the spears from the rising of the morning till the stars appeared."[25]

The memoirs of Ezra are of an inferior quality to this. Their significance in Hebrew historiography lies mainly in their content. For as Nehemiah tells how he built the Jews a city to be safe from their neighbors, Ezra tells how he kept them apart from these same neighbors by refusing to admit intermarriage,[26] and then, in the year 443 or 444, brought forth a book which, if tradition and the surmise of modern scholarship be correct, centred the whole world's history at their very temple.[27] Whatever the exact book was which he expounded, subsequent Jewish tradition believed that it was nothing short of epoch-making, and the name of Ezra, or Esdras, became the greatest among the scribes.[28]

The books of Chronicles, Ezra, and Nehemiah contain these rich historical materials; but their compiler should have little credit for his share in their preservation. His editorial task was done as clumsily and unintelligently as his chronicle is biased and dry. One fact, however, we can deduce from his narrative, which enables us to determine the conclusion of the long process of coöperative authorship by which the Bible story was finally made. As the chronicler apparently used the Pentateuch, Joshua, Judges, Samuel, and Kings in that order, it seems likely that by about

---

[25] Nehemiah 4:17-21. More realistic still is the twenty-third verse: "So neither I nor my brethren nor my servants nor the men of the guard which followed me, none of us put off our clothes, except that every one put them off for washing." Was the last verse a later emendation?

[26] This exclusive policy of Ezra, it has been pointed out, was likely to emphasize the question of descent and so to call forth an interest in genealogies. We see the effect of this in Nehemiah 7 (verse 61), where a list of what one might term pure-blooded, patrician Jewish families is given. One recalls in this connection the fact that P, which is attributed to the time of Ezra, was responsible for the long genealogies of the earlier historical books. Evidently the reëstablished Jews were working up their ancestry with great eagerness. It should be noted, however, that there is a reference in Ezekiel 13:9 to registers of "the house of Israel," at the beginning of the exile. See Josephus, *Against Apion*, Book I, Chap. 5, *sqq*.

[27] The narrative of P, based on the teachings of Ezekiel. See above, pp. 121-122. Thus the Jews began again their national existence, self-centred and isolated, with relatively slight intercourse with the Gentile world.

[28] A considerable literature grew up in his name, and a late tradition went so far as to regard him as the restorer of the law, the author of some seventy works, and finally as the last of writers in the canon of the Old Testament.

300 B.C. they had already been put together in the form in which we have them now.

This ends our survey of what are commonly known as the historical books of the Old Testament, although it by no means covers the entire field of interest to the historian. For in the other works, especially in the prophetic writings, there are narratives of prime importance, if only secondarily historical. The memoirs of a governor like Nehemiah are fully matched, for instance, by the biography of Jeremiah, preserved by his friend and secretary, Baruch.[29] Taken in its setting, along with the words of the prophet, this is a human document of the first order. In personal self-revelation and high religious feeling it has not unaptly been compared with the *Confessions* of Augustine. There are similar poetic or realistic glimpses of the life of the time and the policy of rulers throughout most of this prophetic literature; but, however much it affected history, its purpose was not historical and we must leave it aside.

There is, finally, one supremely good piece of historical writing in that considerable body of Jewish literature which is not included in the Old Testament as known to Protestant readers. The first book of Maccabees is a stirring narrative of the most heroic days of the Jewish nation, a straightforward account, gathered from eye-witnesses [30] and from written sources, of the great war of liberation begun by Judas Maccabaeus, in which the newly vitalized hopes of the Jews were actually realized for a period and political was added to religious liberty. The history of this achievement is given with scientific scruple, and in minuteness of detail and accuracy of information it ranks high among any of the histories of antiquity. One appreciates these qualities all the more when one turns to the second book of Maccabees and sees how the same kind of detail is marred by inaccuracy and distorted by partisanship, until the book becomes a mere historical pamphlet for the Pharisees. The fundamental difference be-

---

[29] See Jeremiah 32, 36:4 *sqq.;* 43:3; 45, etc.
[30] Although written in the second generation after the event.

tween the two books is that in the first, religious interests yield to the historical, while in the second they yield to nothing. It is the same contrast which we have met time and again, of a book that tells the truth as over against one that is meant to edify. But then the latest phase of pre-Christian Jewish thought passed farther and farther away from scientific interest in the facts of a past which offered no more triumphs to record, and turned from the humiliation of reality to that bright dreamland of hope, the kingdom of the Messiah. The two great eras of David and the Maccabees had produced histories worthy of the deeds they recorded; but the last sad age of Jewish national life consoled itself with apocalyptic visions and prophecies of the future. In such a situation, the genuine, old histories themselves suffered as well. They were plundered for texts to buttress belief, and history suffered that faith might live.

The significance of this conclusion of our survey of Hebrew historiography should not escape us, nor should it be misinterpreted. It is a saddening paradox that the higher we treasure ideals the more likely are we to violate ideals for them. The historian devotes himself to the discovery and preservation of the truth. By the truth he means an objective fact or an assemblage of such facts. He is apt to forget that this objectivity upon which he insists as the very basis of their reality does not exist for those who actually use or have used the facts. Hence when he finds high-minded moralists plundering the data of the past to point their morals, he loses respect for both their history and their ethics, without having considered the possibility that the nonhistorical attitude might conceivably have a justification. No one could pretend that the violation of historical standards of truth could be excused today on any basis of morals; for in our appreciation of the value of scientific work we recognize—in theory—nothing higher than truth. But in the prescientific world, where few of the data were established with absolute certainty, the case was different. The idea of objective historical truth could have only a limited appeal, since the medium for the preservation of fact was so imperfect. We have spoken elsewhere of the stimulus to accuracy in modern scholarship caused by the consciousness that others are on our trail. But the heightening of the value of facts brings with it a certain unhistorical failure to appreciate why they should have been so lightly esteemed by men who are apparently inspired by as high ideals—so far as morals go—as the modern critic.

This is the problem which confronts the critic of Hebrew history. For those who wrote the Pentateuch and the books of histories, who edited out their diverse sources and gave them their final form, there was something in the world worth more than annals of the past. The forces of the future were in their hands, forces which determined the fate not only of Jewish history but of the religious outlook of the whole world. The prophets of the eighth century were those great innovators who made religion over from a set of taboos into a moral code and substituted upright living for sacrifice. It is small wonder that the legends of the past were also made over into a form to suit the new outlook. Their own work was of vastly more importance to the men who wrote under the new inspiration than the crude details of an uncertain past. For the modern critic to fail to appreciate the point of view of these Hebrew historians is as grave a sin in historical criticism as to fail, on the other hand, to see the damage they wrought in the ancient sources. It was a point of view which has much to justify it too; for, but for the work of those prophets who sought to carry Israel away from its primitive line of history into new and unhistorical ideals, the history of Israel would never have been worth bothering over at all—except as that of an obscure Oriental people who contributed next to nothing to civilization. In the same way, if the believers in a coming Messiah plundered the documents of the past, the plunder was used for no less a purpose than the documentation of the kingdom of Christ. In short it was the distorters of Hebrew history who made that history worth our while!

Yet the fact remains that, from our point of view, the history was distorted. The paradox is not, however, an antithesis between history and morals, or between science and religion, or between science and theology. It is simply the statement of the difference between the ideals of the scientific and the prescientific eras.

CHAPTER XI

The Formation of the Canon

THERE still remains the question of how this mass of Hebrew writings took the form and shape in which it is known to us, as the Old Testament. The process was a long and slow one, and part of it has already been traced above. We recall how the legends of the earliest days were first thrown into connected written narrative in the eighth or ninth century B.C. in the schools of the prophets as J and E, and how in the close of the seventh century they were combined (JE); how, about the same time, a code was prepared in Jerusalem in the name of Moses (D) then promulgated in the eighteenth year of the reign of Josiah (621 B.C.) and shortly afterward combined with the history (JED);[1] how during the exile a new ritual law, traced to the influence of Ezekiel, was responsible for a new and thorough recasting of the narrative from a priestly standpoint (P) and then how, after various changes, the whole composite mass became our Hexateuch. One might expect from this, that the books of the Jews would go on developing, modified to the changing needs of successive ages, and so, to a certain extent, they did. But there was one influence making strongly against change. The texts themselves became sacred. The use of the Law, as the five "books of Moses" were termed, by the priests in the actual administration of justice may have had something to do with this process of crystallization, but a deeper reason lies in the very mystery of "the written word," which attains an undue authority over all primitive minds and holds its tyranny even in the modern world of encyclopaedias and newspapers. What is written attains a life of its own, and only here and there can one find the unfeel-

---

[1] This incidentally shows how highly the historical texts were regarded, that D should be united with them. For D came with authority.

The Formation of the Canon

ing skeptic indifferent to its fate. But when the word that is written is regarded as the utterance of God—as in practically all early codes of law—the skeptic has little chance to commit his sacrilege.[2]

In Israel this respect for the scriptures attained the dignity of a separate superstition, one which was destined to cast its influence over the whole subsequent history of Jewish and of Christian thought. The early scribes had felt free to arrange and annotate the law as part of their work. Indeed, as we have seen, the law itself was a product of repeated revision and rectification. But from about the middle of the fifth century it became fixed and rigid,[3] the object of religious reverence which protected itself by an enlarged use of old taboos. The books of "the Prophets"—including, it will be recalled, the earlier histories—were stereotyped into their canon by about two centuries later, about 250 B.C. The two lessons read in the synagogue were drawn, one from the law, the other from the prophets, so that the latter shared inevitably the fate of the former. The "scriptures," or "hagiographa," were not so easily moulded into place. The rabbis disputed long over what ones to accept and were unable to come to final conclusions until after the Christians had begun to plunder the sacred arsenal for their revolt.

The difficulty lay in the test of inclusion or exclusion, which was not subject matter but authorship. Only those scriptures were to be admitted which had been written by God through inspired mediums, as in the case of Law and Prophets. Such a test, however, made disagreement inevitable, since there was no ready way of establishing or denying the inspiration. History has never discovered other than two possible lines of evidence for assigning authorship: external evidence, such as that of witnesses who were present when the work was written or had access to knowledge as to how it was written; and internal evidence, from the nature of the text. Although it was obviously presumptuous, involving the danger of blasphemy, for any man to use the second test con-

---

[2] The same authority may attach to spoken words, but their reporters are bound to modify them in terms of their own time and thought. The beliefs about the *logos* occur to one in this connection.

[3] See Nehemiah 8-10.

sciously, since he would in the circumstances be making himself judge of what God should be credited with saying and what not, nevertheless what could not be risked by the individual was done by the mass.[4] A *consensus fidelium*, that "agreement among all those who believe," was arrived at, as is the case with all doctrines truly catholic. In this process, however, the external test of authorship was used to an extent which really led to a study of the contents of the books involved. The books, it must be admitted, were already prepared for such a test or readily adjusted themselves to it. In arrangement of time and circumstance, and miraculous evidences of the presence of the divine Author, the later books even protested somewhat too much, as the apocalyptic literature shows. Two historical devices were also used: ascribing books to authors already accepted in the canon as inspired, and the antedating of works to give them greater claim upon the credulity of the present. Psalms which were perhaps written as late as the Maccabean struggle were grouped with older ones,—all possibly being later than the Exile—and attributed to David. Solomon was made responsible for wisdom of a later day, and thus poetry and proverb enriched the history of the royal period with a new and sophisticated myth. More interesting still to the historian is the antedating of prophecy, such as that of the book of Daniel. We know from its contents that it was written in the time of Antiochus Epiphanes (175–164 B.C.), yet it purports to come from the days of Nebuchadnezzar, over four centuries earlier. Upon the whole, the exigencies of the situation produced a somewhat bewildering misappropriation of texts. But no higher critics were at hand, and the canon of the Old Testament was framed—for two religions.[5]

[4] This is an excellent example of a most important principle, familiar to sociologists and anthropologists, but strangely ignored by historians. All the world's history is affected by it. We have ordinarily considered it as belonging exclusively to a myth-making stage of society; but we are still making myths and resting content with our *consensus fidelium*.

[5] The authoritative form was apparently settled for the Jews at a congress or council of rabbis held at Jamnia, the successor to destroyed Jerusalem, in the year 90 A.D. Josephus, however, in his book *Against Apion* (Book I, Chap. 8), written 93-95 A.D., states that the Old Testament has 22 books, whereas the regular Jewish version has 24. They are: the five books of the Law; eight books of "Prophets," including Joshua, Judges, Samuel, and Kings, "the twelve" major prophets, and the

The Formation of the Canon

The decisions of the rabbis enabled the Christians in their turn to meet pagan criticism entrenched behind a sacred text, and no greater tribute could be paid to the work of rabbi and theologian, or, perhaps, to the weakness of the critical attitude in man, than that from that day of warring creeds to the present the citadel of faith and inspiration has held against the assaults of inquiry and historical skepticism and still asserts an almost undiminished sway. The early Christians, however, did not at first pay any very strict attention to the opinions of the rabbis as to which of the "scriptures" were canonical and which were not. They were eager for them all, especially for those that bore Messianic prophecy; thus a premium was put upon some of the very ones which the rabbis were inclined to discard. As a matter of fact the test of authorship as over against that of the contents of writings again broke down. A new *consensus fidelium* had to be satisfied. "The Christians discovered no reason in the books themselves why Esther, for example, should be inspired and Judith not; or why Ecclesiastes, with its skepticism about the destiny of the soul, should be divinely revealed, and the Wisdom of Solomon, with its eloquent defence of immortality, a purely human production; or, again, why the Proverbs of Solomon were Scripture, and the Proverbs of Ben Sira (Ecclesiasticus) nothing but profane wisdom." [6] Christian scholarship did not challenge this process until Jerome prepared his famous text at the close of the fourth century.

The mention of Jerome suggests the last problem to be considered, the origin of the text as we have it now. The Christians used the Greek, not the Hebrew Bible. This had been translated into the Greek from the Hebrew [7] by the Jews of Alexandria.

---

minor prophets, the latter as one book; and eleven books of "Scriptures," Psalms, Proverbs, Job, Song of Songs, Ruth, Lamentations, Ecclesiastes, Esther, Daniel, Ezra and Nehemiah together, Chronicles. The Christians, by dividing Samuel, Kings, Ezra, and Chronicles and counting the rest separately, reckon thirty-nine books.

[6] G. F. Moore, *The Literature of the Old Testament*, p. 14; C. A. Briggs, *General Introduction to the Study of the Holy Scriptures* (1899), pp. 118 *sqq.;* and articles in *Encyclopædia Britannica* and Hastings' *Dictionary of the Bible.*

[7] A few chapters in Ezra (4:8 to 6:18) and Daniel (2:4 to 7) are in Aramaic.

Legend had it, as also recorded in Josephus,[8] that the law was translated in seventy-two days by seventy-two persons; hence the name Septuagint [9] by which the Greek Old Testament became known. In reality, it was the work of different scholars through different ages and was probably not completed before the second century B.C. It was from this Greek text that the Christian Bible was drawn at first. During the second and third centuries there was some stirring among Christian scholars to have a Hebrew collation. The greatest of these scholars, Origen, drew up a collection of six parallel texts,[10] but it was Jerome who set to work actually to procure a reliable Latin translation for common use in the West, based upon Hebrew texts, in the notion that, being Hebrew, they were more genuine than the Greek version—a notion which turned out, however, to be mistaken, since the Septuagint was in reality from older Hebrew texts than those used by him. In preparing this edition, Jerome took the Jewish point of view as to what books should be included as inspired and what ones should not, thus denying the canonicity of scriptures which were in constant use, and modifying texts by his new translation to the disturbance of the faith of believers—as Augustine, Bishop of Hippo, ventured to admonish him.[11] The Church of the Middle Ages in general tended to follow the liberal view of the churchman rather than the narrower interpretation of the scholar, and when Luther, and Protestantism following him, made the Hebrew Bible the test, reverting to the position of Jerome,[12]

---

[8] *Antiquities of the Jews,* Book XII, Chap. 2.

[9] From the Latin, *septuaginta,* seventy. The name strictly speaking is applicable only to the Pentateuch. But it was loosely extended to cover the whole of the Old Testament.

[10] The famous *Hexapla.* They were: (1) the Hebrew text, (2) transliteration of Hebrew text into Greek letters, and (3) Greek versions of Aquila, (4) of Symmachus, (5) of the Septuagint, (6) of Theodotion; 3, 4, and 6 are from the second century A.D.

[11] This correspondence between Augustine and Jerome offers an illuminating section in Christian historiography. Augustine not only stood for the traditional text, he was in favor of the traditional inclusion of Judith, Tobit, First and Second Maccabees, Ecclesiasticus and the Wisdom of Solomon. Cf. *De doctrina Christiana,* Book II, Chap. 8, written 397 A.D.

[12] Luther placed the Apocrypha between Old and New Testaments, with this further caption, "Books that are not equally esteemed with the Holy Scriptures, but nevertheless are profitable and good to read."

The Formation of the Canon

the Catholic Church at Trent declared on the other hand that these works, *e.g.* Tobit, Judith, Wisdom, Ecclesiasticus, and the Maccabees, were an intrinsic part of the canonical scriptures, adding the usual sanction—"If any man does not accept as sacred and canonical these books, entire, with all their parts, as they have been customarily read in the Catholic Church and are contained in the ancient common Latin edition...let him be anathema."[13]

It is easy to see how the skeptics of the eighteenth century might reverse the doubt of the early Christians and demand not why one should limit the list of inspired books but why one should regard any of them as inspired at all. Such doubts made possible genuine textual criticism, which began with Astruc in the eighteenth century. The development of philology and archaeology supplied the tools for the twofold task of textual studies on the one hand and of external comparison with the rest of ancient history upon the other, with the result that we now know more of how the Bible was put together than the very scribes who copied or rabbis who used it in the immemorial service of the ancient synagogue, as we know more of the history of Israel than the very authors who compiled its last revision.

[13] In the fourth session.

CHAPTER XII

Non-Biblical Literature; Josephus

THE very process just described implied that we have only a portion of the literature of the Jews inside the canon of the sacred scriptures. It remains for us to glance at what lies outside it and finally at the work of a purely secular historian who wrote at Rome, for the Greco-Roman world, the story of Jewish antiquity and the struggle for Jewish freedom—Josephus.

The two chief characteristic products of Jewish thought, legalism and prophecy, which we have seen coloring with more or less different hues the long perspectives of biblical antiquity, continued to determine the quality of the non-biblical literature to a very large degree. The result was that that literature largely consisted of two great developments, corresponding to these two interests: the elaboration of the law in the Talmud and the production of apocalyptic literature. How great these two developments were is something of which Christians are generally grossly ignorant; and yet no student of New Testament history can ever quite get the sense of the setting of primitive Christianity, of the forces which it had to fight and even of those which it incorporated, until he has looked into the teachings of the rabbis and realized the scope of the poetic, rhapsodical dreams of Oriental imaginations fired by fanatic zeal that were prevalent in the closing days of Judaism.

The great body of the "oral" law, as opposed to the "written" law of Moses, was preserved, elaborated, and debated by the rabbis, just as the Christian church has its bodies of ecclesiastical law in addition to the Old and New Testaments. How far back its precepts really go no one can tell; but those who taught it believed that it extended back to Moses and had existed parallel

Non-Biblical Literature; Josephus

with the written law from the time of its deliverance,[1] being passed along by word of mouth from generation to generation. The Talmud, in which this "oral law" was embodied, is to the Jews like the New Testament to Christians, something far more than a mere commentary on the Scriptures, of an authority and influence parallel to them. It is made up of two parts, the Mishnah, which is a collection of texts, begun under the Maccabees and compiled at the end of the second century A.D., and the Gemara, or comments on the Mishnah. The discussions of the Palestinian rabbis were codified in the fourth century A.D. in what is called the Jerusalem Talmud. Those of the schools of Babylonia were codified in the fifth and sixth centuries A.D. This later code, which is about four times the size of the Jerusalem Talmud, is what is meant when "The Talmud" is referred to without further qualification.

This mass of material, as an ostensible body of recorded tradition, might seem to have some claim upon our attention; but we have included it in this survey mainly to emphasize its essentially unhistorical character and the fact that Talmudic training tends to block the path of historical criticism. In the first place, in spite of all the vast literature on the Talmud—and no text has ever been studied with more intensive zeal—it has not received that "higher criticism" which has led us at last to appreciate the historicity of the biblical narratives. Largely because of the very fact that the Talmud was so long oral tradition, it is difficult, perhaps impossible, to determine the origin and first setting of the central texts. In any case this work has not yet been done, and the Talmud remains a practically sealed book to historians, who can use its wealth of descriptive and illustrative material— the Talmudists claim that its texts can meet every possible exigency in life—only in the most general way. Talmudic scholar-

---

[1] As a good example of rabbinical interpretation on which such conclusions rest, a rabbi of the third century A.D. takes Exodus 24:12: "I will give thee tables of stone, and the Law, and the Commandment, which I have written, that thou mayest teach them," and elucidates the text as follows: " 'Tables,' these are the ten words (the Decalogue); the 'Law' is the Scripture; 'and the commandment,' that is the Mishnah; 'which I have written,' these are the Prophets and the Writings (the Hagiographa); 'to teach them,' that is the Gemara—*thus instructing us all that these were given to Moses from Sinai.*" Quoted in article "Talmud" in *Encyclopædia Britannica*. Historical criticism cannot flourish in such an atmosphere.

ship therefore tends to turn the mind toward that type of speculation on words and phrases which results in either hair-splitting quibbles in the application of theological law or the more philosophical moralizing that draws strength from allegory; but neither of these tendencies leads to historical analysis. When one examines the Talmud and considers the influences which it reflects from the dim antiquities of Jewish life, one wonders all the more at the historical product of the Old Testament.

This impression is still further strengthened by a glance at the prophetic literature, which rivalled the Law in influence upon the Jewish mind. We have seen above how this—along with the Law—became the vehicle for so much of that high moral teaching which gave the lasting value to Jewish aspirations—aspirations which otherwise would hardly interest succeeding ages.[2] There was much of this literature, and more still that did not reach the dignity of literature, in the later period of Jewish history.[3] It was a great contribution, poetry fired by passion and rich in dreams, the outpouring of Oriental zealots—the literature of apocalypses. But it gained its best triumphs by its boldest defiance of fact. True, its vision had power at times to supplant the mean realities of actual things by new creations, made real through that conviction which impels to deeds; but the historic forces which it wielded were drawn more from faith in the future than from interest in the past. Prophetism, as we have pointed out elsewhere, blocks the path of scientific inquiry; and yet as we register its impediment to history, we cannot but find in it an expression—one of several, but not the least significant—of that fundamental difference in outlook between the Oriental and the Western mind. The Oriental has remained essentially unhistorical because of his relative indifference as to fact and fancy. His interest is determined more by what he wishes things to be and less by what they are. In the West, in spite of much persistence of the same

[2] This recognition of the lasting message of Jewish theology is the theme of many a recent study, since the critics have destroyed the older basis of canonical authority. As an example may be cited W. F. Badè, *The Old Testament in the Light of Today* (1915).

[3] The chief name among modern scholars in this field is that of R. H. Charles. His contributions need hardly be cited here, however; and the student is referred to articles on "Apocrypha," etc., in Bible dictionaries and encyclopaedias.

Non-Biblical Literature; Josephus

attitude, we have grown interested in things as they actually are and in things as they actually were. History cannot substitute what one wishes to happen or to have happened for what actually happened. Its field is not free and open but sadly circumscribed, marked out by frustration and darkened by the dull walls of fact.[4]

"The Law and the Prophets" are both distinctly Jewish products, for, whatever they borrowed from beyond Jordan, in both cases they are the expression of Palestinian civilization. In the last phase of its history, however, Judaism, especially in the Diaspora or Dispersion throughout the Greco-Roman world, came to a certain degree under the influences of that Hellenic civilization which had permeated so much of the Near East after the conquests of Alexander. The result was that Jew and Gentile were led to look into each other's past. The mutual challenge was hopeful for history. It was such a situation which, as we shall see, had opened the doors to Greek historical criticism in the days of Herodotus, when the antiquity of Egypt became the touchstone for judging that of Hellas. One might have thought that when the two peoples who really could show some achievement in antique history writing—the Greeks and the Hebrews—came to know each other, the effect would be to stimulate a critical appreciation of that achievement and so further the cause of scientific history; that, at least, if the Hebrews did not profit from the contact, the Greeks would. How they escaped doing so—and by so doing to anticipate by twenty centuries the biblical criticism of today—is apparent from a consideration of the work of the two outstanding figures of Hellenic Judaism, Philo the philosopher and Josephus the historian.

Philo Judaeus, as he is commonly termed, was a product of Alexandria, a contemporary of Christ.[5] He comes into our survey,

[4] This inability to distinguish between what things are and what one wishes them to be is a characteristic of all immature or undisciplined minds. It is a factor in current world politics, to be borne in mind in the entry of backward people into the society of nations. They can readily use the same language of political institutions but the sense of fact is not always the same.

[5] We know almost nothing of his life, beyond an incident or two. He was born about the second decade before Christ and was in Rome in 40 A.D. on a mission for the Alexandrian Jews. His works, however, have been preserved in surprisingly full form.

not because of any contribution which he offered to the history of history, but because of his influence in furthering that essentially unhistorical habit of thought to which we have referred above, by interpreting texts by way of allegory. It was a method which Christian writers were to develop to such an extent that we may leave the fuller consideration of it until we come to the work of Origen and the "apologists." But, although Philo seems to have had little *direct* influence upon later Christian writers [6] —probably because he was a Jew,—the contribution which he offered to the world of his time, Jew and Greek, was so distinctive as to demand attention. For Philo applied the familiar device of allegory not simply to explain the texts but to explain them away by boldly taking them over from history to philosophy.

One or two examples, out of an almost unlimited number, will suffice to show how the commentary on the Pentateuch runs, as it takes up the text verse by verse. *The Allegories of the Sacred Laws* begins as follows:

"And the heaven and the earth and all their world was completed." [7] Having previously related the creation of the mind and of sense, Moses now proceeds to describe the perfection which was brought about by them both. And he says that neither the indivisible mind nor the particular sensations received perfection, but only ideas, one the idea of the mind, the other of sensation. And, speaking symbolically, he calls the mind heaven, since the natures which can only be comprehended by the intellect are in heaven. And sensation he calls earth, because it is sensation which has obtained a corporeal and somewhat earthy constitution. The ornaments of the mind are called the incorporeal things, which are perceptible only by the intellect. Those of sensation are the corporeal things, and everything in short which is perceptible by the external senses.

"And on the sixth day God finished his work which he had made." It would be a sign of great simplicity to think that the world was created in six days or indeed at all in time; because all time is only the space of days and nights, and these things the motion of the sun as he passes over the earth and under the earth does necessarily make. But the sun is a portion of heaven, so that one must confess that time is a thing

---

[6] There are almost no manuscripts of his works in mediaeval ecclesiastical libraries (M. R. James, *The Biblical Antiquities of Philo* (1917), Introduction). This is a pseudo-Philo summary of the Pentateuch of the end of the first century A.D.
[7] Genesis 2:1.

posterior to the world. Therefore it would be correctly said that the world was not created in time, but that time had its existence in consequence of the world. For it is the motion of the heaven that has displayed the nature of time.

When, therefore, Moses says, "God completed his works on the sixth day," we must understand that he is speaking not of a number of days, but that he takes six as a perfect number. Since it is the first number which is equal in its parts, in the half, and the third and sixth parts, and since it is produced by the multiplication of two unequal factors, two and three. And the numbers two and three exceed the incorporeality which exists in the unit; because the number two is an image of matter being divided into two parts and dissected like matter. And the number three is an image of a solid body, because a solid can be divided according to a threefold division. Not but what it is also akin to the motions of organic animals. For an organic body is naturally capable of motion in six directions, forward, backwards, upwards, downwards, to the right, and to the left. And at all events he desires to show that the races of mortal, and also of all the immortal beings, exist according to their appropriate numbers; measuring mortal beings, as I have said, by the number six, and the blessed and immortal beings by the number seven. First, therefore, having desisted from the creation of mortal creatures on the seventh day, he began the formation of other and more divine beings.[8]

When one considers that such speculations are the matured contribution of one of the greatest thinkers of antiquity, one sees how far adrift theology might go from the sober world of fact and the processes of history. And theology was to capture the intellectual interests of the age.

Sometimes Philo recognizes the statement of fact in the narrative but even that is the material veil for some divine truth. For instance, the rivers of the Garden of Eden may be real rivers—though the inadequacy of the geography of Genesis is troublesome,—but the escape is always at hand, for the four rivers are the signs of the four virtues, Prudence, Temperance, Courage, and Justice, flowing from the central stream of the Divine Wisdom.[9] Reading such a passage one recalls the jeers of Herodotus at the geographers who held to the Homeric cosmography and

---

[8] Philo Judaeus, *The Allegories of the Sacred Laws*, Book I, Chaps. 1-2 (translated by C. D. Yonge in Bohn's Ecclesiastical Library).

[9] *Ibid.*, Book I, Chap. 19. Cf. also *Questions and Solutions*, Book I, Chap. 12.

especially the Ocean Stream encircling the world; but by no flight of imagination can one think of Herodotus solving his difficulties by transmuting rivers into ideas. The divergence between the paths of history and philosophy is fortunately thus sufficiently clear at the start that we need not stray longer from the one before us.

Flavius Josephus stands out as the very opposite of Philo. He was a man of affairs, warrior, statesman, and diplomatist. He was one of the leaders of the great Jewish revolt but made his peace with Vespasian and became a favorite of the Flavian imperial family, from whom he took his adopted name. After the destruction of Jerusalem he passed most of his life at Rome, and there wrote in Greek,[10] for the Greco-Roman world, a history of *The Wars of the Jews* and a long account of *The Antiquities of the Jews,* as well as a defense of Jewish historical sources and methods against the attacks of Greeks, especially one Apion, in a treatise *Against Apion*.[11] In addition he wrote his own biography, as a reply to attacks upon him by his own people. Thus the man whom the Jews most hated as a betrayer of his country in his own day became the defender of its past. But he has never been popular among the Jews. His readers were mainly among the heathen and the Christian. Among them his vogue was surprisingly large, considering his theme. His works have survived as few from that age have, almost as though he had been a Christian Father.

Josephus' own life enters so much into his writings that it tends to distract one from considering them on their merits. He was born 37–38 A.D. of high-priestly stock and studied for the priesthood. He was a prominent young Pharisee when sent to Rome on a successful mission to plead for some Jews in the year 63–64. Then he was drawn into the Great Rebellion, becoming one of the leaders, but turned to the Roman side after his capture,

---

[10] His early Aramaic account of *Wars of the Jews* is lost. He tells us in the introduction that he translated it into Greek (Sect. 1), but the relation of this Aramaic version to the text we have is not known.

[11] Apion was the leader of an Alexandrian mission opposing Philo. In this incident, therefore, we have a link between the philosopher and the historian.

Non-Biblical Literature; Josephus

saving his life indeed by prophesying that Vespasian would be emperor. The favor of the Flavians never failed him after that, in spite of constant attacks upon him by the Jews. This shifty —and thrifty—career is reflected in the first of his works, the history of the Jewish War, which was written between 69 and 79 A.D., at once a court history and an apology.

The Wars of the Jews is an elaborate work in seven books, of which the first two trace the history of the Jews from the capture of Jerusalem by Antiochus Epiphanes to the war of 67 A.D. In this portion he relies on some previous historians, such as Nicholas of Damascus,[12] and does not venture far afield. The remaining books are based on contemporary sources and personal knowledge and should be read along with his *Autobiography*. He states that he submitted the history to Titus, who indorsed it, as well he might, for Josephus absolves him from blame for firing the Temple[13]—although Tacitus indicates that he gave definite orders to do so—and in general charges the Zealots, who were misguided Jewish patriots, with the real responsibility for the disaster to their nation. Providence is visibly on the side of the great battalions.

The *Antiquities of the Jews,* to which Josephus devoted the major part of twenty years, is a much more ambitious work, one of the longest individual products in antique literature. In twenty long books, Josephus traces, for those who are unfamiliar with the Bible—and the ignorance of the classical world about the Jews was very great—the story of the Jewish past. In the first part of the work, his chief source was the Septuagint, the Greek

[12] Nicholas of Damascus was a Greek savant who became friend and adviser to Herod the Great and who played a considerable part in the diplomacy and politics of the Near East under Augustus. His historical writings included a biography of Augustus of which but slight fragments remain and a *Universal History* in one hundred and forty-two books, dealing with the Assyrians, Lydians, Greeks, Medes, and Persians, and concentrating upon the history of Herod and his own time. Josephus used this latter part in detail, while criticizing Nicholas for his highly flattering and unreliable account of his patron's reign.

[13] An Aramaic version was sent to the "barbarians" of Arabia and beyond, a part of imperial propaganda to show how futile it was for any people to oppose the might of Rome. The reliability of such a narrative was impugned in its own day and today. In general it seems to be accurate, its author was at least convinced of its truth. Its high literary merit must have added to its propagandist value.

edition of the Old Testament,[14] but in addition he drew from that store of tradition passed along among those learned in the law. He also brings in profane testimony, using Herodotus, for instance, for the story of Cyrus, and many Roman sources for the later part. He works these over, however, and fits them into his story so that it is a work of textual criticism—an aspect into which we need not enter—to trace the actual process of composition. In books XVIII and XIX the story shifts to Rome and is an important source on Caligula and Claudius. Especially valuable are the many documents dealing with the legal position of the Jews in the Empire. This represents the nearest approach to systematic archival research which the ancient world affords.

Like Polybius, Josephus is conscious of his weakness in art; but he hopes to make up for it by the content. He promises, in the preface to the *Wars,* to conceal nothing and not to add "anything to the known truth of things." "I have written it down," he says, "for ... those that love truth, but not for those who please themselves (with fictitious relations)." "How good the style is must be left to the determination of the readers; but as for the agreement with the facts, I shall not scruple to say, and that boldly, that truth hath been what I have alone aimed at throughout its entire composition (Book VII, Chap. 11). In the face of such protestations one is reluctantly obliged to come to the conclusion that Josephus was as disingenuous about his style as about the substance,—which, we have just seen, was much twisted for his own defense. For he was a florid writer, trying out successfully all the devices of the literary art of his day with which he was familiar. He invents speeches for the biblical heroes, as for those of later days; he strives for effect by exaggeration, using figures, as some one has said of a statesman of our own time, like adjectives: the Jews killed at Jerusalem number 1,100,000 (Book VI, Chap. 9), whereas Tacitus puts the total number of the besieged at the outside figure of 600,000.[15] He elaborates on the statesmanship of Moses, until one feels that it is just a little overdone. Yet those of his own day liked it, and that is its justifica-

---

[14] It is doubtful if he knew Hebrew.
[15] Tacitus, *Historiae,* Book V, Chap. 13.

tion so that even the little self-apologetic touches, concerning his sad awkwardness in Greek, may have added to the total effect—especially as he deftly combines this with an appeal to take him at his word in the subject matter. Take for instance these closing words of his great *Antiquities:*

> And I am so bold as to say, now I have so completely perfected the work I proposed to myself to do, that no other person, whether he were a Jew or a foreigner, had he ever so great an inclination to it, could so accurately deliver these accounts to the Greeks as is done in these books. For those of my own nation freely acknowledge, that I far exceed them in the learning belonging to Jews; I have also taken a great deal of pains to obtain the learning of the Greeks, and understand the elements of the Greek language although I have so long accustomed myself to speak our own tongue, that I cannot pronounce Greek with sufficient exactness; for our nation does not encourage those that learn the languages of many nations, and so adorn their discourses with the smoothness of their periods; because they look upon this sort of accomplishment as common, not only to all sorts of freemen, but to as many of the servants as please to learn them. But they give him the testimony of being a wise man, who is fully acquainted with our laws, and is able to interpret their meaning; on which account, as there have been many who have done their endeavors with great patience to obtain this learning, there have yet hardly been so many as two or three that have succeeded therein, who were immediately well rewarded for their pains.

Josephus was relatively free from the impediments that blocked the path of more religious natures to the consideration of mere matters of fact. But there is a touch of the difficulty in his comment on Daniel which is worth a passing attention. He says (Book X, Chap. 11) that Daniel "not only prophesied of future events, as did the other prophets, but also determined the time of their accomplishment." The problem was here presented of working out the numbered years of the divine plan, a problem which was to absorb so much of the speculation of later ages and which projected chronology into the future instead of establishing it in the past. Had Josephus been a thinker rather than a student, he would have followed the lead here given, into unhistorical grounds. Fortunately, he was a historian instead of a philosopher.

Josephus published his *Autobiography* as an appendix to a

second edition of the *Antiquities*.[16] The arrangement of this brochure is extraordinary, for more than four-fifths of its eighty pages are devoted to the six months of Josephus' career in Galilee in 66; a preface of five pages leads up to this experience, a conclusion of equal length says a little about the remainder of the war and the rest of Josephus' life, and near the end of the main section is inserted a six-page attack upon a certain Justus of Tiberias. A modern scholar, Richard Laqueur,[17] suggests that this interpolation provides a key, explaining much of Josephus' literary career. Justus had been his rival in 66, and soon after the publication of the *Antiquities* he published a rival history of the Jews. In it he attacked Josephus' reliability and also his conduct during the war; Josephus now replies to this attack. The main section of the reply consisted of the report which he had made to the authorities at Jerusalem in 66 when Justus and others were denouncing his activities in Galilee. This document was therefore the first, not the last, of Josephus' historical writings; it was virtually a contemporary document, written before Josephus went over to the Romans; its narrative differed in important particulars from the later *Wars of the Jews* and was probably more accurate; and it was now published to vindicate the author's activities in that year. This discovery led Laqueur to further considerations which seem well taken. Justus accused Josephus not only of inaccuracy but also of treason to his people, and he was by no means the first or only Jew to do so: the charge had been made regularly by Jews ever since Josephus went over to the Romans, and it cut the aristocratic son of high priests to the quick. He therefore spent the rest of his life trying to prove to his fellow Jews that he was a patriot after all: he had written the *Wars of the Jews*, not merely because he was paid to do so by Titus, but also because he sincerely believed that the course he was urging upon the Jews was the best one (and the terrible repression of the revolts under Trajan and Hadrian showed that he was right); he then devoted twenty years to praising his people in the *Antiquities;* he refuted anti-

---

[16] This paragraph and that on the *testimonium Flavianum* are by Professor Swain.
[17] R. Laqueur, *Der jüdische Historiker Flavius Josephus* (1920).

Non-Biblical Literature; Josephus

Semitic slanders in the tract *Against Apion;* and at last the old man lashed out at Justus in his *Autobiography*. But all was in vain: to the present day Jews have generally regarded Josephus as a scheming, mercenary, and two-faced traitor. He was one of the eight or ten great historians of the ancient world; but if he has not sunk into complete oblivion, as Justus soon did, it is because of the Christians, and more particularly because of a Christian forgery introduced into his history.

Josephus' value to the Christians lay principally in the celebrated *testimonium Flavianum*—the only pagan evidence for the life of Christ.[18] Josephus gave an account of John the Baptist in the *Antiquities* (Book XVIII, Chaps. 116-19) which agrees moderately with the Gospel narrative; later he casually mentioned (Book XX, Chap. 197), James "the brother of Jesus who was called Christ"; and above all is the passage of eight or ten lines (Book XVIII, Chap. 63f.) dealing with Jesus himself. This passage has given rise to much excited controversy. Critics in the nineteenth century unhesitatingly pronounced it a Christian forgery, but scholars today are not so sure. It is indeed scarcely conceivable that Josephus should have written the words as they now stand, for they call Jesus "a wise man, if indeed he should be called a man," record the resurrection on the third day, declare that he had been foretold by the divine prophets, and even state explicitly, "He was the Christ." So ardent a Jew as Josephus would not have made these statements, especially the last one.[19] But it does not follow that Josephus wrote none of the *testimonium* at all. Scholars are coming to the belief that what happened was that a Christian scribe sought to make the passage conform to Christian views by inserting a few words into what Josephus

---

[18] Tacitus and Suetonius both mentioned Christ casually, but only as the alleged founder of the sect of the Christians; Suetonius misspelled his name and seemed to think that he lived in Rome.

[19] Laqueur suggests (*Der jüdischer Historiker, Flavius Josephus*, pp. 274 *sqq.*) that when Josephus found his efforts to reconcile his Jewish compatriots unavailing, he turned to the Christians and inserted the passage as it stands—having his tongue in his cheek all the while, of course—in the hope that they would then purchase and perpetuate his *magnum opus*. The work does, of course, owe its survival primarily to these words, but Laqueur's suggestion is brilliant rather than convincing and seems to be regarded by other scholars as somewhat too fanciful.

had written. The location of the story in the general narrative supports this view: it is the third of a series of five brief, unconnected stories dealing with disturbances, four of which were caused by Jews: it has been rather plausibly suggested that in the course of his researches in the Roman archives, Josephus came upon the *dossiers* regarding these disturbances and made them the basis of his narrative. It has been further suggested—rather fancifully, perhaps—that in the case of Jesus, the *dossier* contained Pontius Pilate's report on the crucifixion. In its original form this narrative may have contained words or phrases uncomplimentary to Jesus, which the Christian scribe saw fit to delete and for which he substituted the words which now cause our difficulties.[20]

There remains one work to consider, and that the most interesting of all to the historian of history, the treatise *Against Apion*, written to challenge the Gentile historians for their failure to appreciate the history of the Jews, and to justify its authenticity. It is anticipating here to quote the criticism of Greek historiography with which the treatise opens, and yet as it contains so much that is still suggestive and sound, it may serve as a connecting link with the next part of our story,[21] and as a discriminating survey of antique historiography in general, it justifies quotation at length: [22]

I cannot but greatly wonder at those who think that we must attend to none but Greeks as to the most ancient facts, and learn the truth from them only, and that we are not to believe ourselves or other men. For I am convinced that the very reverse is the case, if we will not follow vain opinions, but extract the truth from the facts themselves. For you will find that almost all which concerns the Greeks happened not long ago, nay, one may say, is of yesterday and the day before only; I speak of the building of their cities, the inventions of their arts,

---

[20] For a sane discussion of this whole problem see H. St. John Thackeray, *Josephus the Man and the Historian* (1929), Chap. VI. The *testimonium* is also discussed acutely and with great learning by Robert Eisler in his huge but erratic work entitled, ΙΗΣΟΥΣ ΒΑΣΙΛΕΥΣ ΟΥ ΒΑΣΙΛΕΥΣΑΣ, *Die Messianische Unabhängigkeitsbewegung* (2 vols., 1929).

[21] This is a disadvantage due to the treatment of the different national histories as entities rather than in a comparative, chronological survey. But after all the antecedents of the Greco-Roman writers were national.

[22] Josephus, *Against Apion*, Book I, Chaps. 1-6.

Non-Biblical Literature; Josephus

and the recording of their laws; and as for their care about compiling histories, it is very nearly the last thing they set about. Indeed they admit themselves that it is the Egyptians, the Chaldæans and the Phœnicians (for I will not now include ourselves among those) that have preserved the memory of the most ancient and lasting tradition. For all these nations inhabit such countries as are least subject to destruction from the climate and atmosphere, and they have also taken especial care to have nothing forgotten of what was done among them, but their history was esteemed sacred, and ever written in the public records by men of the greatest wisdom. Whereas ten thousand destructions have afflicted the country which the Greeks inhabit, and blotted out the memory of former actions; so that, ever beginning a new way of living, they supposed each of them that their mode of life originated with themselves. It was also late, and with difficulty, that they came to know the use of letters. For those who would trace their knowledge of letters to the greatest antiquity, boast that they learned them from the Phœnicians and from Cadmus. But nobody is able to produce any writing preserved from that time, either in the temples or in any other public monuments; and indeed the time when those lived who went to the Trojan war so many years afterwards is in great doubt, and it is a question whether the Greeks used letters at that time; and the most prevailing opinion, and that nearest the truth, is, that they were ignorant of the present way of using letters. Certainly there is not any writing among them, which the Greeks agree to be genuine, ancienter than Homer's poems. And he plainly was later than the siege of Troy: and they say that even he did not leave his poems in writing, but that their memory was preserved in songs, and that they were afterwards collected together, and that that is the reason why such a number of variations are found in them. As for those who set about writing histories among them, such I mean as Cadmus of Miletus, and Acusilaus of Argos, and any others that may be mentioned after him, they lived but a short time before the Persian expedition into Greece. Moreover, as to those who first philosophized as to things celestial and divine among the Greeks, as Pherecydes the Syrian, and Pythagoras, and Thales, all with one consent agree, that they learned what they knew from the Egyptians and Chaldæans, and wrote but little. And these are the things which are supposed to be the oldest of all among the Greeks, and they have much ado to believe that the writings ascribed to those men are genuine.

How can it then be other than an absurd thing for the Greeks to be so proud, as if they were the only people acquainted with antiquity, the only people that have handed down the truth about those early times in an accurate manner? Nay, who is there that cannot easily gather from the Greek writers themselves, that they knew but little on good foundation when they set about writing, but rather jotted down their own conjectures as to facts? Accordingly they frequently confute one another in their own books, and do not hesitate to give us the most contradictory accounts of the same things. But I should spend my time to little purpose, if I should teach the Greeks what they know better than I already, what great discrepancy there is between Hellanicus and Acusilaus as to their genealogies, in how many cases Acusilaus corrects Hesiod, or how Ephorus demonstrates Hellanicus to have told lies in most of his history; or how Timæus in like manner contradicts Ephorus, and the succeeding writers Timæus, and all writers Herodotus. Nor could Timæus agree with Antiochus and Philistus and Callias about Sicilian history, any more than do the several writers of the Atthidæ follow one another as to Athenian affairs, nor do the historians that wrote on Argolic history coincide about the affairs of the Argives. And now what need I say more about particular cities and smaller places, when in the most approved writers of the expedition of the Persians, and of the actions done in it, there are such great differences? Nay, Thucydides himself is accused by some as often writing what is false, although he seems to have given us the most accurate history of the affairs of his own times.

As for the causes of such great discrepancy, many others may perhaps appear probable to those who wish to investigate the matter, but I attach the greatest importance to two which I shall mention. And first I shall mention what seems to me the principal cause, namely, the fact that from the beginning the Greeks were careless about public records of what was done on each occasion, and this would naturally pave the way for error, and give those that wished to write on old subjects opportunity for lying. For not only were records neglected by the other Greeks, but even among the Athenians themselves also, who pretend to be Autochthons, and to have applied themselves to learning, there are no such records extant, but they say the laws of Draco concerning murders, which are now extant in writing, are the most ancient of their public records, yet Draco lived only a little before the tyrant Pisistratus. For as to the Arcadians, who make such boasts of their antiquity, why need I mention them, since it was still later before they learned their letters, and that with difficulty also?

There must, therefore, naturally arise great differences among writers, when no records existed, which might at once inform those who desired to learn, and refute those that would tell lies. However, we must assign a second cause, besides the former one, for these discrepancies. Those who were the most zealous to write history were not solicitous for the discovery of truth, although it is very easy always to make such a profession, but they tried to display their fine powers of writing, and

Non-Biblical Literature; Josephus

in whatever manner of writing they thought they were able to exceed others, to that did they apply themselves. Some betook themselves to the writing of fabulous narrations; some endeavoured to please cities or kings by writing in their commendation; others fell to finding faults with transactions, or with the writers of such transactions, and thought to make a great figure by so doing. However such do what is of all things the most contrary to true history. For it is the characteristic of true history, that all both speak and write the same about the same things, whereas, these men, by writing differently about the same things, thought they would be supposed to write with the greatest regard to truth. We must indeed yield to the Greek writers as to language and style of composition, but not as regards the truth of ancient history, and least of all as to the national customs of various countries.

As to the care of writing down the records from the earliest antiquity, that the priests were intrusted with that function, and philosophized about it, among the Egyptians and Babylonians, and the Chaldæans also among the Babylonians, and that the Phœnicians, who especially mixed with the Greeks, made use of letters both for the common affairs of life, and for handing down the history of public transactions, I think I may omit any proof of this, because all men allow it to be so. But I shall endeavour briefly to show that our forefathers took the same care about writing their records (for I will not say they took greater care than the others I spoke of) and that they committed that office to their high priests and prophets, and that these records have been written all along down to our own times with the utmost accuracy, and that, if it be not too bold for me to say so, our history will be so written hereafter.

Josephus then goes on to argue the superiority of a people who have "not ten thousand books disagreeing with and contradicting one another, but only twenty-two books, which contain the records of all time and are justly believed to be divine." [23] We cannot follow him further in the argument, but must recall the value of the succeeding chapters for more than Hebrew historiography, since embedded in them are the selections from Gentile writers, especially Manetho and Berossos, which are our only source for them. The pamphlet is the learned work of a clever man.

The last, and greatest, of the Jewish historians, Flavius Josephus, recalls, strangely enough, the last and greatest of the historians of Egypt and of Babylonia-Assyria, Manetho and

---

[23] *Ibid.*, Book I, Sect. 8.

Berossos. Josephus too, as a historian, was more a product of the Greco-Roman world than of the direct antecedents of his own national culture. All three were stimulated to write the history of their countries by the desire to make it known to the Gentile. But Josephus goes beyond them in achievement, and brings to mind still more the last of the great Greek historians, Polybius,[24] whose life, indeed, was singularly like his own. Both wrote their histories at Rome as high favorites of those who had crushed out the last movement of freedom in their native lands, and both profited from being on the defensive among an alien people, whom they had to impress by sound method and weight of evidence. The result was to make of the Greek and the Jew not only historians but historical critics and, to that degree, moderns among the ancients. We see again here another illustration of the point we have touched upon before, that it is not so much the long procession of the centuries which produces the historian as the need to convince one's contemporaries of the truth of what one tells. The mere possession of a mighty past is of less value than a critical audience.

[24] See Chap. XVII.

Part III

GREEK HISTORY

CHAPTER XIII

From Homer to Herodotus

WHEN we come to Greece we at once think of "Homer," and then of the recent discoveries which have remade our perspectives of Greek history, and yet in a way confirm the world-old impression. The archaeologist has unearthed Troys before Troy, but he has found no pre-Homeric Homer. Although now the centuries stretch away beyond the days of Agamemnon in long millenniums, and the ruined walls of Cnossus and Hissarlik are marked with the flow and ebb of many wars and the movements of dim, prehistoric peoples, no trace of Minoan epics has been found. Delicately frescoed walls and masterpieces of the goldsmith's art remain to tell us of the splendor of the sea-lords of Crete or the rich cattle-lords of the Argive plain, but the one great tale which the Greeks preserved of that great past was of its overthrow. What they knew of the ancient civilization which preceded their own was light enough.[1] In the Homeric poems there are lingering traces of the splendor of Mycenae and idyllic glimpses of the island dwellers, but the heroes are of a later day and a different race—they are Greeks of the ninth century B.C. And yet, slight as they are, those traces are so true to what the spade reveals that some source must have kept alive the story from the great days of Crete (Middle Minoan) to those of Homer. Moreover, two of the most scholarly researchers of Greece, still centuries later, Aristotle and Ephorus, speak with such seeming confidence and reasonable accuracy of the age of Minos that one is forced to suppose that Minoan culture left some genuine, historic documents. What they were no

---

[1] "To put the matter epigrammatically, Homer knows almost nothing about the Homeric world." Rhys Carpenter, *The Humanistic Value of Archaeology* (1933), p. 68.

one knows. It is the hope of historians that when Minoan script can be deciphered, the tablets which have been found in the palace of Cnossus will prove to contain, along with business records of the kings, some sort of royal annals like those of Assyria and Babylonia. But so far "Homer" remains, in spite of archaeology, what it has been from long before the days of Herodotus, the earliest account of the Greek past, and, although we shall find the real origins of Greek history writing rather in a criticism of Homeric legends than in the legends themselves, scholars are agreed today that in main outlines the Homeric epics are based upon real events. The tale of the siege of Troy may be a free treatment of diverse incidents from the story of the Hellenic "migrations," and the present text may be but a local variation of rival sagas which chance and Athenian culture secured for posterity, but in the picture of society and in the very tangle of the story there is much of genuine historical value. The *Iliad* throws light upon the finds of the archaeologist just as archaeology throws light upon the historicity of the *Iliad*.[2]

It is no part of a history of history to discuss the still unsolved question, "Who wrote the Homeric poems?"[3] The personality of the blind bard, that dim but pathetic figure, whom all antiquity honored as the supreme epic genius of Greece, has suffered from the attacks of a century of criticism but is apparently recovering once more in a reaction against too sweeping skepticism.[4] It was

---

[2] On these questions see G. W. Botsford and E. G. Sihler, *Hellenic Civilization* (1915).

[3] This problem has often received undue emphasis in the field of historiography. It does not properly belong there, since history began less in the epic than in criticism of the epic. The influence of Homer upon Greek ideas and thought is naturally of supreme interest to historians, but that does not make the *Odyssey* or the *Iliad* history.

[4] G. W. Botsford and E. G. Sihler, *Hellenic Civilization*, Chap. I, Sect. 3. Botsford sums up his position as follows: "We may suppose, then, that songs and perhaps other literature descriptive of the splendors of Minoan life passed down into the Middle Age, which followed the Minoan period, and into the language of the Hellenes, and that Hellenic bards on the Greek mainland and in the colonies continued to sing the glories of gods and heroes, intermingling their own customs and ideas with traditions. The greatest of these bards was Homer, who lived in Asia Minor, perhaps in the ninth or in the eighth century. He incorporated nothing, but created his great poems afresh, making use, however, of much traditional

in 1795 that Friedrich August Wolf (1759-1824) published his epoch-making *Prolegomena ad Homerum* in which the unity of the poems was attacked and "Homer" was dethroned from his supreme position. During the nineteenth century the poems have been studied from every possible angle, and as the study of comparative mythology and folklore developed alongside the progress of philology, the tendency was to view them more and more as folk tales, welded into shape by various poets and at different times. If a note of personal authorship seemed to dominate, one might fall back upon the fact that these were the tales of a folk so keenly individualistic that the quality of personality could not fail but shine through the social expression. Indeed these two elements, the individual and the general, give the poems their double charm and have assured their preservation not only by the Greeks but by those who learned Greek in order to know them. They carry with them the vision of beauty and the living fire of genius and at the same time take on that universal outlook and interest which mark out the folk tale from the individual creation. We have pointed out how records engraved upon stone endure while traditions change; but here was a tradition whose words themselves acquired immortality, engraved not simply in the memory, but in the whole intellectual life, of a people.

The Homeric poems were to the Greeks—so far as history goes—almost what the Old Testament was to the Jews. Their authority was fastened upon the Greek mind down to the era of its full intellectual development. The early Christian Fathers accepted them in this light, devoting their energies merely to prove that the narrative of Moses was prior to that of the Greeks.[5] It is a singular parallel that modern scholarship devel-

---

subject matter. The *Odyssey* was composed after the *Iliad;* yet both may have been the product of one genius. After their completion by Homer the poems were to some extent interpolated."

[5] Not the least interesting passages bearing upon this authority of Homer are the sections of Justin Martyr's *Apology,* in which he places Homer alongside Plato as the two main sources of pagan theology. Justin ingeniously proves, with a display of considerable learning, that Homer as well as Plato borrowed the better side of the Greek system from Moses. This line of argument was followed by many a Christian Father and ultimately worked into systematic shape, as in Eusebius' chronicle.

oped the higher criticism of Homer and Moses side by side [6] and, applying with impartial judgment the same tests to both, has revealed in each case the same art of composite authorship and the gradual formation of canon. Whether Pisistratus, who was credited with having got the specialists in Homer together in the sixth century for the preparation of an orthodox text, was really the Ezra of the Greeks or not, the great scholars at Alexandria seem to have been finally responsible for the text as we have it. For not only are the *Iliad* and the *Odyssey* composite poems built out of materials of various origins, but the poems which have survived are only parts of wide cycles of the "Homeric" saga. Local poets adapted and continued the poems to suit the audience. "Every self-respecting city sought to connect itself through its ancient clans with the Homeric heroes." It is no wonder that many cities claimed to be the birthplace of a legendary poet; doubtless many were!

Alongside Homer stands Hesiod who comes but indirectly within our survey through the influence of his poems upon subsequent writers. Hesiod is no minstrel with a tale, but a peasant moralizer with a gift of homely wisdom and an interest in theology. His poems attempt no sustained and glorious flight. His *Works and Days* are the "works and days" of a simple Boeotian farmer, interested in his crops, the weather, and the injustice of men. The *Theogony,* the opening chapters of a Greek Genesis, tells the story of the birth of the gods and their dealings with men. Neither would be mentioned in a history of history on its own account were it not that in the *Works and Days* one finds the first statement of that familiar scheme of the ages, into the ages of gold, of silver, of bronze, and of iron,[7] which has beguiled the fancy of so many a dreamer in later centuries—in that long "age of iron" in which all dreamers live—and were it not that in the *Theogony* we are given a straightforward account of the myth basis of the ancient Greek idea of the origins of

---

[6] Especially through the influence of F. A. Wolf upon Germany's scholarship at the end of the eighteenth century.

[7] With a Homeric age thrown in between bronze and iron.

society. Hesiod furnishes us, therefore, in the one poem with a framework for the successive epochs of social development, a scheme of world history, and in the other a picture of those divine factors which account for the process itself. In short, we have a philosophy of history—unphilosophical and unhistorical—although in the Hellenic Genesis mankind loses the Eden of the gods slowly and by the very character of successive cultures. There is the germ of a gospel of Rousseau in the outlook of Hesiod.

But none of this is history, Homer no more than Hesiod. It is poetry, romance, art, the creation of imagination, the idealization of both realities and dreams. History began in another and more obscure setting. Indeed, in a sense this poetic material blocked the path of history. From the standpoint of science, art overdid itself; the poems were too well done. They prevented the Greeks from looking for any other narrative—for what could the past offer so satisfactory, so glorious, as the deeds of the saga which everybody knew and the golden age of gods and men in which everyone believed? So the past was clothed with the colors of romance. It held something more than the good old days. A magic of antique Arabian Nights lay beyond its misty boundary, and the tales one told of it were for entertainment rather than for instruction. The present was an age of iron—it always is; but the gleam of the age of gold could still be caught—as it can even today—when the memory was a poem. If the epics stimulated a sense of the past they perverted it as well. The perspective of the early ages of Hellas, as seen in them, stretched by real cities and dealt with real heroes, but they included, as well, so much fantastic material that the genuine exploits could not be distinguished from those invented to suit the audience.

There is another way in which the poetry which was the glory of early Greek literature seems to have hindered the development of history. It placed the emphasis upon individuals. No epic can have as its subject the origins of a civic constitution; it must deal with men, with life and death and great exploits and the rapt tragedy of haunting fate. History may include all this, but it is more. It deals with society as such, with politics and the sober commonplace of business; it records the changes in the administration of the city and the hardships of the debtors in the days of rising prices as well as the raids of robber cattle-lords. Now, whether it was owing to the epics or not, the Greeks, while keenly alert to the politics of the present, were, down to the latter part of the sixth century and even later, satisfied with what Homer had to tell them of their origin. This is long after they had developed more than one complicated political structure. Highly organized states, filled with a critical, inquisitive, and sophisticated citizenship, still accepted the naïve traditions of their past, and continued building upon the general theme still newer myths to connect themselves with the ancient heroes.

It is difficult to realize that no real history, in our sense of the word, was produced in Greece until in the climax of its civilization. The theme of the first prose writers continued to be like that of the poets, less politics than the story of heroes or noble clans. Herodotus himself was the first political historian, the first to deal in systematic form with the evolution of states and the affairs of nations, and Herodotus after all, came late. One forgets that the naïve tales of the Father of History were composed far along in Grecian history, in the age of Pericles and by the friend of Sophocles. Athens had already achieved democracy, the creations of such men as Solon, Cleisthenes, and even Aristides were already things of the past, before a political history was written.

It was not because the Greeks lacked curiosity as to their past that their performance in history writing was so long delayed. The trouble was that their curiosity was satisfied by something other than history. What they needed to develop history and historians was criticism, skeptical criticism, instead of blind acceptance of the old authority. This criticism first showed itself in the cities of Ionia, and with it came into existence not only history but that new intellectual life, that *vita nuova,* which marks out the achievements of the Hellenic genius from all the previous history of the human mind—that philosophy which was science, and that science which was art.

The scene of this renaissance was not Athens nor anywhere on the mainland of Greece. Farther to the east, where the rocky coast of Asia crumbles and plunges into the Aegean, lay the cities of the Ionian Greeks. A little fringe of cities, a dozen or so, on hill crest or by the deep waters of half-hidden bays, these settlements played no role in the political history of the world like that of the states of the Nile or Euphrates valleys. They had no great career of conquest and erected no empire. Few, even today, have ever heard of them. And yet the history of civilization owes to them a debt hardly less than to Egypt or Babylon. It was there that critical thought dawned for the western world. In them began that bold and free spirit of investigation which became the mark of the Hellenic mind.

They held the key between East and West. They had held it some centuries before Darius found them in possession of it, insolently tempting and then suffering his anger. Long before that fateful fifth century when they were to serve as the medium to bring East and West to war, they had been the agents of another kind of intercourse. For, just behind, through the valley of the Maeander and passing the mountain fastnesses of Phrygia and Lydia, lay that overland caravan route which stretched through Asia Minor by old Hittite towns to touch at Carchemish the bazaars of Assyria. Along it moved the Oriental-Western trade. By the southern coast they met Phoenician ships, bringing goods, and perhaps an alphabet. Along the islands to the west and up the coast to the Black Sea their own ships came and went, gathering in that commerce which had brought wealth to Troy and planting their colonies. They were kin with the masters of Attica and held an even larger share than Athens of that still more ancient culture which flourished in Crete and along the Aegean before the days of Homer and the steel swords of the north. They were Greeks, sharing the common heritage. But it was from the barbarians rather than from Hellas that the inspiration came which set going the new scientific spirit. A knowledge of the world outside brought out and fed the native thirst for more, and, as the diversities of civilization opened up before them with possibilities of comparison such as Egyptians or Babylonians never enjoyed, they grew more curious and more skeptical at the same time. They had acquired an external point of view from which to judge of their own traditions. The naïve primitive faith began to suffer from a growing sophistication, and in this movement of intellectual clarification there were some who attacked the Homeric tradition in somewhat the same spirit as that of the philosophers of the eighteenth century who attacked the traditional theologies of Christendom. Before 500 B.C., Xenophanes, the philosopher, denounced the myths of Homer and Hesiod, because such miraculous occurrences are impossible in the face of the regularity of the laws of nature. In such a setting was born "history."

The exact origins are confused and uncertain. As we have seen already, the word "history" (ἱστορίη) was related to "inquiry," but as used by these Ionian Greeks it would apply to the "inquiries" or investigations which characterized the whole intellectual movement rather than to that one branch to which it was ultimately limited. The "historian" was the "inquirer" or truth seeker. The word was already used in this sense in the *Iliad*, where quarrelling parties in disputes at law came shouting "Let us make Agamemnon, Atreus' son, our arbitrator [our 'histor' (ἵστωρ)]." [8] Obviously, by the word "histor" Homer had in mind the wise man who knows the tribal customs and can get at the rights of the case by "inquiring" into the facts. Such skilled "truth seekers" are to be found in all semibarbarous peoples. The Roman *quaestor*—he who inquires—carried the office over into the formal magistracy. But truth seeking is not confined to law courts. One might "inquire" of oracles as well.[9] In spite of the myths with which it had so long to deal, the inquiry was in the world of living men; it was a secular task and a human one. There was in it, apparently from the first, a sense of hard fact, which sooner or later was to get rid of illusions. How it steered clear of philosophy is more difficult to tell. It has been stated that "history" to the Ionians of the sixth century was much what the

---

[8] *Iliad*, Book XXIII, line 486. Cf. Book XVIII, line 501, for similar use.

[9] Cf. Euripides, *Ion*, line 1547. A collection of them was kept for reference in the Acropolis at Athens. See Herodotus, *History*, Book V, Chap. 90.

From Homer to Herodotus 169

Athenians of the fourth century termed philosophy.[10] But the same matter-of-fact quality which swept it far away from the idea of divine inspiration, also kept it from being lost in abstraction. *Philosophia*—love of knowledge—might come to mean speculations about speculations; but *historia* continued at its humbler but more fundamental task of inquiring for the data. There is already a hint of its scientific possibilities in the fact that when Aristotle included in his philosophy an account of the actual, living world he gave to this part of his survey the title *Natural History*. To Aristotle, however, the term still in the main carried with it the connotation of "research." It is only in the work of the last of the great Greek historians, Polybius, that this meaning shifts definitely from inquiry to narrative. To Polybius, intent as he was upon the scientific aspect of his work, this gradual change in usage may have passed unnoticed; but it is nonetheless significant of unscientific possibilities. For if *historia* escaped religion and metaphysics it was captured by literature.[11]

None of these distinctions, however, was possible in the Ionia of the sixth century. The very breadth of the term prevented one thinking of "historia" as mere history. Even Herodotus, although the usage was narrowing in his time, could hardly have imagined himself the Father of History in the later sense of the word.[12] His "inquiry" was geography as well; it included descriptions of physical features of countries with the occupations and achievements of their inhabitants. The whole miscellaneous survey was his "history." But the surprising thing is that those sections which to us are the historical sections *par excellence,* the narratives of hap-

[10] G. Murray, *A History of Ancient Greek Literature* (1912), p. 123. The philosopher Heraclitus declared it necessary for men who were lovers of wisdom (φιλοσόφους ἄνδρας) to be inquirers (ἴστορας) into very many things. See Fig. 35. Hermann Diels, *Fragmente der Vorsokratiker* (5th ed., 1934), I, 159.

[11] As ancient civilization declined, the artistic aspect of *historia* received greater attention until at last, in Byzantine Greek, the word was used for a painting! See Du Cange, *Gloss. ad Scr. med. et inf. Graecitatis* (1688, repr. 1891), I, 523 *svv.* ἱστορεῖν—*pingere;* ἱστορία—*pictura, tabella.*

[12] Herodotus seems to use the word once in the modern sense: "The names of these leaders I shall not mention, as it is not necessary for the course of my History (ἱστορίης); for the leaders of some nations were not worthy to have their names recorded" (Book VII, Chap. 96). Herodotus uses various forms of the root of ἱστορίη a score of times, but nearly always in the sense of "inquiry" conducted by asking questions of someone.

penings beyond the memory of his own time or outside the possibility of his own inquiry, are called by another name. There are several of these embedded in his vast mosaic, large enough to be "histories" by themselves, the story of Croesus and Lydia, of Egypt, of Scythia, or of Thrace; but these narratives of the things really past are termed not "histories" but "sayings"—*logoi*.

This means that they are secondary sources, as it were, narratives of other men, which he cannot verify by his own inquiry or "history." It means more, however. For *logos* was already a technical term;[13] it was what a man had to say—his "story" in about the sense in which the word is used by journalists today—a deliverance in prose. Hence prose writers in Ionia were termed *logographoi*, and it is under this heading that one finds, in most histories of Greek literature, the founders of history.[14]

The prose in history came by way of city chroniclers (ὧροι), who were busied in the Ionian cities, as elsewhere, in carrying back the story to Homer's heroes and Hesiod's gods. Possibly because they took material from temple and civic records,[15] they broke away from verse and put their "sayings" into prose. This in itself was a real liberation, but the results came slowly. The subject seems generally to have been the genealogical story of noble clans—a subject to try the most scientific of tempers, especially if one's livelihood depends upon a successful artistic performance. Yet it was from among the writers of these that the critical impulse came. Among them arose some who grew skeptical of the legends it was their business to relate and so became "truth seekers" through a widening inquiry for the data of the past.

At the head of the list of some thirty of these logographers whose names—but not their works—have come down to us, a Greek tradition placed the "misty figure" of Cadmus of Miletus, to whom some attribute the honor of being the father of Greek

---

[13] The Latin *sermo* (our sermon) has had a somewhat similar history.

[14] Herodotus refers to Hecataeus as "the maker of prose," λογοποιός. Thucydides includes Herodotus among the λογογράφοι. The use of the term by modern writers to apply to these early historians dates from F. Creuzer, *Die historische Kunst der Griechen* ... (1803, 2d ed., 1845). On the subject in general, see J. B. Bury, *The Ancient Greek Historians* (1909), Lect. I.

[15] Such documents and inscriptions as were sure to be found in the important shrines and in the public offices.

prose because of a work he is supposed to have written on *The Foundation of Miletus*. It is, however, impossible for us to go into detail upon the work of these logographers. The writing of prose narrative is no improvement upon verse unless the author avails himself of its freedom to be more exact in what he says, and, to judge from the scornful comment of Thucydides (Book I, Chap. 21), the logographers were little better historians than the poets who preceded them. But perhaps Thucydides' impatience was not altogether justified. However prosy these prose writers became, they should not be blamed too severely for their failure to evolve an adequate chronology; however uncritical they remain, it was something to hand down the stories of the past much as they found them. One must recall the whole situation—the vague chronology, the involved calendar, the unreliable genealogies, the comparative absence of even bad material concerning the past— in order to do justice to these blundering logographers.

At the end of the sixth century a man of genius brought the work of the logographers to its climax and at the same time prepared the way for new and far-reaching developments: he was really the founder of historical writing among the Greeks. This man, whose appearance has been signalized as one of the most important events in the history of early Greek literature and science, was Hecataeus of Miletus. Born towards the middle of the sixth century, Hecataeus belonged to the Greek aristocracy of his city, and after extensive travels he wrote up what he had learned. Two books are attributed to him, an account of his *Travels around the World* and a book of local *Genealogies*, the one a description of the Persian world by a much-travelled subject of the Great King, the other a story of his city's heroes by a patriot Greek. Of the two, the book of travels would seem—and did seem to the Greeks —to be the more important. It revealed the modern world to those who were to take over its heritage. But it is the other book which mainly concerns us here. There was in it the promise of something which makes it, in spite of its obscure and relatively trifling subject, one of the epoch-making contributions in the long story of our intellectual emancipation. It applied the new-won knowledge to criticize the ancient myths. Its opening words seem to mark the dawn of a new era: "Hecataeus of Miletus thus speaks: I write what I deem true; for the stories of the Greeks are manifold and seem to me ridiculous." Ringing words that sound like a sentence from Voltaire! Unfortunately, as has been indicated above, the few fragments in our possession hardly lead one to suppose that the actual achievement of Hecataeus measures up to his ideals. We know that he did not, like Xenophanes, the philosopher, deny the myths in the Homeric legend on the basis of *a priori* scientific impossibility; his criticism was the product of a comparative study of mythology and history rather than an application of Ionian philosophy. It was as a geographer that he brought the comparative method to correct the pseudohistorical. The open world he travelled was responsible for the open mind.

Strangely enough, Herodotus records in a notable passage (Book II, Chap. 143), an incident in the life of Hecataeus which must have contributed largely to produce this first emphatic criticism of historical sources. It is not too long to quote:

When Hecatæus, the historian, was at Thebes, and, discoursing of his genealogy, traced his descent to a god in the person of his sixteenth ancestor, the priests of Jupiter did to him exactly as they afterwards did to me, though I made no boast of my family. They led me into the inner sanctuary, which is a spacious chamber, and showed me a multitude of colossal statues, in wood, which they counted up and found to amount to the exact number they had said; the custom being for every high-priest during his lifetime to set up his statue in the temple. As they showed me the figures and reckoned them up, they assured me that each was the son of the one preceding him; and this they repeated throughout the whole line, beginning with the representation of the priest last deceased, and continuing until they had completed the series. When Hecatæus, in giving his genealogy, mentioned a god as his sixteenth ancestor the priests opposed their genealogy to his, going through this list, and refusing to allow that any man was ever born of a god. Their colossal figures were each, they said, a Pirômis, born of a Pirômis, and the number of them was three hundred and forty-five; through the whole series, Pirômis followed Pirômis, and the line did not run up either to a god or a hero. The word *Pirômis* may be rendered "gentleman."

One must recall the situation. Egypt had been thrown open by Cambyses and had now become the university of the Mediterranean world. How much it had to teach the inquisitive Greeks, as well as the Asiatics, we are only today discovering; but the eager narrative of Herodotus shows how many such interviews as those at Thebes the priests of Egypt had been granting to the half-barbarian Hellenes. Hecataeus had gone there believing in his own traditions, "boasting" of them, as Herodotus implies. The splendors of the river valley from Sais to Thebes—six hundred miles of a museum street—had hardly broken the crust of his Greek provincialism. He could at least offer a rival to Egyptian antiquity in the imaginative conceptions of the Olympian sages. Then came the impressive spectacle of centuries of a human past made visible and real and stretching out before his eyes, and it cast ridicule upon the slight and relatively insignificant Hellenic past. Evidently Hecataeus had described his own confusion or Herodotus would not have referred to it in this offhand way. If so, the incident may well have stood out in his own mind as an experience of decisive importance in the moulding of his point of view. We might not be far wrong, then, if we were to date—so far as such things can be dated—the decisive awakening of that critical, scientific temper which was to produce the new science of history from the interview in the dark temple chamber of the priests of Thebes. Yet we must not forget that it was the Greek visitor and not the learned Egyptian priests who applied the lesson. How much the skepticism of thinkers at home had already predisposed Hecataeus to this critical attitude we cannot tell. But then we need not try to "explain" the mind of one of whom we know little more than what is given here; especially since, even in that little, we see that Hecataeus had a mind of his own.

Hecataeus is the only one of the logographers to whom Herodotus pays tribute by naming as a source. Modern scholarship has interested itself in attempting to estimate how much the Father of History actually was indebted to his pioneering predecessor, but the problem belongs rather to the criticism of Herodotus than to that of Hecataeus and is too detailed for such a survey as this. The general conclusion is that Herodotus was even more in debt than he admitted and that the earlier traveller not only supplied his successor with notes for his history but a guide for his actual travels as well. If this be so, it is all the more remarkable how Herodotus takes particular pains to discredit and ridicule Hecataeus. He repeatedly expresses his scorn of the geographers who adhere to the old Homeric cosmography and believe in the existence of an "Ocean stream" that bounds the world. This attitude of critical superiority is not due to the possession by the critic of any superior technique in research, since he himself could make as grotesque concessions to myth, as, for example, in the accounts of the phoenix and the hippopotamus,—the latter having, according to Herodotus,[16] cloven hoof and horse's mane and tail. It was not in the description of such details that Herodotus could deny the merit of Hecataeus' achievement so much as in the faulty generalizations which tradition had fastened upon Hecataeus—that Homeric map of the world which prevented one from ever forming a correct impression of geography as a whole. Hecataeus had been a great traveller and, we suppose, a shrewd observer, but he was unable to allow the body of fact he gathered to overthrow the preconceived ideas of the world. Herodotus, with much the same technique but greater mastery, could appreciate, as his predecessor failed to do, that where the body of facts runs contrary to theory, the theory must go, even if it had the weight of universal acceptance. Thus, from Hecataeus to Herodotus one passes a further step toward the science of history. Hecataeus after all was only a logographer, Herodotus a historian.[17]

Between Hecataeus and Herodotus, however, stood an event which gave a new direction to the development of Greek historiography and of everything else that was Greek; this event was the war with Persia. Their victories inspired the Greeks with a new confidence in themselves, shook them out of their old manner of life, and gave them a new and wider view of the world. They began to wish to know more about the Persians, and within a few years several little books, called *Persica,* appeared in answer to this demand; among them we may mention those by Dionysius of Miletus and Charon of Lampsacus. The influx of Ionians to Athens and elsewhere brought something of Ionian criticism to the mainland, and old myths were no longer accepted as

---

[16] These stories in Herodotus were probably taken from Hecataeus.
[17] The following two paragraphs are by Professor Swain.

uncritically as before. Then Acusilaus of Argos composed a prose work, later divided into at least three books, in which he retold and rationalized to some extent the stories of Hesiod and other epic writers; he added genealogies, a primitive chronology, and various cosmological speculations and thus made a sort of history. His contemporary, Pherecydes of Athens (fl. c. 480), did much the same thing in his work in ten books on early Athens. These two men were later counted among the Seven Wise Men of Greece. The social, economic, and political changes that followed the war, especially in Athens, gave rise to another very practical type of historical writing: these changes naturally brought the name of the earlier reformer, Solon, into prominence, and as his name was one to conjure with, a heated discussion arose as to the exact nature of his purposes and accomplishments, and a pamphlet literature grew up which was, in part at least, historical. Other pamphleteers wrote tracts for or against the politicians of the day, and these were later regarded as serious histories: five hundred years later Plutarch based his life of Pericles in part upon such a pamphlet written by Stesimbrotus. Out of this exciting century, too, came the two greatest historians of antiquity, Herodotus and Thucydides. But before turning to their immortal works we must devote our attention for a moment to their lesser contemporary, Hellanicus of Lesbos.

We cannot be sure of the dates of Hellanicus' life, but apparently he was born about 485—thus being almost exactly the age of Herodotus—he did his writing during the last third of the fifth century, and he was still working in 407. Though he had travelled considerably in Greece and perhaps elsewhere, he depended much more than his two great contemporaries upon written materials: he therefore might be called the first Greek scholar. Though having no literary style, Hellanicus was a prolific writer and the ancients attributed to him about thirty works—some of which, however, were duplications and others apocryphal. His early writings were mythographical, telling again the ancient myths as history and attempting to connect these heroic times with the present: this work therefore resembled Hecataeus' *Genealogies*. Secondly Hellanicus wrote various ethnographical works, which might be compared to Hecataeus' *Travels*. There are references to works dealing with various parts of Greece (Lesbos, Argos, Arcadia, Boeotia, Thessaly) but whether they formed one book or several we cannot say; he is said to have treated barbarian countries also (Egypt, Persia, Scythia, Lydia, Cyprus, Phoenicia), perhaps in a book called *The Customs of the Barbarians;* but he apparently wrote a *Persica*, and perhaps an *Aegyptica*, as well. The later and most important part of his work consisted in compiling chronicles, an *Atthis* covering the history of Athens from Cecrops to 407 B.C., and a work in three volumes called the *Priestesses of Hera*. He here traced the succession of the priestesses back to a period long before the Trojan War and used it for the chronology at the basis of a general Greek history written in chronicle form. It is true that his computations were far from accurate, but he made a beginning which others improved upon, and his efforts show that he regarded Greek history within a Pan-Hellenic frame of reference. His work brought the first period of Greek historiography to a close.

Such works, which had now left poetry so far behind as to be not merely prose but prosy, were those upon which the Greeks of the great age of Athens rested their ideas of chronology. In the absence of adequate records, history was, even in Hellas, hardly rising above the level of mediaeval annals. It was reserved for a Herodotus of Halicarnassus to combine geography and history narrative with criticism and literature and so to win for history a distinct place in the arts and sciences of mankind for all time.

CHAPTER XIV

Herodotus

THE life of Herodotus coincided almost exactly with the years of the Athenian supremacy, those sixty years or so which lay between the battle of Salamis and the beginning of the end of things in the Peloponnesian war. He was born about 480 B.C., and died after 430 B.C. Practically nothing is known of his life except what can be deduced from his own history. His native city was Halicarnassus, a Dorian settlement on the seacoast of Asia Minor, where, however, inscriptional remains indicate that the Ionic dialect was in use. He had thus accessible for his history the tongue which had already been consecrated to prose literature. But while he wrote their language, he could not rid himself of a strong native prejudice against the Ionians. They are practically the only people in his whole narrative to whom he is almost consistently unfair. They "have built their cities in a region where the air and climate are the most beautiful in the whole world; for no other region is equally blessed with Ionia, neither above it nor below it, nor east nor west of it" (Book I, Chap. 142). Yet, "of all its [Greek] tribes the Ionic was by far the feeblest and least esteemed, not possessing a single State of any mark excepting Athens. The Athenians and most of the other Ionic States over the world went so far in their dislike of the name as actually to lay it aside; and even at the present day the greater number of them seem to me to be ashamed of it" (Book I, Chap. 143). Thus he brings his neighbors into the story, borrowing their tongue to do it! And once in it, they fare no better. His jibes sometimes became a sneer, deftly driven home by the rhetorical device of having some one else—a Scythian for instance—say "by way of reproach" that the Ionians "are the basest and most dastardly of all mankind...

but the faithfullest of slaves" (Book IV, Chap. 142). There is a touch, a shadow, of something Dantesque in this strength of local antipathy, quite out of keeping with the breadth of sympathy and interest he shows elsewhere. The much-travelled Greek never entirely lost the narrow partisanship of his home town. To be sure, as commentators have pointed out, such anti-Ionian sentiments were popular at Athens, which was having its troubles keeping the Ionians in subjection in the days when Herodotus sought its hospitality; but, although the applause of his audience may have led him to polish his darts, he flicked them of his own accord. The Halicarnassus of his boyhood seems to have left its traces in his outlook, whatever else it supplied.

It is unfortunate to have to touch first upon this evidence of smallness in Herodotus, for the work as a whole is marked by a breadth of view in keeping with its breadth of knowledge. Indeed it is doubtful if the wide scope of its information did not depend upon the open mind with which the author-voyager travelled the world, that frank desire to see things as they are, which, when disciplined, leads toward science. Just what disciplines directed the native curiosity of Herodotus no one knows, but they must have been considerable. His work reveals a wide and intimate knowledge of the poetry of Hellas, especially of Homer,[1] and he had readily at hand his predecessors in the new art of prose writing, especially Hecataeus, to cite or refer to on occasion. His education, therefore, must have been almost as extensive as his travels, covering practically the known world. Only a well-born and well-to-do young man could equip himself as he did for his life task. Such a one could hardly keep out of politics in a Greek city, and his travels may have been partly due to exile. But of this he gives no glimpse himself, and the story of participation in a Halicarnassan revolution and subsequent withdrawal to Ionian

[1] "He has drunk at the Homeric cistern until his whole being is impregnated with the influence thence derived. In the scheme and plan of his work, in the arrangement and order of its parts, in the tone and character of the thoughts, in ten thousand little expressions and words, the Homeric student appears; and it is manifest that the two great poems of ancient Greece are at least as familiar to him as Shakespeare to the modern educated Englishman."—G. Rawlinson, *The History of Herodotus* (2d ed., 1862), I, 6. In addition, Rawlinson cites references to some fifteen poets.

Herodotus

no one has attempted to improve upon it. But the assignment of the text to these accepted "books" has not prevented modern scholars from attempting to find "broader, more fundamental and primary" divisions. These, according to the simple statement of the historian of Greek historians, are as follows.[3]

The work falls naturally into three sections, each consisting of three parts. The first section, or triad of Books, comprises the reigns of Cyrus and Cambyses, and the accession of Darius; the second deals with the reign of Darius; the third with that of Xerxes. The first is mainly concerned with Asia including Egypt, the second with Europe, the third with Hellas. The first displays the rise and the triumphs of the power of Persia; the last relates the defeat of Persia by Greece; while the middle triad represents a chequered picture, Persian failure in Scythia and at Marathon, Greek failure in Ionia. And each of the nine subdivisions has a leading theme which constitutes a minor unity. Cyrus is the theme of the first Book, Egypt of the second, Scythia of the fourth, the Ionian rebellion of the fifth, Marathon of the sixth. The seventh describes the invasion of Xerxes up to his success at Thermopylæ; the eighth relates to the reversal of fortune at Salamis; the final triumphs of Greece at Platæa and Mycale occupy the ninth. In the third alone the unity is less marked; yet there is a central interest in the dynastic revolution which set Darius on the throne. Thus the unity of the whole composition sharply displays itself in three parts, of which each again is threefold. The simplicity with which this architectural symmetry has been managed, without any apparent violence, constraint, or formality, was an achievement of consummate craft.

It may be wrong, but as one turns from this schematic arrangement to the narrative itself, an unbidden doubt arises to question if the "architectural unity" of the great work is quite as simple as the analysis seems to imply. As Macan himself confesses,[4] the fourth book is like the first three in the quality which links them all, that encyclopaedic survey by way of vast digressions, which carries the narrative far away from the central theme. The fourth book swings off to the outer confines of the barbarian world and matches with its brilliant sketches of Scythia and Libya the won-

---

[3] J. B. Bury, *The Ancient Greek Historians*, pp. 38-39, based upon analysis of R. W. Macan, though supplying independent criteria.

[4] R. W. Macan, *Herodotus, the Fourth, Fifth, and Sixth Books* (2 vols., 1895), Introduction, Vol. I, pp. xxii-xxiv.

derful second book on Egypt. We leave Darius by Bosphorus or Danube to study the climate, fauna, and flora of the cold northern plains, wander like the Greek traders (whose accounts are woven into the texture of the history) along far rivers through unknown peoples, trace the amber trail to dimmer distances, and, almost incidentally, note the habits and customs of men, until the Scythian *logos* becomes a priceless treasure of anthropological lore. This is surely in the style of the first three books.

The change from the far-reaching discursive style to the narrower treatment of events in the later books is a gradual one; for there are digressions right up to the battle of Thermopylae, but as the Greeks themselves come more and more into the story there is naturally less description and more straight narrative. There was no need to describe the Greeks to themselves, except as the facts were not well known at Athens. The turning point in the history, therefore, inasmuch as one can detect it, seems to be when Athens itself is brought upon the scene, the Athens they all knew. This comes in the fifth book, when, through the great Athenian revolution, we are brought out of the "old regime" to the modern days of the new democracy. All before was ancient history; the overthrow of the tyrants marked, fittingly, the coming of modern times, and from now on Herodotus could be a modern historian. It is hard at this distance to recover the perspectives of the fifth century B.C., and to realize that the Athens and Sparta which had figured in the earlier books were already, to the listeners of Herodotus, about as far away in time as the kingdom of Lydia in space. It takes but a short time for unhistorical peoples to lose their sense of the reality of events; and Solon and Croesus were both alike, the half-historical, half-mythical figures of a bygone era. With Miltiades and Darius the case was different. Though they too already were passing into the heroic past, men who had fought Darius were still alive, and these old veterans sprinkled in the audience would hardly encourage that discursive anecdotal type of narrative which was suitable for the ancient history and for the geography of the earlier part.

The fifth book, therefore, in which the "revolution" is described, may be regarded as furnishing the transition from the "ancient" to the "modern" history of Herodotus. The point is rather obscured by the persistence of downright mediaeval conditions at Sparta, which had yet to be described (Book V, Chaps. 39-48), and, although recent, seem to be on a par with the remoter days of the tyranny at Athens. But everything is shaping up for the dramatic act with which the book closes, the Ionian revolt, which brought the Great War to Greece, henceforth the one dominant theme of the history. The new keynote is struck by the comment with which Herodotus closes the account of the Athenian revolution: "And it is plain enough, not from this instance only, but from many everywhere, that freedom is an excellent thing, since even the Athenians, who, while they continued under the rule of tyrants, were not a whit more valiant than any of their neighbours, no sooner shook off the yoke than they became decidedly the first of all. These things show that, while undergoing oppression, they let themselves be beaten, since then they worked for a master; but so soon as they got their freedom, each man was eager to do the best he could for himself. So fared it now with the Athenians" (Book V, Chap. 78). The path from this to Salamis was thus definitely entered upon, but it was still a long one with many turnings.

Whichever way one views the "architectural plan" of Herodotus' history, whether as a tripartite grouping or a less formal but more intrinsic unity, the plan was apparently not thought out beforehand but grew with the history itself. For internal evidence shows that the first books to be written were the last three, and they were apparently already largely written by the time he went to Athens. His travels—that is, the real expeditions to the outlying world—came later. It was a triumph of art to master the bewildering miscellany which these later years revealed and weave it into a single texture, so that the original story of Xerxes' invasion, with which he came to Athens, was left after all as the fitting climax to the whole.

If the simplicity and perfection of plan were a product of art and not, as might seem, the result produced by the very nature of the circumstances recorded, the same is true of the style. The very artlessness of Herodotus is artful. He is garrulous to a fault and sophistically ingenuous. When unable either to confirm or deny the truth of what he tells, he brings his sources frankly into the narrative and leaves them there. Sometimes—often, in fact—he seems to apologize for them, as in a passage in the seventh book, where he says, "My duty is to report all that is said; but I am not obliged to believe it all alike—a remark which may be understood to apply to my whole History" (Book VII, Chap. 152). So he lets his characters talk; and how they talk! Often he seems to stand by and chuckle. Once in a while he interjects a dry remark—as, when reporting a story that a certain Scyllias swam several miles under water, he adds, "My own opinion is that...he made the passage...in a boat"! (Book VIII, Chap. 8.) Similarly, he often escapes committing himself, as on the question of the sources of the Nile, with regard to which he had found no one among all those with whom he conversed who professed to have any knowledge except a single person. "He was the scribe who kept the register of the sacred treasures of Minerva in the City of Saïs, and he did not seem to me to be in earnest when he said that he knew them perfectly well" (Book II, Chap. 28). Herodotus wishes us to know that he could travel and listen with his tongue in his cheek; yet deftly, at the same time, by his deference to our criticism, and the frankness of his confessions to us, he leaves an impression of simple candor that adds to the charm of the telling.

It must not be forgotten how much of Herodotus' history is a collection of what other people said. Even his moralizing is partly due to what he got from his informants. It is a vast mass of material, drawn from priests and travellers, from tradition and documents, from stories of eyewitnesses and personal observation, all arranged and fitted to a single plan, but not worked over so as to obliterate the nature of the originals. This, to the modern student, is not its least merit. However biased and pro-Athenian Herodotus was, however guides imposed upon his ignorance or sources misled him, he left us largely the means for passing judgment upon himself. And this very fact does much to bring the verdict of even this critical, scientific age in his favor.

It was serious work. Long years of travel were behind the

story, and the author, with proud simplicity, proclaimed himself a savant in the opening line. His narrative "is the showing forth of researches [histories]" by one who is able to make them: the term history is here used in the definite technical sense. His predecessors were "makers of prose," but he is a "historian." Modern criticism denies him the distinction in just the way he claimed it, but it awards him still the distinction which he was awarded in antiquity, of being at once a pioneer and a classic—the Father of History. He combined with the instincts of critical investigation the consummate skill of a great artist. When his work is compared with the histories written before his day, its epoch-making quality is at once apparent. There is not only the deft, elusive touch of a master in the massing of detail, but the narrative never loses its *élan*, however burdened it may be with the weight of fact. It swings along with the strength and grace of a mind unfettered by either the hampering taboos of the primitive or the theories and questionings of too philosophic culture. A tinge of romance from the golden age still lightens the sober path of real events. One must turn to the text itself to appreciate it; commentaries are as inadequate as they are plentiful.

There are one or two further points, however, which are more especially pertinent to this survey. In the first place, we must revert to the point referred to above—the modernity of Herodotus. Nothing is more difficult in the appreciation of history than its perspective, and in judging the achievement of the first historian we are almost sure to find, first of all, our own limitations. Through the long stretch of the intervening centuries, Midas, Solon, Croesus, Cyrus, Darius, and Xerxes all seem to belong to one and the same time. They are all "ancients"; and the short intervals which lie between them do not seem of much importance. Only Egypt reaches out from what seems to us a common age into a different horizon,[5] like the sombre suggestion of the mystery which lies beyond the beginning of the things one knows. But to Herodotus and his audience the perspective was entirely different. It would be as though some one of this generation, writing of the Franco-Prussian war, were to carry back the nar-

[5] As for the legends of Babylon, they bear on the surface the marks of legend.

rative of causes through the long centuries of the national development of Europe in order to treat adequately the questions of today. Herodotus had met and talked with those who lived through these stirring times; the scars of war were in a sense still there; the effects upon the fortunes of Greece, and especially of Athens, were just showing themselves to the full. He built his vast and labyrinthine structure around this main theme of the world conflict; and since it was a world conflict, he brought to bear upon it the history of the world. The treatment varies with the sources. The events at home were known—or at least might be known—to his audience beforehand. There he must be on his guard. On the other hand, the accounts of Egyptians and Orientals are picked up at second-hand: Herodotus marks them off from the rest of his narrative; they are the *logoi*—the tales of the different countries, the extras in his narrative, "histories" by themselves. They are drawn from all kinds of sources, from native priests and dragomans and travellers before his day—Hecataeus especially. It is easy to see why this part is so much less reliable than the other. The priests of Egypt might mislead him or he misunderstand them; but in the Grecian part he knew where he was going. As a matter of fact he did make the mistakes of a traveller. For a glaring instance, he puts down Nebuchadnezzar of Babylon as a woman—Queen Nitocris. But we must recall, as Macaulay reminds us, that Babylon was to Greece about what Pekin was to the Europe of the eighteenth century. The remarkable thing is that Herodotus got as much correct as he did. When one thinks of what tales European tourists are fed on today, what myths are current in this country about the character of foreign peoples, even what persistent misunderstanding there is between different sections of the same country where intercourse is general and constant, one begins to see the canny temper of the Father of History.

It is hard to get a true sense of the Herodotean achievement in terms of any modern parallel. That of a European historian of today writing of the Franco-Prussian war is obviously entirely inadequate. Perhaps it might spur the historical imagination if we were to suppose that our Persians are Russians and our

Greeks Japanese, and that some twenty or thirty years from now an Oriental historian sets to work to immortalize the war which broke the island barriers of Japan and started it on its imperial career of expansion. Port Arthur is Thermopylae, Mukden is Marathon, and Tsushima, Salamis. The Oriental Herodotus travels through the West to gather the materials for a history of the two worlds in conflict. So, in place of that ancient royal road of Persia, he takes the Trans-Siberian railway to the ancient West and wanders through Europe, in search of truth—a genuine "historian." He asks the professors of Oxford for light on history and theology. He listens to talk in the clubs and hotels, and, with little to fall back upon but his Oriental common sense and a few guidebooks in Japanese, tries to work out a reliable account of peoples whose language he cannot read or speak, and among whom he lived only as a travelling guest. His history of Europe might begin with an account of Magellan in search of golden fleeces in the eastern seas, or Marco Polo visiting the great Khan. Beyond Marco Polo, the first historical figure in the annals of Europe, would lie the incredible story of Rome and Greece, and perhaps there would be a passage from Herodotus himself. Beyond this are the blank prehistoric ages, stretching back, according to Oxford anthropologists, to a fabulous ice flood, much farther than the 432,000 years which the priests allotted to ancient Babylon. Suppose that here and there he confused these data of science with the accounts of theologians who believed in the literal inspiration of Genesis. He might, perhaps, suspect and suggest that the material hardly fitted the context, but the theologians were admirable men, with a high sense of morals, so down it would go, with a short note on the character of the informants. As the story drifted on toward modern times, it would grow more complicated, for in a single lifetime Japan passed from feudal society, fighting in armor, to a nation armed with siege cannon and dreadnoughts. Of the age of transition, when the Phoenician Britishers played their role, our Herodotus could gather personal reminiscences and local memoirs—of varying reliability. But when he finally reaches the struggle in Manchuria, he has been over the ground of Mukden himself, and recalls, from his youth, the effects of the war. Here he knows his time and people, for they are his own.

The comparison might be developed farther. But if we have to invent our modern Herodotus in order to appreciate the ancient one, it is better to delay until our impressions of the original are refreshed by a new study of the first single masterpiece in the history of history. To do so one must turn to the book itself, for no series of extracts can do it justice. One instance of his scientific method is perhaps worth quoting in full for another reason.

In an earlier chapter we ventured the regret that Herodotus had not visited Jerusalem about the time the Pentateuch was being edited for the Bible as we have it.[6] It may be of interest to see how near he was to Jerusalem. He had become attracted by the problem of tracing the myth of Heracles throughout non-Greek parallels and tells us how, with curiosity quickened rather than subdued by what he found in Egypt, he pursued his investigations to that borderland of Palestine, Phoenicia (Book II, Chaps. 43-45). A visit inland to the Jewish scholars would not have thrown much light on Heracles, for of the Heraclean labors of Gilgamesh the story of Noah retains no trace. But there might have been significant comments on other matters! The researches in Phoenicia are recorded as follows (Book II, Chap. 44):

In the wish to get the best information that I could on these matters, I made a voyage to Tyre in Phœnicia, hearing there was a temple of Hercules at that place, very highly venerated. I visited the temple, and found it richly adorned with a number of offerings, among which were two pillars, one of pure gold, the other of emerald, shining with great brilliancy at night. In a conversation which I held with the priests, I inquired how long their temple had been built, and found by their answer that they too differed from the Greeks. They said that the temple was built at the same time that the city was founded, and that the foundation of the city took place two thousand three hundred years ago. In Tyre I remarked another temple where the same god was worshipped as the Thasian Hercules. So I went on to Thasos where I found a temple of Hercules which had been built by the Phœnicians who colonized that island when they sailed in search of Europa. Even this was five generations earlier than the time when Hercules, son of Amphit-

---

[6] Chap. IX, pp. 122-123.

ryon, was born in Greece. These researches show plainly that there is an ancient god Hercules; and my own opinion is, that those Greeks act most wisely who build and maintain two temples of Hercules, in the one of which the Hercules worshipped is known by the name of Olympian, and has sacrifice offered to him as an immortal, while in the other the honours paid are such as are due to a hero.

There is no need to appraise the work of Herodotus; history has already done that for us. Until the monuments were deciphered his account was about all we had of some of the greatest empires of the ancient world, and it still remains a constant commentary on them. One might even say that until our own time it has been for antique history as a whole almost what Homer was to the Greek of Athens. But if appraisal of his achievement is gratuitous, it may be well in closing to recall that the achievement involved the two aspects of historiography—criticism, which lies in the field of science, and narrative, which is mainly art—and that while the latter quality has been chiefly of value in the long centuries of the unscientific mind, preserving the story by the very magic of its appeal, yet today it is the other aspect which is of most importance; for the work has now to pass a much more critical audience than ever assembled in Athens, and one that knows more of Greece than they, and more of its antiquity than Herodotus.

It follows that only those conversant with this vast new lore of classical and Oriental archaeology are qualified to speak authoritatively on the critical capacity and the reliability of Herodotus. But, while leaving detailed criticism for textual students, we may at least register the fact that their verdict is growingly in his favor. For the case of the writings of Herodotus is somewhat parallel with that of the records of the Jews. So long as they were taken for more than they could possibly be, they were open to most serious charges of anachronisms, exaggerations, and the like. But when a truer historical perspective enables us to appreciate the *necessary* limitations, in both the implements and the sources of research, of all antique historians, we obtain a juster estimate of their performance because we do not expect too much. So it was with Herodotus. When the data of history from the inscriptions began to run counter to some of his accounts there was a movement of distrust in them,[7] but it has apparently subsided, and we have more discriminating judgments, based on lesser expectations.

It was obviously impossible for Herodotus to write history as we do now. The question is whether he used *his* methods successfully. There was one stern critic of his time, Thucydides, who clearly thought that he attempted too much. Thucydides would probably have held the story down to the original last three books and polished them over and over (as indeed Herodotus did), established every item in them indisputably, and left it at that. But Herodotus chose to add to them the *logoi* or histories which fill the long proem, although he could not establish their accuracy with the precision which characterized the events of his own time. The contrast is significant, and has been taken to show a distinctly less scientific temper on the part of Herodotus, in that he has not that keen appreciation of the boundary line which separates the world of fact from that of fiction. But is the line as firm a one after all as the purely scientific mind imagines it? If Herodotus had been as skeptical as Thucydides, he would have left out of his history some of its most valuable parts, for some of the things most incredible to him contain hints of items established or made intelligible by archaeology. The most striking instance is the comment of Herodotus on the story of the Phoenicians circumnavigating Africa at the behest of Neco, the Egyptian Pharaoh. "On their return, they declared—I for my part do not believe them, but perhaps others may—that in sailing round Libya they had the sun on their right-hand" (Book IV, Chap. 42). Again, in his description of Scythia, he doubts the long northern nights, perhaps because of the exaggerated way the account reached him, that men there slept half the year (Book IV, Chap. 25); he refuses to indorse the existence of any "Tin Islands" whence the tin came which they used,[8] and expressly states that, with reference to the Baltic, "though I have taken

---

[7] Perhaps the strongest statement of this is in A. H. Sayce's *Ancient Empires of the East*. See, by contrast, the judgment summed up in Bury's *Ancient Greek Historians*.

[8] Cf. Book III, Chap. 115.

vast pains I have never been able to get an assurance from an eye-witness that there is any sea on the further side of Europe."[9] It would have given a poorer, and not a more accurate, idea of the world as known to the contemporaries of Herodotus, if all this varied information had been sorted out by a too skeptical mind. The reader who is not upon his guard is constantly reminded,[10] by innuendo, if not openly, that a fact was not finally established simply because it was recorded—a reminder too long ignored—and that the reader should contribute as well some of the critical insight he demanded of the writer. The sources Herodotus used have been analyzed in great detail,[11] and the result is to show that the work is much more the product of scholarly erudition and less of casual hearsay than at first appears. He used documents, such as the acts of the *ecclesia* at Athens, treaties, declarations of war, but more sparingly than a modern historian would, and seems to have been willing to take them secondhand. He could embody genealogies (Book VI, Chap. 53), and use geographies while abusing them. But there was one set of sources which, however essential, was of dubious value: the oracles, especially those of Delphi. They largely furnished the mechanism for that supernatural element which to us lends an air of myth to the narrative, but they were part and parcel of Greek history and Herodotus had no choice but to use them. Unfortunately they helped him to ignore his own chief defect—an absence of the sense of historical causation. He sought only to keep the motives psychologically true and left events to shape themselves under the hand of fate or by the chastening justice of the gods. For while Herodotus did not, like the poets and his pred-

---

[9] *Ibid.*
[10] Cf. Book II, Chaps. 28, 56-57, 131; Book III, Chaps. 115, 116; Book IV, Chaps. 25, 31, 32, 36, 42, 96, 105; Book V, Chap. 10; Book VII, Chap. 152.
[11] See especially the conclusions of R. W. Macan, *Herodotus, the Fourth, Fifth and Sixth Books,* Introduction, Vol. I, pp. lxxiv *sqq.*, and the exhaustive article by Jacoby in Pauly-Wissowa-Kroll, *Realencyclopädie, s. v.* "Herodotos," Sup. Vol. IV. One of the most interesting problems in his use of sources is in his account of Darius' expedition into Scythia, where he omits all mention of the Balkans (Book IV, Chaps. 90-93) apparently, as Macan surmises, because at this point he was following a historical and not a geographical source, and it made no mention of the mountains. But this incident only emphasizes all the more the success with which, upon the whole, Herodotus welded his materials and marshalled the facts.

ecessors, follow the gods to Olympus and "drew ... a very marked line between the mythological age and the historical," he remained throughout a devoutly religious man.

Under the sunny gleam of his rippling narrative there is a substratum of deep melancholy and of the awe concerned with the anger and envy of the gods. King Crœsus, whom the auriferous Pactolus made the richest of men, Polycrates, tyrant of Samos, or Periander, despot of opulent Corinth—their pride and their end are merely iterations and reverberations of the stern melody of human success and divine retribution and the humiliation of man, exemplified most signally in Xerxes himself.[12]

This belief in a Providential scheme of things offered him a clue for tracing the sequence of events which is open now to criticism. But history had to wait from the days of Herodotus to our own for anything approaching a mastery of causation in history. And perhaps our groping may, before long, be classed with such tendency writing as his.

As to style, the varied charm and genial manner are still as fresh and winning as ever; yet one device which Herodotus took over from his logographic predecessors—but which, as we shall see, goes back to the very origins of story telling—the insertion of speeches into the narrative, leaves upon the whole the tone of something antique. What gave an added air of reality to it in ancient Greece lessens its force today. But of this device we shall have more to say when we come to it in a less natural setting and form in the works of Thucydides.

With Herodotus a new art may be said to have begun, that of basing a genuine *epos* upon the search for truth. How potent the touch of the master in it was may be judged from the facts that it still remains among the first of the great creations of history and that it embodied for subsequent centuries the life and movement, thought and action of all that vast antiquity which lay outside the Bible and the other Greek literature. Even Darius and Xerxes owed a large part of their immortality to the traveller-student of Halicarnassus.

---

[12] Botsford, in G. W. Botsford and E. G. Sihler, *Hellenic Civilization*, p. 23.

CHAPTER XV

Thucydides

ALONGSIDE the history of Herodotus stands a work which begins as follows: "Thucydides, an Athenian, wrote the history of the war in which the Peloponnesians and the Athenians fought against one another. He began to write when they first took up arms, believing that it would be great and memorable above any previous war."

In such sober terms does the greatest historian of antiquity begin the story of those eventful years during which occurred what was, in his opinion, the greatest war in all history. This soberness is typical of the whole work, and the consciousness of a high theme even more so. For the author was a different type of man from the sophisticated but garrulous Herodotus. He, too, had travelled before his work was done, being also an exile. But he did not become a citizen of the world, catching with easy familiarity the changeful notes of different countries. He remained throughout a high-born Athenian, a magistrate in history, severe and impartial even when his dearest interests were at stake, proud, isolated, self-contained.[1] There could not well be a greater contrast than that between Herodotus and Thucydides. Thucydides himself knew this. He had a poor opinion of his pred-

---

[1] Thucydides (c. 460?-c. 396) sprang from an old Thracian family on his mother's side, though his father was an Athenian citizen. We have no trustworthy evidence for the date of his birth, some placing it as early as 471, others as late as 455; a late date is generally accepted, however. His family was well-off, possessing the right to work mining properties in Thrace. His early life was spent at Athens, where the influence of the sophists upon him was great. In 424 he was elected one of the two generals to command an expedition into Thrace, which would seem to imply previous military experience. His efforts to save Amphipolis were, however, unsuccessful, owing to his failure to arrive in time; and the incident resulted in his exile. For twenty years he lived on his Thracian estates, and returned to Athens only after its defeat in 404. We cannot be sure of the date of his death, but it seems probable that it took place between 399 and 396 B.C.

ecessors and as much as says so, though without deigning to mention them by name. There is, however, no mistaking a remark like this: "Men do not discriminate, and are too ready to receive ancient traditions about their own as well as about other countries" (Book I, Chap. 20). He classes with the poets those "tales of chroniclers who seek to please the ear rather than to speak the truth" (Book I, Chap. 21). His own ideal is different; it is accuracy and relevancy—a straight story and a true one.[2]

At no place does Thucydides use the word "histor" or any of its derivatives, preferring to describe his work with a word meaning "write down."[3] The important thing for him was the finished product: he knew the truth about the war, and he told it; but except in two introductory passages (Book I, Chap. 22; Book V, Chap. 26), he does not tell how he acquired this information. As a matter of fact, he enjoyed unrivalled opportunities for learning the history of the war. High in affairs of state, he was familiar with the inner history of politics and knew personally the leading men; being in Athens during the early years of the war, he was in a position to know what happened; he tells us that he himself heard some of the speeches which he reports; he participated in one military expedition as commander and probably in others in a less exalted position. For the greater part of his information, however, Thucydides was dependent upon the same sort of "research" that Herodotus used, namely ἱστορία or "inquiry"—though the fact that he was interested primarily in contemporary events made his task simpler, for witnesses who

[2] The following paragraphs owe much to the revision by Professor Swain.

[3] Ξυγγράφω. If it was permissible to treat the ancient λόγοι as "stories" in the journalistic sense of the word (see above, p. 170) we might translate ξυγγράφω by the equally journalistic expression "write up"—except that these words give an impression of lightness or even of flippancy that is utterly foreign to Thucydides. In this case we would translate his opening sentence more literally than Jowett: "Thucydides, an Athenian, wrote up the war (ξυνέγραψε τὸν πόλεμον) of the Peloponnesians and Athenians, how they fought against each other." Thucydides used forms of this word regularly for his own writing (Book II, Chaps. 70, 103; Book III, Chaps. 25, 88, 116; Book IV, Chap. 104, etc.), and in one place speaks of the Ἀττικὴ ξυγγραφή of Hellanicus (Book I, Chap. 97); elsewhere he uses the word for anything written down, especially treaties or laws (cf. Book V, Chaps. 35, 41; Book VIII, Chap. 67). Other examples may easily be found with the aid of M. H. N. von Essen, *Index Thucydides* (1887), which is also authority for the statement that Thucydides nowhere used a word on the root of ἴστωρ.

could speak with authority were easier to find. Even his exile was in a way a blessing, for it enabled him to become acquainted with Spartans (Book V, Chap. 26), with whom he discussed the war at length, and from whom he learned the Spartan point of view. During these years he probably visited Sicily, where the naval power of Athens met its fate.[4] In a few passages, such as that discussing the early history of Sicily, he was dependent upon earlier writers, and sometimes he had copies of the official version of treaties set up in Athens or Olympia.

Thucydides, then, was a modern historian, even more than Herodotus. He tells us explicitly that he began his task as soon as war broke out in 431, and he must therefore have assembled a great pile of notes before the Peace of Nicias ten years later. During the succeeding years of relative peace, he apparently composed a first draft of the present narrative through Chapter 25 of Book V. Then came the renewal of hostilities with the Sicilian adventure, the Decelean war in Greece, and the fall of Athens in 404. Thucydides had probably not published his first account when fighting recommenced, and he now set out to prepare a second book, with a new introduction (Book V, Chap. 26), to deal with the later years of the war. The two books were welded into one, the first being edited and augmented by several passages referring to the catastrophe of 404 and insisting that the fighting of all twenty-seven years, 431–404, was really one war. Thucydides did not live to complete his task, however, for the narrative ends with events in the summer of 411. The last part of the book does not show the literary polish of the rest, and the final sentence is incomplete: one might say almost that the author died, pen in hand. The present division into eight books is of course the work of later scribes or scholars.

After a brief introductory paragraph, the author plunges into a summary account of Greece from Minoan times to the Persian Wars (Book I, Chaps. 1-19), then pausing a moment to criticize his predecessors, the poets and logographers who had never quite done this thing before, with a proud note on his own enterprise, he takes up the theme of his history. The first book deals with

[4] J. B. Bury, *The Ancient Greek Historians*, p. 76.

the origins of the war stated in terms of history. First come the events which involved Athens and Sparta in war (Book I, Chaps. 24-88), but, instead of passing over these immediate causes to the war itself, the author introduces a rather long account of the growth of the Athenian Empire prior to it (Book I, Chaps. 89-117). The first book then closes with the negotiations in Athens, Pericles' speech persuading his fellow citizens to go to war, and the break of diplomatic relations (Book I, Chaps. 118-146).

The whole is the restrained and powerful statement of the origins of the war. The second, third, and fourth books, and part of the fifth, relate the story of the fighting during the Ten Years War and of the negotiation of the peace of Nicias. Here we have not the time to follow him, and even if we had, we may as well confess with Thucydidean candor that few of us would care to do so. For all the art of the greatest historian of antiquity cannot quite reconcile the modern reader—unless he is a Hellenist beforehand—to a prolonged study of the details of the Peloponnesian war. For Thucydides it was the greatest event in history. The Trojan war had found a Homer; the Persian a Herodotus; but these two great epochs of the Hellenic past were, in his eyes, of far less importance than that of the great civil war which involved all of Greece and even disturbed the otherwise negligible barbarian world. The more he studied the past and compared it with the present, the more he was convinced that the greatest theme in history was offered to him by the war of his own lifetime. So he preserved its detailed story with scrupulous care, and it is this very excellence as history against which the modern reader rebels. For the war was long and had many turnings, and Thucydides is no garrulous guide or entertainer. He marches sternly ahead through a world of facts; it is too serious business for one to turn aside and view the scenery; even when the campaign is over for the year and we return home to the city, we must attend the council where plans for next year are on foot. There is only one purpose in life and that is to see the war through. The result is that we are led through years of desultory fighting, raids, skirmishes, expeditions by land and sea, debates in council, strategy in battle, until our memories are fairly benumbed by the variety of incident and the changes in policies, leadership, and fortune.

High drama awaits us, however, in the Sicilian expedition. All critics are agreed that Thucydides' finest writing is to be found in the sixth and seventh books which tell this tragic story with unrelenting realism. A prologue is set in the Melian incident, with the outrageous language of the Athenian ambassadors and the still more outrageous conduct of the Athenian generals—the former proclaiming in brutal terms that might is right, the latter murdering all the men and selling the women and children of neutral Melos into slavery. Then come the proposals to attack Sicily, the memorable picture, full of dramatic irony, of the hopeful departure of the ill-fated Athenian argosy, and the pathetic story of the campaign in Sicily—a story of delay, incompetence, treason, panic, mutiny, the loss of the ships, and the defeat and destruction of the army. The last part of the history, dealing with the Athenian revolution of 411, does not measure up to the rest of the work. Thucydides' fame rests upon his story of the Sicilian expedition, his account of the origins of the war, and a few speeches, notably the one delivered by Pericles in honor of those killed during the first year (Book II, Chaps. 35-46).

Our judgment of Thucydides, however, should not rest upon these sections of the text, but upon the justice of his conception of the history as a whole and the measure of his achievement. On the mastery of his material and his intellectual power, Professor Swain writes as follows:

Never has a historian succeeded better in creating the impression of complete mastery of his materials. Nor has modern criticism shaken this impression: it is of course impossible to check most of Thucydides' statements; occasionally an inscription or other contemporary evidence betrays a slight slip; but a century of hair-splitting criticism has not appreciably impaired his reputation for amazing accuracy. Equally characteristic of Thucydides is his high impartiality: he favors neither side in the great war; he shows good and bad qualities in both Athenians and Spartans, but he never comments upon them; he champions none of the rival parties in Athens; and only in the case of the demagogue Cleon does his Olympian calm forsake him. And yet, if we read attentively, we see how deeply Thucydides felt the tragedy of his native city: we see his hatred of Athenian imperialism, his belief that the follies of the Athenians were responsible for their downfall, his consciousness of their guilt in the case of the Melians and on many other occasions, his humanitarianism and his desire for peace, his admiration of Spartan discipline, and his conviction that Athens was not responsible for the outbreak of the great war. In no place does he argue or defend, yet by sheer intellectual power he imposes his views upon the reader....[5]

The history might perhaps be compared to a Greek statue, stately and serious, restrained and sober, accurate in detail and impressive in composition, yet lacking the vivid coloring and varied background of a modern painting or of Herodotus' history. The whole book centers about one theme, the war: irrelevant digressions such as make the charm of Herodotus are almost entirely lacking, and when Thucydides lets himself go—as he occasionally does for a sentence or two—he does not perceptibly lighten the narrative. The story moves soberly and powerfully along, every episode fitting exactly into its place, comparable perhaps to a troop of hoplites advancing in formation under the leadership of a confident commander.

There is some justice in the remark that the discipline which the author thus imposed upon himself should give satisfaction to

---

[5] As an illustration of his persuasive manner, consider the masterly first book. The reader will probably conclude that innocent Athens fought only because she could not refuse the challenge of her enemies; that Sparta was sincerely devoted to peace; and that the Corinthians were the true aggressors. But if we carefully pick the narrative to pieces and put it together again, we see what Thucydides has done and get a new light on his "impartiality." In a piece of historical writing, arrangement is argument; statements of fact, every one of which is true, can be arranged in many ways; and as some arrangement is always necessary, no historian can be truly "impartial." Suppose that Thucydides had arranged exactly the same materials in a different sequence. Suppose, for instance, that he had adhered closely to the chronological order; that instead of following his preliminary survey of ancient Greece by the Corcyran affair and the formation of the Peloponnesian league against Athens—thus jumping over fifty years—he had followed it immediately by his account of the rise of the Athenian empire, including in the story several of the regrettable incidents which he knew quite well and mentioned in later passages; that instead of simply recording the fact that the Aeginetans "took a leading part in fomenting the war" (Book I, Chap. 67) he had first developed their griefs against Athens as he does several pages later (Book I, Chaps. 105, 108); that he had given more than passing reference to the controversies between Athens and Megara; and that only then had he discussed the activities of the Corinthians and others at Sparta. The reader's opinions on the war-guilt question would then certainly be very different and probably more nearly correct. But then, a thoughtful person, reading the history as it now stands to its end, can scarcely avoid the conclusion that, in Thucydides' opinion, Athenian imperialism, whether it caused the war or not, was a terrible thing and in large measure the cause of the city's woes.

Thucydides

the reader. But, as we have said above, we have as well a sense that, after all, our interest in the world he described is different from that which it stirred in Thucydides, and if the narrative ultimately tires us, it is possible that our weariness is caused less by what is told than by what is left unsaid. Nothing so tires a traveller as to miss the goal of his journey. We can stand long miles of dusty tramping if we are reassured from time to time by glimpses of the delectable mountains. The same is true of mental journeys; fatigue is largely a matter of frustration. And so with Thucydides. The tale he tells is not what we wish most to hear. Its theme is not the greatest in history. Merely as a military event the war was relatively insignificant. Compared with the wars of Rome, of Hun and Teuton, of mediaeval crusaders and modern nations, the struggle between two leagues of city-states has little in itself—merely as war—to attract attention. What makes the Peloponnesian war of lasting interest is not the actual fighting but the issues at stake—Greek civilization and Athenian greatness. Our minds wander from the story of slaughter to what remains untold, the achievements in the art of peace, which alone made the war significant, even for Thucydides.[6] So, if the narrative compels us to follow—and no one can dispute its power—there are seasons when we shoulder the yearly cuirass with reluctance.

As a matter of fact, the greatest theme in history lay right before his eyes, but it was not war; it was the Athens of Pericles and of his own time. There is no glimpse of the Parthenon except as it looms up against the sky where the refugees from Attica watch the flames of Spartan pillagers in their homes. Although the drama of Athens furnished at least the suggestions of the mould in which he made his manual of warfare into the tragedy of Hellas, Thucydides makes no overt allusion to that drama. There is a proud consciousness all the time that the Acropolis is there and that the art and literature of Athens are a shining model to the world, but all references to them are severely sup-

---

[6] Cf. Book I, Chap. 11: "Poverty was the real reason why the achievements of former ages were insignificant" [and the Peloponnesian war so much more important than the Trojan, etc.].

pressed, as not being germane to the subject. Only once does Athens really come into the history, the Athens to which subsequent ages looked back with such wonder and despair—and that is in the funeral oration of Pericles. This is enough, however, to show what we have lost in the refusal of Thucydides to write the history of a people instead of the history of a war. No city ever received a prouder tribute or one more eloquent. It does not describe the monuments, it adds another to them; for it stands like a solitary block of prose, set in the midst of the tragedy of war—a Parthenon itself, hewn to enshrine not the myth goddess of the city but the human spirit of its citizens.

An orthodoxy of appreciation surrounds the works of the old masters in any art; the heretics "fail to understand." But heresy has a moral if not an artistic justification, and we must register the disappointment of the reader of Thucydides who comes to him in the hope of finding in his pages a living picture of the cities which waged the war. To be sure, he did not write for us; he wrote for Athenians, or at least for Greeks, and they took for granted what we wish most to know. But the fact remains that the work lacks for us its central theme. Much has been made recently of the influence of the tragedy of Aeschylus upon the form into which Thucydides threw the materials of his history. It is claimed that this was as much a model to him—consciously or unconsciously—as the epic was to Herodotus. But for the modern audience the rules of the tragedy seem strangely violated. We are continually behind the wings where the killing is in progress. The principals, too, seem to move across the stage at times from insufficient motives, a single speech of rather obvious remarks determining the policy of a city. The real reasons for much of the intricacy of the drama remain undiscovered. We miss a good chorus, made up, if possible, of the business men from the Piraeus, who might explain, if Thucydides did not disdain their foreign accent, the real causes of the war and of the policies of Athens—in terms of economics.

We should not be tempted to elaborate the shortcomings of Thucydides from the standpoint of the modern reader, if it were not for the fact that writers on Greek literature and even historians who should know better, in their enthusiasm over the magisterial performance where the scientific spirit dominates as nowhere else in antique history, give the impression to the student that if he does not find the *History of the Peloponnesian War* completely satisfying his heart's desire, the fault is all his own. There is no fault; there are merely intervening centuries. A work of genius may be universal and for all time; but the form in which it is embodied bears the marks of the local and temporary. This is always true, more or less. In art, as in nature, immortality is of the spirit. That spirit, in Thucydides, was poised in Hellenic balance, between science and art, a model for all time; but the work which it produced shows the limitations of outlook and material which definitely stamp it as antique. To see in the author of the *Peloponnesian War* a "modern of moderns,"[7] facing history as we do, equipped with the understanding of the forces of history such as the historian of today possesses, is to indulge in an anachronism almost as naïve as the failure to appreciate Thucydides because he lacks it! There is a world of difference between the outlook of a citizen of Periclean Athens—however keen and just his judgment, however free from superstition and credulity—and that of a modern thinker supplied with the apparatus for scientific investigation. The whole history of Europe lies this side of Thucydides, and it would be strange indeed if the historian of today had learned nothing from its experience, especially from the nineteenth and twentieth centuries, which have contributed at the same time the implements of historical research and the widened outlook of the social sciences. Yet such is the spell which the spirit of Thucydides still exerts that even Eduard Meyer, the historian who has perhaps done most to reconstruct antique history in the light of those forces which the Greek ignored, is led to assert that there is only one way to handle the problem of history, that which Thucydides first used and in which no one has ever surpassed him.[8]

Were Thucydides alive today, we venture to think that he

[7] Th. Gomperz, *Greek Thinkers* (4 vols., tr. 1901-1912), I, 503.
[8] E. Meyer, "Zur Theorie und Methodik der Geschichte," in *Kleine Schriften* (1910), p. 67.

would be the first to dissent from this judgment, or at least from the general implications involved as to the character of his work. The historian who passed such impatient strictures upon Herodotus would certainly not rest content now with his own performance. There are at least four major elements in his history which he would now recast. In the first place he would have to admit his inability to grapple with the past. He lacked both the implements for dealing with it and a sense of its bearings upon the present. In the second place he failed to give an adequate picture of Greek politics, keeping too close to the definite politics of the war to catch its working as a whole, and he lacked a sense of those economic forces which give significance to the arts of peace. Finally, he put the political and diplomatic elements of his story into the form of speeches by the leading characters—a device common to all antique historians, but one which violates the primary laws of historical work today.

Let us take up these points, hurriedly, in turn. We have said that Thucydides was not at home in dealing with the past; yet his short introduction to the history of Greece before his day was a unique performance. The paradox is not difficult to explain. His sketch of early Greek history is remarkable mainly for what it leaves out. It does not fall into the common fault of early historians, that of romancing. It does not exaggerate as poets and chroniclers did. A skeptical spirit and sound common sense kept Thucydides from yielding to that greatest of all temptations to the storyteller, making a point by stretching the tale. To the antique historian this was much more of a temptation than it can ever be again, for there was little chance that his audience would find him out. When the modern historian tells a great story he is at once asked for his sources, and before the book is fairly started on its career a dozen other historians are on his track, busily verifying the account. In the days of Herodotus and Thucydides, the past was well-nigh unexplored, and the traveller who did not bring back from its dim horizons some trophy of what might have been would miss the applause which he might otherwise so easily win. Thucydides cared nothing for such applause and proudly broke with those who did. He sought the truth because he wished it, not because his readers were clamoring for it; yet his imagination caught the reward of future centuries, when, as he foresaw, his history would be as imperishable as the truth which it contained.

But there is a world of difference between denying the fabulous in the past and appreciating the importance of the obscure. Because the past lacked greatness Thucydides thought it unworthy of his attention. He states his negative conclusions in no uncertain terms: "Judging from the evidence which I am able to trust after most careful enquiry, I should imagine that former ages were not great either in their wars or in anything else" (Book I, Chap. 1). By "former ages" he includes everything down to his own day. Even Salamis had its touch of pettiness; the Greek ships were partly open-decked (Book I, Chap. 14). Compared with the great age in which he lived, all that had gone before seemed poor and insignificant, and therefore, once having convinced himself that this was so, he ignored the past as much as possible. His judgment may have been justified by the achievements of the Athens of his time; but the perspective is, all the same, a barren one so far as history is concerned, for his narrative was limited to the events of his own day. The modern historian has no such outlook. Although he lives in an age incomparably more wonderful in many ways than that of Thucydides, he knows better than to despise the past. On the contrary, he turns all the more to the study of what is obscure in the detail of former civilizations. He does so not to supply lessons to statesmen, which was the main purpose of Thucydides, but from the conviction, forced home by science, that only through a knowledge of how things came about can we understand what they are. Thucydides, in spite of his contempt for the past, thought that the future would be like the present, and had no idea of growth or development, or of the importance of time. The modern historian, on the other hand, has a vision of the eternal linking of past and present, of the progressive creation of evolving societies, which no antique man could possibly have seen. The insignificant gains significance when fitted into such a scheme, just as each stone is necessary in a temple wall. Science builds up its structures out of the neglected data of the commonplace and historians have learned from it never to despise a past, however obscure it seems; for its fragmentary evidence may furnish the clue to the recovery of some vanished civilization or the explanation of otherwise inexplicable elements in a later one.

The fact is that where science has thus determined the outlook of the modern historian, poetry determined that of Thucydides. He would have vigorously denied it, but the case is clear. The epic—or perhaps dramatic—ideal of a great story of great deeds found its way into his ideal of history as well, in spite of all his "scientific" pretensions. The contrast between this and the scientific outlook escapes us, because historians have generally followed the same poetic tendencies down even to our own time, seizing great themes under a sense that they alone were worthy of great histories. Now, however, the men of scientific temper see things differently. They find their theme just where the great masters refused to look—in such a past as that which Thucydides ignored because it was "not great either in wars or in anything else." The result is that, for the first time, history is disclosing its hidden perspectives and the past is taking on some of the color of reality.

Thucydides failed to appreciate these things not from any personal limitations, but because he lived before a scientific study of society was possible. He had the scientific temper, but science demands more than individual genius; it rests upon the coöperative work of many minds, amassing data and preparing implements for others still to use. It is a social phenomenon, indeed the most highly socialized there is, for the economics of the search for truth encounters no such individualistic tendencies as the economics of the search for wealth. So the investigator of today has ready at his disposal a vast array of facts already established and duly classified. Thucydides had no such heritage. He had an archaeologist's eye for the use of monuments as historical sources, for he observed the broken fragments of pillars in the walls of Athens and quoted the fact as a vivid proof of his account of

Thucydides

how those walls were rebuilt after the Persian war.[9] He even used inscriptions when they came his way. But it is a long step from such antiquarian interest—promising as it is—to the systematic investigation of monuments. He could only speculate as to the wealth of Agamemnon, little suspecting that the treasure chambers of Mycenae lay waiting for a spade. Minos was to him but a name from the borderland of legend and history; now the excavations of Cnossus have made it a term in scientific chronology. No prophecy of genius could foretell that, when the search was wide enough and the implements for it sufficiently perfected, the merest trifles of antiquity would take on the significance of historical records; that bits of tombstones and scraps of papyri would enable us to reconstruct the history of vanished centuries or help us to correct the narrative of great historians.

But the chief handicap of the antique historian, in dealing with the past, was an absence of exact chronology. It is hard for us to realize what a handicap this was. Yet the more we examine the history of history the more it becomes apparent that until time was measured it was not appreciated. We have already seen that it took many ages of Babylonian and later Egyptian history for the mathematics of the calendar to straighten out the tangles of days, months, and years, until a systematic chronology became possible. In the Greece of Thucydides' day, the problem had not yet been solved, and the perspective of the past was, as a result, blurred and uncertain. The only historian who had attempted to open it up, by a systematic chronology of Athens, was Hellanicus, and Thucydides soon discovered how unreliable his reckoning was. But it is a remarkable fact that he did not try to correct or improve upon it. He frankly gave up the problem, and fell back upon the most primitive of all methods of reckoning time, that of the old farmer's calendar of the seasons. Summer and winter are all he needs, the summer for fighting, the winter for politics. This

[9] He likewise had a valuable skepticism regarding monuments, which modern archaeologists sometimes lack, as is witnessed by his remark that if nothing but ruins of the two cities remained, men would be very loath to believe that Sparta once ruled half the Peloponnesus but would double the actual power of Athens (Book I, Chap. 10).

is all he needs for the greatest war of antiquity.[10] Beyond those passing years lay obscurity—and relative insignificance. Unlike the historian of today, he saw no long perspectives of the marshalled centuries; instead, he looked but vaguely into "the abysm and gulf of Time," and its darkness almost enveloped the events of his own day.

If Thucydides lacked the prime qualification of a modern historian in his failure to handle time perspectives, his choice of subject bears as well the marks of the limitations of the antique. He had no doubt but that war was the one and proper subject of history. Had this been true, and had the Peloponnesian war been, as he believed it was, the greatest of wars, his work would rank without a rival among the achievements of historians. For the very sternness with which he kept to his theme instead of offering us picturesque details of Greek society, as Herodotus would have done, would be in his favor. Yet even here, a merit may easily develop into a fault. Thucydides did more than cut out the digressions of a storyteller; [11] he concentrated upon the war so intently as not only to exaggerate its importance—the very fault he found with the poets and chroniclers before him—but even to weld the

[10] The comment of Thucydides upon his use of this easy-going method of reckoning time is worth quoting. "Ten years, with a difference of a few days, had passed since the invasion of Attica and the commencement of the war. I would have a person reckon the actual periods of time, and not rely upon catalogues of the archons or other official personages whose names may be used in different cities to mark the dates of past events. For whether an event occurred in the beginning or in the middle, or whatever might be the exact point, of a magistrate's term of office is left uncertain by such a mode of reckoning. But if he measure by summers and winters as they are here set down, and count each summer and winter as a half year, he will find that ten summers and ten winters passed in the first part of the war" (Book V, Chap. 20). This undoubtedly has its advantage for contemporary reckoning; but Thucydides failed to see that the calendar of the war had also to be set in the chronicle of centuries.

[11] It would be an interesting speculation to imagine Herodotus writing the history of the Peloponnesian war. We should know much more of the history of Greece. Thucydides holds himself so closely to the war itself that there are only four digressions of any length in the whole history after he once gets through the introduction. Because he plunges into the war itself (Book I, Chap. 23) at the opening of his narrative, he reverts, in an excursus, to the history of Athens since the Persian war (Book I, Chaps. 89-118). In addition to this he inserts a short account of affairs in Thrace (Book II, Chaps. 96-101), a description of Sicily (Book VI, Chaps. 1-5), and a criticism of the received tradition of the overthrow of the house of Peisistratus (Book VI, Chaps. 54-59). In each place Herodotus would have been tempted to insert a book.

Thucydides

interrupted struggles of the Athenian and Spartan leagues into one and to give the impression that the attention of Greece of his time centred as exclusively upon the war as did his own. Thucydides has even been accused of inventing the war he narrates—in the opinion of his contemporaries there were two or three separate and distinct wars, which he unites into one—and undoubtedly he cherished a fixed idea concerning it; for, as he tells us in the opening sentence, he foresaw its significance from the first, a confession which shows the limitations of his outlook—which is after all but another name for a biased mind. So, although subsequent events to a large degree justified his foresight and approved his perspective, there was perhaps some manipulation of the data to make the continuity clear and to ensure that the national tragedy develop as a tragedy should.[12]

Fortunately, even the story of a war extends beyond the field of battle; it includes as well the politics of the combatants. For one must listen to the speeches in council and watch the moving of the public mind to explain the formation of alliances and the plan of campaigns. So Thucydides interspersed his account of military operations with a history of politics. Indeed he seems to have expended upon it more elaborate care than upon the details of fighting. This, in the eyes of most of his critics, serves at once to distinguish him from all his predecessors. He had left behind the tales of heroes which still evoked the storytelling qualities of Herodotus. Poets and chroniclers "who write to please the ear" are scornfully dismissed for a study of statecraft and generalship. But this is not a history of Greek politics; it is only a history

[12] F. M. Cornford, *Thucydides Mythistoricus* (1907), Part II. Professor Swain comments upon this book as follows: "This book appeared some thirty years ago, and it precipitated a controversy which has not yet died down. Some praised its brilliancy and proclaimed its epoch-making character; others disparaged it with such epithets as 'quaint' and 'smart-aleck.' The book contains three quite separate things. It gives an account of the origins of the Peloponnesian War written in economic terms; this part is full of exaggerations but is valuable as a corrective to earlier views. It puts forward the thesis that Thucydides consciously or unconsciously derived his literary and moral patterns from the tragedies of Aeschylus; here it is unconvincing. And it contains any number of acute comments upon historical writing in general and upon Thucydides in particular, many of which the reader will find enlightening and stimulating. It is the most brilliant work upon Thucydides that has appeared during the present century, but it must be used with extreme caution."

of the politics of the war. The student of history finds in Thucydides almost as little light upon the general character of political constitutions of Greek states as the student of culture does of their life and thought.[13]

We shall, of course, be reminded that Thucydides should not be held responsible for these omissions, for he was not writing constitutional or cultural history. But that is just the point we wish to make. The scope of Thucydides is limited by that of a war which few of us would care to follow—in detail—were it not that the genius of the author holds us to the task, like some inexorable tutor with whom one reads for imaginary examinations. Discipline and profit accrue to the reader, and the text is one of the noblest products of antiquity; but it fails to answer the questions we have most at heart.

The chief trend in this story of politics, however, is a tendency to look to personal motives for causes. To Thucydides this was a world where men willed and wrought, of their own account, through applied intelligence or the impulse of passion and met success or frustration on their own ground. Fortune ($\tau \dot{\upsilon} \chi \eta$) was the unknown quantity, the "x" in the problem; but it was conceived in terms of religion, not of business. It was the inexplicable Power, the Providence beyond the reckoning of history, the Luck which rules the primitive world, decked with the regalia of philosophic mysticism. Thucydides had no idea that Fortune, this substitute for the caprice of the gods, was interested in the price of commodities. Conceiving it in terms of mystery, he noted its action but did not try to explain; for there was no explanation. With us Fortune still plays its major role, but it suggests economics and invites investigation, for it is mainly a synonym for wealth. The very element in history which meant mystery to Thucydides is therefore offering to us the first glimpses of natural law in a natural instead of a spiritual world—the laws of supply and demand and all their implications.

The shortcomings of Thucydides in this matter should not be overstated, for it would be absurd to the point of the grotesque

---

[13] To be sure the modern historian finds much illumination from many passages. But they are mainly incidental in the narrative.

Thucydides

to expect from him an economic interpretation of history. The economic interpretation of history is a very recent thing; it has not yet eliminated the mystery of the individual will and is not likely soon to do so. But it is just as absurd to claim for Thucydides a modern comprehension of universal laws for man and nature and to regard his narrative as one conceived in the enlightenment of modern science. Moreover, Thucydides went further in this direction than any other thinker of antiquity and, primarily in the speeches, dealt with the motivation of political forces.

The result of our survey is the conclusion that the greatest historian of antiquity was uncertain in two of the major requirements of the modern historian: on the one hand, the mastery of time perspectives, the unravelling of the past; on the other hand, the measurement of the forces material and social which modify, if they do not govern, the course of human events. This does not detract from the greatness of his performance; it could not have been otherwise. He did not have the chance to measure economic forces or chronology; the implements for doing so did not then exist.

We must constantly remind ourselves that Thucydides seemed to himself to stand on the very threshold of history. Behind him lay a past which, in comparison with ours, was unimaginably meagre. From beyond the Grecian seas had come nothing but travellers' tales of the eastern wonderland. Within the tiny Hellenic world itself, the slender current of history flashed only here and there a broken gleam through the tangled overgrowth of legend and gorgeous flowers of poetry....[14]

There was nothing to do with such a past but to leave it aside and turn to his great journalistic enterprise of saving the world of fact in which he lived. Skepticism might keep him free from credulity, but it could not forge the tools for investigation.

In short, the mind of Thucydides was neither primitive nor modern; it was antique. No recognition of modern tendencies or capacities should blind us to its limitations. It moved with the precision of supreme self-consciousness, but within narrow confines both of time and space—and by unknown frontiers. To quote Cornford again:

[14] F. M. Cornford, *Thucydides Mythistoricus*, p. 76.

Thucydides lived at the one moment in recorded history which has seen a brilliantly intellectual society, nearly emancipated from a dying religion, and at the same time unaided by science, as yet hardly born. Nowhere but in a few men of that generation shall we find so much independence of thought combined with such destitute poverty in the apparatus and machinery of thinking.... We must rid our minds of scientific terminology as well as of religion and philosophy, if we are to appreciate the unique detachment of Thucydides' mind, moving in the rarest of atmospheres between the old age and the new. Descartes, for all his efforts, was immeasurably less free from metaphysical preoccupation; Socrates appears, in comparison, superstitious.[15]

Finally, there is one element in Thucydides' work which bears the mark of the antique on its face—the speeches which he put into the mouths of his leading characters, and into which he compressed most of the politics and diplomacy of his history. Nothing could be more unmodern than this device. Imagine a Ranke inventing or even elaborating orations for modern statesmen and then embodying them into his narrative! One cannot supply speeches for historical characters unless one has the text, and where the Thucydides of antiquity labored most, the Thucydides of today would give up the task. Even from the standpoint of art, the speeches seem now incongruous and unreal. As Macaulay said of them, "They give to the whole book something of the grotesque character of those Chinese pleasure-grounds, in which perpendicular rocks of granite start up in the midst of a soft green plain. Invention is shocking where truth is in such close juxtaposition with it."[16]

But we must not be too sure of our judgment, either of the antique or of the Chinese. Each must be judged in its own environment. Certainly no one in ancient Greece or Rome could have guessed that a historian would ever object to the writing of orations as a legitimate part of historical narrative. Speechmaking in storytelling is as old as story. It is natural in all primitive narration. All good storytellers put words into the mouths of their heroes. They do this, not as conscious artifice, but simply because their minds work naturally in dramatic mimicry—the mimicry which is a direct legacy from the most primitive form

[15] *Ibid.*, pp. 73, 74.
[16] "Essay on History."

of thought and its expression. This is the explanation of much of what seems to us either naïve or questionable in the Old Testament, where the words of the patriarchs and of Jahveh are given in direct narration by authors of a millennium later than the recorded conversations. There, however, as in Herodotus, the general background of the story was in tone with such primitive dramatizing. In Thucydides the case is different; his mind did not naturally work like that of a gossip or a raconteur, by the impersonation of others. He kept to the old devices and made up speeches to suit his story. The content does not suit the form, and in the ears of a modern the thing rings false; but yet he left us, besides the story of war, a picture of the leadership of men, of great speakers swaying the passions of uncertain crowds, of councils listening to the thrusts of keen debate. If we are always conscious, as we look at these scenes, that we see them through the eyes of an interpreter, we at least have the satisfaction of knowing that our interpreter was, of all who saw them, the one best fitted to transmit them to posterity.

It follows from what has just been said that the speeches were not inserted by Thucydides for mere rhetorical effect, as the quotation from the stylist Macaulay might seem to imply. It was primarily in them that he set forth his philosophy of history. Professor Swain has commented happily upon them as follows:

Thucydides was convinced that ideas are a tremendously important force in history; in that conviction he followed the best Greek tradition. He therefore felt it necessary to portray the state of mind which prevailed at various times. Sometimes he attempted an objective description of this mentality, as when he described the effects of the plague or the revolutionary mentality at Corcyra; sometimes he tried to awaken memories in the reader's mind, as when he described the sailing of the Athenian argosy for Syracuse; and sometimes he put words into the mouths of important people to show what everybody was thinking. It did not matter exactly what disease decimated the Athenians, but the resulting state of mind was very important, and he described it brilliantly; the glowing patriotism expressed in Pericles' funeral oration and the exuberant optimism symbolized by the Syracusan expedition, rather than the intrigues of foreign merchants at Piraeus, were the forces that made the war go on; and the imperialistic mentality which made possible the outrageous conduct of the Athenians in Melos brought the fall of the city. Perhaps Thucydides' methods of depicting these states of mind are not always the most effective with modern readers, accustomed to stenographic reports and footnote references; but few modern historians, with all their advantages, have done better. At any rate, the speeches are the very heart of the book, and it is hard to think of any device by which Thucydides could more effectively have done what he was trying to do. And the mere fact that imitators in succeeding centuries exaggerated this aspect of his work in grotesque fashion should not keep us from appreciating the skill with which he himself performed the task.

A word or two might also be said in criticism of Thucydides' critics. His philosophy of history was not popular in the second half of the nineteenth century, which is probably one reason for many of the attacks upon him and upon the speeches in which he best set forth this philosophy. In these later days it was fashionable to sneer at ideas, to call oratory impotent, and to declare with Bismarck that it is not by speeches and parliamentary resolutions that great things are accomplished, but by blood and iron! This philosophy was shared by the historians of the day—most of whom worshipped, mouth agape, at the shrine of the Iron Chancellor—who liked to think of history as determined by "real" things, such as blood and iron or coal and iron; some of them rather effectively expended huge numbers of words in proving that words are never effective. In our own day we can perhaps notice the beginning of a change away from this attitude. Historians rightly spend great care in the study of economic statistics, but they also study the editorial and news-doctoring policies of the daily press. Moreover, if we pause for a moment to reflect, we see that the celebrated reference to blood and iron was itself nothing more than a very effective—one might almost say, a terribly effective—piece of Bismarckian bombast. Had Thucydides omitted the speeches he would have given a falser impression of what happened than would a modern historian writing an account of America's part in the World War with no mention of Woodrow Wilson's speeches about making the world safe for democracy or of the Fourteen Points. Of course Thucydides was unable—as he points out himself—to give the exact words used by the speakers, but he did the best he could. A modern historian can and must use different methods to set forth the idealistic forces at work in peace and war, but if he fails to do so—tacitly assuming that all men, or at least all leaders, are either caricatures of the "economic man" of classical economists or else mere fools—he gives a very false history of his period. Thucydides, careful student of society that he was, realized better than his critics, and tried to show in his history, that ideas are a prime force in human affairs. And he wrote his book to encourage certain ideas and to make clear the terrible consequences of others.

Thucydides

Thucydides began his history with the expression of haughty scorn for the tales of poets in the youth of Hellas; prose, not poetry, is the medium for truth. With this judgment the modern critic agrees, and prosy historians have found in it much consolation and encouragement. But prose in the hands of Thucydides was not a bare shroud upon dead facts to ensure them decent burial in ponderous books; it was a work of art in itself, as nervous with life and energy when moving with the war bands or the fleet as it was keyed to the eloquence of Athenian oratory when dealing with politics and diplomacy. His work was the result of long and painstaking researches—at times he breaks his impersonal reserve to tell us so—but he did not consider it complete until the elements of which it was composed were worked over so as to lose their outlines in the structure of the whole. Unlike Herodotus he tried to obliterate his sources in the interest of art.[17] Fortunately the art was noble enough to compensate for the loss of the materials and secured for the facts themselves an immortality which they alone could never have attained. But there was danger in this polishing of text. Thucydides himself was not the victim of rhetoric; he lived and wrote before the schoolmen had fettered language into styles, and he could hardly have surmised that the very passages upon which he concentrated the mastery of his art would exemplify a tendency hardly less fatal to history than the naïve credulity of the early poets, a tendency to sacrifice substance for form—in prose. How real the danger was, the subsequent chapters of antique historiography show. But Thucydides stands out in as strong contrast against the age of rhetoric as against that of poetry. In him the antique spirit is revealed at its best; but it was antique.

[17] So definitely is this the case that one can readily detect where his hand had not given the final touch.

CHAPTER XVI

Rhetoric and Scholarship

THUCYDIDES left no such impress upon subsequent Greek historians as might have been expected. He remained a great name; but few read and fewer imitated him. His severe yet lofty style and his passion for the truth were foreign to the taste of the age that followed.[1] For although history did not revert to poetry, it passed into the field of rhetoric, where the ideal was a striving for effect rather than for fact. It was not until in the first century B.C., when the old Greek classics were revived, that Thucydides became once more an influence, or, rather, an ideal. But to trace this farther carries us to Rome. Moreover between Thucydides and the rhetoricians lay another historian, known to all those who even begin the study of Greek, to whom we must now turn, though only for a hurried glance.

Alongside Herodotus and Thucydides, the ancients placed Xenophon, the three forming the trio of great Greek historians. Modern criticism has a much lower opinion of Xenophon. Soldier of fortune, student of philosophy, intimately acquainted with the men and events of an age fateful both for Greece and for the history of the world, he caught no gleam of its larger meaning, gained no sense of the causes and little appreciation of the results of the happenings he chronicled. The sudden fall of Sparta, for instance, he attributed not to its own rather obvious faults, but to the direct action of the gods. Neither Greek nor Persian history was clear to him in its tendencies and significance.

To quote the discriminating judgment of Professor Bury:

[1] J. B. Bury, following Wilamowitz-Möllendorff, points out that it was not an age favorable to the composition of political history in any case. The engrossing intellectual interest was then political science. And one need only look into the treatises on political science written by the theorist today to see how history suffers.

In history as in philosophy he was a dilettante.... He had a happy literary talent, and his multifarious writings, taken together, render him an interesting figure in Greek literature. But his mind was essentially mediocre, incapable of penetrating beneath the surface of things. If he had lived in modern days, he would have been a high-class journalist and pamphleteer; he would have made his fortune as a war-correspondent; and would have written the life of some mediocre hero of the stamp of Agesilaus. So far as history is concerned, his true vocation was to write memoirs. The *Anabasis* is a memoir, and it is the most successful of his works. It has the defects which memoirs usually have, but it has the merits, the freshness, the human interest of a personal document. The adventures of the Ten Thousand are alive forever in Xenophon's pages.[2]

This adverse judgment of the modern critic would seem to leave Xenophon but slight claim to consideration in a history of history. But we cannot get rid of him with quite so summary a dismissal. For the historical, as contrasted with the purely biographical, treatment demands of us that we keep in mind not simply the appraisal of his work today, but also the opinions of the successive generations of readers who have rendered a verdict different from ours. The very contrast between the high regard in which Xenophon was held by the ancients and the slight esteem of his modern critics is itself a fact of real significance—perhaps the most significant one which the work of Xenophon presents for us. To Cicero, for instance, and to the great cultured world for which he spoke—and still speaks—Xenophon was one of the world's classics. Why?

First of all there was his style, graphic, entertaining, harmonious, "sweeter than honey" as Cicero said, not heavy with ill-assorted facts nor dulled by too much philosophy. But apart from style, there was his happy gift of portraiture and his descriptive concreteness. If he failed to get at the inner connection of events, he brought out all the more the personality of the individual leaders. And after all, it is a fair question in some stages of history whether the events that offer themselves to the narrator are as much worth considering as the characters of the actors. However unenlightened Xenophon may have been as to the processes

[2] J. B. Bury, *The Ancient Greek Historians*, pp. 151-52.

of history, as a memoir writer he contributed largely to the little there was of that high-class journalism which draws its charm from an interest in people. The appreciation of Xenophon by the ancients was therefore based upon real qualities, and, although they are insufficient to enable him to hold his place in the present, when the standards of history reflect the wider vision of the social sciences and demand a control of causal perspectives, still they are qualities which endure.

Xenophon was born about the opening of the Peloponnesian war and died when the power of Macedonia was already threatening to close the last troubled era of Greek freedom (c. 430–354 B.C.). As a young Athenian noble he became a disciple of Socrates and preserved his "recollections" (*Memorabilia*) of his teacher in four books, which present the homely detail recorded by an observer rather than by a thinker and the less abstruse side of Socrates' philosophy. It is unfortunate for him that Plato's account lies alongside to invite comparison. Very few historians, not to mention journalists, would measure up well with such a rival. As it is, however, the *Memorabilia* is an invaluable human document. It also affords precious glimpses of the social life of the time. But though this unenlightened pupil of Socrates failed to get at the inner connections of events, he brought out all the more the personality of the individual leaders.

Of vastly different content is the *Anabasis,* a narrative of the war of Cyrus the Younger against Artaxerxes, his royal brother, and of the retreat of the Ten Thousand Greek mercenaries in the service of Cyrus. Xenophon was elected their general after the death of Cyrus, and his narrative—the best known manual to beginners of the study of Greek—remains a clear picture of the marching soldiers and of the hinterland through which they passed. Moreover, his description of places and his geography generally have the merit—rarer than one would suspect—of being relatively accurate.

The formal effort of Xenophon at the writing of history, however, was not the *Anabasis* but the *Hellenica,* an attempt to carry on the history of Thucydides—completing the Peloponnesian war from the autumn of 411 B.C. and terminating at Mantinea in

362. But it is very unlike Thucydides, in both outlook and style. It moves in lively narrative and, where a bare story of intricate events would pall, it interjects personal descriptions drawn to the life. Indeed, so well are these done that the reader's interest is kept stimulated where otherwise it would flag. So, although there is an undue proportion of this descriptive material, it is so successfully handled as almost to turn a defect into a merit. There was an excuse as well in the theme itself. It lacked that large, compelling epic quality which lay inherent in the Persian wars of Herodotus and that dramatic unity which Thucydides revealed in the struggle against Athenian supremacy. The pattern of Greek history was becoming more puzzling, the isolation of even the more inland states was giving way, and their interaction was becoming more varied. If a Thucydides failed to estimate the economic forces behind the fortunes and policies of his time, Xenophon should not be blamed too much for sharing the weakness of all antiquity in this regard. The *Hellenica* was written while he was in exile from Athens and presents the later history of Greece from the Spartan point of view. The Peloponnesians were having their day, as the Athenians had had theirs when Thucydides wrote. But the times were no longer great. When one recalls what Sparta was—its arid intellectual soil, its unadjustable hardness, its parochial militarism—one is surely justified in tempering justice with charity in judging the limitations of outlook shown by a writer living under its domination; even if, beyond the narrowing horizon of politics and culture, he could, looking back, recall the inspiration of a great adventure with ten thousand Greeks in Asia, or, better still, could treasure as a lasting possession the personal memories of Socrates.

In spite of what has just been said, the fact remains that Xenophon was one of those historians who, by writing history, helped to make it. At the time when intellectuals like Isocrates were looking for someone against whom a successful war might be waged, in order to promote Greek unity, statesmen like Philip of Macedon and Alexander were not likely to miss the point conveyed in Xenophon's writings that the Persians of his day were utterly decadent. Supplemented, of course, by other evidence and propaganda, there was that in Xenophon's writings which encouraged the kings of Macedon to turn their forces against the East. It was not merely the march of the Ten Thousand, but also Xenophon's brilliant and popular description of it which prepared the way for Alexander. Professor Swain says:

> Thucydides wrote his history to instruct statesmen and others who might wish to know the social consequences of given acts, but it is extremely doubtful whether anyone ever learned statesmanship from him. Xenophon was less ambitious, and his history has been roughly handled by the nineteenth-century admirers of Thucydides, from Niebuhr through Grote and Freeman to Bury; but his historical writings —like those of many moderns (Michelet, Treitschke, Froude) who have failed to win the highest academic approval—were a factor in determining the subsequent course of human events.

Between Xenophon and Polybius we come upon a period, difficult for us to appreciate justly, which has been termed the age of the rhetorician.[3] The very name is forbidding. Formal rhetoric not only repels the scientist, it has even lost its charm as an art. We find it hard to be patient with mere words when we have so rich a world of real experience to draw upon, and few who study the evolution of history can repress condemnation of the pupils of Isocrates. The condemnation is justified from the standpoint of science; rhetoric played too great a role in the antique culture, and facts too little. But the historian of history must temper his condemnation or run the risk of becoming unhistorical. Given the antique world as it was, he should not expect it to achieve the modern method. The art of Demosthenes was as fitting and as noble an expression of the maturity of Greek genius as was the Homeric epic of its youth. From the standpoint of science, the Greek mind was always hampered by its art. This was true of a philosopher like Plato and a historian like Thucydides; it could hardly fail to be true, in a different sense, of those who lived in an age when the great creations of that art were already their heritage.

[3] R. C. Jebb, *The Attic Orators from Antiphon to Isæus* (2 vols., 1876; 2d ed., 1893).

Rhetoric and Scholarship

Rhetoric is to us largely a subject for school children, and is branded in later life with the scorn of things immature; but the Greek ideal was not altogether vain. The great art of expression by words is surely as worthy of one's study as arts which live in color or stone. At once plastic and monumental, preserving the form and color of reality by the choice of the clear-cut word or the finely moulded phrase, rhetoric elevates the prose of literature to replace the vanishing art of poetry. Its field in antiquity, however, was limited. The ancient city lacked the varied scope of modern journalism; its interests were mainly local, and its literature was spoken rather than written. In a country where the theatre took the place of our libraries, and where even philosophy was largely dialogue, it was but natural that rhetoric should, in its higher forms, tend to be practically a synonym for oratory.[4] Moreover, oratory, in a Greek city, was a real force. The arena of politics was hardly larger than the amphitheatre or the agora, and it was possible to control it almost as definitely by the voice and personality of a speaker. But oratory was not confined to politics. It was an art cultivated for itself, like music today, and "people went to hear an oratorical display just as we go to hear a symphony."[5] It was therefore inevitable that speechmaking should overrun the narrative of history and the play upon language overrun speechmaking; as inevitable as that the histories of the nineteenth century should be couched so largely in the terms of national politics, or those of the twentieth should include the survey of economics and the sciences. The invention of orations in history, which, as we have seen, has its origins in primitive storytelling, and which Thucydides took over from his predecessors as a natural part of his expression, became, in the age which followed, a definite part of the historian's trade, and not more in Greece than in Rome, which was to receive much of its education at the hands of the Greek rhetor. So Livy clogged his moving narrative with long discourses, and even Caesar, orator as well as soldier, would halt the charge, as it were, to

---

[4] On the other hand, the rhetor's work in the general art or discipline of speaking was almost synonymous with education.
[5] J. B. Bury, *The Ancient Greek Historians*, p. 174.

deliver through the mouth of the general some unnecessary harangue.

Yet, as we have seen in the case of Thucydides, what seems to us artifice was often genuine art. The orations which are now so futile and unreal gave to the antique mind the very reflection of reality. We must judge the antique historian only by living through the politics of agora or forum in the small Mediterranean cities where the living voice was both journalism and literature, and where the destiny of a state might at any time be decided by the power of a ringing speech. Yet one may carry the historic imagination too far and excuse too much. The rhetoric which brought popularity to the historian of the third century B.C. brought him just as surely the neglect of later times.

Formal rhetoric, however, did not limit itself to the speeches. Such obvious devices did perhaps less damage to historiography than the general tendency which they represented to sacrifice accuracy for effect. History, at best a poor enough mirror of reality, is readily warped by art; and rhetoric is art of the most formal kind. It distorts into ordered arrangement the haphazard, unformed materials which chance produces or preserves. It sets its pieces like an impresario and completes with convincing elegance the abrupt and incomplete dramas of reality. All history writing does this to some degree, since it is art. But rhetoric passes easily over into the sphere of conscious distortion. A phrase is worth a fact, and facts must fit the liking of the audience, or serve to point a moral. As few facts in reality do lend themselves readily to these moral and aesthetic purposes, the rhetorician readjusts the story to his needs.[6]

We must be careful, however, not to allow the trend away from rhetoric in the present day to blind us to the fundamental purposes of those Greeks who used it to become the schoolmasters of the antique world. Their purpose was at bottom the same as that of Thucydides, to instruct their readers by the lessons which thoughtful men might draw from history. It was a moral purpose, rather than merely an aesthetic ideal, which dominated the

---

[6] W. v. Christ, *Geschichte der griechischen Litteratur* (5th ed., 1908-1913), II, 228-35, 348-67.

Rhetoric and Scholarship

later Greek historians. The delight of a Cicero in the mastery of speech must not blind us to the fact that even for the orator, the criterion of success was the ability to sway the mind of his listener towards some chosen end. In the eyes of an unsympathetic and critical age, the rhetoricians overplayed their hand, but after all, they had something to say. This at least is true of those who wrote history. The trend was not toward art for art's sake, but toward education.

As we have just indicated, this trend was nothing new in the history of history. The earliest historians had used their art for the entertainment of the primitive mind, and entertainment remains a constant purpose in all good historical writing. But the border between it and instruction is illusive. The Homeric tales which thrilled their listeners by a recital of great deeds also led them to emulate the exploits of the heroes. There were no primitive psychologists conscious of the fact that the pleasure of listening was due partly to the way in which the listeners made of the recital a school for valor as they identified themselves with the heroes whose exploits they admired. Education gains through entertainment, however, in proportion as the free play of the imagination, which gives so much of the charm to primitive storytelling, makes way for the settled purpose of moulding the mind of the listener. This, as we have seen, was the difference between the outlook of Herodotus and that of Thucydides, but the path which leads from entertainment to instruction is also that which led from instruction to propaganda.[7]

In a sense, all education is propaganda; but the propagation

---

[7] It is only in recent years, and perhaps to a large degree as a result of the controversies arising out of the War, that propaganda has become a subject for scientific study. Nowhere else could it be analyzed to such advantage as in the study of antique education and the importance which rhetoric occupied in it. Nothing is more enlightening than to see how the interest of the author shifts from things as they were to things as they should be. Once he has assumed the latter attitude, his next step is to study how he can influence the largest number of people to take his point of view, and this leads to embellishment of the text and manipulation of the content. Thus the later Greek historians did not risk following in the footsteps of Thucydides, who let the examples of the past point their own moral, for they could not rest satisfied with a method which, in less competent hands, would leave the story chaotic and meaningless. They had to mould it so as to make the lesson clear.

of knowledge can be either dogmatic or critical. As dogma, it attempts to impose its point of view upon the reader or the listener; as criticism, it tends to put the reader on his guard, not only against the beliefs which it attacks, but against the innate tendency to accept the plausible and the commonplace as true. Now, criticism can hold its own much more easily when the aim of the writer is to entertain than when his purpose is an ethical one; for entertainment has no such serious consequences as when we attempt to control the conduct of others. Instruction is serious business, and those engaged upon it are likely to become conscious or unconscious propagandists for the things they teach. Using new knowledge to buttress up the old, they instinctively turn aside from criticism.

Greek history was saved from dogma because its content was continually refreshed by an ever-changing world. Its last historians had tales to tell that far outrivalled those of Herodotus; so the curiosity which bred criticism of local myths in the days of Hecataeus continued to stir the minds of the Greek savants after Greece itself had been merged in the Roman Empire. But the task which confronted these Greek scholars of the later day was infinitely more difficult than any which historians had dealt with hitherto. The breakup of the ancient city-state system furnished no easy pattern for those whose past was bound up in it. Viewed from a later age, the conquests of Alexander and of the Caesars furnished a unity in the light of which the previous history was read. It is to the high credit of the Greek historians of the fourth century that, lacking the finished picture, they were already beginning to see its outlines and were already escaping from the narrow parochialism which had limited even the horizon of Thucydides. Although some still saw history within the confines of Greek civilization, there were those who, carrying their survey outside it, became pioneers in the movement to view the world as one.

The new era challenged consummate art and competent scholarship. In the art of expression the historians had to hold the attention of sophisticated readers whose lives were passed in a

Rhetoric and Scholarship

rapidly changing world and who, therefore, were more likely to be interested in the things taking place around them than in the obscure processes of the past. It was but natural, therefore, that they should use the same kind of appeal that the orators had developed in what still remains the greatest age of oratory. In this they succeeded, to judge by the popularity which they enjoyed. But scholarship proved to be a more difficult field. The implements of historical research which Thucydides found lacking were improved by those who spent their lives in archives and libraries; but the tests for evidence were never worked out systematically as they have been by the historians of today, and in our eyes there is a certain naïveté to the way in which the sources were handled even by the best of them.

Rhetoric and scholarship are by no means irreconcilable, if by rhetoric we mean the use of language appropriate to the occasion. But the researcher tends to concentrate upon the facts which he finds in his source material and to have little patience with the restatement of them. These two trends, so clearly marked in modern historians, are already seen in the Greek historians of the fourth century.

To judge by the comments of the ancient critics, both Greek and Roman, few men have impressed themselves upon an art more profoundly than the rhetorician Isocrates.[8] His canons of style were not only to prevail in the Greece of his day, but to pass on, through the rich rhythmic periods of Cicero, to mould

---

[8] This remarkable man was born of well-to-do parents in the same Attic deme as Xenophon in 436. As a youth he was a pupil of the Sophists, especially Gorgias, and—if we are to believe a statement in Plato's *Phaedrus*—Socrates predicted great things for him as an orator and philosopher. After the fall of Athens he spent a short time in exile and then for several years earned a living by writing speeches for others. The weakness of his voice prevented the realization of his ambition to become a public orator and statesman. But in 392 he opened a school for training orators, which was an event of importance in the history of Greece: more real leaders came out of that school, remarked Cicero, than ever issued from the Trojan horse. Isocrates did not merely teach his pupils the art of oratory: he gave them a liberal education as well and inspired them with his own literary and political ideals. The literary ideal was the creation of a smooth and perhaps somewhat florid prose style capable of popular appeal: the political ideal was Pan-Hellenism. After other leaders had failed him, Isocrates at last favored Philip of Macedon and died, aged 98 years, shortly after Philip's victory at Chaeronea.

the prose of many a modern author. Isocrates wrote no formal history himself, but he used it largely as a persuasive force in his orations.[9] Fortunately, mastery of style went along with the widened outlook in the history of the whole Hellenic world. He viewed the politics of Greece as essentially one and sought to inspire a common patriotism by appealing to the pride of all in the achievements of a single city.[10] The glory of Athens, its services to Greece and the lessons of its democracy, were held up to other states as an ideal for the future. But the forces of the world today are never those of yesterday, and when the long spears of Macedon wrecked, instead of realizing, the dreams of the great orators who shed such lustre upon the last age of Greek liberty, there was left only history in which to embody the new ideal.

The first general historian of the Hellenic world, and one of the most popular in antiquity, was Ephorus, to whom, according to Photius, Isocrates assigned the task of preserving the more distant past in fitting mould.[11] He was, as Polybius remarks, the first and only writer to attempt a general history of the Greek world. His narrative began with the fall of Troy and continued down to 341. He was not uncritical when dealing with both chronology and myth,[12] but he rejected the ideal of Thucydides to keep his speeches closely modelled upon the originals. He frankly made them up and was especially fond of harangues upon the field of battle. Yet he seems to have had a sense of their proper use, for Polybius, who was a keen judge, says that he has "a most elegant and convincing digression on this very subject of a comparison between historians and speech-makers."[13]

---

[9] His encomium on Euagoras may share with Xenophon's similar work on Agesilaus the distinction of being among the first formal biographies. This type of literature was much developed by his successors, its more crudely encomiastic qualities were refined, and early in the Christian era it became, in the hands of Plutarch, Suetonius, and Tacitus, a worthy and important form of historical writing.

[10] In his insistence upon the need of a general war of all Greece with Persia in order to unite the Greeks, using Philip as the weapon and instrument, Isocrates' reliance upon a military salvation reminds one of Bismarckian tactics.

[11] Photius, *Bibliotheca*, Chap. 176. Diodorus and Strabo also relied largely upon Ephorus for the field he covered. H. Peter, *Wahrheit und Kunst* (1911), pp. 151 sqq.

[12] E. Meyer, *Forschungen zur alten Geschichte* (1892-1899), I, 186 sqq.

[13] Polybius, *Histories*, Book XII, Chap. 28.

Polybius also characterizes the work of Ephorus as a whole as "admirable throughout in style, treatment, and argumentative acuteness."[14]

The name most commonly linked with that of Ephorus is Theopompus, to whom, according to the story cited above, Isocrates assigned the "modern" field, while he gave the past to Ephorus.[15] In any case, he wrote two important histories, a continuation of Thucydides—the *Hellenica* (in twelve books)—and a survey of contemporary Greek politics in the time of Philip—the *Philippica* (in fifty-eight books). He was gifted with a lively style and he employed all the artifices of rhetoric to secure effect—a Greek Macaulay or Treitschke. Placed by the ancients in the front rank of historians, his work has suffered unduly from the ravages of time and changing taste. Little of what he wrote remains, his works not having been copied from their papyrus rolls into the codices which might have insured their preservation.[16] He travelled extensively and saw things at first hand; he was an insa-

---

[14] Here, mention should be made of the fragment of a *Hellenica*, of greater value than that of Xenophon, which was published in 1908 by B. G. Grenfell and A. S. Hunt in *Oxyrhynchus Papyri*, Part V, pp. 143 sqq. The twenty pages of the work which we now possess show that its author was a historian of no mean ability. The fragment, which was written about 200 A.D., is devoted to the events of about eighteen months in 396-395, which shows that this history was written on a much larger scale than the *Hellenica*. A reference indicates that an earlier passage had dealt with the closing years of the Peloponnesian war; chronology is arranged by summers and winters, and the general development of the topic resembles the manner of Thucydides: it therefore seems rather clear that the author of this work was consciously continuing Thucydides. The fullness and accuracy of his narrative, his breadth of view, and his comprehension of politics—in which he greatly excelled Xenophon—shows that he was a worthy pupil of the great master. We have no evidence as to the length of his history or the end of the period covered, but had the book been very long, other fragments would probably have been preserved. Our section of it apparently was composed between 387 and 356. This *Hellenica Oxyrhynchia*—as the history is sometimes called—was one of the best historical productions of the first half of the fourth century; fortunately it became Ephorus' main source for its period, and he preserved to us much of what the anonymous historian said.

[15] Cicero's chief comment deals with the contrast in the style of the two pupils of Isocrates (*De oratore*, Book III, Chap. 4): "Isocrates, an eminent teacher of eloquence, used to apply the spur to Ephorus, but to put the rein on Theopompus; for the one, who overleaped all bounds in the boldness of his expressions, he restrained; the other who hesitated and was bashful, as it were, he stimulated."

[16] Diodorus already, in the first century B.C., reported the loss of rolls of Theopompus (*Bibliothecae historicae*, Book XVI, Chap. 3, Sect. 8).

tiable investigator; yet the exigencies of style and a biased mind vitiated his work.[17]

Standing apart from the influence of Isocrates, and keenly criticizing Ephorus and Theopompus, was Timaeus, the Sicilian, who passed fifty years of his life at Athens busied with antiquarian researches. The attitude of the scholar toward the rhetorician is expressed in his protest that "history differs from rhetorical composition as much as real buildings differ from those represented in scene-paintings," and, again, that "to collect the necessary materials for writing history is by itself more laborious than the whole process of producing rhetorical compositions."[18] It was Timaeus who instituted in history that dating by Olympiads which henceforth became the Greek standard of chronology for historians and the learned world, although it never was adopted into common use.[19] He was an indefatigable worker and investigator, and if he was a pedant who lacked discrimination and that knowledge of the world which enables one to judge men and describe events, he furnished the historians who followed with much information otherwise lost. But he was biased and unfair, lacking not only the larger vision but the judicial mind, and his attack on his predecessors was the text of a more crushing attack upon himself by Polybius, who devotes his whole twelfth book to little more than this purpose. Polybius scorns this mere dryasdust who spent his time in libraries and never saw the world, and who is a stickler for small points while he fails to see the large ones. But, as we have indicated, the methods of historical research had not yet been worked out, and grappling with source material—the scholar's task—was in itself a not unworthy aim.

At this point our narrative comes definitely to grips with the

[17] Fragments in C. Müller, *Fragmenta historicorum Graecorum* (5 vols., 1841-1873), I, 289-333; IV, 643-45.
[18] Quoted by Polybius, *Histories*, Book II, Chap. 28.
[19] These researches of Timaeus in chronology naturally bring up a very knotty problem, that of the material upon which he could draw. We have seen the general character of the work of Hellanicus, the one standard authority in chronology. After him chronicles of Athens (Atthides) continued to be written, and grew in scope to include all kinds of happenings. A line of Atthid writers developed, somewhat like the Pontifical annalists at Rome (J. B. Bury, *The Ancient Greek Historians*, p. 183).

Rhetoric and Scholarship

problem which has partly emerged from time to time in earlier chapters: how far should the history of history go to include those of whose performance we have little or no adequate record? From the fourth century on there are many names in the annals of Greek historiography. Some of them, to judge by the fragments we possess, were craftsmen worthy to be listed here. But for those whose interest lies in tracing the science and art of history as a whole, instead of using it to fill out the record of a given time, these dimmer figures in the great gallery of historians may be left aside.

There is, however, one document which is of special interest both on account of its contents and on account of its author, *The Constitution of Athens,* which Aristotle wrote between 329 and 322. This treatise was discovered in 1890 in a papyrus from Egypt. The first half of the essay is a sixty-page sketch of the constitutional history of Athens from early times down to the revolutions of 404–403; the second half describes the constitution as it was in Aristotle's day. Stiffly formal, it is probably the work of a pupil thrown hastily together by the master. While it is slight enough as history, the peculiar interest that attaches to it has led to much discussion on the part of modern historians of Greece and furnishes an excellent example of historical criticism in this field. Professor Swain has summarized the results as follows:

> Aristotle drew the historical material for this essay largely from the Atthides and the political pamphleteers of the fifth century; he mentioned Herodotus by name and referred explicitly to a passage in Thucydides, but his version of several events differed considerably from theirs. Thus, in his account of Harmodius and Aristogeiton (Chap. 18) he generally followed Thucydides (Book I, Chap. 20; Book VI, Chaps. 54-56), but he did not hesitate to amplify and rectify that authority in several particulars, in spite of the fact that Thucydides went out of his way to boast of his accuracy and special information concerning the episode. On several occasions Aristotle took the trouble to deny charges brought against Solon or others by the pamphleteers, and it is therefore somewhat disturbing that he should prefer them to Thucydides. Sometimes he apparently preferred one source to another because its author's political views resembled his own; but on other occasions he showed himself far in advance of other ancient historians by a high respect for contemporary documents. Thus he quoted at length from

a poem written by Solon in justification of his reforms: unfortunately he took the poem as it stood, without further investigation of its truth —but it is well to remember that there are still historians who are willing to accept the memoirs and *apologiae* of statesmen as historical sources of primary value. In Chapters 29 to 40, dealing with the years 413 to 403, Aristotle depended upon one authority, otherwise unknown to us, who apparently wrote his narrative soon after the events described: the author was a partisan of Theramenes, but he included in his narrative several resolutions and laws enacted at the time. Aristotle seems to have selected his authority on this basis, for he introduced these contemporary documents into his own narrative; but modern critics believe that in a few cases he was fooled by propagandist forgeries. At any rate, it is clear that Aristotle appreciated the importance of documents and that he sought to make his study in part at least a collection of documents.

This regard for documentary sources was closely connected with Aristotle's scientific interests and his emphasis upon objective fact. At the same time his methods of work facilitated the collection of such materials. As has been pointed out, Aristotle used his students as collaborators and directed them in assembling information on all sorts of topics—such as the constitutions of the 158 cities. Some of these collections (συναγωγαί) were published, others were made the basis of Aristotle's own writings. Thus, the first book of the *Metaphysics* contains many quotations from previous writers on the subject, and much of what we know about the early history of the Athenian drama is derived from the *Poetics*. Diogenes Laertius, writing in the third century A.D., gave a long list of Aristotle's writings, mentioning among them works on the victors in the Olympic and Delphic games and in the dramatic contests at Athens. An inscription found at Delphi in 1895 confirms the statement about the list of Delphic victors, records the fact that a copy of the book was ordered preserved in the temple there, and adds that Callisthenes collaborated with Aristotle in preparing it.[20] These works are interesting in more ways than one. Earlier historians, such as Thucydides (Book III, Chap. 8; Book V, Chap. 49) had sometimes dated events by the athletic victors of the year; perhaps Aristotle intended these works to be reference books on chronology. It must be remarked, however, that neither he nor Callisthenes used this system of chronology in their histories; it was only fifty years later that Timaeus established the reckoning by Olympiads which received general acceptance. In the second place, Aristotle and his collaborators,

---

[20] Diogenes Laertius (Book V, Chap. 1, Sect. 26); cf. Plutarch, *Solon*, Chap. 11; W. Dittenberger, *Sylloge*, No. 275. See also Th. Homolle, "Un Ouvrage d'Aristote dans le Temple de Delphe," in *Bulletin de Correspondance Hellénique*, XXXII (1898), 260 ff.

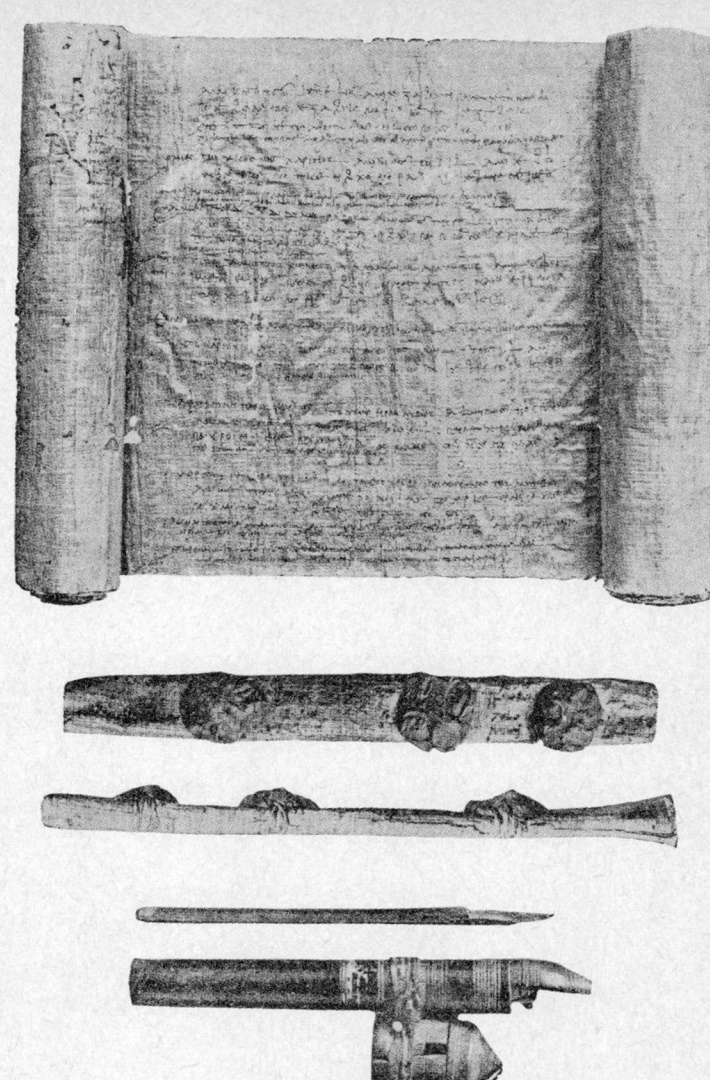

PAPYRUS ROLLS, OPEN FOR READING AND CLOSED (SHOWING SEALS), TOGETHER WITH A PEN AND WITH A PENHOLDER AND INKWELL.

Rhetoric and Scholarship 229

in preparing these lists, must have made researches in official records at Olympia, Delphi, and Athens. Here at last we find Greeks engaged in "research" after the manner of Ranke and his disciples! But this promising start was not followed up. It is certain that no research in the archives underlay Aristotle's own *Constitution of Athens,* and there is no evidence that Callisthenes engaged in it before writing his *Hellenica.* In fact, only a few historians in all antiquity can claim to have based their writings upon official archives, and we shall see that their researches were very scanty.

No Greek historian arose to handle the greatest political achievement of the Hellenic race—the Alexandrine empire—with any of that high competence which marked the Thucydidean story of the tragedy of Athens. Ephorus had written the national story down to 356, and Theopompus had covered the age of Philip. There they stopped. To the Hellenistic world this was like the Old Testament story of Judaea to the Christians. But the story of the great Diaspora, of the spreading of the Greeks through all the Orient, of the building of new cities and planting of Hellenic colonies over to the heart of Asia, of the widening of language and the vital contact with Oriental science, religion and philosophy, all this remained unwritten by competent hands. The Greeks, at the moment when their history seemed ended, emerged upon the theatre of world history, not as local patriots or the art creators of single cities, but as the trained and competent interpreters of the more universal phases of antique culture. The conquest of Alexander made possible a Hellenic Orient —as great an event in the history of civilization as the Romanization of the West. But the epic of that conquest was never written, not even the prose of it, by men worthy of the theme. Fairylike stories of Oriental splendor revealed in Susa or Babylon found ready credence, at a time when truth itself was so incredible, and alongside of them are narratives of some of Alexander's generals and subsequent rulers, like blue books among fiction. Yet the Herodotus of the *revanche* was missing. Instead, the last great Greek historian was a hostage at Rome, writing in the house of Scipio the story of the rise of the western imperial republic whose armies he himself saw sacking the treasures of Corinth when Greece became a Roman province.

CHAPTER XVII

Polybius

THE historian of history need hardly describe the works or narrate the lives of Herodotus, Thucydides, Livy, and Tacitus, for their achievement is universally known, their works the common possession of the whole cultured world. But the case is different with Polybius. Art withheld from him the Hellenic heritage; he was no master of style; his history is not among the world's best literature. He is generally known to the modern reader as a name in footnotes. And yet in the long line of great historians he ranks among the first. He is par excellence the historian's historian of antiquity, and in our own day, when the scientific ideals for which he fought have at last won their way to power, his figure emerges from the comparatively obscure place to which his literary achievement entitles him, and reveals itself as a modern among antiques, critical but not blankly skeptical, working toward constructive principles and conscious of the exacting standards of science.

Polybius was a noble Greek, born at Megalopolis in Arcadia about 198 B.C. His father, Lycortas, was the friend and successor of Philopoemen, the patriot leader of the Achaean league—that last effort of united Hellas—and Polybius himself had hardly reached manhood before he was intrusted with high responsibility both as ambassador and magistrate. But the policy with which he was identified—that of strictly maintaining the formal alliance with Rome, neither yielding to encroachment nor furnishing pretexts for aggression—had little chance of success while the Roman armies were reducing the neighbors of Greece and Greek warring factions were inviting trouble. Pretexts for aggression can always be found, and accordingly, after the battle of Pydna in 168 B.C., Polybius was carried off to Rome, along with a thousand

Polybius

others, nominally as prisoners to await a trial which never came, but really as hostages to insure a freer hand for practical imperialism. Polybius himself fared the best of these, for he was taken into the family of the victorious general, Aemilius Paulus, and so stayed not only in Rome, but in company of the Scipios, in daily intercourse with the leading spirits of that masterful aristocracy into whose hands had fallen the destinies of the Mediterranean world. This favored position seems to have been won more by his personality than by his distinguished ancestry or position in Greece, for he tells us with winning frankness how the young Scipio Aemilianus, who was later to be conqueror of Africa, sought his friendship and became his pupil (Book XXXII, Chap. 10).

Situated thus in the centre of things, Polybius became fired with the ambition to write the history of the tremendous epoch in which he was living. "Can any one," he asks at the opening of his work, "be so indifferent or idle as not to care to know by what means, and under what kind of policy, almost the whole inhabited world was conquered and brought under the dominion of the single city of Rome, and that too, within the period of not quite fifty-three years?" (Book I, Chap. 1.)[1] For those who are not "so indifferent or idle," Polybius left to the world a scientific achievement of undimmed and perpetual worth. Forty books of history carried the story from "the first occasion on which the Romans crossed the sea from Italy," in 264 B.C., through the varying fortunes of the Punic wars, down to the close of the history of Carthage and of Greece in 146 B.C. Of these forty books only the first five have come down to us entire, but lengthy portions of some of the others enable us to form a fairly clear idea of the work as a whole. Moreover, conscious of the intricacy of his subject, and of the difficulty of handling intelligibly

[1] H. Peter remarks that Polybius begins with Greek readers in mind but as his work progresses he turns to the Romans (*Wahrheit und Kunst*, p. 263). Note the frankness of this admission, "If what I say appears incredible to any of my readers," let him remember that the Romans will read it and "no one ... would voluntarily expose himself to certain disbelief and contempt" (Book XXXII, Chap. 8). The extent to which he could win thoughtful Romans may be measured by the fact that Brutus made excerpts from him during the campaign of Pharsalus (Plutarch, *Marcus Brutus*, Chap. 4).

such a mass of detail, Polybius like a true schoolteacher furnishes us with explanatory notes and even, in the opening of the third book, with a sort of syllabus of the whole plan, in order to make sure that the reader will not miss seeing the woods for the trees. These directions and hints are so thoroughly characteristic of the author, as we shall see later on, that we cannot do better than quote from them Polybius' own conception of his field of work. Apart from their value as guides, they at once afford a glimpse of the half-apologetic, half-proud attitude and the wholly intimate relationship which Polybius assumes and establishes with the reader:

> My History begins in the 140th Olympiad. The events from which it starts are these. In Greece, what is called the Social war, the first waged by Philip, son of Demetrius and father of Perseus, in league with the Achæans against the Ætolians. In Asia, the war for the possession of Cœle-Syria which Antiochus and Ptolemy Philopator carried on against each other. In Italy, Libya, and their neighbourhood, the conflict between Rome and Carthage, generally called the Hannibalic war.
> My work thus begins where that of Aratus of Sicyon leaves off. Now up to this time the world's history had been, so to speak, a series of disconnected transactions, as widely separated in their origin and results as in their localities. But from this time forth History becomes a connected whole: the affairs of Italy and Libya are involved with those of Asia and Greece, and the tendency of all is to unity. This is why I have fixed upon this era as the starting-point of my work. For it was their victory over the Carthaginians in this war, and their conviction that thereby the most difficult and most essential step towards universal empire had been taken, which encouraged the Romans for the first time to stretch out their hands upon the rest, and to cross with an army into Greece and Asia (Book I, Chap. 3).

The real history, therefore, begins with the third book; the first and second are but a laborious and massive prelude. The fifty-three years whose unparalleled achievements he proposes to chronicle are those from 220 to 168 B.C. That would bring the narrative down to the year in which the author himself was carried off to Rome, when the victory of Pydna ended forever any reasonable hope of the independence of Macedon or Greece. The rank subjectivity of Polybius' outlook [2] is reflected in this original plan. He proposed to stop the survey of politics where he himself had stopped; not consciously for that reason, but because from the home of the Scipios it had seemed as if the Roman conquest were over. He had become an imperialist and shared the imperialistic conviction in an "inevitable destiny." It was from this point of view that he conceived his history. Fortuna—part chance, part goddess—had "made almost all the affairs of the world incline in one direction, and forced them to converge upon one and the same point." So his history was to culminate in the unification of the Mediterranean world. He knew that intrigue and hot revolt still broke out in the subdued territories but such things, properly reduced in size by distance, are always to be expected on the verge of the imperialist's perspective. Later, however, Polybius saw that the task of imperialism was not completed but only begun by its conquests, and so he carried his narrative down to include the burning of Carthage and the sack of Corinth—at both which events he was present.[3]

The reason which Polybius gives for adding this later survey is interesting and important. It furnishes us with the clue to his conception of the mission of the historian. We may as well quote him in his own downright way. It is clear enough, he says, that in the fifty-three years "the Roman power had arrived at its consummation," and that the acknowledgment of her supremacy had been extorted from all, and her commands obeyed:

But in truth, judgments of either side founded on the bare facts of success or failure in the field are by no means final. It has often happened that what seemed the most signal successes have, from ill management, brought the most crushing disasters in their train; while not unfrequently the most terrible calamities, sustained with spirit, have been turned to actual advantage. I am bound, therefore, to add to my

---

[2] "He is always on the stage himself, criticizing, expounding, emphasizing, making points, dotting the i's and crossing the t's, propounding and defending his personal views." J. B. Bury, *The Ancient Greek Historians*, p. 211.

[3] His presence at the sack of Corinth has been disputed. In any case, his account has survived in such poor fragments that the question is of secondary importance. He was evidently there, or near there, shortly afterwards. Book XXXIX, Chap. 13: "I saw with my own eyes pictures thrown on the ground and soldiers playing dice on them."

statement of facts a discussion on the subsequent policy of the conquerors, and their administration of their universal dominion: and again on the various feelings and opinions entertained by other nations towards their rulers. And I must also describe the tastes and aims of the several nations, whether in their private lives or public policy. The present generation will learn from this whether they should shun or seek the rule of Rome; and future generations will be taught whether to praise and imitate, or to decry it (Book III, Chap. 4).

Here we come upon the practical aim of all Polybius' work—the pragmatic character of it, which he insists upon time and again. History was to him no mere antiquarianism. He is a practical politician, and history is simply past politics. It is justified by its utility; it is philosophy teaching by experience.[4] A knowledge of history, he says in another place, is no mere graceful accomplishment but absolutely essential as a guide to action. Only history can supply the statesman with precedents. The present offers no such chances as the past for judging the relative forces of circumstances or the motives of men:

In the case of contemporaries, it is difficult to obtain an insight into their purposes; because, as their words and actions are dictated by a desire of accommodating themselves to the necessity of the hour, and of keeping up appearances, the truth is too often obscured. Whereas the transactions of the past admit of being tested by naked fact; and accordingly display without disguise the motives and purposes of the several persons engaged; and teach us from what sort of people to expect favour, active kindness, and assistance, or the reverse. They give us also many opportunities of distinguishing who would be likely to pity us, feel indignation at our wrongs, and defend our cause—a power that contributes very greatly to national as well as individual security. Neither the writer nor the reader of history, therefore, should confine his attention to a bare statement of facts: he must take into account all that preceded, accompanied, or followed them. For if you take from history all explanation of cause, principle, and motive, and of the adaptation of the means to the end, what is left is a mere panorama without being instructive; and, though it may please for the moment, it has no abiding value (Book III, Chap. 31).

[4] This time-worn phrase is already found in *Ars rhetorica* (Chap. XI, Sect. 2), attributed to Dionysius of Halicarnassus, in a paraphrase of Thucydides, Book I, Chap. 22.

Polybius

The keynote of this is that history must "instruct." It is no mean task that it has in hand; the lesson which the tutor of the Scipios would draw from it is nothing less than a science of politics. The story of Hannibal's march upon Rome and of the firmness of the Romans in the crisis is told with equal and generous admiration for both sides, "not ... for the sake of making a panegyric on either Romans or Carthaginians, ... but for the sake of those who are in office among the one or the other people, or who are in future times to direct the affairs of any state whatever; that by the memory, or actual contemplation, of exploits such as these they may be inspired with emulation" (Book IX, Chap. 9). Perhaps the clearest statement of this conviction of Polybius that history is philosophy teaching by experience—a conviction stated many times over—is his comment on the narrative of the defeat of Regulus in the first Punic war:

> I record these things in the hope of benefiting my readers. There are two roads to reformation for mankind—one through misfortunes of their own, the other through those of others: the former is the most unmistakable, the latter the less painful. One should never therefore voluntarily choose the former, for it makes reformation a matter of great difficulty and danger; but we should always look out for the latter, for thereby we can without hurt to ourselves gain a clear view of the best course to pursue. It is this which forces us to consider that the knowledge gained from the study of true history is the best of all educations for practical life. For it is history, and history alone, which, without involving us in actual danger, will mature our judgment and prepare us to take right views, whatever may be the crisis or the posture of affairs (Book I, Chap. 35).

It must be admitted that such a "pragmatic" point of view is not altogether reassuring. A historian who is avowedly intent on the lessons history supplies would be given short shrift today in the courts of historical criticism. But Polybius was saved as a historian by his very commonplaceness as a philosopher. He never really got the upper hand of the facts. He does not even achieve a systematic conception of cause and effect, so necessary to the brilliant distortions of philosophers. He talks about causes, and allows himself as much as two chapters in one place to point out that a "cause" and a "pretext" are not the same thing (Book III, Chap. 3). But he gets little farther than a negative criticism of his predecessor, Fabius Pictor, who had not even seen this. In spite of the best pedagogical intentions, Polybius did not lose sight of actualities in the search for final causes. He is too matter-of-fact to leave the facts. His intensely practical outlook makes him incapable of sympathy with abstractions and keeps him down to the task of securing accurate and full data in the field of realities—which is the first and indispensable qualification for the historian. Polybius is intent upon supplying statesmen with lessons from experience, not with theories of what might have happened. In a discussion of the constitution of Sparta he says that it would not be fair to class the Republic of Plato "which is spoken of in high terms by some philosophers" among the systems which have actually been tried out:

> For just as we refuse admission to the athletic contests to those actors or athletes who have not acquired a recognized position or trained for them, so we ought not to admit this Platonic constitution to the contest for the prize of merit unless it can first point to some genuine and practical achievement. Up to this time the notion of bringing it into comparison with the constitutions of Sparta, Rome, and Carthage would be like putting up a statue to compare with living and breathing men. Even if the statue were faultless in point of art, the comparison of the lifeless with the living would naturally leave an impression of imperfection and incongruity upon the minds of the spectators (Book VI, Chap. 47).

This sounds less Greek than Roman. But it also reassures us that the author is not the man to be drawn into the realm of theory so long as the world is full of things for him to study. He wastes no time over "final causes," in spite of a constant desire to bring up the question.[5] Indeed his own philosophy of history is not quite settled. He begins by attributing to Fortune the great drift of events which resulted in the imperial unity; but, while paying a formal tribute to the goddess of luck, he in practice reserves her for the more unexpected turns of affairs, the sudden surprises and the inexplicable (Book XXIX, Chaps. 21-22). "It

---

[5] See, for instances, Book I, Chaps. 63-64; Book III, Chaps. 7-9, etc.

was *not* by mere chance or without knowing what they were doing that the Romans struck their bold stroke for universal supremacy and dominion, and justified their boldness by its success. No: it was the natural result of discipline gained in the stern school of difficulty and danger" (Book I, Chap. 63). The theology of Fortune shares the fate of all the other abstractions at the hands of Polybius. He is not interested in it, but in the facts.

In keeping with this attitude was the method of work. Polybius was a student rather than a scholar; a student of men and the world around rather than of books. To be sure he spared himself no pains in his investigations, and that meant much scholarly research; but he always regarded that as of secondary importance compared with a first-hand knowledge of how things had been, and were being, done. If anything could shock the complacency of the modern research-historian who sees the world so often through the barred windows of an alcove in the archives, it is that attack upon Timaeus, the learned antiquarian, which fills most of the twelfth book, and to which we shall revert later. Polybius holds Timaeus up to scorn, because "having stayed quietly at Athens for about fifty years, during which [time] he devoted himself to the study of written history, he imagined that he was in possession of the most important means of writing it" (Book XII, Chap. 25, Sect. d). One must have served in war to know how to describe it accurately and well; one must have watched the political movements of one's own day to be able to handle those of the past. These qualifications Polybius had in a superlative degree. Of a good deal of his story he had been "an eye-witness,... in some cases one of the actors, and in others the chief actor" (Book III, Chap. 4). He was present at the last great tragic moment of Carthage; it was to him that Scipio turned to confide his presentiment that Rome would some day suffer the same fate (Book XXXIX, Chap. 5). He knew not only Romans and Greeks but leaders on all sides, Massanissa, for example, and Carthaginians themselves (Book IX, Chap. 25). Then, instead of staying comfortably in Rome, he set out, like a Herodotus of the West, to see the new world which was just opening up to civilization. It was a scientific exploration. He tells us that he confronted "the dangers and fatigues of my travels in Libya, Iberia, and Gaul, as well as of the sea which washes the western coast of these countries, that I might correct the imperfect knowledge of former writers" (Book III, Chap. 59). His experience leads him to a wholesale distrust of former geographers; but then, as he adds, none of them enjoyed the opportunities for finding out about the world which the *pax Romana* now afforded. His curiosity was insatiable. He himself traversed the pass by which Hannibal crossed the Alps; at the other end of Italy he deciphered Hannibal's inscription on a pillar on a promontory of Brutium in order to establish the distribution of the Carthaginian forces. He mapped out cities, examined records,[6] transcribed treaties,[7] and studied earlier historians. But he seldom found an authority with whom he did not become impatient, and perhaps his most striking personal note is his persistent criticism and distrust of historians and his frequent disgust with them. It was impossible for one of his direct, businesslike temperament to accept the rhetorical historians of his day, but in his scorn of rhetoric and his impatience of bookishness, he went so far as to miss the real achievements of his predecessors.

This attitude, moreover, had a personal significance; it reflects

[6] See the chance remark (Book XVI, Chap. 15) that a document at Rhodes bears out his account.

[7] See Book III, Chaps. 22 *sqq.* This passage gives the texts of six treaties between Rome and Carthage, Polybius having copied them from bronze tablets preserved in the treasury of the quaestors beside the temple of Jupiter Capitolinus. Unfortunately, however, Polybius apparently fell into grievous error here because of his lack of insight into the devious ways of diplomats—and this in spite of all his boasting about his superiority to other historians because of his practical experience with men! He takes his predecessor Philinus, the Sicilian historian, severely to task (Book III, Chap. 26) for saying that Rome and Carthage had once concluded a treaty by which the Romans promised to keep away from Sicily and the Carthaginians from Italy, and that the Romans had violated this treaty when they invaded Sicily at the beginning of the First Punic War. Polybius states definitely that there never was any such treaty. As a matter of fact, Livy mentions the treaty twice, and modern historians are virtually unanimous in supporting Philinus against Polybius. The latter apparently assumed that, had there been such a treaty, even if the Romans had broken it, they would nevertheless have kept a copy of it on exhibit in the treasury for more than a hundred years—as a perpetual memento of their own infamy! Unfortunately Polybius was not the last historian of diplomacy to fall into the error of assuming that the diplomatic documents published in an official "blue book" are necessarily authentic and unexpurgated.

the weak side of Polybius. For, in spite of all his prodigious labor, he never learned how to tell his story effectively. He was no artist. He had none of the easy grace of Herodotus or the masterful touch of Thucydides. It is rather characteristic of him, by the way, that he never referred to the former and mentioned the latter only in a casual remark. He had nothing to learn; he chose to work out his own salvation—and almost failed to win it. For he could not weave the intricate and elaborate pattern of world history without frequently tangling the threads in the effort not to lose them. He knew this as well as we do and time and again came into the narrative himself with digressions which are excuses and explanations.[8] This is what gives that intimate, personal character to his history, which is so unantique. Herodotus swung into his theme with the abandon of one who knows how to tell a great story well. Thucydides worked like a dramatist, objectively, submitting only the finished product to the audience. Neither of them invited you into his workshop or interrupted a war to discuss scientific methods. But Polybius cannot keep himself out of the narrative, and once in it, he gives free rein to his feelings as well as his views. He consistently loses his temper when he finds things wrong in his sources, and once heated, he becomes garrulous. Untrained—for a Greek—in literature, a man of action who had turned schoolteacher, he faces his subject like a problem and presents his research like solutions. He lectures his contemporaries and berates his predecessors [9] when they fail to come up to his standard—which is generally the case. Then he apologizes for the digression and settles down to a little more narrative. But the digressions are much more than apologies; for, after all, Polybius had thought deeply on his own task. They rise to the dignity of a treatise upon history, the first and the noblest statement of scientific ideals for the historian until the days of Ranke. Indeed, it is these excursuses rather than his great theme which

---

[8] The following passages are especially valuable for their comments upon style and method of handling: Book II, Chap. 56; Book III, Chaps. 57-59; Book IX, Chap. 1; Book XV, Chap. 36; Book XVI, Chap. 17; Book XXXVII, Chap. 4; Book XXXIX, Chap. 1. Perhaps the most thoroughly apologetic is this opening of the thirty-ninth book.

[9] See J. B. Bury, *The Ancient Greek Historians*, Lect. VI.

give to Polybius so high a place in the history of history. How incredible it would have seemed to him that any one should read his history for the sake of its asides instead of for the compelling interest of the theme! Yet there are some to whom even the rise of the Roman Empire is of less significance than the rise of the scientific method. After all, the one is in the past, its potentialities are well-nigh spent; the other is of the future and all time, and capable of untold possibilities.

This treatise is scattered throughout the whole history as we have indicated and indeed is exemplified in the structure and method of work. Polybius demands the truth which is "the eye of History," and insists that the historian must give up all partisanship, all personal bias, and making himself a judge, proceed to master the facts—as they actually were. "Directly a man assumes the moral attitude of a historian he ought to forget all considerations," such as love of one's friends, hatred of one's enemies.... He must sometimes praise enemies and blame friends. "For as a living creature is rendered wholly useless if deprived of its eyes, so if you take truth from History, what is left but an idle unprofitable tale?" (Book I, Chap. 4.) These are noble words, worthy to be held in everlasting memory. Unfortunately they were almost never heard and, in spite of good intentions, not applied even by those who studied Polybius—Cicero, for instance. Polybius does not say that historians are given to conscious falsification—though he does strike that note at times—but he is keenly alive to the bias that partisanship is sure to give to a narrative even in honest hands. "I would beg my own readers, whether of my own or future generations, if I am ever detected in making a deliberate misstatement, and disregarding truth in any part of my history, to criticize me unmercifully; but if I do so from lack of information, to make allowances: and I ask it for myself more than others, owing to the size of my history and the extent of ground covered" (Book XVI, Chap. 20). This strain runs all through the work, but it is especially concentrated in the famous twelfth book in which Polybius attacks his predecessor Timaeus. This digression comes near to being a treatise in itself. The student of history who fails to be stirred by it—considering its time and circumstances—has little to hope from anything that follows in this survey.

Polybius believed in the pragmatic character of the historian's office. History must edify, must be of *use*. But it loses its pragmatism if it is not true; it is only an "idle tale." And this is the pragmatic test of his own work. We are not much edified by the details of the wars in Greece. No one is now likely to become excited over the institutions of the Locrians or the policy of Diaeus. But as long as history endures the ideals of Polybius will be an inspiration and a guide.

CHAPTER XVIII

Later Greek Historians

ALTHOUGH Polybius may justly rank as the last of the great Greek historians, his name is by no means the last in Greek historiography. There were many historians, of varying degrees of importance, among those Greek scholars who became the teachers of the Roman world, and while individually their achievement is perhaps not such as to warrant any detailed examination of it here, yet, taken as a whole, it offers some striking generalizations.

In the first place the incentive to history writing was no longer connected with that first stimulus which produced it, patriotism or national sentiment. The transplanted scholar, living an exile in foreign lands, could hardly take his own antiquity along; and if he did, few would care to know about it. On the other hand he could not acquire the antiquities of the country of his residence with the same sentimental appreciation of their bearing upon history as if he had been born to their inheritance. The result was a certain detachment upon the part of later Greek scholars which, in some cases, seems to have made for indifference as to those movements of cause and effect that intrigued the keen intelligence of Polybius and thus left them rather dilettante antiquarians. On the other hand, it also made for an enlargement of view that carried the better minds beyond the narrow confines of purely Roman patriotism and gave them a glimpse of world history.

It is hard to say why the obvious advantages of such a detached position were not exploited more. The Hellenistic Greek could view many of the historical problems of antiquity with much the same kind of aloofness as that which the modern scholar brings to the study of the Middle Ages. One might even expect

Later Greek Historians

that the economic stimulus of earning a living by one's wits would have stirred the Greek intellectuals, who graced the households of the masters of the world as slaves, freedmen, or dependents, to notable achievement in that kind of research which leads to systematic results along scientific lines. But rhetoric, on the one hand, and philosophy, on the other, proved to be the winning rivals.

Mention of Greek philosophy in this connection recalls the fact that we have hardly spoken of it before. Rhetoric and the influence of Isocrates have come very largely to the fore; but what of the influence of philosophy upon Greek historiography? Plato has so far escaped any but casual mention, and Aristotle has come within our survey with scarcely more than a footnote! Yet the greatest creations of Greek thought could not but affect the outlook of historians, even if they contributed little directly. Truth was an ideal of philosophy as of history, and in the recognition of social virtues as historic forces, or even in the whole pragmatic quality of such a work as that of Polybius, there may be as much an index of Stoic influence upon the writer's trend of thought as of his direct power of observation.[1] The lessons which history supplies to one trained in the principles of such a philosophy are not the same as those which it would bring to a Herodotus.

To follow these suggestions would lead one into intricate fields of scholarship, far beyond our bounds. The history of the philosophy of Greek historiography may best be left for the specialist. This, of course, implies that the contribution of philosophy to history was a limited one. For while it offered points of view to historians, it failed to provide that apparatus of criticism which is the basis of science. Aristotle, it is true, made a beginning; but the influence of Plato told in the other direction. Although it was a great thing to have justified the supremacy of reason, as he did, and to have insisted upon the identity of truth and good, the abstract tendency of his speculation unified that assemblage of

[1] An excellent short account of this subject is to be found in H. Peter, *Wahrheit und Kunst* (1911), Chap. VII: "Die Stoa, Polybius, Poseidonios und Strabon,"

data, which is the investigator's universe, by means of the most unhistorical line of thought imaginable, his theory of ideas. Metaphysics and history have not much in common.

But the interest of thinkers in ideas rather than in facts was less responsible for the limited progress of antique historiography than the failure to recognize the value of mechanism. There is a striking passage in *Phaedrus* in which, according to Plato, Socrates laments the passing of that time when the only known facts about the past were those treasured in memory and the coming of that degenerate age when people no longer bother remembering things they can read in books.[2] He deprecates above all the invention of writing. Reliance on such devices lessens the capacities of the user for distinguishing truth from its semblance. It is a specious argument; and one might think that his pupil Plato, recording it—in writing—might do so with a sense of the humor of the situation. But there is no sign of it. For, as a matter of fact, this objection of Socrates to alphabets was but a single expression of something reaching deeply through the whole trend of Plato's mind. That mind was fundamentally poetic. It recoiled from mechanism temperamentally. It felt instinctively that making black marks on papyrus from Egypt or skins from Asia—those skins the merchants of Pergamum later made into parchments—is an operation inferior to reciting an epic. It is the same kind of protest that we have today on the part of those who prefer hand labor to machinery. Socrates, one supposes, would have preferred to tell the time by a guess at the lengthening shadow on the square rather than by using a watch. By ignoring inventions one keeps "close to nature."

This is an attitude to be found through the whole history of culture. Its most earnest advocates have been the artists, of every kind of expression, impatient of anything interposed between nature and the individual. It partly springs from the concentration of a creator on his creation—that concentration which is joy—leaving him relatively indifferent as to its preservation. Idealism, drawn to this romantic sentiment, has often denied itself

[2] *Phaedrus,* 274-275 D.

the means of achievement by holding aloof from the processes by which ideas are realized. It is curious how shortsighted it has been. For, in the larger view, mechanism itself is an art creation. The invention of an alphabet is a work of art to rank beside poetry. In its use it is part of the clothing of thought, like the words themselves, and shares the immortality which it assures. Even machinery, which supplants the motions of the hand of the worker, incorporates thought in its materials, just as marble bears the impress of a sculptor's imagination or the massing of pigment on a painter's canvas preserves the suggestion of nature. Since it is, however, a social rather than an individual creation, the appreciation of it is more difficult.

Greek philosophy missed the great point that the power of ideas works itself out in a grimy world, the world of daily life. History depends upon that mechanism which transfers thought from brains to material substances and so enables thought to endure while thinkers come and go. It is rather sobering to recall how much depends upon the substance. We know, for instance, that the burning of the library at Alexandria blotted out for all time much of the culture of that distant antiquity which it had gathered in the papyri on its shelves. We know, as well, that the last classics of Greece and Rome perished in the mouldy rolls of papyrus which could not last in the climate of the northern Mediterranean. The book trade of the ancients was careless of the future—as ours is today. But had it not been for papyrus rolls dealt in by those astute traders who brought their goods to the wharves of the Piraeus and Ostia, it is doubtful if the literature of classic Greece and Rome would have been produced at all. Had there been nothing better than clay tablets to scratch, how would the Augustan age have achieved what it did? Imagine Polybius or Livy accumulating the mud cylinders necessary for their histories! Or, to bring the matter down to our own time, what would our modern literature and journalism amount to if the art of making paper had not been brought to Europe by the Arabs? A printing press without paper is unthinkable; and modern literature cannot exist without them both. We need a *Sartor Resartus* in the history of literature to show us how naked and helplessly limited is thought except when provided with mechanism.

There have been two great creative epochs in the history of our civilization: that of ancient Greece and that of today. The one produced critical thought; the other applied it to invent machines. Beside these two contributions to secular society, all others rank as minor. The one stirred into activity that critical intelligence upon which rests our whole apparatus of knowledge; the other made nature our ally not merely by applying its power to do our work, but also by supplying the means for extending knowledge itself, almost to the infinite. And the point to which this history returns again and again is that even the genius of a Plato could hardly anticipate the merest fraction of the results to be obtained by the slow, minute processes of the mechanism of science.

It is perhaps fortunate for us that we are spared the temptation of tracing these suggestions in subsequent Hellenic historians, by the fragmentary character of the literary remains of most of those who might offer themselves for such a study. We shall, however, have it before us as we turn to Rome. It remains now for us merely to pass in rapid review the work of the more outstanding figures among those gifted Greeks who supplied the cultured world of their time with the kind of histories it demanded.

The history of Polybius was continued by the Stoic Posidonius, who applied himself to the task with somewhat the same appreciation of the distortions of narrative due to rhetorical adornment as Polybius himself. He had also, like Polybius, travelled widely on the outskirts of the known world, from Spain to Rhodes and Syria, and wrote voluminously on all kinds of topics. His *Geography* and his *History* are the only works of interest here. The latter was begun in 74 B.C. and continued the universal history of Polybius, in fifty-two books, from 144 B.C. to the Dictatorship of Sulla in 82 B.C. It was a notable performance, and although Posidonius does not belong with the rhetoricians, but in the succession of Timaeus and Polybius, Cicero deferred to him as to a master of style, when trying himself to write the account of his

Later Greek Historians

own consulate in Greek. The modern critic has not less praise for this Stoic historian, his learning, and his critical capacity.[3]

Strabo (c. 64 B.C.–19 A.D.), the great geographer, was also a continuator of Polybius and wrote as well some *Historical Memoirs*, which included a treatment of the deeds of Alexander. The *Geography*, too, had a historical introduction covering the history of geography and the work of geographers to his own day—almost our only source for such important figures as Eratosthenes. Moreover, historians are so much in evidence as authorities in the *Geography* that it may almost be said to embody the descriptive phase of antique historiography, that phase so evident in the excursuses of Herodotus. But Strabo has a further interest for us. His method, in line with the traditions we have just seen maintained by Posidonius, was to cite largely from his authorities and so preserve fragments of them for his less scholarly readers and, in part, for us. A travelled Greek, he also knew Rome and is an outstanding example of those "philosophers"—for so he is termed by Plutarch—who held to the saner lines of criticism and respected facts. He was more a scholar than a historian, as his predilection for geography indicates. The events of history require an added dimension. It is easier to describe the world in space than in time,[4] and for that great synthesis which recreates in intelligence the happenings of chance he lacked the full stature of genius. On the other hand, it was to his credit that he did not try to reach that synthesis by that facile use of words and phrases to which a rhetorician would have yielded.

It was just this synthesis, in the widest possible sense, which Diodorus Siculus (c. 80–29 B.C.), Strabo's older contemporary, had tried to reach in his general history (*Bibliotheca historica*) in forty books—tried and failed, for the chief value of his

---

[3] Cicero, *Epistularum ad Atticum liber secundus*, Letter I, Sects. 1 and 2.

[4] In this connection, mention should be made of those Greek chronographers who drew together comparative lists of events in world chronicles. The basis of chronology, laid by Eratosthenes of Alexandria in the third century B.C., was built upon by Apollodorus of Athens, whose four books of chronicles reached down to 119 B.C. Then Castor of Rhodes gathered the threads together into a synchronistic table or "canon," ending with the year 61 B.C. Castor's chronicle was destined to prove of great importance later to the Christian chronologists. He is plentifully in evidence in Eusebius.

work to us is in the fragments of sources which he built into it, not the bold unifying conception of which he was chiefly proud. He began with the mythical accounts of ancient Egypt and the Orient and carried the story of Greece and Sicily down to the close. But—fortunately for the preservation of his sources—he did not see the interconnection of events and simply made a sort of world-chronicle out of a series of chronicles of different countries, cutting and trimming the authorities to meet the exigencies, but still leaving them to substantiate the narrative. To this clumsy, but imposing, monument of erudition Diodorus added some of the unrealities of rhetoric, and it is hardly to be wondered at if he failed to receive the attention of those of his day for whom he wrote. It was only later, when Christian scholars in the third century began to look back across the pagan past for an account of the whole world, and not of Rome merely, that Diodorus proved to be of enough importance to secure the preservation of part of his world history.

It was in the line of these great world histories that Nicholas of Damascus wrote the one hundred and forty-four books of universal history to which reference has been made above in the chapter on Josephus. The favorite of Herod the Great knew how to win as well the favor of Augustus, and his detailed account of contemporary events was apparently not lacking in rhetorical polish. But his work was more a compilation, like that of Diodorus, than an independent history.

By a strange coincidence, it was the city of Herodotus which produced the historian who most vitiated the scientific possibilities of this kind of scholarship by acceptance of the standards of rhetoric. Dionysius of Halicarnassus, born about the middle of the first century B.C., came to Rome in the year 30 B.C., and, as he proudly relates in the introduction to his *Archaeologia,* spent twenty-two years in preparation for his great work, which was published in the year 7 A.D. He moved in the best circles of Rome, and it was his ambition to rival Livy by the wealth of his detailed information concerning the Roman antiquities. In addition, he tried to satisfy Greek pride by making much of the Greek origins of Rome. Two such divergent purposes could be welded into a single history only by the greatest creative capacity upon the part of the historian; instead of this, Dionysius brought a scholarship limited by the devices of rhetoric. Even these devices were not all his own; for he embodied expressions from the Greek classics, where they could aptly apply to his narrative; but recent study has increased the respect for his conscientious and careful workmanship.

Under the Roman Empire, Greek scholarship continued at its various tasks, and after the golden age of Latin literature was over, Greek became once more, under the Antonines, the medium for culture. Into the details of this story we shall not enter; but we should at least recall in passing the lasting importance to history of Plutarch's *Lives*. Few books have done more to determine the reputation of historical characters for subsequent ages. The forty-six *Parallel Lives* are arranged in pairs, namely Roman and Greek, and the personalities they depict are typical of the times and customs of their environment or of their own professions and careers. There are generals and statesmen, patriots and lawgivers; a gallery of the great figures whose names were already more or less legendary and who now become fixed in the imagination of the world as real, living characters. Plutarch was a native of Boeotia, and, although he travelled widely, he seems to have written his biographies after his return to the little town of Chaeronea, where he was born. It is a striking fact that, writing as he does in this isolated village, he shows a larger and more catholic mind than his brilliant contemporary, Tacitus, writing at Rome. This is a point to which we shall revert later, when we come to see the influences which made for provincialism at Rome under the Caesars; but it is well to recognize here that in Plutarch we have a genuine "historian" in the first sense of the word, an inquirer on the paths of truth, as interested in comparative religion as in morals, and lacking only in the social and political interests which bind these elements of personality and mystery into the complex processes of society and so make history.

Finally, passing by such notable figures as Appian of Alexandria, of whose accounts of the various provinces of the Empire in twenty-four books, written under Trajan and Hadrian, almost half have been preserved, and Arrian of Bithynia, the favorite of Hadrian and the Antonines, the worthy disciple of Epictetus and historian of the Persian wars, we come to the last of the list in Cassius Dio Coccejanus, the historian of Rome, of the third century. He was born in Nicaea in Bithynia about 155 A.D. and passed a long life in high offices of state—consul, proconsul of Africa, legate to Dalmatia and Pannonia. He died about the year 235. His history of Rome, in eighty books, was divided into decades after the manner in which Livy's was then preserved, and it stretched over the whole field from the arrival of Aeneas in Italy to the reign of Alexander Severus. It was a work of long researches—ten years spent in collecting the materials, twelve more in composition—and was to the Greek-speaking East much what Livy was to the Latin West. It expounded the great theme of Roman history in the spirit of a Roman official. At the close, therefore, Greek historiography fused and lost itself in that theme of empire which was to perpetuate its outlook, however changed and dimmed, in a new state creation at Byzantium.

Looking back over the whole of the history of history by the Greeks, we find that in spite of the unique quality of the Greek genius, their achievement in this field could not wholly escape the mould in which it was cast by other and less gifted people. It is true that no others who have been so poorly equipped with the instruments of research have left anything to compare with the Greek reconstruction of the past. This was chiefly because the Greek was interested in man himself, in the things he does or likes to do; therefore, even when the facts were wrong they were interesting and might even be instructive. But from the time Greek genius reached maturity, in the days of Pericles, the most serious of the Greek historians conceived their task, not as that of mere antiquarians rescuing isolated facts from oblivion, but as that of the interpreters of processes or trends. In Thucydides this was seen in almost static terms, for the same set of circumstances and the same type of actors would bring the same results. The historians of the later age, although they lived in the midst of change, were not able to improve upon this social science that rested upon a direct observation of human nature. For, after all, life in the ancient world did repeat itself, although in different terms. The farmer's calendar remained unchanged; life went on essentially the same, generation after generation; even in politics, which was the theme of history, wars might change the fate of cities or of peoples, but after the Roman conquest this was little more than moving chessmen on the board. The same game might be played over and over again for all they knew of its underlying laws. And yet their purpose was to study its rules.

In this limited sense, therefore, it is hardly straining the point to say that Greek historiography repeats that of the Jews. We have already seen how the high purpose of the Hebrew prophets made the study of Hebrew history worth while by the very distortions which they made of it, for out of a past which often seemed to deny the very interpretation they put upon it, they built their great concept of a world in which human justice was developing under Divine rule. The Greek student of the human drama had no such unifying doctrine for which he could marshal the data of history. Rather, he limited his vision to the actors on the stage; hence, his outlook was more varied and, therefore, more open to the challenge of criticism. But both the Jew and the Greek—and as we shall see later on, the Christian as well—sought in history the guide to a way of life.

Part IV
ROMAN HISTORY

CHAPTER XIX

History at Rome; Oratory and Poetry

IF POLITICS be the main theme of history in the antique world, it might seem reasonable to look for the greatest historians among the people who achieved the greatest political creation, the Romans. But although Rome furnished the lesson in practical statesmanship, both for antiquity and for succeeding ages, its achievement in history writing is, upon the whole, poor and disappointing. It was a Greek, Polybius, who, as we have seen, wrote in the city of the Scipios the story of the emergence of the Latin people upon the theatre of world empire. Although Sallust, Livy, and Tacitus rise to the height of national monuments—Tacitus even higher still—yet the two outstanding figures of Roman literature, throughout the Middle Ages as in modern times, are Vergil, the epic poet, and Cicero, the philosophic orator. There is a real significance in this; for in them, rather than in the historians, are typified the interests and attitudes of the intellectual Romans themselves—in them and in that other, still greater creation of the Latin genius, the Roman law. The extent of the failure of the Romans in history writing, when they had a theme the like of which had never before been even dreamed of in the world, is obscured by the individual genius of Tacitus. But from his time—excepting Suetonius, who was partly contemporary—to the fall of the empire at the end of the fourth century, when a simple, straightforward soldier, Ammianus Marcellinus, told of the wars on the frontier and the troubles at home, there "was not one author of talent to preserve in Latin the memory of the events that stirred the world of that period; but it was a Bithynian...Dion Cassius of Nicæa, who, under the Severi, narrated the history of the Roman people." [1]

Our sense of loss is probably lessened by the poor consolation that had a second Tacitus appeared and devoted himself to the larger theme disclosed by the passing centuries, he could hardly have succeeded, however great his genius, in dealing alone with so vast a subject. History, as has become clear from our survey of Greece, differs absolutely from poetry or philosophy in that it needs an apparatus for investigation. Philosophy may get a new grip upon the questions of reality from a Descartes divesting himself—or trying to do so—of the inheritance of past systems. But the historian can never work in isolation. The conditions under which Thucydides wrote justify the revisions in his story of the Peloponnesian war which may be made by any editor of the merest selections for college textbooks; since the Romans failed to develop historical apparatus any more adequate for their purpose than that of the Greeks was for Thucydides, we should, at best, have had the same kind of exploit over again. From Thucydides to Ammianus Marcellinus stretch almost eight hundred years, during which ran the whole drama of the classic world. Yet little, if any, progress was made in the work of the historian. On the other hand, from the day of Niebuhr, hardly a century ago, to the present, the whole perspective of that antiquity has been remade and a multitude of facts established which the antique historians should have known but had no way of finding out. Surely no greater proof is needed that history, to be adequate, differs from the rest of literature in that it is more science than art, a social rather than an individual product.

The sense of the mediocre character of the historical writings of Romans during the Republic is brought out by Cicero in the one treatment of history and its possibilities which has come down to us in Latin literature. The setting is significant, for it occurs in his treatise, *On the Orator*,[2] an imaginary dialogue, placed by Cicero at the Tusculan villa of Crassus in the year 91 B.C. The principal disputants were the two great orators Lucius Licinius

---

[1] F. Cumont, *The Oriental Religions in Roman Paganism* (tr., 1911), p. 7, where the debt of Rome to the Orient is brilliantly summarized.
[2] Cicero, *De oratore*, Book II, Chap. 12.

Crassus and Marcus Antonius.[3] The passage which deals with history occurs in a most incidental way. Antonius has been speaking of the fact that no special training is needed by the orator to quote official documents in his speeches—a point with which his interlocutor, Catulus, agrees:

"Well, then, to proceed," said Antonius, "what sort of orator, or how great a master of language, do you think it requires to write history?" "If to write it as the Greeks have written, a man of the highest powers," said Catulus; "if as our own countrymen, there is no need of an orator; it is sufficient for the writer to tell truth."

This depreciation of the old Roman historiographers—for so mere truthtelling was regarded—is apparently brought in to indicate the general opinion in which they were held in Cicero's day. It draws from Antonius, however, the following justification of the Romans by way of a slight historical survey. The most noticeable point in this survey is the recognition upon the part of Cicero—for of course it is Cicero who speaks—that the development of historiography in Greece and Rome took place along exactly similar lines:

"But," rejoined Antonius, "that you may not despise those of our own country, the Greeks themselves too wrote at first just like our Cato, and Pictor, and Piso. For history was nothing else but a compilation of annals; and accordingly, for the sake of preserving the memory of public events, the pontifex maximus used to commit to writing the occurrences of every year, from the earliest period of Roman affairs to the time of the Pontifex Publius Mucius, and had them engrossed on white tablets, which he set forth as a register in his own house, so that all the people had liberty to inspect it; and these records are yet called the Great Annals. This mode of writing many have adopted, and, without any ornaments of style, have left behind them simple chronicles of times, persons, places, and events. Such, therefore, as were Pherecydes, Hellanicus, Acusilas, and many others among the Greeks, are Cato, and Pictor, and Piso with us, who neither understand how composition is to be adorned (for ornaments of style have been but recently introduced among us), and, provided what they related can be understood, think brevity of expression the only merit."

---

[3] Grandfather of the triumvir.

We shall revert later to this account of the Annales Maximi, for it is a prime source; what interests us here is to follow the clue which Cicero offers as to the reasons for the mediocrity of Roman history writing. His whole interest is in the style of the writers. The first step forward was, in his eyes, when Antipater, the instructor of the orator Crassus, adorned his narrative with rhetoric. Admittedly Antipater overdid it,[4] but yet history at Rome did not amount to much before his time. The implication is clear, and is developed by Antonius. History is an art, and as such is to be compared with oratory; and the point is made that the Romans have failed to do it justice because they have concentrated too excessively upon forensic eloquence:

"It is far from being wonderful," said Antonius, "if history has not yet made a figure in our language; for none of our countrymen study eloquence except to display it in pleading and in the forum; whereas among the Greeks, the most eloquent men, wholly unconnected with public pleading, sought to gain renown in other ways, such as writing history; for of Herodotus himself, who first lent distinction to this kind of writing, we hear that he was never engaged in pleading; yet his eloquence is so great as to delight me extremely, as far as I can understand Greek. After him, in my opinion, Thucydides has certainly surpassed all historians in the art of composition; for he has such a wealth of material, that he almost equals the number of his words by the number of his thoughts. He too, so far as we know, although he was engaged in public affairs, was not one of those who engaged in pleading; and he is said to have written his books at a time when he was removed from all civil employments, and, as usually happened to every eminent man at Athens, was driven into banishment. He was followed by Philistus of Syracuse, who, living in great familiarity with the tyrant Dionysius, spent his leisure in writing history, and, as I think, principally imitated Thucydides. Afterwards, two men of great genius, Theopompus and Ephorus, coming from what we may call the noblest school of rhetoric, applied themselves to history by the persuasions of their master Isocrates, and never attended to pleading at all. At last historians arose also among the philosophers; first Xenophon, the follower of Socrates, and afterwards Callisthenes, the pupil of Aristotle and companion of Alexander. The latter wrote in an almost rhetorical manner; the former used a milder strain of language, which has not the animation of oratory, but, though perhaps less energetic,

---

[4] Cicero, *De oratore*, Book II, Chap. 13.

is, as it seems to me, much more pleasing. Timæus, the last of all these, but, as far as I can judge, by far the most learned, and richest in subject matter and variety of thought, and not unpolished in style, brought a large store of eloquence to this kind of writing, but no experience in pleading causes." [5]

There is a good deal to think about in this slight sketch. It is a chapter of the history of history in miniature, the first and only one in Latin literature. Yet it deals with Greeks! Rome had as yet produced no such line of great historians. Sallust, Livy, and Tacitus were yet to come. Cicero knew only one Latin name to match the Greeks, the elder Cato, and in judging him he used Hellenic standards. He recognized that the field of history is one by itself, and he had a real appreciation of its dignity, but after all, it did not interest him as did philosophy. He did not attempt to transmit to Rome the ideals of Thucydides, as he did those of the Platonic school of thinkers to whom he owed so much.[6] Thucydides is "a wise and dignified narrator of facts," but he "was never accounted an orator," and used hard and obscure sentences in his speeches; as for Xenophon, though "his style is sweeter than honey," it is "as unlike as possible to the noisy style of the forum." It is therefore a mistake, says Cicero, to imitate, as some do, the one or the other in the training of an orator.[7]

Once having got our bearings, that history is a useful art and that its chief use is to furnish inspiration or "points" to the orator, it is clear that rules should be at hand for its production, rules that the orator might readily apply. Yet no such treatment can be found among the works on rhetoric; and this leads Cicero to supply the need, in an oft-quoted passage:

Who is ignorant that the first law in writing history is that the historian must not dare to say anything that is false, and the next, that he must dare to tell the truth? Also that there must be no suspicion

[5] *Ibid.*, Book II, Chaps. 13-14.
[6] Cicero, *De oratore*, Chaps. 3-4. "I confess that I have been made an orator (if indeed I am one at all, or such as I am), not by the workshop of the rhetoricians, but by the works of the Academy." It is philosophy that stirs the imagination of the great orator, and imagination is the main thing in eloquence (not facts!).
[7] Cicero, *De oratore*, Chap. 9. The admission of this vogue is as significant as Cicero's comment.

of partiality or of personal animosity? These fundamental rules are doubtless universally known. The superstructure depends on facts and style. The course of facts (*rerum ratio*) requires attention to order of time and descriptions of countries; and since, in great affairs, such as are worthy of remembrance, we look first for the designs, then the actions, and afterwards the results, it should also show what designs the writer approves; and with regard to the actions, not only what was done or said, but in what manner; and when the result is stated, all the causes contributing to it, whether arising from accident, wisdom, or temerity. As to the characters concerned, not only their acts should be set forth but the life and manners of at least those eminent in reputation and dignity. The sort of language and character of style to be observed must be regular and continuous, flowing with a kind of equable smoothness, without the roughness of judicial pleadings, and the sharp-pointed sentences used at the bar. Concerning all these numerous and important points, there are no rules, do you observe, to be found in the treatises of the rhetoricians.[8]

It is perhaps somewhat confusing, in an introductory chapter, to have the doors thus thrown open upon the central theme. But Cicero reveals more than he intends, and one sees from these slight sketches what there was in the Roman attitude toward history which determined its whole character. Two things stand out: the practical bent of the Roman, and his Greek education. History is an aid to statesmen and orators, furnishing examples of actions to emulate or avoid, or illustrations for speeches, which the user—if not the historian himself [9]—may improve to suit the needs of an idea or a phrase.[10] Truth for truth's sake is all right in its way; but truth that is apt and to the point, in debate or in practice, is worth more to a Roman. Now history abounds in truths that may be applied; the trouble is that in applying them one is likely to destroy the nexus of events and lose the sense of historical relationships, of that *process,* in short, which gives

---

[8] Cicero, *De oratore,* Book II, Chap. 15.

[9] Cf. Quintilian's dictum, *De institutione oratoria,* Book X, Chap. 1, Sect. 31: *Historia ... scribitur ad narrandum non ad probandum.*

[10] Cf. Cicero, *Brutus,* Chap. 11. "It is the privilege of rhetoricians to exceed the truth of history that they may have the opportunity of embellishing the fate of their heroes." Collections of historical anecdotes were compiled to aid the rhetorician in his praise of virtue and denunciation of vice. The best known of these collections was made by Valerius Maximus in the days of Tiberius, under the title, *Nine Books of Memorable Deeds and Sayings.* It consisted of short, pointed, and highly embellished stories drawn largely from Cicero, Livy, and Sallust.

History at Rome; Oratory and Poetry

meaning to the whole.[11] Pragmatic history, in spite of the plea of Polybius,[12] is dangerous business. The practical Roman, however, was not so much interested in any other kind. And his native bent was not corrected by his Greek education. "Greece captive, captured Rome," as the saying ran. And the Greeks who achieved this cultural triumph were the grammarians and rhetoricians who taught the Latins the arts of elegance and sophistication. The effect of Greece upon Rome was seen in history as in poetry and in religion, a constant influence reaching all the way from the transformation of its early legends to embellishments of style in the later writers.

The legendary element in Roman history is the most unhistorical product imaginable, being made up of sophisticated and late inventions in imitation of Greek mythology rather than of folk myths and supplanting the simple annals of the poor by suggestions of strange adventures that linked the origins of Rome with the great days of Troy. To the Roman there was little worthy of record in the humble story of his little farmer-state, struggling with its neighbors of Latium. There are no contemporary legends of the long period of history in which Rome grew from a group of villages on the hills by the swampy backwater of the Tiber, to be the chief city of the western plain. Contemporary data begin only when Rome was already conquering the Mediterranean.[13] And as both Polybius and Livy "recognized as the chief principle of historical criticism that there can be no trustworthy and sincere history where there have not been contemporary historians," we may frankly and shortly dismiss, as not germane to our subject, the legendary heritage which Rome possessed from its earliest days. It remained for a Wissowa or a Fowler in our own day to recover from the fragmentary remains of cult and myth, of law and custom, the living picture of that quaint, if unheroic, life of wattled hut and marketplace which left its traces on the Roman character, but which the glamour of

---

[11] In other words, destroy the *history*. See Chap. I, for definition.
[12] It would be interesting to speculate as to how much of Polybius' pragmatism is a reflection of Roman influences.
[13] Only the scientific mind has a sense of the significance of the obscure. So long as history is considered as primarily one of the literary arts such things escape it.

Greece and of Rome's own great career obscured until the critics of the nineteenth century began their destructive and reconstructive work.[14]

If the legends of early Rome were unreal, even as legends, we need hardly delay over the way in which the epic poets immortalized them. And yet, this was history to Romans, almost, if not quite, as the Homeric poems were to Greeks. Indeed, the epos of Rome was a recurring echo of the great voice of Homer. It was not necessarily due to any inherent weakness of the Roman imagination, as is often supposed, nor to any abstract nature of the Italian gods; it was rather due to the absence of a great adventure. There was no racial sense among the dwellers of Latium as among the Greeks; they had no "barbarian" world against which to sharpen their national consciousness. Moreover, they were conquered by Etruscans and the greatest age of the early period was under foreign kings. Hence there was little chance for an epic of glorious war. As for the abstract deities, the gods of early peoples are not abstract; we are beginning now to understand better the cults and faith of early Rome. There were no great divine happenings, simply because the worshippers had done nothing heroic; for the myth of the gods is a reflection of the human story. The deities of Rome were obscure, not abstract. Later, there was no need to invent new epic poetry when that of Greece had been captured and brought home along with the rest of the booty.[15]

---

[14] This is not the place for a comprehensive survey of the remaking of early Roman history. The groundwork of historical criticism was laid by Louis de Beaufort, in his *Dissertation sur l'incertitude des cinq premiers siècles de l'histoire romaine* (1738). B. G. Niebuhr's great work is still of absorbing interest. The first two volumes of his *Römische Geschichte* appeared in 1812, a third in 1832, and his *Lectures* in 1846. The reaction against his negative criticism has generally taken the line that the growth of Rome might be traced fairly well through an analysis of its institutions. T. Mommsen's *Römische Geschichte* (1st ed., 1854-1856) deliberately ignored the early period as unhistorical, but even the credit which he was willing to allow the later sources on the regal era (in his various studies), has been denied by the vigorous skepticism of E. Pais, *Ancient Legends of Roman History* (1905), Chap. I, "The Critical Method."

[15] There is no argument for any native lack of inventive capacity in the Romans because they appropriated Greek culture. Compare America today, which copies everything European, down to millinery. Yet we like to think that our inventive faculties are still available and could be shifted to other uses than those of busi-

History at Rome; Oratory and Poetry 263

The first of the predecessors of Vergil was Livius Andronicus (c. 284-204 B.C.), a Greek from Tarentum who translated the *Odyssey* into Latin. The wanderings of Ulysses into those western seas which wash the shores of Italy—rather than the siege of Troy itself—was the suggestive theme for Italians. Then came Naevius (d. c. 199 B.C.), a true Roman, who adapted several plays from the Greek and composed a few of his own dealing with subjects drawn from Roman history (Romulus and Remus, a victory over the Gauls) and who, towards the end of his life, wrote a history of the first Punic War, which he had himself seen, in "the style of a mediaeval chronicle but with a mythological framework after the Homeric manner (Juno as the enemy, Venus as the friend of the Trojans, Jupiter and Apollo taking personal part in the action)." [16] But the one who, more than any other except Vergil himself, fastened the poetic legend of Trojan origins upon Roman history was Ennius (d. 169 B.C.), whose *Annales* were placed by Cicero on the plane of the history of Herodotus for reliability,[17] whom Livy used as a source, and upon whom Vergil built. He traced the history of Rome from the landing of Aeneas in Italy down to his own time, the end of the second century B.C. Ennius was considerably more of a historian than one would at first suspect from the medium he used, for he availed himself of the Homeric device of accumulating lists and exact data in order to record not imaginary but historical, or at least legendary, material. His narrative was influenced by his intimate relations with the older Scipio Africanus and tends to take the side of the Scipios in the politics of the great Roman houses, as against the Fabians, who had as their exponent the first Roman historian—to be considered in the following chapter—Q. Fabius Pictor. Ennius was successful in outbidding Pictor in popularity, and the story of the old families as preserved in later days obscured the exploits of the Fabians. But the creator of the Latin hexameter—for Ennius has that distinction—did not allow these

---

ness in case of need. The point is that circumstances, rather than natural capacity, dictate our activities.

[16] W. S. Teuffel and L. Schwabe, *History of Roman Literature* (tr., 1891-1892), Vol. I, Sect. 95, *n.* 8.

[17] Cicero, *De divinatione,* Book II, Chap. 56.

clannish interests to obscure the main one, which was the history of Rome itself. We come at the outset, therefore, upon the striking fact that in poetry as in prose, from first to last, the chief aim of Latin literature, responsive to the demands of national outlook, is the exaltation of the state.

The culmination of the poetic legend in Latin was, of course, Vergil's *Aeneid*. Merely to recall it here shows how far from the narrow paths of history those delusive, quasi-historical interests take us, which linked the Rome of Augustus with the story of its origins. It was a work of genius to carry into the sophisticated age of the Principate the simplicity and charm of a tale of the olden time; to recreate Homer, as it were, consciously, and to impress both for his own time and for succeeding ages a sense of reality upon mere poetic imaginings by the sheer, inevitable quality of art. Yet this assent which he won for a fabricated myth was secured less by the Homeric power of narrative than by stirring the emotions of readers over the fate of his characters. St. Augustine tells us how deeply he was affected, as a youth, by the story of Dido dying for the love of Aeneas, a tale with a charm to rival the Christian epos.[18] Vergil shows how human sympathy may translate even the grotesque into the field of experience. Next to this emotional suggestiveness must be mentioned the religious quality of Vergil's mind, that *pietas* or reverence, which calls forth a responsive note wherever the universal "will to believe" is supported by emotion. It was reverence for the greatness in Rome's destiny which tinged even the remote distances with dignity, while the spell of the past lent, in turn, to the present a gleam of poetry and romance. Moreover, the narrative, varied as it was from simple, natural scenes in keeping with the quiet of the poet's own temper to the splendor of imperial visions, offered a pageant of life and color which until then was unknown in Latin literature. It is small wonder, therefore, that the myth content of the *Aeneid* became fixed upon Rome as a substitute for history.[19]

[18] Augustine, *Confessiones*, Book I, Chap. 13.
[19] The first edition turned at this point to Lucretius. The following two paragraphs of appreciation of Vergil were contributed by Professor Swain.

History at Rome; Oratory and Poetry 265

The author of this mighty epic was born near Mantua in 70, and died in 19 B.C. He passed his young manhood during the civil war, made the acquaintance of Maecenas and Augustus who encouraged him in his work, and wrote his great poem during the decade that followed the battle of Actium (31 B.C.). Nominally, the *Aeneid* tells once more the story, already told by Ennius and others, of how Aeneas carried his ancestral gods (civilization) from Troy to Italy and became the founder of the Roman people. But the poem contains much besides. It is a glorification of Rome and her world mission and of Augustus; and it is a sermon and exhortation addressed to the Romans of Vergil's day. As was natural for a poet writing in the early days of the Empire, Vergil hopefully looked forward to a glorious future; but his spirit had been deeply chastened by the miseries of the civil war, and a strain of sadness runs through his poem, giving it at once a wistful charm and a high seriousness of purpose. *Sunt lacrimae rerum et mentem mortalia tangunt*—"Here are tears for man's fate, and man's lot touches the mind!" In the midst of the miseries of his own day, Vergil sought to hearten and reform his compatriots by reminding them of their glorious yet difficult past. Time and again he finds occasion to describe events, places, and persons celebrated in Roman history, and we see the whole story of the city, from Romulus and Remus suckled by the wolf down to Octavian at Actium. In the midst of incredible dangers and difficulties, these men, like their ancestor, the "pious" Aeneas, had remained true to their duty and had built up the greatness of Rome. *Tantae molis erat Romanam condere gentem*—"So great was the labor of founding of Roman race." Of course much of the history thus told was scarcely true, and it all was embellished for increased effectiveness; but Vergil was one of the most scholarly of poets, deeply read in history, and—like the Roman orators mentioned above or the historian Livy to be mentioned below—he found in the heroes of Rome's past an appropriate inspiration and model for the Romans of his own day. The memory of their deeds should be preserved forever. In stirring words he addressed the brothers Nisus and Euryalus, who had died bravely:

> *Fortunati ambo! Si quid mea carmina possunt,*
> *Nulla dies umquam memori vos eximet aevo,*
> *Dum domus Aeneae Capitoli inmobile saxum*
> *Accolet imperiumque pater Romanus habebit.*

"Fortunate both, if my words can accomplish aught, you will never pass from memory while the house of Aeneas holds the changeless rock of the Capitol and Father Rome retains his sway" (Book IX, lines 445-49).

These words are highly reminiscent of the opening sentence of Herodotus but they also suggest more remotely, Thucydides' expression about "a possession forever." In each case the everlasting possession was a story of deeds—facts—which both author and reader believed to be true—or essentially so—which were well told, and which seemed to have an importance for the life of the day in which they were told. The event showed that Vergil's type of history was the more powerful, and that he came closer than Thucydides to producing a possession forever. He perfected the major outlines of Rome's marvellous epic, and his statement of it was accepted until modern times as the outline of Rome's history. More prosaic historians merely fitted details into this outline.

If consideration of the myths of Rome has carried us over into the field of Latin poetry before we have so much as secured a foothold in that of history proper, we may as well profit by the occasion, before turning to the sober beginnings of prose annals, to consider here a poem which stands apart from all others, not only in Latin, but in the world's literature, and which is of deep and lasting interest to thoughtful students of history—the poem of Lucretius, *On the Nature of Things* (*De rerum natura*). If Vergil stands with Homer in epic power and universality of appeal, Lucretius suggests comparison with Dante or Milton, both in the sombre "fanatical faith" in his scheme of the universe, and in his sense of a religious mission to rid the world of superstition. But the vision of the world which he proposed to substitute for that of popular imagination was not, as in the case of Dante or Milton, merely a reinterpretation of accepted beliefs, refined through Aristotelian or biblical media. Lucretius proposed to dispense with myth entirely, and, many centuries before its day, wrote in terms of science. It is a poem for the twentieth century, in this sense perhaps the most marvelous performance in all antique literature. Any survey of antique processes of mind as they bear upon the development of historical outlook would be sadly incomplete without an examination of *De rerum natura*.

Of the life of Lucretius Carus (c. 95–55 B.C.) little is known.[20] The one poem which has been left us appeared just before Vergil's day, and, "though it not only revealed a profound and

---

[20] The brief notice in St. Jerome's *Chronicle,* stating that he lost his reason through a drug and wrote in the intervals of sanity and that Cicero with his own hand edited the poem, while practically the only account we have, is open to suspicion on each of the three supposed facts which it supplies.

History at Rome; Oratory and Poetry

extraordinary genius, but marked a new technical level in Latin poetry, stole into the world all but unnoticed,"[21] whereas the *Aeneid* was produced (and even preserved)[22] under the direct patronage of Augustus. In neither style nor message was there any of the appealing charm of Vergil, but a scheme of the world based upon Epicurean philosophy, cast into a ringing, if metallic, verse. Much of this lies outside our field; we are not concerned here with atomistic theories nor with the fate of the dead, nor even with the effort to justify man's place in the universe by displacing superstition and the fear of the gods. But there is more than a philosophy of history in the marvellous fifth book, which traces the birth of the world and then, after the scientific postulates of creation, attempts a survey of the beginnings of life, of men, and of civilization. Strongly countering that natural tendency to look backward to a golden age, a dawn of innocence in an Eden of the gods, such as the Jews or Greeks had accepted, Lucretius begins with the slow evolution of life from lower forms to higher; first vegetable, then animal, then primitive man, suffering much but living a wild and hardy life. The beginning of civilization and the central fact of social origins according to Lucretius, as also according to the sociologists today, was the discovery and use of fire; it came, not as a gift of a god, but either from lightning setting trees aflame, or from the friction of dry boughs in the wind. No Vulcan brought fire and its blessings to men; natural causes led to its discovery. Then control of metals brought an ever-enlarging control over nature, and with settled life came politics and the state, the arts and sciences. Even religion had a natural origin, for, terrified by dreams at night and filled with the awe engendered by mystery, mankind created its gods by its own imaginings and so obscured the patent but elusive truth. This generalized plan of human advance is not history in the narrower sense; but where such a genius as that of Lucretius illustrates the process, it offers the historian more suggestion than he sometimes proves worthy of receiving.

[21] J. W. Mackail, *Latin Literature* (1895; repr. 1907), p. 40.
[22] Vergil, dying before he had the chance to work it over as he wished, had left instructions that it should be destroyed. Augustus countermanded these orders.

We may, therefore, close this chapter by quoting a section or two from the one poet-critic and philosophic thinker of antiquity who eliminated from his mind that entire myth picture of social origins which, in one form or another, obscured with its mirage the vision of all antiquity; and who, by so doing, anticipated much of modern discovery.

Quotation from Lucretius is difficult, both because the expression itself is often involved and because the poem so holds together that extracts fail to carry the argument. But one may catch a glimpse of its graphic power from the lines which describe the various possible ways in which the smelting of metals may have been learned:

> ... copper and gold and iron were discovered, and with them the weight of silver and the usefulness of lead, when a fire had burnt down vast forests with its heat on mighty mountains, either when heaven's lightning was hurled upon it, or because waging a forest-war with one another men had carried fire among the foe to rouse panic, or else because allured by the richness of the land they desired to clear the fat fields, and make the countryside into pastures, or else to put the wild beasts to death, and enrich themselves with prey. For hunting with pit and fire arose first before fencing the grove with nets and scaring the beasts with dogs. However that may be, for whatever cause the flaming heat had eaten up the forests from their deep roots with terrible crackling, and had baked the earth with fire, the streams of silver and gold, and likewise of copper and lead, gathered together and trickled from the boiling veins into hollow places in the ground. And when they saw them afterwards hardened and shining on the ground with brilliant hue, they picked them up, charmed by their smooth bright beauty, and saw that they were shaped with outline like that of the several prints of the hollows. Then it came home to them that these metals might be melted by heat, and would run into the form and figure of anything, and indeed might be hammered out and shaped into points and tips, however sharp and fine, so that they might fashion weapons for themselves, and be able to cut down forests and hew timber and plane beams smooth, yea, and to bore and punch and drill holes. And, first of all, they set forth to do this no less with silver and gold than with the resistless strength of stout copper; all in vain, since their power was vanquished and yielded, nor could they like the others endure the cruel strain. Then copper was of more value, and gold was despised for its uselessness, so soon blunted with its dull edge. Now copper is despised, gold has risen to the height of honour. So rolling time changes the seasons of things.

What was of value, becomes in turn of no worth; and then another thing rises up and leaves its place of scorn, and is sought more and more each day, and when found blossoms into fame, and is of wondrous honour among men.[23]

Then follow a disquisition on the art of war and a rapid series of pictures of the various stages of social development, pastoral, agricultural, and urban, ending with the luxuries of civilization.

So, little by little, time brings out each several thing into view, and reason raises it up into the coasts of light."[24]

The pathway to those coasts of light, which Lucretius pointed out, unhappily lay untravelled, and there was ample justification for the poignant lines which he interjected into the sketch of history, when treating of the origins of religion—lines which match the noblest protests of reason in the face of mystery in all literature:

Ah! unhappy race of men, when it has assigned such acts to the gods and joined therewith bitter anger! what groaning did they then beget for themselves, what sores for us, what tears for our children to come! Nor is it piety at all to be seen often with veiled head turning towards a stone, and to draw near to every altar, no, nor to be prostrate on the ground with outstretched palms before the shrines of the gods, nor to sprinkle the altars with the streaming blood of beasts, nor to link vow to vow; but rather to be able to contemplate all things with a mind at rest.[25]

But the mind of Lucretius was not "at rest." Such gloomy might is not serenity. Its very poise is protest—protest against that "will to believe" which is the universal barrier to science. No wonder the world at large shrank from such stern rationalism, and preferred the genial, mythical stories of Vergil.

[23] Lucretius, *De rerum natura*, Book V, lines 1241-1280, translated by C. Bailey, 1910 (reprinted by permission of the Clarendon Press).
[24] *Ibid.*, Book V, lines 1454-55.
[25] *Ibid.*, Book V, lines 1194-1203.

CHAPTER XX

Roman Annalists and Early Historians

IN THE last chapter much was made of the Greek characteristics of the Latin legends of origin. It is possible, however, that the taste for indigenous historical materials was stronger in Rome than one would suspect from the slight remains we possess. Cicero tells us how the Roman nobles loved to be glorified in poetry.[1] The ancestral cult of Rome, combined with this aristocratic tendency of noble houses to exalt their deeds, was, naturally, one of the mainsprings of Roman history. It was a tainted spring, but bountiful.

It was customary [says Cicero in another place [2]] in most families of note, to preserve their images, their trophies of honor, and their memoirs, either to adorn a funeral when any of the family died, or to perpetuate the fame of their ancestors, or to prove their own nobility. But the truth of history has been much corrupted by these laudatory essays, for many circumstances were recorded in them which never happened, such as false triumphs, a pretended succession of consulships, and false connections and distinctions, when men of inferior rank were confounded with a noble family of the same name; as if I myself should pretend that I am descended from Manius Tullius, who was a Patrician, and shared the consulship with Servius Sulpicius, about ten years after the expulsion of the kings.

Such records of noble families, reaching back to primitive tradition and written down later by slaves or dependents, formed one of the chief sources for Roman historians when dealing with the early period. They knew, as Cicero did, that the material was

---

[1] Cicero, *Pro Archia Poeta*, Chaps. 9-11. The description given here of the means taken by the Roman dignitaries to preserve their names and exalt their glory reminds one somewhat of the inscriptions of Egypt or Babylon.

[2] Cicero, *Brutus*, Chap. 16.

not worth much [3]; but they did not know how to apply the canons of historical criticism so as to move surely and safely through the treacherous offerings.

By way of these specious antecedents of history we pass from poetry to prose, that farthest flung line of the scientific advance. Prose literature, developing slowly and late in Rome as elsewhere, naturally came more directly under Greek influence than poetry. Written Latin prose did not rise to rival the spoken Latin until Cicero's day, which partly explains why there is so much about orators in Cicero's essays and the echo of a similar interest in the historians—even in Tacitus. Moreover, Latin prose literature had a short period of flower, declining after the first century of the empire, partly because the formalism of the patrician periods was out of keeping with the realism of business, and partly because the men of the provinces developed their varied forms of speech. History writing among the Romans did not, therefore, develop its own natural media of expression but, like a borrowed or captured piece of art, remained more or less out of place in its setting. The façade was Attic, or affected by Attic influences; yet the structure of most Roman histories was of the simplest and homeliest of designs—that of the annal.

The starting point for this annalistic treatment was that register of annual events kept by the Pontifex Maximus in the Regia, which has been described above in the passage from Cicero. It was there where "all the people had the liberty to inspect it." So important was it that its style "was adopted by many" of the earlier Roman historians, a style "without any ornaments," "simple chronicles of times, persons, places and events." In the eyes of Cicero, history at Rome developed mainly along the lines of this annalistic writing; and so it had up to his time. The description he gives is confirmed by an examination of the available references to obscure authors and by the traces they have left upon the method of Livy and Tacitus themselves.

[3] In this connection mention should be made of the use of the old inscriptions by the later historians. Monumental inscriptions were used by both Greek and Roman historians of early Rome, but they were sometimes misled by what they saw, and the monuments became foundations for new myths, as is likely to be the case anywhere if full contemporary records are missing.

The extract from Cicero on the *Annales Maximi*, slight as it is, is matched by only one other paragraph in the Latin literature which has come down to us. In the closing part of the fourth century of our era, Servius, a grammarian who wrote an exhaustive commentary on Vergil, described the pontifical annals as follows:

> The annals were made in this way. The pontifex maximus had a white tablet (prepared) every year, on which, on certain days,[4] he was accustomed to note, under the names of the consuls and other magistrates, those deeds both at home and in the field, on land or at sea, which were deemed worthy to be held in remembrance. The diligence of the ancients inscribed 80 books with these annual commentaries, and these were called *Annales Maximi* from the Pontifices Maximi by whom they were made.[5]

The starting point for our survey is therefore the Regia, or house of the head of that college of priests, the *pontifices*, who had perpetuated the religious duties of the abolished kingship, having charge of the calendar and the archives, that is, both the measurement and the record of time. The *album* or white wood tablet which our sources describe—and the two quoted are practically all there are on the *Annales Maximi*—was, therefore, but one of several records in their keeping. In addition to those which dealt more especially with sacred science, the *Libri pontificum* and the *Commentarii pontificum*, there were also *Fasti calendares* or *Fasti consulares*, with the names of officials and items for the calendar. The *Annales* differed from the rest in that they were prepared for the public. How extensive they were is a matter of conjecture. Cicero rhetorically dates them from the very origin of Rome. The repeated destruction of the Regia by fire really left the later Roman antiquaries in the dark as to their actual extent. It seems likely, however, that no contemporary pontifical annal *of the kind described* was kept during the long period when

---

[4] *Per singulos dies*, not *every day*, but when the event happened. Hence the *acta diurna*, or official daily bulletin from the time of Julius Caesar, was not a continuation of this.

[5] *Servii Grammatici qui feruntur in Vergilii carmina commentarii*, edited by George Thilo and Hermann Hagen (3 vols., 1878-1887), Vol. I, Bk. I, line 373. This paragraph occurs only in the manuscript published by Daniel in 1600 and may belong to a later commentator.

Rome grew from a group of farming villages to be the chief city of Latium. In any case, the sack of Rome by the Gauls (390 B.C.) destroyed whatever the pontiffs had preserved. Livy tells us that "whatever was contained in the commentaries of the pontiffs and other public and private records, was lost, for the most part, in the burning of the city" (Book VI, Chap. 1). The great pile of dry wood in the Regia was right at hand for the Gauls to warm themselves, and the tablets must have made good fuel.[6] The result was that, whatever historical data the early pontiffs prepared, the later Romans could not profit from them. Year by year, however, during the robust period of the republican expansion, the Pontifex would hang up the white tablet on the wall of his house for the citizens to see and, for such as could, to read. The practice lasted until about 120 B.C., when, owing to the growth of the histories by private individuals, it became superfluous. Then P. Mucius Scaevola published the whole extant collection in one volume of eighty books, as Servius intimates in the extract above. Upon the whole it would seem that this official history shared the defects of such compositions as we have noted them elsewhere with only this in its favor, that in a republic the rival claims of leaders and clans act in some degree in the place of criticism. Whether or not it was the prominence of these official annals which, in the absence of genuine historical literature, made the annalistic—or at least the chronological—structure the chief orthodox form for history writing in Latin, the fact remains that Roman historiography is strikingly held to the annalistic mould. Even Tacitus' *Annales* bear (though disguised) the common impress.[7] Indeed the word *annal* was much more the synonym for "history" than *historia*. Not only was it used in that general sense which it has in such English phrases as "the annals of the poor" or "the annals of the Empire,"[8] but in the eyes of the grammarians it was the only correct term for

---

[6] O. Seeck, *Die Kalendertafel der Pontifices* (1885), p. 74.
[7] On the influence of the old annalistic forms on Tacitus' works, see E. Courbaud, *Les Procédés d'art de Tacite dans les Histoires* (1918), p. 34 and references.
[8] So Ennius called his epic *Annales;* and when Vergil refers to the content of early history he uses the same general term (*Aeneid*, Book I, line 373: *Et vacet annales nostrorum audire laborum*).

history of the past. *Historia* was properly used only of contemporaneous narrative.⁹ So, indeed, we find the works of Tacitus which deal with his own day termed *Historiae* and those dealing with an earlier period *Annales,* although these titles probably do not come from Tacitus' own hand.¹⁰

The official annals, therefore, seem to have played a considerable role in early Roman historiography. Of the remaining books of the priesthood, the *Fasti* are, perhaps, the most important. These began as lists of days for the calendar, the lucky and unlucky days—*dies fasti* and *dies nefasti*—and as such remained, through a varied history, the basis of calendarmaking, even through the Julian reform and into the Christian era. The name was, therefore, naturally transferred as well to denote annalistic chronicles, lists of years giving the names of consuls, etc. (*Fasti consulares*) and the lists of triumphs (*Fasti triumphales*). Two such lists were drawn up in the reign of Augustus.

In addition to the *Annales Maximi* and the *Fasti* of the pontiffs, there were lists of secular magistrates, such as the *Libri magistratuum* or *Books of the Magistrates,* reminding one of the Eponym lists of the Assyrians. Some of them were written on linen (*libri lintei*) and kept in the temple of Juno Moneta, the Goddess of Memory, on the Capitol. Livy may have these in

---

⁹ Thus Servius, commenting on the line of Vergil quoted here, says: "There is this difference between history and annals: history deals with these times which we witness or have been able to witness. The word comes from ἱστορεῖν, that is 'to see' [dicta ἀπὸ τοῦ ἱστορεῖν, id est videre (!)]; but annals are of those times of which our age is ignorant. Hence Livy consists of both annals and history. Nevertheless they are freely used one for the other, as in this place where he says 'annals' for 'history.'" Aulus Gellius had earlier (*Noctes atticae*, Book V, Chap. 18) cited the authority of Verrius Flaccus the lexicographer for this distinction of meaning and adduced practically the only fragment we have of Sempronius Asellio, one of the later annalists, to show that the narrower meaning of the word, a yearly list of happenings, was their ideal of history. Asellio is impatient with the narrowness of those who do not connect the isolated items of war or conquest with the broader theme of politics and who do not show the motives and reasons for which things were done. He terms such annals *fabulas pueris,* unworthy of the name of history. "For annals cannot in any way make men more eager to defend their country, or more reluctant to do wrong."

¹⁰ It is doubtful if they bore any such titles; more likely, as in the case of Livy, whose work was termed *Ab urbe condita libri,* the annals of Tacitus were *Ab excessu d. Augusti.*

Roman Annalists and Early Historians

mind when he refers repeatedly to the *libri magistratuum* (Book II, Chap. 4; Book IV, Chaps. 7, 20), or he may use the term to cover all similar sources and even the *Annales Maximi*. For by the end of the republican era there were a number of such collections, and antiquarians were already working on them.

When we turn from these materials for history to history itself, we find, significantly enough, that the line of Roman historians is headed by one who wrote in Greek. Q. Fabius Pictor is commonly recognized as the first Roman historian.[11] Born about 254 B.C. of distinguished family, he played a leading part in the wars with Ligurians and Gauls before the war with Hannibal, in which he also took part. His *History* (ἱστορία), which carried the story of Rome from the days of Aeneas to his own time, was enriched by access to the archives of his family, in which—as has been the case so often in our day—the official documents of official members of the family had found a resting place. He wrote for the nobles, not for the commonalty (as did his contemporary Plautus, the author of comedy), and memoirs of nobles are also traceable in his work. In fact, history writing in Rome remained, down to the days of Sulla, a privilege of the upper class, from which it drew its readers and to which it appealed, leaving a perspective upon Roman social history which only modern scholarship has been able (in part) to correct. As for Fabius Pictor, he furnished Polybius with his main guide for the second Punic war, in spite of Polybius' uncomplimentary remarks about him, due, perhaps, as has been suggested, to the rivalry of the Scipios (Polybius' patrons) with the Fabii (Book III, Chaps. 8-9). While Livy apparently included him in the indefinite references to the "most ancient writers," he also twice refers to him specifically as "the oldest historian" and once as

[11] Professor Swain adds the following note: "In reality he was merely one of the Hellenistic historical writers, comparable to Berossos and Manetho, who wrote Greek histories of their respective countries. A few other Romans—among them L. Cincius Alimentus, A. Postumius Albinus, and A. Acilius—wrote histories in Greek during the second century; though these works were of no great value as histories—in which they differed from that of Fabius—they attracted a certain attention, and at least one of them was later translated into Latin."

the trustworthy contemporary of the events described, whose name cited in the texts would substantiate the narrative (Book I, Chap. 44; Book II, Chap. 40; Book XXII, Chap. 7). After Livy's day he ceased to be known to Roman authors, although he was still used by Greek historians.

The real father of Roman history, however, was M. Porcius Cato, that most Roman of Romans, who fought the influence of Greece, yet revealed a mind saturated in Greek thought, and who, according to Cicero and Nepos, learned Greek itself late in life. Born about 234 B.C., he lived a busy public life, holding the highest offices, and meanwhile writing earnestly and much at those earliest books of Latin prose, his treatises on agriculture, war, oratory, as well as history. His history, the seven books of *Origines,* was a national work but it repeated the Greek myths of origin.[12] The prefaces to his books recall the school of Isocrates which he ridiculed,[13] and his pragmatic outlook, recommending history for practical uses, while natural enough in a Roman, was also to be found in the Greeks, from whom he professedly turned away. Again, although he kept to the annalistic form, he found it admirably suited for the insertion of orations in the formal style—especially orations which he had delivered himself—and he inserted them to such an extent that the speeches were even brought together as a special collection by themselves.

Cato was a thorough and careful worker; all Latin writers bear witness to that. Cicero refers to his study of the inscriptions on tombstones,[14] which may also reflect a lesson from the Greeks. But his interest did not extend to the varied data of the social life; it was strictly limited to politics. A citation preserved by Aulus Gellius, a chatty antiquary of the second century A.D., is worth quoting:

> They [the Romans] were not very strenuous in their endeavours to explore the causes of the eclipses of the sun and moon. For M. Cato,

---

[12] The first three books gave the old legends regarding the origins of Rome and other Italian cities, while the last four dealt with the two Punic Wars and the events of Cato's own day; the first two and a half centuries of the Republic were therefore treated rather sketchily, if at all.

[13] See Plutarch, *Marcus Cato,* Chap. 23.

[14] Cicero, *Cato maior,* Chap. 11, Sect. 38; Chap. 7, Sect. 21.

who was indefatigable in his researches after learning, has spoken upon this subject indecisively and without curiosity. His words in the fourth book of *Origins* are these: "I have no inclination to transcribe what appears on the tablet of the Pontifex Maximus, how often corn is dear, how often the light of the sun or moon is, from some cause or other, obscured." [15]

From the valuable treatise on agriculture which he left us, we can imagine that Cato followed the grain quotations of the Regia very closely, and as he brought to the task of history writing the training of a practical man, we have every reason to regret that he did not do exactly the thing he here refuses to do. The one thing, however, which the whole of this survey teaches, is that history reflects the major interests of the society which produces it, and that the insight of historians into the importance of events is relatively slight, except as they are interpreters of their own time. The dominant interest of the men around Cato was no longer agriculture, as in the early days of the farmer state, but war and politics and the struggle with Carthage. Hence the trivial incidents of the priestly annals were to be ignored.

Subsequent historians at Rome agreed with Cato in this, but they ceased to struggle as he did against the Greek invasion, and as rhetoric gained the day more and more, Cato was less and less read until, in Cicero's day, he was almost entirely left aside. It is interesting, therefore, to find Cicero himself turning to Cato's defense, for it shows what solid worth there must have been in the first of the Roman historians:

Not to omit his [Cato's] *Antiquities,* who will deny that these also are adorned with every flower, and with all the lustre of eloquence? And yet he has scarcely any admirers; which some ages ago was the case of Philistus the Syracusan, and even of Thucydides himself. For as the lofty and elevated style of Theopompus soon diminished the reputation of their pithy and laconic harangues,[16] which were sometimes scarcely intelligible from excessive brevity and quaintness; and as Demosthenes eclipsed the glory of Lysias; so the pompous and stately elocution of the moderns has obscured the lustre of Cato. But many of us are deficient in taste and discernment, for we admire the Greeks for their

---

[15] Aulus Gellius, *Noctes atticae,* Book II, Chap. 28 (tr. Beloe).
[16] Thucydides eclipsed by Theopompus!

antiquity, and what is called their Attic neatness, and yet have never noticed the same quality in Cato. This was the distinguishing character, say they, of Lysias and Hyperides. I own it, and I admire them for it; but why not allow a share of it to Cato? They are fond, they tell us, of the Attic style of eloquence; and their choice is certainly judicious, provided they do not only copy the dry bones, but imbibe the animal spirits of these models. What they recommend, however, is, to do it justice, an agreeable quality. But why must Lysias and Hyperides be so fondly admired, while Cato is entirely overlooked? His language indeed has an antiquated air, and some of his expressions are rather too harsh and inelegant. But let us remember that this was the language of the time; only change and modernise it, which it was not in his power to do; add the improvements of number and cadence, give an easier turn.... I know, indeed, that he is not sufficiently polished, and that recourse must be had to a more perfect model for imitation; for he is an author of such antiquity, that he is the oldest now extant whose writings can be read with patience; and the ancients, in general, acquired a much greater reputation in every other art than in that of speaking." [17]

There was another reason, however, besides the severity of his style, for the neglect of Cato's history by the contemporaries of Cicero. If history was prized at Rome by the aristocracy for the glory it reflected on their noble houses, there was little use in preserving Cato's *Origins*. For this confirmed enemy of the upper class made it a point to omit the names of leaders in describing the achievements of Roman arms and carried his grim humor so far, on the other hand, as to preserve for future generations the name of an especially fierce elephant which fought bravely in the line of battle.[18]

We must leave it to more detailed surveys to describe the writers who carried the story of Rome down to the last years of the republic, writers such as P. Mucius Scaevola, who in 123 B.C., as Pontifex Maximus, ended the old *Annales Maximi* and published them; L. Coelius Antipater, the jurist, who broke with the old annalistic style; thoughtful scholars like Sempronius Asellio, who sought, in the manner of Polybius, to establish the causes of

---

[17] Cicero, *Brutus*, Chaps. 17-18.
[18] See Pliny, *Naturalis historia*, Book VIII, Chap. 11; Plutarch, *Marcus Cato*, Chap. 25.

events;[19] Q. Claudius Quadrigarius and the more popular but less critical Valerius Antias; L. Cornelius Sisenna, the historian of the period of Sulla; or C. Licinius Macer, whose *Annales* seem to have been more controversial than accurate. Although these writers were gratefully used by later Latin historians, and above all by Livy, so little has been left of their works or about them as to render comment a matter of minute erudition, out of place in a study like this. Cicero, however, viewing history from the standpoint of literature, offers an illuminating comment on Antipater, who wrote at the close of the second century. Historians up to that time, says Cicero, were simply makers of annals (*annalium confectiores*) and for him history in the proper sense began with Antipater, the first to adorn his tale with art or artifice (*exornator rerum*) instead of being, as his predecessors were, mere narrators.[20]

L. Coelius Antipater was a distinguished jurist and teacher of oratory, who lived a scholarly and retired life during the closing decades of the second century. Perhaps owing to this retirement, he gave up the pragmatic principle and substituted for his aim rather that "pleasure to the ear" (*delectare*) which Thucydides had once denounced but which the followers of Isocrates had made the vogue. He lacked, however, the restraint and good taste of the Greek; carried rhythm to extreme; introduced not only speeches, but also anecdotes; and broke the narrative with all kinds of diversions so that the reader should not suffer ennui. For instance, instead of giving the figures of Scipio's expedition to Africa, he tells us that birds fell from heaven at the noise of the shouting soldiers. As Thucydides had done, he chose a single war, the second Punic, as his theme, rather than the whole story of Rome. In his preface he tells frankly that he takes his material from those authors who are deemed reliable, meaning Fabius Pictor and Cato; but he read widely in Greek and Latin writers. The seven books of this history were used as texts for criticism in the days of Cicero's youth, and where

---

[19] See above, p. 274 *n.* 9.
[20] *Ceteri non exornatores rerum, sed tantummodo narratores fuerunt.*—Cicero, *De oratore*, Book II, Chap. 12.

rhetoric flourished more than history, Antipater flourished with it. An epitome was prepared by Marcus Brutus, and the Emperor Hadrian is said to have preferred him to Sallust—the student of Thucydides, the first real Roman historian in the eyes of the modern.

CHAPTER XXI

Varro, Caesar, and Sallust

IF THE achievement of Roman historians was disappointing, the fault did not lie altogether in a lack of interest about the past, as is witnessed by the list of historians of the closing era of the Republic which has been given in the last chapter; and historians were not the only ones to contribute antiquarian lore. There were, in addition to poets and historians, other scholars as well at work on all kinds of curious investigation, interpreting auguries or the archaic hymns of the Salii, studying the history of law or philosophy or the etymology of words, or simply writing encyclopaedic surveys of things in general. This movement of scholarship forms a notable supplement to Roman historiography, reaching as it does all the way from Cato through Varro to the elder Pliny. Partly in the form of practical manuals, partly in erudite volumes, it preserved a mass of data for the learned society of Cicero's day and later, and it helped to satisfy curiosity as to striking events of unusual customs. But the essentials of criticism were lacking, that is, adequate tools; and it need not surprise the reader of this study to find that the work of these scholars was, upon the whole, on a lower plane than that of the historians. The test of success for the antiquarian at Rome seems to have been what it was for the American capitalist in the nineteenth century, mere amount of output. Varro, for instance, wrote some seventy-five works in over six hundred books. The author of so many works could not examine with care the sources from which such a past store of learning was drawn. The credulous, uncritical character of Pliny's great *Natural History*, the final summing up of this encyclopaedic historical literature, is a fair indication of its inability to sort out fact from fiction; due to the absence not only of historical discipline, but also of those of the other sciences which deal with human evolution: the sciences of language, philology; of society, anthropology; of comparative religion. Yet, inaccurate or not, these collections of the data of history were at hand for the Romans to read, and as the reader is generally still less critical than the writer, there were probably few who had any idea of how thin the line of established fact really was. On the contrary, at least from the day of Varro, it must have seemed to them more like an enveloping, if hazy, sea, in which only the most expert could find his bearings.

We should have a better idea of the situation if the works of Varro had come down to us in anything like the way in which those of Cicero were preserved. But whether it be, as Augustine suggests, that the appeal to the lover of words is stronger than that to the lover of facts,[1] or that the facts ceased to have any meaning by themselves, there remain but slight fragments of the many writings of Varro. Born in 116 B.C., and therefore Cicero's senior by ten years, Varro lived a long and busy life, not as a hermit-scholar, but as a man of affairs, taking an active part in politics; a somewhat whimsical man, as his satirical miscellany shows. The only work which concerns us, however, is his treatise on *Roman Antiquities,* published in 47 B.C. There were twenty-five books dealing with human and sixteen with "divine" antiquities. The data were grouped into large sections under Persons, Places, Times, and Things. There was no attempt to establish their interconnection historically, but simply an amassing of curious facts. Strangely enough, while the part dealing with human affairs was lost, portions of the religious section, the *Antiquitates rerum divinarum,* were destined to be passed down to us because of the interest of Christian theology in combating the pagan deities. Augustine's *City of God* quoted, in order to ridicule them, Varro's accounts of the early cults of Rome. Modern scholarship, correcting Varro in places, is upon the whole able to profit better from the data he offers than were the Fathers of the Church and also better than the believing pagans. To these Varro supplied something like a "counterblast" to the negative criticism of Lucretius, and helped to restore that emphasis upon the good

[1] Augustine, *De civitate dei,* Book VI, Chap. 2.

old Roman virtue of *pietas*, upon which the Vergilian epic was so strongly to insist.

But however much this work of Varro may have served its purpose, we find in the attitude of Cicero towards him an indication that those days were strangely like our own; that literary men sometimes did not read the works of scholars. Cicero did not quote Varro, whose works were not to be found in his library. His friend, Atticus, the bookpublisher and author, had them, however, and urged Cicero to use them; but when Cicero and Varro both made their peace with Caesar and returned to their literary pursuits, Cicero's letters to Varro are still general and somewhat formal.[2] Even under the stress of having to exchange dedications to some of their works, the mutual regard of scholar and man of letters is none too cordial.

This is all the more evident when one turns to the little manual on the history of eloquence which Cicero wrote at this time, under the title *Brutus*. The book itself is of interest to us, for it is the nearest to history of Cicero's writings. It passes in review about two hundred orators, Greek and Roman, but all in the form of a pleasant dialogue, suitably held under the statue of Plato on a quiet lawn, by Brutus, Atticus, and Cicero. But the incident with which it opens is most significant. Atticus had written a short, general outline of universal history. From all that we can gather, it was a poor enough affair, an annal based, like that of his predecessor Cornelius Nepos,[3] upon the Athenian chronicle of Apollodorus, and hence in the direct line that leads through Eusebius, to Christian monastic annals. But it got away from the beaten path of purely Roman antiquities and presented the world as one, and perhaps its very slightness, combined with its extended perspectives, constituted its chief charm. There is no subtler appeal to our intellectual *amour propre* than to have great and difficult truths in science or philosophy made obvious by keeping us unaware of the difficulties. In any case, Cicero hails this manual with lyric joy; it has restored his drooping spirits

---

[2] E. G. Sihler, *Cicero of Arpinum* (1914), pp. 249, 334. This is a suggestive book, crowded with facts but hard to follow.

[3] Atticus' chronicle was written about 47 B.C., that of Cornelius Nepos about 63 B.C. On Apollodorus see above, p. 73 *n*. 12.

and made life worth living in these dark days; it opens out the obscurities of the past to the daylight and furnishes a sure guide where all was so confused! In short, Atticus' outlines have done for Cicero what H. G. Wells' *Outline* has done for the modern busy reader, led him to that "peak in Darien" where he might discover the expanse of Time, not so much with the shock of wild surmise, as with the comfortable assurance that he already had the chart for its exploration. The significance of the incident is not that Atticus had written a manual of general history, but that Cicero needed it so badly.

Reference to this general history naturally recalls at this point the works of the later Greek historian described above, and we may perhaps anticipate here enough to mention the one attempt to carry over into Latin the scheme for universal history, which we met first in Ephorus and Theopompus. Pompeius Trogus, the younger contemporary of Livy, covered the history of the Near East in forty-four books, beginning with Ninus and including the Macedonian Empire. The title of the work, *Historiae Philippicae*, sufficiently indicates the Greek point of view, for the culminating figure was Philip of Macedon. Rome came in only incidentally, and rather as seen by her enemies. This was not the kind of history to rival Livy; and it would have perished utterly had not a certain M. Junianus Justinus made a synopsis of it which was destined largely to satisfy the meagre curiosity of the Middle Ages in the great story of the pagan world. For it was to this that Orosius, the pupil of Augustine, mainly turned for his materials when writing the story of the sufferings of the pre-Christian era which was the historical counterpart to the *City of God*.[4]

Consideration of works like these has carried us somewhat afield from the main lines of Roman historiography. But before we proceed to the first of the great historians of Rome, Sallust, whose figure already stands before us, we must pause for a moment more to consider the historical writings of another class, not scholars this time but men of action.

For in the controversial atmosphere of late republican politics most statesmen who could write left narratives to justify their

---

[4] *Historiarum adversum paganos libri septem.*

conduct, and those who could not write them themselves employed others to do so. The dictator Sulla (138–78 B.C.) after his retirement from public life wrote an autobiography, which seems to have resembled the semifabulous narrative of an Oriental rather than that of a sober Roman; for it points to a series of miraculous occurrences coincident with his public work to show that the hand of the goddess Tyche was visible throughout.[5] Yet such a narrative could impose upon Plutarch. Lucullus also (114–57 B.C.) early in life wrote a history of the war with Marius; but the use of current narrative as apologetic pamphlet literature reached its height in the last years of the Republic, when Pompey on the one side and Caesar on the other defended their actions at the bar of history. Pompey did not plead himself, but maintained a "literary staff"[6] to present his story in the light of hero-worship. For this purpose, slaves or Greeks were best, and Theophanes of Mytilene described the third Mithradatic War as a repetition of the conquest of Asia by Alexander, repeating the hero myth even down to a conflict with Amazons.[7]

It is only when we turn from nonsense like this to Caesar's *Commentaries* that we suddenly realize the full measure of achievement of these war memoirs.[8] Few books, however great, can stand the test of use in school and still retain a hold upon us in later life, and it was a questionable gain to Caesar that he wrote in such simple, lucid phrase as to make his works the object of the desolating struggles of the young with Latin prose. But if one does, by any chance, go back to Caesar after years of absence from the schoolroom, one finds a surprise awaiting him. For these works, written primarily to justify himself before the Roman people, dictated in camp and in the midst of the

---

[5] It bore the title *Commentarii rerum gestarum*.

[6] The expression used by H. Peter, *Wahrheit und Kunst*, p. 323. See also his *Die geschichtliche Literatur über die römische Kaiserzeit bis Theodosius I und ihre Quellen* (1897), I, 163 *sqq*. Varro wrote for Pompey.

[7] The use of slaves or freedmen to exalt the fortunes of the great was common in Rome as elsewhere. But none of the achievement is notable enough to come within this survey.

[8] Caesar's *Commentarii* are ostensibly merely "sketches" for a history to be written later; but this was partly a stylistic self-depreciation, recognizable among the rhetorical devices of the day. Cicero wrote the account of his consulate in the same vein.

world's affairs, contain not a word of open eulogy of the author and present the narrative as if from an impersonal observer, interested not only in the war but in the manners and the customs of peoples; in short a detached, objective account such as Thucydides himself might approve. This is the external, however; for so happily is the illusion of impartiality maintained that it is only when one has read the story through that one realizes the possibility of another point of view. It was a work of genius to use the quality of self-restraint to increase the impression of reality and so, after all, to make what was left out speak for the writer.

For the ten or eleven years following the murder of Julius Caesar in 44 B.C. there was living in retirement, in his luxurious villa on the Quirinal, the first notable historian whom Rome produced, Gaius Sallustius Crispus, known to us as Sallust. He had been a partisan of Caesar, and his great wealth, which showed itself in the elaborate gardens (*horti Sallustiani*) which he laid out on the northern hillsides of the city, was probably partly due to his having held the governorship of the province of Numidia for a while after Caesar's victories. But during the hot factional fights and the civil wars of the period of the Triumvirate and the founding of the imperial Principate of Augustus, he withdrew from present politics to devote himself to a narrative of those of the age which had just passed away.

Such a course of action needed, in the eyes of a practical Roman, some apology, and the two works of Sallust which have come to us, *Catiline* and the *Jugurthine War*, begin with such apologies. Since they supply the point of view from which he wished us to judge of his performance, we may first listen to what he has to say on the matter. The third and fourth chapters of the *Catiline* run as follows:

> It is a fine thing to serve the State by action, nor is eloquence despicable. Men may become illustrious alike in peace and war, and many by their own acts, many by their record of the acts of others, win applause. The glory which attends the doer and the recorder of brave deeds is certainly by no means equal. For my own part, however, I count historical narration as one of the hardest of tasks. In the first place, a full equivalent has to be found in words for the deeds narrated,

Varro, Caesar, and Sallust

and in the second, the historian's censures of crimes are by many thought to be the utterances of ill-will and envy, while his record of the high virtue and glory of the good, tranquilly accepted so long as it deals with what the reader deems to be easily within his own powers, so soon as it passes beyond this is disbelieved as mere invention.

As regards myself, my inclination originally led me, like many others, while still a youth, into public life. There I found many things against me. Modesty, temperance, and merit had departed, and hardihood, corruption, and avarice were flourishing in their stead. My mind, a stranger to bad acquirements, contemned these qualities; nevertheless, with the weakness of my youth, I was seized and held amid this throng of vices by ambition. I presented a contrast to the ill behaviour of my fellows, none the less I was tormented by the same craving for the honours of office, and the same sensitiveness to popularity and unpopularity as the rest.

At last, after many miseries and perils, my mind was at peace, and I determined to pass the remainder of my days at a distance from public affairs. It was not, however, my plan to waste this honourable leisure in idleness and sloth, nor yet to spend my life in devotion to such slavish tastes as agriculture or hunting. I returned to the studies I had once begun, from which my unhappy ambition had held me back, and determined to narrate the history of the Roman people in separate essays, wherever it seemed worthy of record. I was the more inclined to this by the fact that my mind was free alike from the hopes and fears of the political partisan.

In his second work, *The Jugurthine War*, Sallust is even more on the defensive:

Among the tasks that occupy the intellect, historical narration holds a prominent and useful place. As its merits have been often extolled, I think it best to leave them unmentioned, and thus escape any imputation of arrogantly exalting myself by praise of my own pursuit. And yet I have no doubt that there will be some who, because I have determined to pass my life at a distance from public affairs, will apply the name of indolence to my long and useful task. At any rate, the men to whom it seems the height of energy to court the mob, and buy favour by their public entertainments, will do so.

In both these sections his defense involves a characterization of the politics of Rome—the other alternative field for his activity—which is, in a word, the essence of his history as well. For he dealt as a historian with just that corrupt and vicious political life of the closing years of the Republic from which he sought refuge in the polite society of his friends and the delights of intellectual intercourse. The choice of the conspiracy of Catiline for a subject to be immortalized, revealing—as it did in his depiction—the degradation of Roman ideals and the failure of its social, as well as of its political, system, was typical of his outlook. The story of the war against Jugurtha, his other theme, has a constantly recurring note as to the venality of Roman senators, and if we lose the thread of home affairs in the graphic—though sometimes fanciful—descriptions of battle in the wilds of Numidia, the climax of the tale is less the fate of Jugurtha than that striking passage which closed the disreputable manoeuvres of the king and his partisans in Rome, in which, as he was leaving the city, "he is said, after looking back at it in silence, at last to have cried: 'a city for sale, soon to fall if once it find a buyer'" (Chap. 35). There is no wonder that, in dealing with characters and events such as these, Sallust should find history difficult.

But the difficulty was enhanced by the fact that he never quite saw the perspective as a historian. He was intent upon preserving "the memory of gallant deeds that kindled a fire in the breasts of brave men, that cannot be quenched until their own merit has rivalled their ancestors' fame and renown" (Chap. 4), and so he sought to bring out, partly by contrast against that dark background, the patriotism of a Cato or the military genius of a Metellus. Yet he was too much of a historian to do this at the expense of the narrative as a whole; the episodes are not allowed to dominate as they would in the case of a mere writer of memoirs. The attempt to be impartial prevents him from that brilliant sort of sketching which would have distorted the narrative for the sake of a few strong effects. On the other hand, the background never becomes really clear. He did not set himself, in these works at least, the larger theme of which they furnished the notable illustrations—the theme of Roman government in the days when an outworn oligarchy was attempting to rule through an outworn constitution, and the democratic statesmen had not yet found their Caesar.

If, therefore, there is something inherently weak about the work of Sallust, why is it held in such high regard? For, not only have we the praise of the one most competent to pass judgment in Rome, Tacitus himself,[9] but modern critics are agreed that Sallust stands out distinctly above his predecessors and remains, with Livy and Tacitus, one of the three best-known Latin historians. The reason is mainly that he applied to Rome the standards of Thucydides and Polybius, whom he took as his masters, and, cutting adrift from the current of complacent rhetorical compositions, honestly tried to tell the truth. Moreover, in style as well as in content, he held himself aloof from the florid or oratorical traditions, wrote with dignity, and gave a certain fitting, archaic flavor to his narrative.[10] Like Thucydides, he polished and repolished his phrases, and the speeches he introduced, even when he had the text before him,[11] were rewritten in keeping with the rest of his work. Fortunately one orator, Cicero, saved him the trouble of so doing with his particular orations, by rewriting and polishing them for posterity himself.

It is generally held that one of Sallust's chief merits is his depiction of character, and it is true that his characters are for the most part drawn with real impartiality and are lifelike. But the qualities assigned them seem to smack a little of formula; they are not subtle combinations of temperament and capacity, capable of swiftly surprising the reader but share the element of the commonplace which makes so much of antique literature seem more or less like stage property.[12] However, it is open to the classicist to take exception to this, for the full merit and charm of Sallust's art demand more time and study than his subject matter makes otherwise profitable.

Finally, there are two frank weaknesses in Sallust as a historian. In the first place he is weak in chronology and geography.

[9] Tacitus, *Annales,* Book III, Chap. 30.
[10] A good example of a deftly turned phrase, even were it not original, is the crisp comment on the Numidians who were "protected rather by their feet than by their swords" (*Bellum Jugurthinum,* Chap. 74).
[11] As, for instance, that of Cato against Catiline or that of Memmius against Jugurtha. His speeches are admittedly well done, and if there are too many for us and the moralizing is overdone, they suited the age for which they were written.
[12] The portrait of Marius is perhaps an exception. See Sallust, *Bellum Jugurthinum,* Chap. 63 *sq.*

His editors have all pointed out how incredibly careless he is in both respects. He uses vague phrases for lapse of time and even then gets hopelessly wrong, while his geography of Africa is a fanciful bit of writing, displaying such errors as putting cities near the coast that should be forty miles inland. This would have shocked Polybius, and if Sallust found Thucydides vague in his time reckoning, Thucydides would have never failed, as Sallust did, where the data were at hand.

The second weakness of Sallust came from his very advantages. A retired capitalist, living in elegant ease, employing scholars to do the drudgery of research,[13] he missed some of that keen sense of the value of accuracy which comes from constantly feeling the iron discipline of the scientific method. But, more than this, he saw the world much as such a one would today through the windows of a Pall Mall or Fifth Avenue club. His philosophy, which he outlines in his preface, is one of self-denial, but it is the kind of self-denial that goes with club life. It reminds one of Polonius. It does not reach out to grapple with the real problems of a workaday world. It is placid and sure of itself, properly censorious, but lacking in grasp of fundamentals.

Whether Sallust's other work, a history of the whole era just preceding his own, was ever finished or not,[14] we have traces of only a few fragments, and the fact that he proposed to concentrate on certain main features as a rule for historical composition, leads us to surmise that his performance in the larger task was hardly one to cause us to revise our judgment upon him. Yet he may have suffered from the fact that in the ages that followed, particularly in the closing period of imperial history, it was the charm of his style and the power of his portrayal which preserved for us what it did, rather than any more solid merit in historical synthesis.

[13] He employed scholars to do the "grubbing" for him (Suetonius, *De illustribus grammaticis*, Chap. 10). Yet he should get due credit for recognizing the value of scholarly aids. "Such pains were seldom taken by a Latin historian." See J. W. Mackail, *Latin Literature*, p. 84.

[14] It bore the title *Historiae* and apparently covered from about 78 to 66 B.C., continuing where L. Cornelius Sisenna had left off.

CHAPTER XXII

Livy

WHATEVER opinions one may have as to the place of Sallust among historians, that of Livy remains unchallenged. He was the national historian of Rome, the only one who successfully handled the long and intricate story of war and politics from the establishment of the city to that of the Empire. Others worked at portions; he took over the whole. Even in mere size his history was monumental. It has no less than one hundred and forty-two books, and a book in Livy is a small work in itself. But apart from its vastness, the conception which underlay the history of Livy was so consistently developed, the outlines of his structure so clear and so harmonious that it is hardly too much to say that it was the impress which he gave to the history of the Republic that lasted down to the day of Niebuhr and the nineteenth-century critics. He carried the idea of the fated mission of Rome as the unifying centre of the civilized world back across the centuries of its obscurity, and linked together past, present, and future in one culminating perspective. In a sense it was merely the reflection in history of the greatness of the writer's own times. But the fact that those times were great made the faith in Rome itself—which was Livy's creed —almost the same as a belief in human progress or a vital interest in organized society. Thus his patriotism became catholic and remained an inspiration to succeeding ages, even after the Roman world had passed away.[1] Whatever criticism may have to say as to his methods of work, it cannot shake the place of Livy as one

---

[1] See A. Molinier, *Les sources de l'histoire de France* (1901-1906), I, 36, for the influence of Livy's perspective upon the historical ideas of the Middle Ages. This influence, however, was rather indirect, while from the days of the humanists to our own Livy has again his place among "the classics."

of those few historians whose works have lived rather than endured. Judged in this light, the national historian of Rome stands high among the old masters.

Titus Livius (59 B.C.–17 A.D.) was born at Padua but passed most of his life at Rome and wrote under the direct patronage of Augustus. Indeed, he represented in history that effort toward reform in morals in which Augustus was so much concerned, by the strong emphasis which he placed upon the ancient virtues and the depiction of heroic acts and patriotic sacrifice. But the very sincerity of character which revealed itself in this moral attitude of Livy kept him independent in spirit, so that although at court he was no courtier. He did not, like Horace and Vergil, place Augustus among the gods and indeed only mentioned him incidentally, "once to mark a date, again to prove a fact." A sturdy provincial, without any of the ties that made partisanship a family virtue, he came to Rome just when the hot feuds of the latter Republic were quenched in the great Civil War, and the era of violence, corruption, and intrigue which determined the perspectives of Sallust was apparently over. While he came to see in the Principate a continuation of these elements in the Roman past which made for greatness, he did not share the high enthusiasm of Vergil and Horace for the new regime. He ventured to praise Brutus and Cassius, and Augustus, as a friendly joke, used to call him a "Pompeian."[2] Livy, like Sallust, thought of his own times as decadent, and, again like his predecessor and many other Romans, he placed the Golden Age in the period between the Second and Third Punic Wars. So far as we can judge, the story from Marius to Actium was one long tale of horror. But while his character and outlook are clearly shown in his works and in the few references we have concerning his life, those references are so few that, as in the case of Herodotus, we are left with a history rather than a historian. As Taine has somewhat sententiously summed it up: "A date in Eusebius, some details scattered in Seneca and Quintilian, two words thrown by chance in his own work; that is all that is left us on the life of Titus Livius. The

[2] Tacitus, Book IV, Chap. 34.

historian of Rome has no history."[3] The fragments we have show him to have been modest in the midst of his vast popularity;[4] his work reveals the fact that he travelled little and read much; and his style bears the marks of the training of a rhetor. In other words, he was a cultured gentleman of studious habits. Beyond that we can hardly go.

When we turn from the man to the history, we may as well begin at the beginning and let Livy describe his purpose and his conception of the work, as he does, frankly enough, in the Preface to the *Ab urbe condita:*

Whether the task I have undertaken of writing a complete history of the Roman people from the very commencement of its existence will reward me for the labour spent on it, I neither know for certain, nor if I did know would I venture to say. For I see that this is an old-established and a common practice, each fresh writer being invariably persuaded that he will either attain greater certainty in the materials of his narrative or surpass the rudeness of antiquity in the excellence of his style.

However this may be, it will still be a great satisfaction to me to have taken my part, too, in investing, to the utmost of my abilities, the annals of the foremost nation in the world with a deeper interest; and if in such a crowd of writers my own reputation is thrown into the shade, I would console myself with the renown and greatness of those who eclipse my fame.

The subject moreover is one that demands immense labour. It goes back beyond 700 years, and, starting from small and humble beginnings, has grown to such dimensions that it begins to be overburdened by its greatness. I have very little doubt, too, that for the majority of my readers, the earliest times and those immediately succeeding will possess little attraction; they will hurry on to those modern days in which the might of a long paramount nation is wasting by internal decay. I, on the other hand, shall look for a further reward of my labours in being able to close my eyes to the evils which our generation has witnessed for so many years; so long, at least, as I am devoting

---

[3] H. Taine, *Essai sur Tite Live* (1856), p. 1.
[4] The younger Pliny tells us a striking story, apparently current in his day, which sufficiently indicates the contemporary fame of Livy. "Have you never read [he says to Nepos] about a certain man from Cadiz, who came from the very end of the world to see Livy, moved thereto by the latter's name and fame, and immediately after seeing him went back home again?" (*Epistulae,* Book II, letter 3.)

all my thoughts to retracing those pristine records, free from all the anxiety which can disturb the historian of his own times even if it cannot warp him from the truth.

The traditions of what happened prior to the foundation of the City, or whilst it was being built, are more fitted to adorn the creations of the poet than the authentic records of the historian, and I have no intention of establishing either their truth or their falsehood. This much licence is conceded to the ancients, that by intermingling human actions with divine they may confer a more august dignity on the origins of states. Now, if any nation ought to be allowed to claim a sacred origin and point back to divine paternity, that nation is Rome. For such is her renown in war that when she chooses to represent Mars as her own and her founder's father, the nations of the world accept the statement with the same equanimity with which they accept her dominion.

But whatever opinions may be formed or criticisms passed upon these and similar traditions, I regard them as of small importance. The subjects to which I would ask each of my readers to devote his earnest attention are these—the life and morals of the community; the men and the qualities by which, through domestic policy and foreign war, dominion was won and extended. Then, as the standard of morality gradually lowers, let him follow the decay of the national character, observing how at first it slowly sinks, then slips downward more and more rapidly, and finally begins to plunge into headlong ruin, until he reaches those days in which we can bear neither our diseases nor their remedies.

There is this exceptionally beneficial and fruitful advantage to be derived from the study of the past, that you see, set in the clear light of historical truth, examples of every possible type. From these you may select for yourself and your country what to imitate, and what, as being mischievous in its inception and disastrous in its issue, you are to avoid. Unless, however, I am misled by affection for my undertaking, there has never existed any commonwealth greater in power, with a purer morality, or more fertile in good examples; or any state in which avarice and luxury have been so late in making their inroads, or poverty and frugality so highly and continuously honoured, showing so clearly that the less wealth men possessed the less they coveted. In these latter years wealth has brought avarice in its train, and the unlimited command of pleasure has created in men a passion for ruining themselves and everything else through self-indulgence and licentiousness.

But criticisms which will be unwelcome, even when perhaps necessary, must not appear in the commencement, at all events, of this extensive work. We should much prefer to start with favourable omens, and if we could have adopted the poets' custom, it would have been much pleasanter to commence with prayers and supplications to gods and goddesses that they would grant a favourable and successful issue to the great task before us.

Nowhere else in antique historiography have we so winning an appeal. It has the personal note of Polybius without his pedagogical airs, the moral atmosphere of Sallust but not his censorious declamation, and a promise of the charm of a Herodotus in the *logoi* about old, forgotten things that take the mind off the sordid cares of the present. The light touch, which brings one at the close to the borderland that lies between humor and poetry, shows at once the sure hand of a master. The omens are favorable when the historian has in mind the frailties of his readers to the point of not recalling them unduly but can leave the heroic past to convey its own lesson.

The history of Livy bore the simple title, *From the Foundation of the City (Ab urbe condita)*, and it properly begins with Aeneas, whose deeds are hurriedly sketched on the basis of the "generally accepted" legend. There is little indication of enthusiasm for this or the story of Romulus which follows. There is even a rising doubt as to the divine paternity of the founder of Rome and a naturalistic alternative to the tales about him. Indeed, the narrative hardly gets under way in the legends of origin. It is not until we have the struggle of Rome against Alba Longa, culminating in the dramatic duel of the three Horatii against the Curiatii (Book I, Chap. 25), that we are conscious of the swing of unfettered movement and the play of the historical imagination. The problem of origin is left unsolved; the case is given away to neither the credulous nor the skeptical; details hardly matter; for, in any case, says Livy, "in my opinion, the origin of so great a city and the establishment of an empire next in power to that of the gods was due to the Fates" (Book I, Chap. 4).

This at once suggests the phase of Livy's history which is most open to question in our eyes. It is so religious in tone as to be frankly mediaeval in the inclusion of the supernatural as an intrinsic part of the human story, and especially in the handling of crises, when by miracle or portent the gods reveal themselves. Omens and prodigies abound; when the gods are not on the scene they are just behind it.[5] Herodotus by comparison is almost modern, for, although the oracles play a great part in his narrative, the gods remain aloof. Livy, on the contrary, in the spirit of Augustus' religious reforms, made piety the very core of patriotism. There is a flavor of Stoic doctrine in the way Fate "disposes the plans of men, and blinds their minds, yet leaves their wills free." But the philosopher yields to the historian, as he relates the narratives in the way he finds them in his sources and realizes how fully his characters believed in all the apparatus of official magic, and the uncanny presences that heralded disaster or victory. In a sentence which is practically unmatched in antique history for penetrating historical imagination, he admits the influence which the old faiths exert over him as he sinks himself into the past and learns to think and feel the way his ancient heroes did.

I am quite aware [he remarks (Book XLIII, Chap. 13)] that the spirit of indifference which in these days makes men in general refuse to believe that the gods warn us through portents, also prevents any portents whatever from being either made public or recorded in the annals. But as I narrate the events of ancient times I find myself possessed by the ancient spirit, and a religious feeling constrains me to regard the matters which those wise and thoughtful men considered deserving of their attentions as worthy of a place in my pages.

This is certainly the most that can be said in his defense. If the gods reveal the future, as they do in the instance which calls forth this aside, they are moving in the pages of Livy as they did through the brains of his heroes and to that degree the supernatural is the more natural history.

The story of Rome was one of constant war, and Livy is at his best describing campaigns and battle scenes. A man of letters

---

[5] Occasionally, however, Livy seems to have his doubts. "Many prodigies were announced that year, and the more readily men of simple and pious minds believed them the more numerously they were reported" (Book XXIV, Chap. 10); "other ridiculous things [*ludibria*] which people imagined they had seen or heard were believed to be true" (Book XXIV, Chap. 44); "in the anxiety of the strain caused by such a serious war, when men referred every fortunate or unfortunate event to the gods, numerous portents were announced" (Book XXVIII, Chap. 11). Nevertheless, he carefully copied out the numerous reports of prodigies which he found in the ancient annals.

and not a soldier himself, he is deficient in military science and inaccurate in geography, and his sense of numbers is poor; yet his narrative of action is nervous, swift, and forceful. While in argumentative sections his style is often involved and sometimes drags, here he has the art of securing speed and yet combining it with the picturesque. The only thing that spoils his best portions is the chance that he will interrupt them to insert just such an argument in the shape of interminable speeches or harangues. These were undoubtedly, in Livy's eyes, the high points of his art; for the influence of that form of rhetoric which Romans most admired was dominant in his style. There are over four hundred speeches in the thirty-five books which have come down to us, and they were adjudged, by no less a critic than Quintilian, to be unsurpassed in diction and content.[6] It must be admitted, indeed, that they are not vapid declamations but real, characteristic speeches; but they are often long and labored.

It was not the speeches which Livy feared might drive readers away, but the long succession of the wars themselves. After ten books of them he is moved to exhort the tired reader to continue as a patriotic task: "What sort of a man must he be who would find the long story of those wars tedious, though he is only narrating or reading it, when they failed to wear out those who were actually engaged in them?" (Book X, Chap 31).

In this apprehension Livy was justified. It was the greatest tribute to his genius that antiquity preserved, well into the Middle Ages, so vast a repertory of archaic wars. If only relatively small portions of the great work have come down to us,[7] it was not until those dark ages after the seventh century that the missing books disappeared, and even some parts of them are preserved in extracts by later authors. Why the long story of obscure struggles was preserved when so much more important parts were lost is, of course, impossible to say; but perhaps the historian's love for

---

[6] Quintilian, *De institutione oratoria*, Book X, Chap. 1, Sect. 10.

[7] The extant books are I-X, XXI-XLV, of which XLI and XLIII are incomplete; they cover the history of Rome from the beginning to 293 B.C., and from 218 to 167; in addition we have the *Periochae* or epitomes of all the books except two, which vary in length from two lines to a whole page. There was once a much fuller abbreviation, now lost.

those quaint, far-off days had something to do with preserving them.

When we turn from the art of Livy to his criticism and use of sources, we at once come upon his weakness. Criticism was contrary to his nature. He was a narrator. He gives one the impression that he used criticism only superficially and because it was the fashion. He did not discriminate among his sources, but took what best fitted with the scheme of the story. Polybius was used, but not consistently; Cato, perhaps, and Licinus Macer, Antias and Claudius Quadrigarius; but second-hand annalists were good enough so long as they contained the data. While hardly going so far as to apply the adage *se non e vero e ben trovato,* Livy did not interest himself in those researches in either philology or antiquarian lore which the new scholarship of his day had made available. It is enough to say that he shows no trace of having read Varro.

There are, however, signs of the distinct sense of dependence upon the sources which he found available. The most notable is the difference in tone after the narrative of the burning of the city by the Gauls. The sixth book, which begins the new era, starts as follows.

The history of the Romans from the foundation of the City to its capture ... has been set forth in the five preceding books. The subject-matter is enveloped in obscurity; partly from its great antiquity, like remote objects which are hardly discernible through the vastness of the distance; partly owing to the fact that written records, which form the only trustworthy memorials of events, were in those times few and scanty, and even what did exist in the pontifical commentaries and public and private archives nearly all perished in the conflagration of the City. Starting from the second beginnings of the City, which, like a plant cut to its roots, sprang up in greater beauty and fruitfulness, the details of its history both civil and military will now be exhibited in their proper order, with greater clearness and certainty (Book VI, Chap. 1).

The promise in these latter lines was made good rather in a literary than in a scholarly sense. Where all his authorities agree, he is happy; where they disagree he is without any principles of criticism to guide him. An interesting instance of this is in a passage to which reference has already been made. After stating that his readers will doubtless tire of his Volscians, he goes on to say:

> But they will also be struck with the same difficulty which I have myself felt whilst examining the authorities who lived nearer to the period, namely, from what source did the Volscians obtain sufficient soldiers after so many defeats? Since this point has been passed over by the ancient writers, what can I do more than express an opinion, such as anyone may form from his own inferences? (Book VI, Chap 12.)

The point to be noted is that Livy does not dream of questioning the fact of the great size of the Volscian army, in view of the agreement of his authorities. He can only turn aside to theories which may help to rationalize the account so as to make it more credible. The modern historian must first do what Livy seems not to have done at all, determine the value of his various sources.

If Livy was not a scholarly historian, neither was he qualified by that experience in practical affairs which Polybius preferred to scholarship. His failure to see the value of that wider knowledge of men and places shows itself not only in his lack of exactness in geography, to which reference has been made, and in a deplorable weakness in constitutional matters, but it narrows as well his view of history and of Rome. As Pelham has so ably put it:

> With Polybius, the greatness of Rome is a phenomenon to be critically studied and scientifically explained; the rise of Rome forms an important chapter in universal history, that must be dealt with, not as an isolated fact, but in connexion with the general march of events in the civilized world.... Livy writes as a Roman, to raise a monument worthy the greatness of Rome, and to keep alive, for the guidance and the warning of Romans, the recollection alike of the virtues which had made Rome great and of the vices which had threatened her with destruction.[8]

Livy's history is, therefore, intensely patriotic. The rise of Rome was due to the sterling virtues of the good old days; above all, to piety. The fathers of the Republic are men of courage and

---

[8] H. F. Pelham, "Livy," in *Encyclopædia Britannica* (11th ed.).

firmness, and of unshaken faith in the greatness of their destiny. Fortunately, these are virtues of general application, and however inadequate they may be as an explanation of the Roman triumph, they offered to subsequent moralists much inspiration to apply the lessons elsewhere. It is only in our own day that civic virtues have ceased to be impressed upon the young by the model supplied from the pages of the classics. And it is sufficient tribute to Livy in this regard to recall that he was the one writer of antiquity singled out by that most realistic political thinker of the humanistic era, Machiavelli, to drive home to his age the lessons of the past.[9]

[9] See *Discorsi sopra la prima deca di Tito Livio* (various editions, English translations 1836 and 1883).

CHAPTER XXIII

Tacitus

FROM Livy to Tacitus is somewhat like passing from Herodotus to Thucydides. Tacitus, too, was an artist in history. His style is the result of the maturity, not only of individual, but also of national, achievement. The charm of the naïve is lost. The storytelling power that carries one through interminable detail by making narrative entertaining is no gift of Tacitus. His appeal, like that of Thucydides, is to intelligence. But the intelligence of the age of the Flavians was not the same as that of the age of Pericles; and beyond the general standards which they set themselves, there is little resemblance between the work of the greatest of Greek historians and that of the greatest of the Latins. For both, history was a tribunal, the final one; but where Thucydides was a magistrate, Tacitus was an advocate—the most brilliant, perhaps, who ever sought to determine the judgment of Time, but an advocate all the same. His client was Rome itself, and the stake was human liberty; but these impersonal ideals were less in evidence in the handling of his case than the dangers they encountered, dangers embodied in real men and women, not envisaged as abstractions. It was the tyrant, not tyranny, that Tacitus attacked; the immoral men or women whom he could name, rather than immorality in general. But, however powerfully he drove home his argument, he recognized the dignity of the court in which he was pleading and asked only the judgment which the facts would warrant. Thus, while Thucydides sought to establish the truth alone, Tacitus sought to maintain that truth which would be of service to the world. How far the two methods coincided would depend upon one's conception of both truth and the pragmatic values of history.

Of the life of Cornelius Tacitus we know very little, our knowledge being confined to what he tells himself—and he is most uncommunicative—and to the letters of the younger Pliny, his intimate friend, who addressed no less than seven epistles to him. The date of his birth has been fixed, by a surmise as to his probable age upon appointment to political office, at about 54 A.D., and he must have lived through approximately the first two decades of the next century. The marked stages of his political career are indicated by him in somewhat enigmatic fashion at the opening of his *Histories:* "My political position was begun by Vespasian, augmented by Titus, and carried still higher by Domitian." This has been taken to mean that Vespasian made him quaestor; that he became aedile or tribune of the people under Titus and praetor under Domitian. His marriage with the daughter of Agricola calls out a passing comment but, although he immortalized his wife's father, he is practically silent about his home life. He indicates that he left Rome for four years upon the completion of his praetorship [1] but nowhere does he indicate where he spent this time. Conjecture naturally connects it with his famous monograph on Germany—although this did not appear until some six years later (98 A.D.)—and still further surmise, hunting for a suitable post of observation, would give him the governorship of Belgic Gaul. However this may be, he was back in Rome in 93 A.D., and there is ample evidence in his *Histories* that from then till the close of Domitian's reign, he lived through the very heart of "the terror." [2] He was consul the year after the tyrant's death and then began to publish his shorter studies, the life of *Agricola* in 97 or 98, and the *Germania* in 98. His histories, the fruit of years of study, favored by the quiet resulting from his forced dissimulation under the tyranny of Domitian, were published piecemeal, as he completed them. Boissier has inferred from a letter of Pliny that the *Histories* probably began to appear about 105 A.D. and that it was because they had taken Rome by storm that Pliny suffered a sudden and sore temptation to try his own hand at history as a

---

[1] *Annales,* Book XI, Chap. 11; *Agricola,* Chap. 44.
[2] *Agricola,* Chaps. 3, 44.

means of achieving immortality.[3] A chance remark in the *Annals*, that the Roman Empire "now extends to the Red Sea" through Egypt (Book II, Chap. 61), implies that these words were written about ten years later (c. 115 A.D.), when Trajan had carried the frontiers that far.[4] Finally, an inscription discovered in modern times in Caria indicates that toward the end of Trajan's reign, Tacitus held the great post of proconsul in Asia.[5]

Such is the meagre framework for the life of Tacitus, except for the indications furnished in the letters of Pliny, which are less separate facts than a picture of the society in which they moved and of the interests of the two men. Pliny tells us that when he began his career at the Roman bar, Tacitus was "already in the prime of his glory and renown" as a celebrated pleader (Book VIII, Letter 20); and he still practiced pleading after Domitian's death, for we know of one important lawsuit which he conducted jointly with Pliny. But the eloquence to which Pliny bears generous witness (Book II, Letter 1) awakened even less admiration than the histories. These, he asserts, will live forever; and fortunate is the man who can secure mention in their enduring pages (Book VI, Letter 16; Book VII, Letter 33). Reading Pliny, one might suppose that Tacitus belonged to those whom contemporaries already have marked out for immortality. But if so, they were content to let him achieve it by his own works, unaided by biographers.

So much for the outlines of Tacitus' life. But if the external facts are lacking, the more intimate picture of his education and outlook, of the society he frequented, and of the influences of its morals, manners, and politics upon him is relatively clear. He was an aristocrat, not of the old nobility of Rome, for they had almost

---

[3] Pliny, *Epistulae*, Book V, letter 8. See G. Boissier, *Tacitus and Other Roman Studies* (tr. Hutchison, 1906), p. 93.

[4] The *Histories* were written first and covered the period from 69 to 96 A.D. in fourteen books; of these we now have only the first four and half of the fifth, dealing with the events of about two years. The *Annals*, in their original title *Ab excessu divi Augusti*, covered the years from 14 to 68 A.D. in sixteen books; we now have Books I-IV (14-28) parts of V and VI (29, 31-37), and XI-XVI with gaps at the beginning and end (47-66).

[5] *Bulletin de Correspondance Hellénique*, XIV (1890), 621-23.

all disappeared; but of the newer gentry, drawn from the provinces or from the official classes.[6] It was a wealthy and polite society, like that of the old regime in France; one where wits counted, where literature was a passport to elegant salons and clever repartee might make, or unmake, fortunes. It was more a school for scandal than for history. There was much floating gossip which Tacitus, as a man of the world, could hardly fail to pick up—mostly malicious gossip, concerned with personalities rather than with political movements, spiteful guesses as to what was going on by those who wished to pose as knowing and who felt aggrieved that they did not, or generally depreciating comments by the politically unemployed. The only thing to recommend this unlovely growth of scandalmongering was its contrast with the still more unlovely output of adulation on the other side. Fortunately such a school brings its own remedy in the sophisticated skepticism which it breeds in those who indulge in its sensational curriculum, so that its worst effects are attenuated. But the skepticism it breeds is not of that inquiring kind which leads to science; it is more the dulling influence of surfeited sensationalism, tending to bring indifference. It is not a happy soil for scientific history. In a mind like that of Tacitus it bred a sort of saturnine melancholy which pervades all his work.

Tacitus himself belonged by sentiment to the senatorial faction, although in practice accepting office and favor from the emperor. His prejudices are not concealed; the only point in doubt is how far his sense of scientific obligation to historical truth kept him within the restraints of accuracy.[7] It is a problem which will probably never be solved, for we have little but Tacitus himself upon which to base our judgment. Moreover, it is the one subject

---

[6] The elder Pliny in his *Naturalis historia,* Book VII, Chap. 17, refers to a Cornelius Tacitus, a Roman knight, who was a financial administrator in Belgic Gaul. It has been conjectured that he was either father or uncle to the historian. See G. Boissier, *Tacitus and Other Roman Studies,* p. 2.

[7] Tacitus' feeling for his class comes out on all occasions. He upholds its dignity even against itself. For instance, when some nobles so far forgot themselves as to go into the imperial Neronian vaudeville to retrieve their fortunes, he turns the incident against the emperor, who would bring such disgrace upon the victims. As for themselves he comments, "As they have ended their days, I think it due to their ancestors not to hand down their names" (*Annales,* Book XIV, Chap. 14).

upon which the commentators upon Tacitus have almost invariably concentrated their remarks. Hence we shall not delay here over it or such related questions as that of the real character of Tiberius, whether the *Germania* was mainly a moral lesson to the Romans, or other well-worn themes of criticism. The mere fact that such questions do persist in offering themselves to readers of Tacitus is itself an indication of the character of his work as a whole.

The social prejudices of Tacitus were responsible for more than his partiality; they also account for the details as to the fate of prominent citizens with which he clogs his narrative of imperial history. No one now cares much about these ill-starred victims or unwise plotters. But the audience for which Tacitus wrote had a personal interest as keen as his own in the interminable stories of intrigue. These were something like family tales of one's ancestors, cherished in a smothered desire either for justification or for posthumous vengeance. Tacitus found it hard to make up his mind to omit any of these crimes, and the result was to give much of his narrative something of that savage flavor which seems most appropriate in a Gregory of Tours. One might almost fancy, reading such a long succession of horrors, that the scene was at a Merovingian, semicivilized court, or among Nibelungen heroes, instead of the court and capital of all the world. It is rather too much to be convincing; for, however true the facts might be, they could hardly be the central theme of history.

Tacitus was aware that all was not right with such a narrative but could not discover the remedy. He was too close to the scene for that, too much involved in the petty issues of family politics. He knew that the stage was overcrowded and the action a long-drawn-out succession of intrigues or atrocities and from time to time commented on his embarrassment at being obliged to repeat continually such stories as these. But, on the other hand, since the events had happened, and since in his eyes they had formed the chief content of imperial history, he felt that his obligation to historic accuracy and fulness prevented curtailment. As a historian he was happy to gather all the facts he could, however difficult it made the literary task of exposition. This comes out in such comments as the following:

> Many authors, I am well aware, have passed over the perils and punishments of a host of persons, sickened by the multiplicity of them, or fearing that what they had themselves found wearisome and saddening, would be equally fatiguing to their readers. For myself, I have lighted on many facts worth knowing, though other writers have not recorded them.[8]

But if a sense of scholarship tempted him to tell the whole story, how could he retain the interest of his reader? It was Livy's question over again. And Tacitus, mindful of how well Livy had maintained that interest by digressions and incidental matter thrown into the serious current of his work, tried the same devices.[9] The narrative of what was happening in the city was varied by constant reference to events on the frontiers or in the provinces. These glimpses of the wider current of imperial affairs in the eyes of the modern historian give the meaning to the whole[10]; to Tacitus they rather gave relief from the oppressive quality of his chief subject, the fate of men of his class. For instance, after an account of one of the Parthian wars he adds: "I have related in sequence the events of two summer campaigns as a relief to the reader's mind from our miseries at home."[11] This is hardly the way to conceive history greatly.

[8] *Annales*, Book VI, Chap. 7. If they were not recorded, they must have been repeated by word of mouth. In any case such a reference shows what vague traces we have as to the sources of Tacitus.

[9] Not merely to entertain, however. As he states himself, "he will studiously refrain from embroidering his narrative with tales of fabulous marvels, and from diverting his readers with fictions; that would be unbecoming the dignity of the work he has undertaken" (*Historiae*, Book II, Chap. 50). G. Boissier, *Tacitus and Other Roman Studies*, p. 75; H. Furneaux, *The Annals of Tacitus* (2 vols., 2d ed., 1896-1907), I, 40-41.

[10] The best illustration is, of course, Mommsen.

[11] *Annales*, Book VI, Chap. 37. The remark is all the more significant since the chapter on the phoenix having been seen again in Egypt occurs just before the account of the Parthian campaigns. One might have thought it sufficient diversion!

But even foreign wars became monotonous in time. See Book XVI, Chap. 16: "Even if I had to relate foreign wars and deaths encountered in the service of the State with such a monotony of disaster, I should myself have been overcome by disgust, while I should look for weariness in my readers, sickened as they would be by the melancholy and continuous destruction of our citizens, however glorious to themselves." This is surely personal history, lacking in perception of larger issues.

Tacitus himself recognized the shortcomings of his work in this regard, without ever quite learning how to overcome them. He fancied that the trouble lay in the subject itself, which is but another way of saying that the subject was too great for him. This comes out in a remarkable passage in which he frankly compares his task with that of Livy, although avoiding mention of his predecessor's name:

> Much of what I have related and shall have to relate, may perhaps, I am aware, seem petty trifles to record. But no one must compare my annals with the writings of those who have described Rome in old days. They told of great wars, of the storming of cities, of the defeat and capture of kings, or whenever they turned by preference to home affairs, they related, with a free scope for digression, the strifes of consuls with tribunes, land and corn-laws, and the struggles between the commons and the aristocracy. My labours are circumscribed and inglorious; peace wholly unbroken or but slightly disturbed, dismal misery in the capital, an emperor careless about the enlargement of the empire, such is my theme. Still it will not be useless to study those at first sight trifling events out of which the movements of vast changes often take their rise.
>
> All nations and cities are ruled by the people, the nobility, or by one man. A constitution formed by selection out of these elements, it is easy to commend but not to produce; or, if it is produced, it cannot be lasting. Formerly, when the people had power or when the patricians were in the ascendant, the popular temper and the methods of controlling it, had to be studied, and those who knew most accurately the spirit of the Senate and aristocracy, had the credit of understanding the age and of being wise men. So now, after a revolution, when Rome is nothing but the realm of a single despot, there must be good in carefully noting this period, for it is but few who have the foresight to distinguish right from wrong or what is sound from what is hurtful, while most men learn wisdom from the fortunes of others. Still, though this is instructive, it gives very little pleasure. Descriptions of countries, the various incidents of battles, glorious deaths of great generals, enchain and refresh a reader's mind. I have to present in succession the merciless biddings of a tyrant, incessant prosecutions, faithless friendships, the ruin of innocence, the same causes issuing in the same results and I am everywhere confronted by a wearisome monotony in my subject matter. Then, again, an ancient historian has but few disparagers, and no one cares whether you praise more heartily the armies of Carthage or Rome. But of many who endured punishment or disgrace under Tiberius the descendants yet survive; or even though the

families themselves may now be extinct, you will find those who, from a resemblance of character, imagine that the evil deeds of others are a reproach to themselves. Again, even honour and virtue make enemies, condemning, as they do, their opposites by too close a contrast. But I return to my work.[12]

In so many words Tacitus puts his case, and, as a skilled pleader, he puts it well. But a little examination of the extract shows how, in reality, he simply gives his case away. "Peace wholly unbroken or but slightly disturbed, dismay in the capital, an emperor careless about the enlargement of the empire, such is my theme." Its history is bound to be "circumscribed and inglorious." These words, however, indicate not its limitations as he imagines, but his own. For just as Thucydides failed to leave us the history of the greatest theme of Greece, Athens at the height of its glory, so Tacitus failed adequately to describe that greatest political creation of antiquity, which for the first time in history was extending a common citizenship throughout the world, building up a common law and policing the routes of commerce for the arts of peace. It was, again, the failure of the pre-scientific mind to appreciate the importance of the commonplace and obscure—which is the major theme of life and society. There is, however, this difference between Thucydides and Tacitus, that the former had personally a keen appreciation of the Athens he took for granted; while Tacitus, in spite of all his insight, seems hardly to have seen the Roman Empire. He saw and traced its external fortunes, and his vivid picture of details, on distant frontiers as well as at home, lends to his work that appearance of reality to which the modern journalist aspires. But the deeper facts of statesmanship escaped him, the living forces of a busy world intent upon the security of its heritage, a world that was something more than a victim of intrigue. Granting that he could not analyze in terms of sciences yet undiscovered, he might at least have brought to the problem more of that antique substitute for science, the open mind. He had seen too much of life to be capable of its greatest gift—the sense of wonder, which, as Plato said, is the beginning of philosophy.

[12] *Annales*, Book IV, Chaps. 32-33.

The more one examines the *Histories* and *Annals* the more one feels that such an adverse judgment is justified. Compare the outlook of Tacitus upon the problems of his day with those of even the most mediocre modern historian of the imperial history, and one sees at once what was lacking in the work of the Roman. But again, on the other hand, as we have so often insisted in the course of these studies, the conclusion does not follow that Tacitus' failure to grasp the essentials of his age is to be judged in the light of *our* knowledge. If he failed to rise to the full height of the real theme of his age, it was partly because history had not yet learned to deal with generalized and abstract forces. It dealt with men instead; with nations as aggregations of individuals, where character and chance are at grips with destiny— with policies determined by personalities, incidents settled by single appeals or by acts of force. There are passing references here and there in Tacitus to the business side of politics, but they are generally incidental. The most notable exception is the description of "The Panic of the Year 33," [13] as it has been aptly termed by a modern writer. This was too serious a social crisis to be ignored. Moreover, it affected many private fortunes. There are, as well, references to the dangers of excessive luxury in Rome, as in the case when Tiberius addressed a letter to the Senate on the subject.[14] But, upon the whole, questions of economics are as few and far between as those of general politics.[15] As for the process of social evolution, Tacitus is almost naïvely conservative. In a society so advanced as that in which he lived it almost required a certain wilful ignorance of history to insist, as Tacitus does, that:

Mankind in the earliest age lived for a time without a single vicious impulse, without punishment and restraints. Rewards were not needed when everything right was pursued on its own merits; and as men de-

---
[13] *Annales,* Book VI, Chaps. 16-17.
[14] *Ibid.,* Book III, Chaps. 52-55.
[15] There is the repetition of old complaints about the decline of Italian farm supplies (*ibid.,* Book XII, Chap. 43); similarly rather dubious comments on Nero's proposed reforms in taxation (Book XIII, Chap. 51), with sometimes an interest in the supply of metal, as in the silver mines at Nassau (Book XI, Chap. 20). See also references to Nero's spell of economy (Book XV, Chap. 18), or his extravagance (Book XVI, Chap. 3).

sired nothing against morality, they were debarred from nothing by fear. When however they began to throw off equality, and ambition and violence usurped the place of self-control and modesty, despotisms grew up and became perpetual among many nations.[16]

"Man is born free; and everywhere he is in chains" was the way Rousseau put it, in the ringing challenge of the opening words of the *Social Contract*. Tacitus, too, was writing an indictment of society; but a misreading of history excusable in a prophet is less easy to pardon in a historian.

Tacitus at least had not much of a generalized conception of historical processes. And that is why he did not know how to manipulate the vast and often obscure interrelation of events so as to show its larger meaning. It is perhaps too much to say that he never saw his history as a whole; but he never saw it in the whole of its setting. He was a great artist rather than a great thinker, a wonderful observer and analyst of motives, but fundamentally a master of detail. In effect his depiction reminds one of the old Dutch masters: of features drawn with minutest care, yet deftly and swiftly; of landscapes enriched with everything really there. What makes his greatness as an artist is that he combines this mastery of detail with a freedom and breadth of movement, a grave and sombre power which gives to his work the high quality of tragedy. It always speaks with dignity, however trivial the incident. It never rings false, no matter how strained and rhetorical the phrase. Sentences are compressed into phrases and phrases into single words; but the crabbed text challenges the reader—and remains with him.

Yet in spite of all this richness of detail, power of depiction, mastery of expression, and dignity of spirit, Tacitus remained an annalist, whose narrative was held together by that most primitive of all links, the time nexus. Things are mentioned when they happened, because they happened when they did. There is no such attempt to trace the complex of events through cause and effect as we find in the Greeks. To be sure there are commonsense remarks as to why this or that incident arose, but the wider

---

[16] *Ibid.*, Book III, Chap. 26.

sweep of history, which gives it its meaning, is lacking.[17] Year by year, or event by event, the facts are noted as they occur in the sources, and the items jotted down are mostly quite isolated from those which precede or follow. Only the extent of detail on each one prevents the almost mediaeval quality of such a plan from appearing at first glance. That it does not do so is due to the skill with which the author used his artistry of expression to cover the defects of his plan.

It is typical of such a historian that his best work should be, in addition to the depiction of character—as in the marvellous portrayal of Tiberius—the description of great cities, when events so concentrate in a single time or place as not to involve a problem in perspective. Of these, the most outstanding instance is the opening portion of the *Histories*, where the revolutionary year 69 is described in such graphic detail that, as the translator of the text has put it, we know no other year in all antique history as we do this. In the rapid passage of events, the play and counterplay of emotion, the sudden changes of fortune, mob action uncertain yet determining the wavering of its leaders, soldiery in control but not sure of itself, and the empire the prize of disorder, we have a scene painted with masterful power and scrupulous care. It is Tacitus at his best.

When we turn from the choice of handling of the subject to the more technical problem of the use of sources, we find Tacitus about as much at sea as in the shaping of his general plan. In the first place there is the question of oral tradition and rumor.[18] How can it be tested? What criteria are there for the contemporary historian by which to substantiate what he hears?

---

[17] This general comment stands in spite of various passages which might be cited against it, as, for instance, the closing words of the second book of the *Annals*, with reference to Arminius: "He is still a theme of song among barbarian nations, though to Greek historians, who admire only their own achievements, he is unknown, and to Romans not as famous as he should be, while we extol the past and are indifferent to our own times" (Book II, Chap. 88). But if Tacitus had been working in the spirit of Herodotus, the *Germania* would have been incorporated in the history as one of the *logoi*.

[18] "Rome with its love of talking" (*Annales*, Book XIII, Chap. 6).

Time and again he confronts this problem. For instance, he tells us that the measures taken to avenge the death of Germanicus were "a subject of conflicting rumors, not only among the people then living but also in after times. So obscure are the greatest events, as some take for granted any hearsay, whatever its source, others turn truth into falsehood, and both errors find encouragement with posterity."[19] More flat-footed still is the attack upon such unsupported rumor as had fastened the crime of Drusus' murder upon Tiberius. After giving the story of that crime as he finds it in the narratives of most of the best historians, in which Tiberius is not implicated, he relates at length the accusing rumor to disprove it, adding: "My object in mentioning and refuting this story, is, by a conspicuous example, to put down hearsay, and to request all into whose hands my work shall come, not to catch eagerly at wild and improbable rumors in preference to genuine history which has not yet been perverted into romance."[20]

This seems clear and straightforward; but current history simply cannot ignore current gossip, and Tacitus' histories are constantly fed by its sediment-bearing stream. Indeed, as the written sources he consulted were themselves often but the composite result of similar rumors, it is not to be wondered at if such phrases as "it was said" or "many say" run through the narrative as substantiating references. Sometimes he definitely admits the importance of such source material, as in connection with the description of Piso's death at Tiberius' instigation:

I remember to have heard old men say that a document was often seen in Piso's hands the substance of which he never divulged, but which his friends repeatedly declared contained a letter from Tiberius with instructions referring to Germanicus, and that it was his intention to produce it before the Senate and upbraid the emperor, had he not been deluded by vain promises from Sejanus. Nor did he perish, they said, by his own hand, but by that of one sent to be his executioner.

Neither of these statements would I positively affirm; still it would not be right for us to conceal what was related by those who lived up to the time of my youth.[21]

---

[19] *Ibid.*, Book III, Chap. 19.   [20] *Ibid.*, Book IV, Chap. 11.
[21] *Ibid.*, Book III, Chap. 16.

In short, it was inevitable that much of Tacitus' work would have to depend upon oral testimony. How much this was the case is impossible to state definitely, for except in the matter of official documents or when his sources disagree and he must choose between them, he does not mention them individually.[22] However, it should be recalled that he himself had been contemporary with most of his narratives, for he was about fourteen years old when Nero died, and as a boy he must have heard many a reminiscence of the days of Tiberius and even of Augustus. The influence of these experiences upon his histories must extend far beyond single incidents which might be attributed to this or that source; they would largely determine his whole outlook.

As to written sources, Tacitus falls back upon the well-accepted principles which we have seen followed by his predecessors, especially Livy. Where his sources agree, he accepts the narrative —unless denied by more authoritative personal or oral accounts. "Proposing as I do [he says], to follow the consentient testimony of historians, I shall give the difference in their narratives under the writer's names."[23] But he does not follow these sources blindly. He checks one by another, and does not always adhere to the same one in different parts of his works. When there is little to choose between contradictory sources he is plainly at a loss. For instance, take a comment like this: "I can hardly venture on any positive statement about the consular elections, now held for the first time under this Emperor, or indeed subsequently, so conflicting are the accounts we find not only in the historians but in Tiberius' own speeches."[24]

This extract is interesting as indicating Tacitus' occasional use of documentary material as well as narrative. But only once did

---

[22] Even this is greatly to his credit. Boissier, commenting on it, says (*Tacitus and Other Roman Studies*, p. 55): "He is the ancient historian who most frequently cites the authors and documents he has consulted. He does not do so out of a kind of erudition run mad, as is so often done nowadays to make a show of being better informed than other people, since ... no one then deemed it any merit in an author, and since consequently he could reap no glory therefrom."
[23] *Annales*, Book XIII, Chap. 20.
[24] *Ibid.*, Book I, Chap. 81.

he cite the *Acta Diurna*,[25] for it never occurred to him to exploit this fund of information systematically; he rarely quoted other official documents; however, he did consult the memoirs of notable characters.[26] The problem in criticism as to what he most relied upon, whether he simply rewrote some of the more excellent historical accounts before his day, or completely remade the story, can hardly ever be settled, since the authorities he used have practically all perished. It is abundantly clear, however, that, lacking a knowledge of the principles of source criticism which leads the modern scholar to trace the history of his documents before he risks the story of the events they record, he nevertheless made up by literary genius for the shortcomings of science, in so far as that could well be done.

That with all his handicap Tacitus takes rank still in the forefront of the world's historians is due not only to his genius as a word painter, or his insight into character—the two gifts in which he excels—but also to his idea of history itself. He has a most exalted conception of it. There is small tolerance for the dilettante outlook of those "elderly men who amuse themselves comparing present and past." [27] He holds, in common with all earnest thinkers of antiquity, that it is "history's highest function to let no worthy action be uncommemorated, and to hold the reprobation of posterity as a terror to evil words and deeds." [28] This is to be done without bitterness or favor (*sine ira et studio*).[29] There was also more of the poet in his make-up than in any other antique historian. His sense of words, his use of compressed, epigrammatic phrases are genuinely poetical devices. And still more poetical than these implements of expression are the wealth of color and the variety of action which give the illusion of life to his pages. In a remarkable passage, a great modern Hellenist has described the masterpieces of Greek history as suggestive of basreliefs, thin in outline and low in tone.[30] They are conceived in

---

[25] *Ibid.*, Book III, Chap. 3.
[26] *Ibid.*, Book IV, Chap. 53.
[27] *Ibid.*, Book XIII, Chap. 3.
[28] *Ibid.*, Book III, Chap. 65.
[29] *Ibid.*, Book I, Chap. 1.
[30] A. and M. Croiset, *Histoire de la littérature grecque* (5 vols., rev. ed., 1910-1921), II, 568.

one dimension, as it were—lacking in depth and motion. This is just what Tacitus supplies to antique historiography. He is a romanticist as opposed to their classicism; a genius with the creative grasp of a Victor Hugo but holding himself in, consciously, from that "folly of extremes" which is the danger fronting those who can carry their art so far.

Restraint with power behind it; in this respect at least, the genius of Tacitus is a living embodiment of that of Rome.

CHAPTER XXIV

From Suetonius to Ammianus Marcellinus

THERE were two of Tacitus' contemporaries who rivalled him in that part of his work where he was most successful—portraiture; Plutarch, the Greek, and Suetonius, the Roman biographer, were both of his time; and all three used to some degree the same materials. Indeed there is so much resemblance between Plutarch's lives of Galba and Otho and the description of the reigns of these two Emperors by Tacitus in his *Histories,* that critics, after the most minute analysis of the two texts, are still unable to agree as to whether one of them was dependent upon the other, and, if so, which one; or whether both depend upon a common source; and the relation of Suetonius to them, and in general to Tacitus, remains one of the most interesting problems in source criticism. However that may be, the vogue of biographies in this age is characteristic of the second century of the Empire. It is not merely the interest in character or characters which is significant; that is peculiar to no one age, since it belongs to all. It is the concentration of interest upon individuality to the exclusion of the larger social or political view; individuals no longer felt able to influence social and political development, and consequently took little interest in it.

Suetonius Tranquillus (c. 75–160 A.D.) was, like Tacitus, an upper-class Roman who devoted himself to scholarship; by no means so much of a personage as Tacitus, but perhaps more of a scholar. In his researches he reminds one of Varro, for he had a perfect mania for finding and noting all kinds of details, physical peculiarities, trivial incidents, obscure situations—in short all the miscellany that might go into an encyclopaedic *Notes and Queries* dealing with biography. He ultimately held a posi-

From Suetonius to Ammianus Marcellinus

tion where his insatiable curiosity could have full play, as secretary to Hadrian's praetorian prefect, Septicius Clarus, a position which opened to him the secret documents of the imperial cabinet. The result was a work as different as possible from Tacitus', yet sharing the same immortality by reason of the subjects of which it treated.

The Lives of the Caesars (*De vita Caesarum*) is a collection of biographies in eight books. The first six books are each devoted to the life of a single emperor (Caesar to Nero), but the seventh book covers the revolutionary year 69 with the three emperors it produced, and the Flavians make up the eighth. It was published in the year 120 A.D., and so Tacitus, in his old age, after "enjoying the serene glory of a great and serious historian,"[1] may have enjoyed reading that anecdotal counterpart to his grave and unbending narrative. For the work of Suetonius is the very antithesis of the *Annals*. It is, indeed, something of a new *genre*. As Boissier has so well put it:

> We plainly perceive in reading the *Lives of the Cæsars*, that the author has aimed at making a work of a new order; he has avoided including what was to be found in history as it was understood before him. He has not arranged events in chronological sequence, which is a rule of the historic art; rhetoric is quite absent; political views and general reflections occupy small space; he has made no pretence of teaching. On the other hand, anecdotes abound, told simply, without any attempt at effect or pictorial treatment. We read in his pages original documents, letters especially, when they throw some light on the great man he is describing; the witticisms fathered on him and those made at his expense; the monuments he has erected or restored are enumerated; the games he has given the people, a universal passion at the time; the signs which have announced his death, for the author is very superstitious and his readers still more so; finally, we are provided with his physical portrait, in which nothing is omitted, from the dimensions of his figure to the colour of his eyes. Suetonius has no compunction in telling us without any reticence all known of his infirmities; how Cæsar combed his hair over his forehead to conceal his baldness, how Claudius sputtered and jogged his head in speaking, how Domitian, who had been a very handsome lad when young, was afflicted towards

---

[1] G. Boissier, *Tacitus and Other Roman Studies*, p. 78. The extract quoted precedes this remark.

the end with a huge stomach borne on thin legs, and only found consolation in saying, "that there is nought more pleasing than beauty, but also nought that passes more quickly." Here, obviously, we were at the antipodes of ancient history. It is highly probable that works of this order held no very high place in the hierarchy of literary forms drawn up by the grammarians of the time. Never would Pliny, who knew and liked them both, have committed the impropriety of putting Suetonius on a level with Tacitus. Tacitus is a great personage, a serious man, a senator, a consul, who "graves for eternity." Suetonius is but an advocate, a student (*scholasticus*), who wants to divert his contemporaries. And yet Suetonius has created a form which is to last so long as the empire and he survive. History shall scarce be written henceforth save on the model he has designed; on the contrary, whilst Tacitus is always admired, he will never again be imitated. He was almost the last of the historians who wrote in the ancient fashion.

From the day of Hadrian, the decline in Latin literature which had already set in proceeded rapidly. Greek historians, it is true, to some extent made up for the deficiency, as we have already seen, although very hurriedly. But there were no western counterparts to Appian, Arrian, or Cassius Dio; and, apart from the pleasant miscellany of the *Attic Nights* (*Noctes Atticae*) of Aulus Gellius (born c. 130), with their scraps of information and some epitomes of history, paring down the old masters, we have little but biographical continuations of Suetonius to record, until the very closing days of imperial history.

Of these, a certain Marius Maximus (c. 165–230), carried the biographies of emperors down from Nerva to Elagabalus thus continuing the work of Suetonius to his own day. His work seems still to have been a creditable performance. Others continued at this popular substitute for history; and finally, some one gathered together a collection from Hadrian to Numerianus (117–284 A.D.), the so-called *Scriptores historiae Augustae*.[2] These are frankly mediaeval in style and content. Servile in tone, they are both trivial and self-contradictory in a helpless sort of way. It is hardly an apology for them to say that,

---

[2] The tradition that this was drawn from the works of six authors has been discarded. Recent criticism shows the slight historical value of this composite work, which includes many forged documents, a discovery which calls for the elimination of many notes from Gibbon's first volume.

after all, "they mean well and intend to state what is, or what they believe to be, the truth. Where they go astray, they are rather dupes than impostors."[3] The great age of antique historiography was over. The way in which it sank to the level of the Middle Ages has been outlined by Professor Swain as follows:

> In the later part of the fourth century Sextus Aurelius Victor composed a brief history of the Roman Empire in the form of biographical sketches of each emperor from Augustus to Constantius (d. 361). To this was prefixed—either by Victor or by an editor—a history of the Roman Republic by an unknown author written in the form of similar sketches of distinguished Romans of the period; it bore the appropriate title, *De viris illustribus urbis Romanae*. A brief summary of the earliest period, *Origo gentis Romanae*, written in ordinary narrative form, was then added and the whole history of Rome was thus presented, largely in biographical form, under the title *Historia Tripartita*. Another contemporary of these two men was the Christian scholar St. Jerome. Far superior in scholarship and intellectual ability to Victor or the authors of the *Augustan History*, he continued, nevertheless, the Latin tradition of Suetonius. His work *De viris illustribus* was modelled upon, and much of it drawn from, Suetonius' work of the same name; other of Jerome's writings were in much the same style and he was thus influential in carrying the Suetonian form over into the Middle Ages, where it underwent a new development in the *Acta Sanctorum*.
>
> Brief mention must also be made of one other form of historical writing which became popular in these centuries of decline—the epitome. Ever since the Greeks began writing big books there had, of course, been epitomes, made either for convenience or for economy: thus Theopompus epitomized Herodotus, Theophrastus epitomized some of Aristotle's works, Brutus epitomized Polybius, and an epitome of Livy soon appeared, perhaps in the days of Tiberius. We have also seen that throughout antiquity historical "research" frequently consisted in nothing more than finding and epitomizing earlier literary historians; but the better writers, such as Livy, when dealing with times long before their own, would epitomize many writers, weaving facts from different sources into one narrative, while second-rate writers like Diodorus would occasionally add facts from other sources to those from the principal one they were epitomizing. Now, however, epitomizers took an easier course: frequently—as in the case of Justin—they abbreviated a single author, selecting episodes here and there on the basis of their anecdotal

---

[3] Teuffel-Schwabe, *History of Roman Literature*, Vol. II, Sect. 392.

or moral value; sometimes—as in the cases of Florus and Licianus, both in the second century—they selected from three or four writers and arranged the episodes according to a system of their own, thus being original authors after a fashion; and sometimes they completed the work by bringing it down to their own day but in the same abbreviated style, as did Eutropius, who managed to compress more than 1100 years of Roman history—from Romulus to Valens—into about seventy-five pages. Such works as these somewhat resembled the *Outlines* of this and that which have appeared in such numbers in America in recent years, and they were apparently what the reading public of that day demanded, for they were multiplied while the works of the great historians were allowed to fall into decay or to be lost completely. Florus, Justin, and Eutropius were the pagans who handed down a knowledge of classic history to the Middle Ages.

From such a foretaste of mediaevalism, it is with distinct surprise that, just as we are entering those ages in reality, we come upon the single, outstanding figure of a good historian—a Greek but writing in Latin a continuation, not of Suetonius but of Tacitus.

Ammianus Marcellinus (c. 330–400 A.D.) was a native of Antioch who fought with the Roman armies all along the threatened frontiers, east and west. He knew the world of the barbarians as well as the culture of the empire, and his rich and varied experiences but strengthened his large share of native common sense. The combination of plentiful information and good judgment did not produce a work of genius; but the *Rerum gestarum libri,* which carried the story of Rome from Nerva to the death of Valens (96–378 A.D.), was a performance worthy of the best company in antique historiography. Only the more contemporary sections (Books XIV–XXXV) have been preserved. As they cover but the years 353 to 378 A.D., it is evident that either the early books were relatively slight and introductory, or that those we have belong only to a division of the whole series, dealing with contemporary history—much as Tacitus separated his *Histories* from his *Annals.* In any case, all that we have of Ammianus is the history of the last twenty-five years preceding the battle of Adrianople.

This last work of Roman history is frankly that of a soldier—

From Suetonius to Ammianus Marcellinus

a blunt, sincere man, honest and open-minded; a pagan, yet tolerant of Christians; not thoroughly at home in his study, yet proud of his scholarship; writing with the colloquial turn of a man of affairs and still turning it to use by preparing a history which was to be read in public. There is almost a touch of romance in the fact that this is so; that the last of the antique histories was to be declaimed, in competition with the output of the rhetoricians, the way the history of Herodotus was given to his age. Ammianus seems to have tried hard to brush up his Latin for such public presentation, but, in spite of his residence at Rome while he was writing it, his expressions remain clumsy, and obvious affectations even render the text obscure. It is only when one compares him with any other Latin historian for centuries before or after him that one appreciates his value as a straightforward, if somewhat awkward, witness to the truth. No fitter tribute has ever been paid him than that by the greatest historian who has ever dealt with the fortunes of Rome. For when Gibbon parted company with him, at the year 378, he took the occasion to bid Ammianus the farewell of a fellow craftsman worthy of mastership in the guild of history.[4]

---

[4] E. Gibbon, *The Decline and Fall of the Roman Empire,* Chap. XXVI (J. B. Bury's edition, III, 122): "It is not without the most sincere regret that I must now take leave of an accurate and faithful guide, who has composed the history of his own times without indulging the prejudices and passions which usually affect the mind of a contemporary."

PART V

CHRISTIANITY AND HISTORY

CHAPTER XXV

The New Era

THE great historians of antiquity were writers of modern history. Herodotus, Thucydides, Polybius, Tacitus, were interested in what had happened because of what was happening, and great things were happening in their day. Herodotus writing, as he said, "in order that the great and wondrous deeds of both Greeks and barbarians may not be effaced by time," massed his facts around that world-stirring crisis, which had taken place a half century before, the Persian wars. Thucydides, persuaded that "former ages were not great either in their wars or in anything else," believed the war that had passed before his eyes was the greatest event in the world's history, and he bent his life's energies to describing it. Polybius, too, carried off to Rome in the track of her victorious armies, saw as a captive the miraculous dawn of that first empire of the Mediterranean world, and he wrote his history to explain it. Livy's vision was also always fastened upon the imperial present and the calm, clear-headed patriotism which had brought it about. Tacitus lacked this generous enthusiasm, but his interests were not antiquarian; the great age in which he lived drew his observation and supplied him with his task. From the clash of East and West in the Ionian cities in the sixth century B.C., whereby the critical curiosity of men and societies was first made active, to the tragic close of the drama of the ancient world, almost a thousand years later, history was centred upon the great events and the characters that dominated the world in which each writer lived.

But there was one event of supreme importance that had no Herodotus to gather up its details, no Polybius to weld it into the world's history with scientific insight and critical acumen—the rise of Christianity.¹ The product of obscure enthusiasts in an obscure and despised Oriental people, it did not win more than a disdainful paragraph (in Tacitus) at the hands of pagan historians. Its own writings were but poor attempts at history compared with what other lesser events produced. When the scanty texts of the sayings and doings of Jesus were taking the shape in which we have them now, a Plutarch was writing biographies of all the pagan heroes. But no Christian Plutarch appeared for another three centuries; and then all that the learned Jerome was able to preserve for us was three or four paragraphs on the lives of the leading apostles.²

There were several reasons for this. In the first place Christianity began in a most humble way and among the unlettered. It did not burst out in a flame of conquest like Mohammedanism but crept, half-hidden, along the foundations of society. Its very obscurity left little to chronicle. If it changed the lives of men, they were lives too insignificant to be noticed by history. Only in the present age, after democracy itself has learned to read and begun to think, is the historian awakening to the spiritual forces in the lives of the obscure. But even now we pay little attention to such seemingly extraneous elements as the beliefs of foreign immigrants settled in our city slums—the class that furnished the majority of the early converts to Christianity. In any case the Greco-Roman world troubled itself little about the history of the Jews and less still about that of the Christians.³

Even when Christianity had penetrated the society of the learned, moreover, it stimulated little historical investigation.

[1] H. von Soden, "Das Interesse des apostolischen Zeitalters an der evangelischen Geschichte," in *Theologische Abhandlungen* (1892), pp. 113-169.

[2] Jerome's *De viris illustribus*, written after the model of the work of the same name by Suetonius.

[3] The emphasis which subsequent ages has placed upon references to Judaism and Christianity in pagan writers has given those passages an altogether factitious prominence. There are at best only a very few, and those are mostly either incidental or pointed with ridicule. See T. Reinach, *Textes d'auteurs grecs et romains relatifs au judaïsme, réunis, traduits et annotés* (1895); the opening sections of the important work of J. Juster, *Les Juifs dans l'empire romain, leur condition juridique, économique et sociale* (2 vols., 1914). E. Schürer's *Geschichte des jüdischen Volkes im Zeitalter Jesu Christi* (3 vols. and index, 3d and 4th eds., 1901-1911, tr. 1897-98) remains the standard work on the period. See also articles in the *Jewish Encyclopædia* dealing with the Diaspora.

The New Era

Pagan savants, like Celsus,[4] sometimes challenged the sources of Christian tradition and scripture,[5] but for the most part the great controversy between Christian and pagan writers took place in fields that lay beyond the scope of history. Christianity was a religion, not a thing of politics, and although, as we shall see, the problem of fitting it into the Jewish, and then into the Gentile, setting did involve historical conceptions, yet the main interests awakened by it were theological. This meant that history, as a record of mere human events, was bound to suffer; for theology, in so far as it concerned itself with those events, sought to transfer them from the realm of human action to that of divine grace, and so to interpret the phenomena of time and change in terms of a timeless and unchanging Deity.[6] The western world has since gratefully built its theology upon the conceptions so brilliantly worked out by the Fathers, and the historian whose business it is to register the judgments of society cannot fail to appreciate their great formative influence in the history of thought. But their very success was a loss to history; for it placed the meaning of human effort outside the range of humanity and thus impressed upon the western world a fundamentally unhistorical attitude of mind.

The motive force which accomplished this theological victory was faith. Faith was the chief intellectual demand which Christianity made of its converts.[7] By it the mind was enabled to view events in a perspective which reached beyond the limits of time and space into that imaginary overworld which we know as Eternity. Faith did more than remove mountains, it removed the whole material environment of life. There have been few such triumphs of the spirit as it achieved in those early days

---

[4] See below, pp. 342 *sqq*.

[5] As Apion did those of the Jews.

[6] It is significant to see how the conception of the essential unhistoricity of God, as a Being beyond the reach of change, has been growingly modified in modern times. The increase in the number of those mystics who have revised their theology in terms of modern science and philosophy (especially Bergsonian) is, from the standpoint of the history of pure thought, the most decisive triumph of the historical spirit. The Deity himself becomes historical; eternity disappears; all is time—and change.

[7] Charity was hardly an intellectual virtue, at least as conceived by the Fathers.

of the new religion. But the fact remains that this achievement was largely at the cost of history. Faith, one can see from the criticism of those first really conscious historians, the Ionian Greeks, is an impediment to genuine history, unless the imagination which it quickens is kept within control. The historian needs rather to confine his imagination by skepticism and to be more upon his guard against believing whenever he feels the will to believe than at any other time—which, in the realm of religious virtues, has sometimes been mistaken for a sin.[8] Moreover, over and above the fact that faith puts a premium upon credulity,[9] it indicates an absence of any real, serious interest in historical data. When one "takes a thing on faith," it is because one is intent upon using it for something else of more importance—so important, indeed, that often while still unrealized it can clothe with reality the very condition upon which it depends. Thus the "will to believe" can master phenomena in a way not permitted to historians. Faith and scientific history do not readily work together.

If this is clear in the dawn of Greek history, when science first challenged faith, it stands out even more clearly still in that very antithesis of the creations of Hellas, as we may best term the gospel according to Paul.[10] Nowhere else in the world's literature is there a call to faith like that of Paul, and few, even of the great creators of religious doctrine, have been more indifferent than he to the historical data upon which, in the order of nature, that faith would seem to rest. The Apostle to the Gentiles cared little for the details of the life of Jesus and boasted of his indifference.[11] He learned of the divinity of Christ by a flash of

---

[8] There are all kinds of faith, to be sure. We are speaking only of religious faith which transfers phenomena from the natural to the supernatural world and is, therefore, the chief opponent of rationalism.

[9] As Celsus, the pagan critic, so cogently suggested.

[10] And we must regard Paul as the intellectual creator of Christian theology.

[11] See the first, second, and third chapters of the Epistle to the Galatians.

A word might be added here on the origin of the Gospels. One or more collections of the sayings of Jesus were written in Aramaic about 60 A.D. or soon after. The Gospel of Mark was written about the year 70, those of Matthew and Luke about fifteen or twenty years later, based on Mark and the sayings of Jesus (commonly known as Q, for *Quelle*, source), and other documents for the infancy of Jesus. The Gospel of John was written later by a philosophically minded Greek.

revelation which marked him out as one of the prophets. Then the desert, rather than Jerusalem, furnished him that tremendous plan of Christian doctrine upon which Christian orthodoxy still rests, which included the whole drama of humanity from the Creation and the Fall to the Redemption and the vision of its meaning, revealed on the road to Damascus. The plan was based upon the Law and the Prophets, but only because Paul's thought ran in terms of their teaching. His scheme was one that needed no verification from the sources even of sacred scripture, if once it could carry conviction by inner experience.[12]

Finally the faith of early Christianity was largely involved in a doctrine which centered attention not on this world but on the world to come, and the world to come was about to come at any moment. Immortality for the individual was a doctrine shared by other mystery religions of the pagan world; but only Christianity developed—out of the apocalyptic literature of the Jews—the vaster dream of an imminent cataclysm in which the world to come should come for all at once. While this doctrine appears in full force in Christian circles only from the latter part of the first to the middle of the second century and was most developed in circles given over to what might be viewed, even by ecclesiastics, as extreme spirituality, it undoubtedly had a large and damaging influence upon Christian historiography. There is nothing which so effectively destroys our interest in the past as to live under the shadow of a great and impending event. It would not have been the same had each individual convert merely been keenly aware of the shortness of his own life and the vision of the coming day of judgment. That is still and has always been a perspective before religious minds, and, however strange it may seem, it does not entirely kill the interest in the origin and evolution of these things which are so soon to vanish from before

---

"Historians," says Professor Swain, "might well ponder over the causes of the undeniable fact that the least reliable of the Gospels has been the most influential." Luke, as the *Acts of the Apostles* shows, was an educated man who compiled his history out of various sources, was accurate in geography and painstaking, and his work stands easily alongside the best pagan histories of his time.

[12] The Pauline doctrine involved a conceptual parallel to history, which apparently furnished a better past to the world, one more reasonable and more probable than that which actually had been the case.

the eyes of death. Such is the vital instinct in us.[13] But it is a different thing for heaven and earth and all mankind to pass away at once as these early Christians expected them to do at any time. A few years ago we were to traverse the tail of a comet and there was some speculation as to whether its deadly gases might not exterminate all life on this globe. Had the probability been more probable, had astronomers and men of science determined the fact by some experimental proof, with what breathless and hypnotic gaze we should have watched the measured coming of that star across the gulfs of space! Our vast, unresting industries would have ceased; for there would have been no tomorrow to supply. Our discoveries in science, our creations in art would have been like so many useless monuments in an untenanted world—and science and art would have had no incentive to go on. The one interest for us all would have been that growing point of light—that doom, swift, inevitable, universal. Here comes a problem of psychology. For as a matter of fact that same doom is coming; we know it with absolute certainty; we know there can be no escape. How many of those who saw that comet pass will be alive fifty years from now? In a century, at most, the earth will be the sepulchre of all—just as much a sepulchre as if the race had perished in one grand catastrophe. And what a little interval is a century! Yet our mills work on, our discoveries continue, our art goes on producing its visions of beauty, and above all, we increase our interest in the distant past, digging for history in the hills of Crete and Asia and working as never before to rescue and reconstruct the past from archives and libraries. Why? Because humanity is more to us than our individual lives, and the future is a reality through it. If humanity were to disappear and no future be possible, we should lose our reckoning, along with our sense of values, like Browning's Lazarus, who has had a vision of eternity but has lost track of time.

So it was in the millennial atmosphere of the early Church.

[13] The influence of the belief in immortality upon historical perspectives invites our attention here, but the subject is too intricate for hurried consideration. Undoubtedly the emphasis upon a contrast between time and eternity obscured the meaning of phenomena in their time-setting.

The New Era

However vaguely or definitely the triumph of "the Kingdom" was reckoned,[14] the belief in its approach carried the mind away from earthly affairs and their history. Men who drew their inspiration from it had but little interest in the splendor of a Roman state or in the long procession of centuries when were painfully evolved the institutions of pagan law and government, institutions which not only safeguarded the heritage of antique culture but made possible the extension of Christianity.

The only history of importance to the Christian was that which justified his faith, and it all lay within the sacred writings of the Jews. So, as the vision of the Judgment Day became fainter and

[14] The conception of a millennium, drawn from the later Jewish literature, was that Christ and his saints would rule for a thousand years; but in spite of much calculation the belief was never quite reduced to successful mathematics. It is interesting, in passing, to see how it drew upon that other interest in chronology, the plotting out of a future instead of a past, which astrology best illustrates. In fact the millennium may be said to be a sort of Christian equivalent for astrology. In the earlier prophets the Messianic kingdom is to last forever (cf. Ezekiel 37:25, etc.), a conception found also in the apostolic age (John 12:34). Jeremiah, however, had risked a prophecy of Jewish delivery from captivity at the end of seventy years (25:12), but when his dream of deliverance was not realized, the later prophets had to find an explanation, and apocalyptic literature developed a reckoning which should save the validity of the earlier. This was definitely the occasion of Daniel's attempt (9), which has taxed the mathematics of every apocalyptic dreamer to the present day. The conception of a thousand years came late, and perhaps rests on very extended use of symbolic interpretation. According to Psalms 90:4, a day with God is as a thousand years. Combine this with the six days of Creation in Genesis and by analogy the world's work will go on for six such days, or six thousand years, and then the Messiah will reign for a Sabbath of a thousand years. This idea is found only once in the Talmud. It was developed for Christians in Revelation (see 20:4: "They lived and reigned with Christ a thousand years"). Through Jewish and Christian apocalypses the doctrine was taken up, sometimes with, sometimes without, the mathematical data. By the middle of the second century it began to subside, and although Montanism in the early third century revived it, it was henceforth regarded as somewhat tinged with heresy and Judaism. In the learned circles, Neoplatonic mysticism, as taught by Origen, superseded the crudities of the millennistic faith. "It was only the chronologists and historians of the church who, following Julius Africanus, made use of apocalyptic numbers in their calculations, while court theologians like Eusebius entertained the imperial table with discussions as to whether the dining-hall of the emperor—the second David and Solomon, the beloved of God—might not be the new Jerusalem of John's Apocalypse" (A. Harnack, article "Millennium" in *Encyclopædia Britannica* (11th ed.). This article furnishes an admirable survey and bibliography. See the treatment of Christian eschatology in the various works of R. H. Charles in the field of apocalyptic literature.)

the Church proceeded to settle itself in time and not in eternity, it looked back to a different past from that which lay beyond the pagan world. The sacred scriptures of the Jews had replaced the literature of antiquity. A revolution was taking place in the history of history. Homer and Thucydides, Polybius and Livy, the glory of the old regime, shared a common fate. The scientific output of the most luminous minds the world had known was classed with the legends that had grown up by the campfires of primitive barbarians. All was pagan; which meant that all was delusive and unreliable except where it could be tested in the light of the new religion or where it forced itself by the needs of life into the world of common experience.

There is no more momentous revolution in the history of thought than this, in which the achievements of thinkers and workers, of artists, philosophers, poets, and statesmen, were given up for the revelation of prophets and a gospel of worldly renunciation. The very success of the revolution blinds us to its significance, for our own world view has been moulded by it. Imagine, for instance, what the perspectives of history would have been had there been no Christianity, or if it had remained merely a sect of Judaism, to be ignored or scorned! Religion carried history away from the central themes of antiquity to a nation that had little to offer—except the religion.

The story of Israel could not, from the very nature of its situation, be more than an incident in the drama of nations. The great empires of the east lay on either side of it, and the land of promise turned out to be a pathway of conquering armies. From the desert beyond Jordan new migrations of Semite nomads moved in to plunder the Jews, as the Jews themselves had plundered the land before. On the west, Philistine and Phoenician held the harbors and the sea. Too small a nation for a career of its own, exposed and yet secluded, the borderer of civilization, Israel could produce no rich culture like its more fortunately situated neighbors. When unmolested for a time, it too could achieve rapid progress in its fortress towns. But no sooner was its wealth a temptation than the Assyrian was at the gates. It is small wonder, then, if in spite of the excellence of much of the historical literature

The New Era

embedded in the Old Testament, even the best of it—such as the stories woven around the great days of Saul and David—when compared with the narrative of Polybius or even with that of Herodotus, leaves a picture of petty kinglets of an isolated tribe, reaching out for a brief interval to touch the splendors of Tyre and Sidon and vaguely aware of the might and wealth of Egypt.

The main contribution of the Jews to the world was in a field which offers history few events to chronicle. As we have insisted above, it was a contribution of the first magnitude, to be treasured by succeeding ages above all the arts and sciences of antiquity. But its very superiority lay in its unworldliness, in its indifference to the passing fortunes of man or nations which make up the theme of history. This, at least, was the side of Judaism which Christianity seized upon and emphasized. But there could be little for history in any case in a religion born of national disaster and speaking by revelation. The religion which is born of disaster must either falsify realities by a faith which reads victory in defeat or it must take refuge in the realm of the spirit, where the triumphs of the world, its enemy, are met with indifference or scorn. In either case the perspective is distorted. Revelation may save the future by stirring hope and awakening confidence; but with the same calm authority with which it dictates the conduct of the present, it will falsify the past—falsify, that is, in the eyes of science. In its own eyes it is lord of circumstance and master of phenomena, and the records of the centuries must come to its standards, not it to theirs.

It was, therefore, a calamity for historiography that the new standards won the day. The authority of a revealed religion sanctioned but one scheme of history through the vast and intricate evolution of the antique world. A well-nigh insurmountable obstacle was erected to scientific inquiry—one at least which has taken almost nineteen centuries to surmount.

Not only was the perspective perverted, and the perversion made into a creed, but the stern requirements of monotheistic theology placed a veritable barrier against investigation. The Christian historian was not free to question the data as presented to him, since the source was inspired. He might sometimes evade the difficulty by reading new meanings into the data and so square them with the rest of history, a device employed by every Father of the Church whose erudition and insight brought him face to face with the difficulties of literal acceptance of the scriptures. But however one might twist the texts, the essential outlines of the scheme of history remained fixed. From the prophets of Jahveh, with their high fanaticism, and from Paul, the prophet of Jesus, there was but one world view, that dominated by the idea of a chosen people and a special dispensation. The only difference between Jewish and Christian outlook was that what had been present politics became past history. The apostle to the Gentiles did not give up the Jewish past. Pre-Christian history was in his eyes the same narrow story of exclusive providence as it was in the eyes of the older prophets. Gentiles had had no share in the dispensations of Jahveh; it was only for the present and future that they might hope to enter into the essential processes of historical evolution. The past to Paul was what it was to a Pharisee.

This exclusive attitude of Christianity with reference to the past was in striking contrast with the attitude of contemporaneous paganism, which was growing liberal with increasing knowledge. To attack the story of Jahveh's governance of the world was, for a Christian, sacrilege, since the story itself was sacred. A pagan, with a whole pantheon to turn to, placed no such value upon any one myth and therefore was free to discount them all. His eternal salvation did not rest upon his belief in them; and, moreover, he did not concern himself so much about his salvation in any case. When the belief in an immortality was bound up with the acceptance of a scheme of history, the acceptance was assured. What is the dead past of other people's lives, when compared with the unending future of one's own? History yielded to the demands of eternity.

Moreover in its emphasis upon the Messiahship of Jesus, Christianity fastened upon one of the most exclusive aspects of Jewish thought. Such history as the proof of this claim involved was along the line of a narrow, fanatic, national movement.

The New Era

Christianity, it is true, opened the Messianic kingdom to the whole world, but it justified its confidence in the future by an appeal to the stricter outlines of a tribal faith in the past. And yet that appeal, in spite of its limitations, was the source of such historical research as Christianity produced. For, when pressed by pagan critics to reconcile their claims with those of Greeks or Egyptians, the Fathers were obliged to work out not merely a theory of history—their theology supplied them with that—but a scheme of chronology. The simple problem, so lightly attacked, as to whether Moses or the Greeks should have the priority as lawgiver forced the apologists to some study of comparative history. While in this particular issue they had a somewhat easy triumph,[15] there was a danger, which is obvious to us now, in too much reliance upon the chronology of the Old Testament, and especially in placing an emphasis upon the literal text. The trenchant criticism of their opponents, therefore, led the Fathers to adopt that allegorical type of interpretation, which they learned from the Greeks themselves, and which is so useful wherever there is a need for holding fast to a text while letting the meaning go. We shall, therefore, find the chief developments of Christian historiography during the first three centuries following these two lines of allegory and symbolism on the one hand, and comparative chronology on the other.

[15] One of the earliest and best short statements of this claim is that made by Tatian in his *Address to the Greeks,* Chaps. 31-41. It is strikingly in line with Josephus' protest in *Against Apion.*

CHAPTER XXVI

Allegory and the Contribution of Origen

IN spite of what has been said as to the weakness of Christian historiography, it is possible to maintain the thesis that, among religions, Christianity is especially notable as resting essentially on a historical basis.

In so far as Christianity was a historical religion, that fact was due, as has just been said, to the Messianic element in it. Indeed it can be said to have claimed from the beginning that it was a historical religion—a fulfilment of history, one fitting itself into the scheme of social and political evolution in a particular state. The apostles themselves, in their earliest appeal, demanded that one "search the scriptures"—a demand unique in the founding of religions. There is a vast difference, however, between studying history and studying historically. That they did study it, the one fact that the Christians retained the Old Testament is ample evidence. That they failed to deal with it adequately, the New Testament is also ample evidence. But since the Christian Messiah was offered to the whole world as well as to the Jews, Christian historiography had two main tasks before it: to place the life of Jesus in the history of the Jews, and, also, to show its setting in the general history of antiquity. The latter problem was not forced upon the Church until the pagan world began to take the new religion seriously, and its answer is found in the works of the great apologists. The relation of Christianity to Judaism, however, the Messianic problem proper, was of vital importance from the beginning, for it involved the supreme question whether or not Jesus was the one in whom the prophecies were fulfilled.[1]

---

[1] The coming of the Messiah was the main continuation of Jewish national history. Messiahship was to the Jews of the time of Christ the embodiment of some-

Allegory and the Contribution of Origen

One "searched the scriptures," therefore, for the evidences of the signs by which the advent could be recognized. The invitation to search them was, in appearance at least, a challenge to a scientific test, that of verification. If the data of the life of Jesus corresponded with the details of the promises, there was a proof that the promises had been fulfilled. But since the fulfilment was not literal, the interpretation could not be literal either. The spiritual Kingdom of the Messiah had to be constructed out of fragmentary and uncertain references, and the only satisfactory way to apply many of them was by symbolism and allegory. Modern critical scholarship has now discarded Messianic prophecy, on the basis that the texts so confidently cited as foretelling the life of Jesus had no such purpose in the minds of their authors. But orthodoxy has held, through all the history of the church, that the texts were applicable and that the proof was thereby established of the harmony of the old and the new dispensations.

We cannot turn, however, to the problems of higher criticism. The significant thing for history writing was the creation of what might be called a new *genre*—that of the allegorical interpretation of texts. The use of allegory to explain, or explain away, texts was not a creation of Christian historians, for the device was not unknown to pagan literature or philosophy. As far back as the sixth century B.C., Homer was interpreted allegorically by Theagenes of Rhegium, and pagan philosophy had constant recourse to allegory to harmonize myth with reason. The Jews too were past masters in its use. We have seen how the allegorical interpretation of the Old Testament had been developed by the Jewish scholars, especially those of the Diaspora, who found themselves thrown into contact with Gentile scholars

---

what the same thought as stirred the Frenchman of the close of the nineteenth century at the recollection of 1870 and the lost provinces or lent such inspiration in embittered Poland to the prophetlike poetry of Mickiewicz. It was the dream of a deliverer, a belief strengthened, rather than crushed, by failure and disaster. The whole sad drama of Jewish history may be said to have concentrated its expression in the Messianic hope—a hope against hope itself. Christianity, in offering itself as the realization of that hope, was stepping into a definite place in Jewish history, but it was a place to which the Jewish nation as a whole has never admitted it.

338 Allegory and the Contribution of Origen

and felt the need of harmonizing Greek thought with their own intellectual heritage; we have seen to what extent it was carried in the writings of the greatest Jewish philosopher of antiquity, Philo of Alexandria.[2] But it is to be found as well in the Old Testament itself, especially in the prophetic literature, where it runs alongside that elusive trace of the unattained which gave the prophecies their fascinating charm. One could trace it back farther still to the mind of primitive man, where symbol and reality are often confused into a single impression. But in the hands of the Christian theologians, symbolism emerged from the background of thought to dominate the whole situation. The story of realities depended upon the interpretation of the unrealities; and that story of realities was nothing short of a history of the world itself.

The greatest master of Christian allegory was Origen, the Alexandrine Greek, who, in the third century, contributed so much to the formulation of a scheme of theology for the Fathers of the Church. Origen was a scholar as well as a philosophic thinker, and it was his work on the text of the Bible, to which reference has been made above, which won for him the praise of one so unlike him in point of view as St. Jerome. In that limited gallery of illustrious men which St. Jerome has left for us, the *De viris illustribus*, Origen stands out clearly: [3]

Who is there, he asks, who does not know that he was so assiduous in the study of Holy Scriptures, that contrary to the spirit of his time, and of his people, he learned the Hebrew language, and taking the Septuagint translation, he gathered in a single work the other translations also, namely those of Aquila of Ponticus the Proselyte, and Theodotian the Ebonite, and Symmachus an adherent of the same sect who wrote commentaries also on the gospel according to Matthew, from

---

[2] The influence of Philo upon the Christian Fathers is a matter of great interest. The admiration of speculative minds for the Jewish thinker is echoed in the comment which Eusebius prefixes to his list of the works of Philo (*Historia ecclesiastica*, Book II, Chap. 18): "Copious in language, comprehensive in thought, sublime and elevated in his views of divine Scripture, Philo has produced manifold and various expositions of the sacred books" (A. C. McGiffert's translation in the *Library of Nicene and Post-Nicene Fathers*).

[3] Jerome, *De viris illustribus*, Chap. 54. Also in the preface of his *De nominibus Hebraicis*, Jerome speaks of him as, "Origen, whom all but the ignorant acknowledge as the greatest teacher of the churches, next to the Apostles."

Allegory and the Contribution of Origen 339

which he tried to establish his doctrine. And besides these, a fifth, sixth, and seventh translation, which we also have from his library, he sought out with great diligence, and compared with other editions. And since I have given a list of his works in the volumes of letters which I have written to Paula, in a letter which I wrote against the works of Varro, I pass this by now, not failing, however, to make mention of his immortal genius, how that he understood dialectics, as well as geometry, arithmetic, music, grammar, and rhetoric, and taught all the schools of philosophers, in such wise that he had also diligent students in secular literature, and lectured to them daily, and the crowds which flocked to him were marvellous. These, he received in the hope that through the instrumentality of this secular literature, he might establish them in the faith of Christ.

This tribute by Jerome summarizes the lengthy account of Origen by Eusebius in the sixth book of the *Ecclesiastical History*, to which we may still turn for a full account of the life and influence of one who, while not a historian in the stricter sense, contributed to Christian historiography one of its most remarkable chapters.

Origen was as courageous in his interpretations as he was thorough in his scholarship. Not only did he deny the literal truth of much of Genesis and explain away the darker happenings in the history of Israel, but, even in the New Testament, he treated as parables or fables such stories as that of the Devil taking Jesus up into a high mountain and showing him the kingdoms of the world. One reads Origen with a startle of surprise. The most learned of the Fathers of the third century was a modern.[4] His commentaries upon the Bible might almost pass for the product of the nineteenth century. The age of Lyell and Darwin has seen the same effort of mystic orthodoxy to save the poem of Creation, by making the six days over into geological eras and the story of Adam and Eve a symbol of human fate. Many a sermon upon the reconciliation of science and religion —that supreme subject of modern sermons—might be taken almost bodily from Origen. For his problem was essentially like that which fronts the modern theologian; he had to win from a rationalism which he respected the denial of its inherent skepti-

---

[4] Too modern to be entirely orthodox. Hence his subsequent eclipse.

cism. Like Philo, a resident of that cosmopolitan centre, Alexandria, that meeting place of races and religions, Origen was a modern among moderns. He was a Greek of subtlest intellect and vast erudition, one of the finest products of the great Hellenic dispersion.[5]

Interpretation of the scriptures by allegory is not, in Origen's eyes, an unwarranted liberty. The scriptures themselves sanction it—allegorically! There is a "hidden and secret meaning," he says, "in each individual word, the treasure of divine wisdom being hid in the vulgar and unpolished vessels of words; as the apostle also points out when he says, 'We have this treasure in earthen vessels.' "[6] Quaintly naïve as such reasoning seems when based upon a single text, its weakness becomes its strength when sufficient texts are adduced to convey the impression that the scriptures themselves do really proclaim their own symbolic character. This Origen endeavors to do. "If the law of Moses had contained nothing which was to be understood as having a secret meaning, the prophet would not have said in his prayer to God: 'Open thou mine eyes and I will behold wondrous things out of thy law'" (Psalms 119:18). What, he asks, can one make out of the prophecy of Ezekiel except allegorically?[7] Prophetic literature implies allegory in its very structure. But the strongest proof of the legitimacy of allegorical interpretation is its use in the New Testament, and so largely by St. Paul.[8]

The modern critic sees the vicious circle in which such reasoning moves. But he sees it because he denies the hidden meaning, the secret lore, which to the "intellectuals" of the third century was the real heart of phenomena. Symbolism has deeper roots than one suspects. The mysterious efficacy of numbers is as wide as savagery; the secret value of words is a doctrine as universal as speech. They come from untold ages beyond Pythagoras or Heracleitus. The Christian emphasis upon the logos—the word which became God and the word which was God—but put the stamp of supreme authority upon a phase of thought intelligible to all antiquity. Gnosticism took hold of that phase and, by

[5] See Eusebius, *Historia ecclesiastica*, Book VI, for details of Origen's life.
[6] *De principiis*, Book I, Chap. 1, Sect. 7.
[7] *Contra Celsum*, Book IV, Chap. 50.
[8] *Ibid.*, Book IV, Chap. 49.

Allegory and the Contribution of Origen

insisting upon an inner doctrine which was concealed from the uninitiated, attempted to harmonize Christianity with the parallel cults of paganism. Neoplatonism was doing much the same for paganism itself. The cults of Asia and Egypt were drawn together and interpreted in the light of the worship of Demeter or Dionysus. Origen's point of view is not so naïve as it seems. It was in line with that of his age. The world was becoming one, and yet at the same time it was a medley of different and divergent civilizations. The only way the ancient could think of overcoming this antithesis between an ideal which sought for unity and phenomena which differed was by denying the essential nature of the differences. We should do the same if it were not for our hypothesis of evolution and the historical attitude of mind. Only when one sees the impasse into which the thinkers of antiquity were forced in their attempts to syncretize a complex and varying world, does one realize by contrast what a tremendous implement of synthesis the evolutionary hypothesis supplies. The only alternative method by which to realize the harmony which does not appear is by symbolism.

If we once grant that texts are not what they seem, there is only one way to learn their true meaning. We must find a key, and that key must be some supreme fact, some fact so large that the content of the text seems but incidental to it. Christianity supplied such a clue to the interpretation of the Old Testament, and the Old Testament, for its part, supplied Christianity with the authority of a long antiquity. The value of that antiquity for the basis of a story of obscure, recent happenings in Jerusalem was felt by all apologists and has been a convincing argument until the present. It was left for the nineteenth century to substitute for symbolism the tests of historical criticism and thus to see the whole scheme of allegorical theological interpretation fade away. But we should not forget that, false as it seems to us in both method and results, the symbolic method made the theologian somewhat of a historian in spite of himself, and we should not expect of the savant of the third century the historical and evolutionary attitude of today—which was, so far as we can see, his only alternative.

Symbolism may twist the texts; but a mind like Origen's does not miss the essential point that the texts must be there to twist. Nothing is more interesting in the historiography of early Christianity than to see how Origen came to realize, after all, the paucity of his sources and their inadequacy, particularly of those dealing with the history of Christianity itself. He shows this with scholarly frankness in a passage in his famous apology, *Against Celsus*. Celsus was a pagan Greek who wrote the most notable attack upon Christianity of which we have record from those early times. His treatise was a powerful and learned criticism of the Christian writings and teachings, especially emphasizing their unscientific character and the credulity of those who believed in them. Origen's reply reveals in more places than one how in him a genuine historical critic was lost in the theologian. To illustrate: Celsus had claimed that before writing his attack he had taken the trouble to acquaint himself with all the Christian doctrines and writings. Origen, drawing on his prodigious knowledge of the Bible, shows time and again what a superficial acquaintance it had been—that is, judged according to Origen's method of interpretation. But when Celsus charges the Christians with obscurantism, stating that their teachers generally tell him not to investigate, while at the same time exhorting him to believe, Origen takes another tack.[9] He is apparently a little ashamed of the emphasis taken from reason and placed upon faith by his Christian colleagues. He does not actually say as much, but he reminds Celsus that all men have not the leisure to investigate. After this weak admission, however, he turns round, in what is one of the most interesting passages of patristic writing, and demands if Celsus and the pagans do not follow authority as well. Have not Stoics and Platonists a teacher too, whose word they go back to? Celsus believes in an uncreated world and that the flood (Deucalion's) is a fairly modern thing.[10] But what authority has he? The dialogues of Plato? But Moses

---

[9] *Ibid.*, Book I, Chaps. 12 and 10. The order of citations has been reversed here for clarity.

[10] Celsus also had the idea of a common evolution of ideas and customs and of the borrowings of one nation from another, *e.g.*, circumcision from Egypt, *ibid.*, Book I, Chap. 22.

Allegory and the Contribution of Origen

saw more clearly than Plato. He was in incomparably better position to be informed. Why not prefer the account of Moses?

The value of a controversy is that each side sees the other's weak points. It seldom results in admitting the inferiority of one's own position; but once in a while a fair-minded man will be courageous enough to state that, through no fault of his own, he is unable to be more accurate than his opponent. This is about what Origen does, in taking up the charge of Celsus that the narrative of the baptism in the Jordan is so improbable a story as to require confirmation of first-hand witnesses before he as a thinking pagan could accept it. In reply Origen frankly admits the paucity of sources for the history of Christianity, but demands to know if Celsus is willing to give up pagan history because it contains improbable incidents. The passage is worth quoting, for it shows how the most learned of all the Fathers, the most subtle and comprehensive intellect, with one exception, which Christianity enlisted to its cause, recognized the weakness of Christian historiography but failed to see how it could be remedied:

Before we begin our reply we have to remark that the endeavour to show with regard to almost any history, however true, that it actually occurred, and to produce an intelligent conception regarding it, is one of the most difficult undertakings that can be attempted, and is in some instances an impossibility. For suppose that some one were to assert that there never had been any Trojan War, chiefly on account of the impossible narrative interwoven therewith, about a certain Achilles being the son of a sea-goddess Thetis and of a man Peleus, or Sarpedon being the son of Zeus, or Ascalaphus and Ialmenus the sons of Ares, or Æneas that of Aphrodite, how should we prove that such was the case, especially under the weight of the fiction attached, I know not how, to the universally prevalent opinion that there was really a war in Ilium between Greeks and Trojans? And suppose, also, that some one disbelieved the story of Œdipus and Jocasta, and of their two sons Eteocles and Polynices, because the sphinx, a kind of half-virgin, was introduced into the narrative, how should we demonstrate the reality of such a thing? And in like manner also with the history of the Epigoni, although there is no such marvellous event interwoven with it, or with the return of the Heracleidæ, or countless other historical events. But he who deals candidly with histories, and would wish to keep himself also from being imposed upon by them, will exercise his judgment as to what statements he will give his assent to, and what he will accept figuratively, seeking to discover the meaning of the authors of such inventions, and from what statements he will withhold his belief, as having been written for the gratification of certain individuals. And we have said this by way of anticipation respecting the whole history related in the Gospels concerning Jesus, not as inviting men of acuteness to a simple and unreasoning faith, but wishing to show that there is need of candour in those who are to read, and of much investigation, and, so to speak, of insight into the meaning of the writers, that the object with which each event has been recorded may be discovered.[11]

In so many words Origen admits that since the sources for Christian history cannot be checked up by external evidence, there is nothing left but to accept their main outlines on faith—the same faith the Greek has in the existence of Troy or the Roman in the early kings. But being a Greek—and above all a Greek in argument—he qualifies his faith by reason and explains away what seems improbable. In a way, therefore, we have before us a sort of sophisticated Herodotus after all, who eliminates myth to suit his perspective.[12]

[11] *Ibid.*, Book I, Chap. 42 (F. Crombie's translation in the "Ante-Nicene Christian Library.")

[12] In addition to Celsus, Porphyry entered the lists against Origen from the pagan side. Of his attack, the following extract, quoted, with cautionary comment, by Eusebius in the sixth book (Chap. 19) of the *Historia ecclesiastica* (A. C. McGiffert's translation), is worth repeating as an indication of the controversial atmosphere in which we are here moving:

" 'Some persons [says Porphyry], desiring to find a solution of the baseness of the Jewish Scriptures rather than abandon them, have had recourse to explanations inconsistent and incongruous with the words written, which explanations, instead of supplying a defense of the foreigners, contain rather approval and praise of themselves. For they boast that the plain words of Moses are enigmas, and regard them as oracles full of hidden mysteries; and having bewildered the mental judgment by folly, they make their explanations.' Farther on he says: 'As an example of this absurdity take a man whom I met when I was young, and who was then greatly celebrated and still is, on account of the writings which he has left. I refer to Origen, who is highly honoured by the teachers of these doctrines. For this man, having been a hearer of Ammonius, who had attained the greatest proficiency in philosophy of any in our day, derived much benefit from his teacher in the knowledge of the sciences; but as to the correct choice of life, he pursued a course opposite to his. For Ammonius, being a Christian, and brought up by Christian parents, when he gave himself to study and to philosophy straightway conformed to the life required by the laws. But Origen, having been educated as a Greek in Greek literature, went over to the barbarian recklessness. And carrying over the learning which he had obtained, he hawked it about, in his life conducting himself as a Christian and contrary to the laws, but in his opinions of material things and of the Deity being like a Greek, and mingling Grecian teachings with foreign fables. For he was continually studying Plato, and he busied himself with the writings of Numenius and Cronius, Apollophanes, Lon-

Allegory and the Contribution of Origen 345

Had the Christian world been and remained as sophisticated as Origen, the conception of biblical history for the next fifteen hundred years would have been vastly different. But, although the allegorical method of biblical interpretation was used by nearly all the Fathers—by none more than by the pope whose influence sank deepest into the Middle Ages, Gregory the Great—and still forms the subject of most sermons, the symbolism and allegory came to be applied less to those passages which contained the narrative than to the moralizing and prophetic sections. The stories of the Creation, of the Flood, of Joseph, of the plagues in Egypt, of Sodom and Gomorrah, were not explained away. But about them and the rest of that high theme of the fortunes of Israel were woven the gorgeous dreams of every poetic imagination from Origen to Bossuet which had been steeped in miracle and rested upon authority. One turns to Sulpicius Severus, the biographer of the wonder-working Martin of Tours, for the Bible story as it reached the Middle Ages. The narrative of the Old Testament was taken literally, like that of the New; the story of a primitive people was presented to a primitive audience. Allegory was not allowed to explain away passages which would have shocked the critical intelligence of Hellenic philosophers, for those were the very passages most likely to impress the simple-minded Germans for whose education the church itself was to be responsible.

There was, however, a better reason than mere credulous simplicity why Jewish and Christian history were not allegorized

---

ginus, Moderatus, and Nicomachus, and those famous among the Pythagoreans. And he used the books of Chaeremon the Stoic, and of Cornutus. Becoming acquainted through them with the figurative interpretation of the Grecian mysteries, he applied it to the Jewish Scriptures.'

"These things are said by Porphyry in the third book of his work against the Christians. He speaks truly of the industry and learning of the man, but plainly utters a falsehood (for what will not an opposer of Christians do?) when he says that he went over from the Greeks, and that Ammonius fell from a life of piety into heathen customs. For the doctrine of Christ was taught to Origen by his parents, as we have shown above. And Ammonius held the divine philosophy unshaken and unadulterated to the end of his life. His works yet extant show this, as he is celebrated among many for the writings which he has left. For example, the work entitled 'The Harmony of Moses and Jesus,' and such others as are in the possession of the learned. These things are sufficient to evince the slander of the false accuser, and also the proficiency of Origen in Grecian learning."

away. It was because that history had been made credible by an exhaustive treatment of chronology. Christian scholars took up the task of reconciling the events of Jewish history with the annals of other histories, and worked into a convincing and definite scheme of parallel chronology the narrative from Abraham to Christ. Mathematics was applied to history—not simply to the biblical narrative but to all that of the ancient world—and out of the chaos of fact and legend, of contradiction and absurdity, of fancy run riot and unfounded speculation, there was slowly hammered into shape that scheme of measured years back to the origins of Israel and then to the Creation which still largely prevails today. This is one of the most important things ever done by historians. Henceforth, for the next fifteen centuries and more, there was one sure path back to the origin of the world, a path along the Jewish past, marked out by the absolute laws of mathematics and revelation. An account of how this came about will carry us back into that complicated problem of the measurement of time which we have considered before in its general aspects. Now, however, we come upon the work of those who gave us our own time reckoning, and who, in doing so, moulded the conception of world history for the western world more, perhaps, than any other students or masters of history.

CHAPTER XXVII

Chronology and Church History; Eusebius

THE history of history repeats itself. Tradition and myth, epic and genealogy, priestly lore of world eras and the marking of time, criticism and history follow each other or fuse in the long evolution of that rational self-consciousness which projects itself into the past as it builds up the synthesis of the present. Similar pathways lie behind all developed historiographies. Indeed, the parallel between the histories of the history of different nations is so close as to rob the successive chapters of much of the charm of novelty. When we have reviewed the historiography of Greece, that of Rome strikes us as familiar. The same likeness lies already in the less-developed historiographies of Oriental cultures. They all emerge from a common base, and, to use a biological expression, ontogeny recapitulates phylogeny—that is to say, the individual repeats the species. The law of growth, it seems, can apply to history-writing as though it were just an actual organism with an independent evolution, instead of what it really is, a mere reflection of changing societies.

The explanation apparently lies at hand, in the similar evolution of the societies which produce the history. But from such premises one would hardly expect the historiography of a religion to exhibit the same general lines of development. Yet in the history of Christian history we have much the same evolution of material as in that of Greece or Rome. Naturally, the priestly element is stronger, and the attempts at rationalizing the narratives more in evidence. But it is the absence rather than the presence of sophistication which strikes one most. The genealogies play their role for the kingdom of the Messiah as for the cities of Hellas,[1] Hesiods of Jewish and Christian theology present their schemes of divinely appointed eras, and through the whole heroic period of the Church legends of saints and martyrs furnish the unending epic of the unending war, where the hosts of heaven fought with men—not for a vanished Troy but for an eternal city. Finally, the work of Christian logographers in the apologists—and every theologian was an apologist—reduced the scheme to prose. The parallel would not hold, however, beyond the merest externals if it had not been for the development of Christian chronology; for the thought of writing history was but little in the minds of theologians, and hardly more in those of martyrologists. From the apologists, face to face with the criticism of the unbelieving world, came the demand for more rigid methods of comparative chronology, by which they could prove the real antiquity and direct descent of Christianity. The same kind of practical need had produced similar, if more trivial, documentation by pagan priests and was later to repeat itself in mediaeval monasteries. So that in the Christian Church, as in the antique world generally, history proper was born of the application of research and chronology to meet the exacting demands of skepticism as well as of the desire to set forth great deeds.

The path to Christian historiography lies, therefore, through a study of Christian chronology. The basis for this was the work of the Jewish scholars of the Diaspora. When the Christian apologists of the second and third centuries attempted to synchronize the Old Testament history with that of the gentiles, they could fall back upon the work of a Jewish scribe, Justus of Tiberias, who wrote in the reign of Domitian.[2] He prepared a chronicle of Jewish kings, working along the same uncertain basis of "generations" as had been used in Gentile chronicles and so claiming for Moses an antiquity greater than that of the oldest figures in Greek legend. The difficulties in the way of any

[1] Julius Africanus' pioneer work in this direction, in harmonizing the variant genealogies of Christ in the Gospel, quoted by Eusebius, *Historia ecclesiastica*, Book I, Chap. 7.

[2] The connection of Christian chronology with that of the Greeks, *e.g.* Castor, has been referred to above. See Eusebius, *Chronicorum liber primus*.

Chronology and Church History; Eusebius

counterproof lent this statement great value in argument, especially since it was merely a mathematical formulation of a belief already established in the Church. But, although the argument of priority was familiar from early days, the first formally prepared Christian chronology did not appear until the middle of the third century when Julius Africanus wrote his *Chronographia*. It was a work in five books, drawing upon the writings of Josephus, Manetho, and pagan scholars, and arranging the eras of the old dispensation in a series symbolical of creation itself. The duration of the world is to reach six thousand years, after which is to come a thousand-year Sabbath. The birth of Christ is put five thousand five hundred years from Adam, which leaves five hundred more before the end. Halfway along this stretch of centuries, three thousand years from the creation, we come upon the death of Peleg, under whom the world was parcelled out, as is recorded in Genesis.[3]

A scheme like this is a chronology only by courtesy, and yet a glance at the dating along the pages of the authorized edition of the Bible will show how relatively close to it has been the accepted dating of the world's history down to our own time.[4]

---

[3] Genesis 10:25. See the monumental study of H. Gelzer, *Sextus Julius Africanus* (2 vols., 1880-1885), which has disentangled the fragile threads of his chronology, as preserved in various ways. Julius Africanus was a Christian layman of great learning who knew Latin, Syriac, and Hebrew as well as Greek. He served in the Roman army under Septimius Severus, to whom he dedicated one of his books; he died after 240.

[4] These same chiliastic ideas dominated the chronology of Archbishop Ussher, in the seventeenth century, and are still printed in the margin of many Bibles. The celebrated year 4004 B.C. for the date of creation is exactly four "days" before the birth of Christ in 4 B.C. The archbishop had a little trouble in arriving at this date, for the figures in the Hebrew text of the Old Testament add up to 153 years more than this and he had to allow himself several rectifications. He tried to put the call of Abraham in 2004 B.C. but could not quite manage it. Had he been successful, human history would again have fallen into six periods or "days" of a thousand years each, two without the Law, two under the Old Law of Judaism, and two under the New Law of Christ, and the Second Coming might be expected in 1996 A.D. At about this time, too, the learned John Lightfoot, the greatest Hebrew scholar of his day if not of his century, made the oft-repeated declaration that God created Adam out of the dust of the earth on the morning of Friday, September 17, at 9 o'clock. This was the sixth day of a week beginning September 12, upon which day the equinox fell under the old style calendar: the world was presumably created in a state of balance, and as the fruit was ready for Adam, it must have been created at the fall equinox; the 9 o'clock was deduced

Critically considered, it was merely a variation of the symbolism of Origen—an allegory of the general scheme of history instead of an allegory of details. It was symbolism on a bolder and larger scale, all the more convincing because, while it supplied the framework for events it did not have to harmonize or explain them away. Three main influences made for its success. The absence of any continuous Jewish chronology offered it open field; theology demanded that the world's history should centre upon the life of Christ and the coming of the kingdom; and the idea of world eras was just in line with the ideas of pagan savants who had attained a rude conception of natural law in the movement of history. A treatment of history which could appeal to the great name of Varro for its pagan counterpart was not lightly to be rejected. The best minds of antiquity saw—though dimly—the outer world as a reflection for the human reason; but what Platonic idea ever mastered recalcitrant phenomena so beautifully as this scheme of Christian history with its symmetry established by a divine mathematics?

One is tempted to turn aside to the absorbing problems of philosophy which these crude solutions of world history open up. But before us stands a great figure, a Herodotus among the logographers of the early Church. Eusebius of Caesarea, the Father of Church History, worked out from materials like these the chronology of the world which was to be substantially that of all the subsequent history of Europe to our own time and preserved the precious fragments of his predecessors in the first history of Christianity.[5]

Eusebius meets the two qualifications which Polybius prescribed as indispensable for the historian. He was a man of

---

from that later Friday when Jesus was judged at 9 o'clock, nailed to the cross at noon, and died at 3; similarly Adam was created at 9, sinned at noon, and was ejected from the Garden at 3 P.M. (John Lightfoot, *The Whole Works,* 1822 edition, VII, 372-77). In such a manner distinguished scholars created chronology less than 300 years ago! (Note by Professor Swain.)

[5] The name Eusebius was a very common one in the records of the early Church. There are forty Eusebiuses, contemporaries of the historian, noted in Smith and Wace's *Dictionary of Christian Biography,* and, in all, one hundred and thirty-seven from the first eight centuries. Eusebius of Caesarea took the surname Pamphilus after the death of his master Pamphilus, out of respect for him.

Chronology and Church History; Eusebius 351

affairs, of wide knowledge of the world, and he held high office in the state whose fortunes he described. He it was who at the great council of Nicaea (325 A.D.) sat at the right hand of Constantine and delivered the opening oration in honor of the emperor.[6] Few historians of either church or state have ever had more spectacular tribute paid to their learning and judicial temper. For it was apparently these two qualities which especially equipped Eusebius for so distinguished an honor. At least one likes to think so; but perhaps the distinction fell to him because he was, as well, an accomplished courtier and as much the apologist of Constantine as the historian an apologist of the Christian faith.

This incident fixes for us the life of Eusebius. Born about 260 A.D., he was at the fulness of his powers when the Church gained its freedom, and he lived on until 339 or 340. He had studied in the learned circle of Pamphilus of Caesarea, whose great library was to furnish him with many of his materials,[7] and there came under the spell of Origen, whose influence was supreme in the circle of Pamphilus. Nothing is more difficult in criticism than the estimate of one man's influence upon another—and nothing more light-heartedly hazarded. It would be hard to say what Eusebius would have been without the works of Origen to inspire him, but that they did influence him is beyond question. Eusebius was not an original thinker. He lacked the boldness of genius, but to witness that boldness in Origen must have been an inspiration toward freedom from ecclesiasticism and traditionalism.[8] His history is no mere bishop's history; it is the record of a religion as well as of a church. Its scholarship is critical, not credulous. From Origen, too, may have come the general conception which makes the first church history a chapter in the

[6] Sozomen, *Historia ecclesiastica*, Book I, Chap. 19.
[7] Eusebius, *De martyribus Palæstinae*, Chap. 4; Jerome, *De viris illustribus*, Chaps. 75, 81.
[8] These at least are the two main influences of Origen upon Eusebius according to McGiffert and Heinrici. See A. C. McGiffert's edition of the *Church History*, p. 7, and C. F. G. Heinrici, *Das Urchristentum in der Kirchengeschichte des Eusebius* (1894). Heinrici here presents the case against F. Overbeck's view (*Über die Anfange der Kirchengeschichtsschreibung*, 1892), that Eusebius follows the hierarchical, episcopal thread in a sort of constitutional history of the church.

working out of a vast world scheme, the "economy" of God.[9] But the time had now come for such a conception to be commonplace. It was no longer a speculation; the recognition by the empire was making it a fact.

If one were to search for influences moulding the character of Eusebius' history this triumph of the Church would necessarily come first. No history of Christianity worthy of the name could well appear during the era of persecutions. Not that the persecutions were so severe or so continuous as has been commonly believed. Eusebius himself, for instance, lived safely through the most severe persecution and, visiting Pamphilus in prison—for Pamphilus suffered martyrdom—carried on his theological works in personal touch with his master. But though the persecutions have been exaggerated, the situation of the Church was not one to invite the historian. Constantine was its deliverer; in a few years it passed from oppression to power. And in the hour of its triumph Christian scholarship was to find, in a bishop high at court, a historian worthy not only of the great deeds of the saints and martyrs, but of the new imperial position of the Church.

Eusebius was a voluminous writer, "historian, apologist, topographer, exegete, critic, preacher, dogmatic writer."[10] But his fame as a historian rests upon two works, the *Church History* and the *Chronicle*. Both were epoch making. The one has earned for the author the title of Father of Church History; the other set for Christendom its framework in the history of the world.

The *Chronicle* was written first.[11] It is composed of two parts, the *Chronographia* and the *Chronological Canons*. The first of these is an epitome of universal history in the form of excerpts from the sources, arranged nation by nation, along with an argu-

[9] C. F. G. Heinrici, *Das Urchristentum in der Kirchengeschichte des Eusebius*, p. 13.

[10] See "Eusebius of Cæsarea" by J. B. Lightfoot in Smith and Wace's *Dictionary of Christian Biography*, a brilliant article.

[11] He already refers to it in the opening of his *Historia ecclesiastica* (Book I, Chap. 1), also in the *Eclogae propheticae* (Book I, Chap. 1), and in the *Praeparatio evangelica* (Book X, Chap. 9), which were both written before 313. As the *Chronicle*, when it reached Jerome, was carried down to 325, it is conjectured that there may have been a second edition.

Chronology and Church History; Eusebius

ment for the priority of Moses and the Bible. It is a source book on the epochs of history, much like those in use today as manuals in our colleges. The second part consists of chronological tables with marginal comments. The various systems of chronology, Chaldaean, Greek, Roman, etc., are set side by side with a biblical chronology which carries one back to the Creation, although the detailed and positive annals begin only with the birth of Abraham. The *Canons* therefore presents in a single, composite form the annals of all antiquity—at least all that was of interest to Christendom. It presented them in simplest mathematical form. Rows of figures marked the dates down the centre of the page; on the right hand side was the column of profane history; on the left hand the column of sacred history.[12]

The fate of this work is of peculiar interest. It is doubtful if

[12] In the present text some profane history notes are on the left side, but this was due to the fact that the comments on profane history were fuller than those on sacred history and were crowded over for reasons of space.

Eusebius was largely indebted for his plan to Castor, whom he invokes at the beginning and end of the lists for Sicyon, Argos and Athens. H. Gelzer, *Sextus Julius Africanus,* Part II, pp. 63 *sqq.* On the relations between Eusebius and Julius Africanus, on whose work the *Chronicle* was based, see H. Gelzer, *Sextus Julius Africanus,* Part II, pp. 23-107.

In his use of the Old Testament Eusebius preferred the Septuagint because this was the version traditionally used in the Church, but the reasoning by which he defended his choice is, to say the least, amazing and casts a bright light upon antique historical criticism. (1) Since the two Jewish versions (Hebrew and Samaritan) disagree, the presumption is that both are wrong and the Greek right. (2) The Hebrew says that the earlier patriarchs begat their children at a younger age than the later ones did, whereas the Greek says that they did so at a more advanced age, which seems a more probable development. Eusebius suspects that the Jews lowered the figures for the early patriarchs lest men postpone marriage too long in the hope of thereby attaining a patriarchal age! See the German translation of the Armenian version (all we have) by J. Karst, pp. 37-40 (Vol. V of the series "Die griechisch-christlichen Schriftsteller der ersten drei Jahrhunderte," Vol. XX). Augustine too favored the Septuagint, but he settled the matter very simply by invoking divine inspiration (*De civitate Dei,* Book XVIII, Chap. 43). When Jerome translated the *Chronicle* into Latin, he took over the Greek figures, but twenty years later, when translating the Vulgate, he retained the Hebrew figures. The two works therefore differed in chronology, but the variation was not serious, for the *Chronicle*—beginning only with Abraham— differed markedly from the Hebrew in only one place—regarding the length of the captivity in Egypt, where the Greek figures are undoubtedly right. In the Preface to the *Chronicle,* however, Jerome gives the Greek figures of 2242 years from Adam to the Flood (instead of 1656) and 942 years (instead of 292) from the Flood to Abraham (*Eusebii Pamphili chronici canones, Latine . . . Hieronymus,* ed. J. H. Fotheringham, 1923, p. 11).

any other history has ever exercised an influence comparable to that which it has had upon the western world; yet not a single copy of the original text has survived; the Latin West knew only the second part, and that in the hasty translation of Jerome. Modern research has unearthed a solitary Armenian translation of the work as a whole, and modern scholars have compared this with the fragments preserved by Byzantine chronographers [13] until finally, in the opening of the twentieth century the work is again accessible—if only to the learned. If, however, recovery of the chronicle is a work of archaeological philology, like the recovery of an ancient ruin, yet all the time that it had lain buried this little book of dates and comments had been determining the historical outlook of Europe.[14] For the next thousand years most histories were chronicles, and they were built after the model of Jerome's translation of Eusebius' *Canons*. Every mediaeval monastery that boasted of enough culture to have a scriptorium and a few literate monks was connecting its own rather fabulous but fairly recent antiquity with the great antiquity of Rome and Judaea through the tables of Eusebius' arithmetic.

This anonymous immortality of the great *Chronicle* is easily accounted for. It was not a work of literature, but of mathematics. Now mathematics is as genuine art as is literature, art of the most perfect type; but its expression, for that very reason, is not in the variable terms of individual appreciations. It is not personal but universal. It does not deal with qualities, but with numbers; or at best it deals with qualities merely as the dis-

---

[13] Especially Georgius Syncellus. These chronographers preserved such large extracts that Joseph Scaliger was able to risk a reconstruction of the text from them alone. Scaliger's first edition was published in 1606, the second edition in 1658. The Armenian version, with a Latin translation, was published at Venice in 1818 by J. B. Aucher. The text in Migne, that by Cardinal Mai (1833), is based upon this; but the classic work on the *Chronicle* is that of A. Schoene, *Eusebii chronicorum libri duo* (Vol. I, 1875; Vol. II, 1866), while the Armenian text has recently been published with parallel German translation, by J. Karst in the great edition of Eusebius' works now appearing in the series, "Die griechisch-christlichen Schriftsteller der ersten drei Jahrhunderte." It has also the version of Jerome, edited by R. Helm.

[14] Joseph Scaliger refers thus to the influence of Eusebius. *Qui post Eusebium scripserunt, omne scriptum de temporibus aridum esse censuerunt, quod non hujus fontibus irrigatum esset* (Quoted in J. P. Migne, *Patrologiae Graecae*, XIX, 14).

Chronology and Church History; Eusebius

tinguishing elements in numbers. The structure is the thing, not the meaning nor the character of the details. And the structure depends upon the materials. Hence there is little that is Eusebian about Eusebius' *Chronicle*, except the chronicle itself. It has no earmarks of authorship like the style of a Herodotus or a Thucydides. But all the same its content was the universal possession of the succeeding centuries.

There is, however, a simpler reason for the fate of Eusebius' *Chronicle*. It has a forbidding exterior. It had even too much mathematics and too much history for the Middle Ages; they were satisfied with the results of the problem. But behind this forbidding exterior the modern scholar finds a synthesis of alluring charm. Parallel columns of all known eras extend up and down the pages; eras of Abraham, David, Persia, Egypt, Greece, Rome, etc. It is interesting to see this tangle of columns simplify as the diverse nations come and go; and finally all sink into the great unity of Rome. At last the modern world of Eusebius' own time was left but four columns, the years of Rome (A. U. C.), of Olympiads, of Roman Consuls, and of Christ. The rest was already ancient history. As one follows the sweep of these figures and watches the steady line of those events where the Providence of God bore down the forces of the unbeliever, one realizes that in this convincing statement lay the strongest of all defenses of the faith. Here, compressed into a few pages, lies the evidence of history for the Christian world view. Origen's great conception that pagan history was as much decreed by Jehovah as sacred history finds in the *Chronicle* its most perfect expression; the facts speak for themselves.[15] No fickle Fortuna could ever have arranged with such deliberate aim the rise and fall of empires. History is the reservoir not of argument, but of proof, and the proof is mathematical.[16]

---

[15] This view of universal history places Eusebius on a distinctly higher plane than that of a mere apologist. It enabled him to have somewhat of the Herodotean sweep and breadth. See C. F. G. Heinrici, *Das Urchristentum in der Kirchengeschichte des Eusebius*, pp. 13 sqq.; Eusebius, *Historia ecclesiastica*, Book I, Chap. 8.

[16] The translation of the *Canons* by Jerome, while apparently superior to the Armenian version, bears the marks of careless haste. He tells us himself (Preface, lines 13 sqq.) that it is an *opus tumultuarium* and adds that he dictated it most

The human element of humor, however, comes into the situation when one turns back to the opening paragraph and learns the attitude of Eusebius himself.

> Now at the very beginning, I make this declaration before all the world: let no one ever arrogantly contend that a sure and thorough knowledge of chronology is attainable. This every one will readily believe who ponders on the incontrovertible words of the Master to his disciples: "It is not for you to know the times or the seasons, which the Father hath put in his own power" [Acts 1:7]. For it seems to me that he, as Lord God, uttered that decisive word with reference not merely to the day of judgment, but with reference to all times, to the end that he might restrain those who devote themselves too boldly to such vain investigations.[17]

We have left ourselves little space for the work by which Eusebius is chiefly known, the *Ecclesiastical History*. So far as students of theology and church history are concerned, little space is needed, for the work itself is readily accessible and that, too, in an English edition and magnificently translated.[18] The general student of history seldom reads church history now, and the achievement of Eusebius shares the common fate. Yet it is a great achievement, and a genuine surprise awaits the reader who turns to it. One might expect that the age of Constantine would produce a history of the obscure, unstoried institution which had suddenly risen to the splendor of an imperial church, but one could hardly expect to find out of that arena of fierce theological conflict the calm and lofty attitude of generous reserve and the sense of dominating scholarly obligation for accuracy which characterize the first church historian. The judgment of Gibbon,

---

hurriedly to a scribe. He must have meant, so A. Schoene thinks (*Die Weltchronik des Eusebius*, 1900, p. 77), that he dictated the marginal comments, not the rows of figures. Probably a *notarius* translated the figures into Latin, and Jerome added the notes.

A great deal of discussion has arisen over the fact that in the *Ecclesiastical History* Eusebius differs decidedly from the chronology of the *Chronicle*.

[17] Eusebius, *Chronicorum liber primus*, Preface.
[18] *The Church History of Eusebius* by A. C. McGiffert, in the "Library of Nicene and Post-Nicene Fathers," 2d Series, Vol. I, pp. 81-403. The same volume contains a translation of the *Life of Constantine* by E. C. Richardson and an exhaustive bibliography.

Chronology and Church History; Eusebius

that the *Ecclesiastical History* was grossly unfair,[19] is itself a prejudiced verdict. To be sure it lacks the purely scientific aim; it is apologetic. But Eusebius is not to be blamed for that; the wonder is that he preserved so just a poise and so exacting a standard in view of the universal demands of his time. We should not forget that the apologetic tone of Christian historiography was also sanctioned by the pagan classics. Even Polybius had demanded that history be regarded as a thing of use, and Cicero, Sallust, Livy, and Tacitus had applied the maxim generously. Christian historiography should not bear the brunt of our dissatisfaction with what was the attitude of nearly all antiquity.[20]

The task of Eusebius was a difficult one. Only those who have tried themselves to extract historical data from theological writings can appreciate how difficult it was; but even they have an advantage over the Father of Church History. For now the principles of scientific, objective criticism of sources are well understood, and the historian can stand apart from the data aware that his criticism may be frankly skeptical without injury to his standards of religion. But Eusebius could not go far upon that path without arousing more serious doubts as to his general canons of belief. His history was, after all, intended to contribute proof of the truth of the central doctrines in the literature it used. He had to combine discriminating judgment with the "will

[19] *The Decline and Fall of the Roman Empire* (J. B. Bury edition), II, 135: "Eusebius, himself, indirectly confesses that he has related whatever might redound to the glory, and that he has suppressed all that could tend to the disgrace of religion," adding in a footnote, "Such is the *fair* deduction from I:82, and *De Mart. Palest.* c. 12."

[20] This point is well made by H. O. Taylor in *The Mediaeval Mind*, I, 78-81.

At the same time Eusebius advances principles of historical composition against which it is well to be on one's guard, as for instance in the following extract, with reference to the divisions among the Churches: "But it is not our place to describe the sad misfortunes which finally came upon them, as we do not think it proper, moreover, to record their divisions and unnatural conduct to each other before the persecution. Wherefore we have decided to relate nothing concerning them except the things in which we can vindicate the Divine judgment. Hence we shall not mention those who were shaken by the persecution, nor those who in everything pertaining to salvation were shipwrecked, and by their own will were sunk in the depths of the flood. But we shall introduce into this history in general only those events which may be useful first to ourselves and afterwards to posterity" (*The Church History of Eusebius*, A. C. McGiffert edition, Book VIII, Chap. 2).

to believe." There is therefore more than rhetoric, though that is not lacking, in the apology with which he enters upon his narrative:

> But at the outset I must crave for my work the indulgence of the wise, for I confess that it is beyond my power to produce a perfect and complete history, and since I am the first to enter upon the subject, I am attempting to traverse as it were a lonely and untrodden path. I pray that I may have God as my guide and the power of the Lord as my aid, since I am unable to find even the bare footsteps of those who have traveled the way before me, except in brief fragments, in which some in one way, others in another, have transmitted to us particular accounts of the times in which they lived. From afar they raise their voices like torches, and they cry out, as from some lofty and conspicuous watch-tower, admonishing us where to walk and how to direct the course of our work steadily and safely. Having gathered therefore from the matters mentioned here and there by them whatever we consider important for the present work, and having plucked like flowers from a meadow the appropriate passages from ancient writers, we shall endeavor to embody the whole in an historical narrative, content if we preserve the memory of the successions of the apostles of our Saviour; if not indeed of all, yet of the most renowned of them in those churches which are the most noted, and which even to the present time are held in honor.
>
> This work seems to me of especial importance because I know of no ecclesiastical writer who has devoted himself to this subject; and I hope that it will appear most useful to those who are fond of historical research. I have already given an epitome of these things in the Chronological Canons which I have composed, but notwithstanding that, I have undertaken in the present work to write as full an account of them as I am able. My work will begin, as I have said, with the dispensation of the Saviour Christ—which is loftier and greater than human conception,—and with a discussion of His divinity; for it is necessary, inasmuch as we derive even our name from Christ, for one who proposes to write a history of the Church to begin with the very origin of Christ's dispensation, a dispensation more divine than many think.[21]

In spite of the touch of rhetoric in such passages as this, the *Ecclesiastical History* does not live by grace of its style. Eusebius had no refined literary taste; he wrote, as he thought, in rambling and desultory fashion. But he combined with vast erudition a

---

[21] *The Church History of Eusebius* (A. C. McGiffert edition), Book I, Chap. 1.

Chronology and Church History; Eusebius 359

"sterling sense," and a "true historical instinct" in choosing the selections from his store of facts and documents.[22] Conscious of the value of the sources themselves, he weaves into his narrative large blocks of the originals, and in this way has preserved many a precious text which would otherwise be lost. The *Ecclesiastical History* is less a narrative than a collection of documents, for which every student of Christianity is devoutly thankful, and more thankful yet that the author was so keenly conscious of his responsibility. Wherever his references can be verified, they prove correct—which gives a presumption of accuracy for those found in his work alone.

Such instances of scholarly caution occur time and again in the *Ecclesiastical History*, in some cases revealing a discriminating use of sources in the effort to get to originals. This is especially the case where the incident narrated may seem in itself improbable, or where the skeptic is likely to challenge the evidence. For example, he narrates a story of Marcus Aurelius as follows:

It is reported that Marcus Aurelius Cæsar, brother of Antoninus, being about to engage in battle with the Germans and Sarmatians, was in great trouble on account of his army suffering from thirst. But the soldiers of the so-called Melitene legion, through the faith which has given strength from that time to the present, when they were drawn up before the enemy, kneeled on the ground, as is our custom in prayer, and engaged in supplications to God. This was indeed a strange sight to the enemy, but it is reported that a stranger thing immediately followed. The lightning drove the enemy to flight and destruction, but a shower refreshed the army of those who had called on God, all of whom had been on the point of perishing with thirst.

This story is related by non-Christian writers who have been pleased to treat the times referred to, and it has also been recorded by our own people. By those historians who were strangers to the faith, the marvel is mentioned, but it is not acknowledged as an answer to our prayers. But by our own people, as friends of the truth, the occurrence is related in a simple and artless manner. Among these is Apolinarius, who says that from that time the legion through whose prayers the wonder took place received from the Emperor a title appropriate to the event, being called in the language of the Romans the Thundering Legion. Tertullian

---

[22] See the fine characterization by A. C. McGiffert in the Prolegomena to his edition of *The Church History of Eusebius*, pp. 46 *sqq*.

is a trustworthy witness of these things. In the Apology for the Faith, which he addressed to the Roman Senate, and which we have already mentioned, he confirms the history with greater and stronger proofs. He writes that there are still extant letters of the most intelligent Emperor Marcus in which he testifies that his army, being on the point of perishing from thirst in Germany, was saved by the prayers of the Christians. And he says also that this emperor threatened death to those who brought accusations against us.[23]

This scholarly accuracy was combined with a vast learning. Eusebius had enjoyed the freedom of the great library of Pamphilus at Caesarea, in his earlier days. He tells us that he gathered materials as well in the library at Jerusalem founded by Bishop Alexander [24] and Constantine seems to have opened his archives to him.[25] But he learned not less from the busy world in which he lived. He was no recluse; he lived at the centre of things, both politically and ecclesiastically. His genial nature blinded him to men's faults, and his judgments on contemporaries—particularly on Constantine—are of little value.[26] But even at his worst he seldom recorded any marvellous event without the Herodotean caution of throwing the responsibility back upon the original narrative. There is no better example of this than the account in the *Life of Constantine* of the emperor's vision of the cross. It was an incident all too likely to find ready that credence in Christian circles which it found in subsequent ages. But, however much a courtly panegyrist Eusebius could be, in matters of fact he is on his guard. His account runs soberly enough:

And while he was thus praying with fervent entreaty, a most marvellous sign appeared to him from heaven, the account of which might have been hard to believe had it been related by any other person. But since the victorious Emperor himself long afterwards declared it to the writer of this history, when he was honored with his acquaintance and society, and confirmed his statement by an oath, who could hesi-

---

[23] *The Church History of Eusebius* (A. C. McGiffert edition), Book V, Chap. 5.
[24] *Historia Ecclesiastica*, Book VI, Chap. 20.
[25] *Ibid.*, Book V, Chap. 18.
[26] The *Life of Constantine* is a panegyric rather than a biography, and it is unreliable even in questions of fact.

tate to accredit the relation, especially since the testimony of after-time has established its truth? (Book I, Chap. 28.)

For two centuries Christian worship had laid hidden behind the "Discipline of the Secret." The uninitiated knew little of what was held or done by the adherents of this intolerant mystery, "after the doors were shut." Constantine brought the new regime, when persecution and secrecy ceased. Eusebius had lived through the dark days of Diocletian, and although he himself had escaped (a fact sometimes held against him), his dearest friends and, above all, his great teacher Pamphilus had been martyred. Free now to speak, therefore, he turns back from the "peace of the church" to the years of persecution with a feeling for martyrs like that of Homer for heroes, of the Middles Ages for wonder-working saints.[27] He depicts their sufferings, however, not simply as the material for heroic biography, but as forming the subject of a glorious page of history, that of the great "peaceful struggle" by which the Kingdom of the Messiah was to take its place among and above the powers of this world. The martyrs of Palestine are fighting the Punic Wars for the kingdom of Christ:

Other writers of history record the victories of war and trophies won from enemies, the skill of generals, and the manly bravery of soldiers, defiled with blood and with innumerable slaughters for the sake of children and country and other possessions. But our narrative of the government of God will record in ineffaceable letters the most peaceful wars waged in behalf of the peace of the soul, and will tell of men doing brave deeds for truth rather than country, and for piety rather than dearest friends. It will hand down to imperishable remembrance the discipline and the much-tried fortitude of the athletes of religion, the trophies won from demons, the victories over invisible enemies, and the crowns placed upon all their heads.[28]

It was reserved for a greater intellect—that of Augustine—to carry this conception of the Church as the realization of the temporal Kingdom of Christ to its final form. But the outlines of Augustine's *City of God* are already visible in the opening chap-

[27] C. F. G. Heinrici, *Das Urchristentum in der Kirchengeschichte des Eusebius*, p. 3.
[28] *The Church History of Eusebius* (A. C. McGiffert edition), Book V, Introduction, Sects. 3, 4.

ters of the *Ecclesiastical History,* as its foundations were placed by Eusebius' master, Origen. The Messiah is not a recent Christ, but comes to us from the beginning of the world, witnessed to by Moses and the prophets. And when "in recent times" Jesus came, the new nation which appeared was not new but old, the Nation of God's own Providence—Christian and universal. The paean of the victorious Church is sounded at the opening of its first history; "A nation confessedly not small and not dwelling in some corner of the earth, but the most numerous and pious of all nations, indestructible and unconquerable, because it always receives assistance from God." [29] This is the historical prologue to the *City of God.*

Before we turn to the work of the two great Latin Fathers who contributed to the Middle Ages both the philosophy of history and its annals—Augustine and Jerome—we must pass in rapid survey the historiography among the Greek Fathers of the church. It was not the field in which the greatest of these did their best work; for Greek love of disputation was dominant in the eastern Church, where heresy and orthodoxy fought out their confusing and never-ending battle. Cappadocia, the homeland of the greater theologians, produced the first of the successors of Eusebius, Philostorgius. His *Church History*—wrongly so-named —published about 425, a century after Eusebius, is known to us only through the epitome of the Byzantine Photius, the scholar-patriarch of Constantinople of the ninth century. These excerpts show a real interest in profane history and an apologetic for Christianity similar to that of Augustine. Recent critics have rescued him from obloquy which his heretical views—that of a minor sect, the Eunomians—condemned him until the advent of modern scholarship.

We have only a few fragments left of another work produced at Constantinople at approximately the same time, the *Christian History* of Philip of Sides, a history of the world from the Christian point of view, a Byzantine parallel of the contemporary work of Orosius to which we shall come presently. To judge from

[29] *The Church History of Eusebius* (A. C. McGiffert edition), Book I, Chap. 4.

the references to it, it seems to have been an enormous mass of all kinds of material, filling nearly a thousand papyrus rolls. Except for the chronographers, to whom we shall return later, this covers the last phase of antique historiography at the Greek capital of the Roman world.

If the pagan past was thus being left aside, the history of the Church was carried on from where Eusebius left it by three scholars who each covered approximately the same period, 325–439, thus bringing the record down to their own day. These were Socrates, who was born and lived most of his life at Constantinople; Sozomen, a native of Palestine but also a resident of the eastern capital, and Theodoret, born in Antioch but a bishop of Eastern Syria. Of these, Socrates was the best historian, Theodoret the best stylist but poorest in substance. Since they wrote about the same time and covered the same ground, it was but natural that a century later Cassiodorus, the Roman senator, monk, and scholar, to whose collecting zeal we owe the preservation of many of the ancient classics, had the three writers translated in one connected story called the *historia tripartita*. It was in this form that they were passed on into the Middle Ages.

CHAPTER XXVIII

The City of God

THE revolution in the history of history which paralleled the rise to power of the Christian church in the early fourth century reached its culmination a century later in the works of Augustine and Jerome. It was a revolution in the fullest sense of the word; for not only was the content changed from Greek or Roman to Jewish, but the temper and attitude ceased to be scientific as faith reasserted itself against the critical ideals of Hecataeus or Thucydides. Doubt of accepted tales, which leads to a criticism of evidence, is at the opposite pole from scholarship searching for proof of beliefs to which one has already given full allegiance. The triumph of faith, on which the Pauline structure of theology was based, made history subservient to religion, much as we have seen to be the case in that other revolution carried on by the prophets of Israel long before. For those who lived through the period when the civilized world, nerveless and disorganized, was facing final ruin, the chief intellectual interest lay in either distraction, as for instance Neoplatonism, or in the interpretation of life in terms that carried the mind away from the impotence of the present and the impermanence of its institutions to contemplate the power and glory of a World Everlasting.

We have already seen how the story of the pagan past was slipping out of the purview of both Greeks and Romans, the great historians making way for secondary figures and the broadening stream growing shallower until finally it dried down to the texts of the epitomists. In its place was set the story of the world force, which was taking the place of a decadent paganism, and of that small fraction of antiquity from which it sprang—the Jews. This process, slow at first, had back of it the embattled strength of the mightiest army of propaganda ever marshalled in any cause, the Fathers of the Church. Not that they cared for the effect of their writings upon historiography as a medium for the human story, but that they urged along the trend of their times, that *Zeitgeist* which all followers of Ranke recognize as largely determining the outlook of history. By the time Alaric was at the gates of Rome the Christian point of view had become dominant in both the philosophy of history and in history itself. Three centuries more were to pass before the pagan models were quite lost to sight. But from the seventh century to the seventeenth—from Isidore of Seville and the English Bede for a thousand years—mankind was to look back along a line of Jewish priests and kings to the Creation. Egypt was of interest only as it came into Israelite history—Babylon and Nineveh were to illustrate the judgments of Yahveh, Tyre and Sidon to reflect the glory of Solomon. The "Gentiles" were robbed of their legitimate history as they became lay figures for the history of the Jews. Although the Christian dispensation invited them within its divine economy for the present and future, their past lay with those "who knew not Yahweh"; it furnished neither texts for morals, as the Scriptures did, nor authority for dogma. The result of this indifference was a cultural loss parallel to the barbarian devastation. The pagan creators and inheritors of antique society became and remained almost to our day, in sermons and Sunday schools and in common opinion, not living men nor nations appreciative of the arts and sciences, but outcasts who did not enter into the divine scheme of the world's history. When a line was drawn between pagan and Christian back to the Creation of the world, it left outside the pale of inquiry nearly all antiquity. That such a narrow prospect should persist was largely due to the fact that the German nations, both those who settled within the Roman Empire and those beyond its frontier, had no interest in the antique past; it was not theirs. The politics of Greek city-state or of the Gracchi was essentially unreal to them. The one living organization with which they came in touch was the Church. So Pompey and Cicero paled before Joshua and Paul. Diocletian, for all his organizing achievements, became a mere persecutor of the martyrs. Constantine, stained with murder and shrewd to measure the main chance in religion as in war, became a saint.

The firmest hand that ever drew this line between the two worlds—paganism ruled by the powers of darkness and Christianity ruled by divine grace—was that of Augustine, Bishop of Hippo in Africa, whose life covered the momentous years of the second half of the fourth century and the first of the fifth. Both he and his contemporary, Jerome, were trained as young men in rhetoric and both of them have testified to the hold which the poets and the great stylists had upon them before they turned from the love of such vain delights to the uncouth style of the scriptures, which "seemed to me," says Augustine in his *Confessions,* "to be unworthy to be compared to the stateliness of Cicero." "Lord thou knowest," wrote Jerome, "that whenever I have and study secular manuscripts, I deny Thee." This appeal of the classical culture to the brilliant young rhetorician who was to mould the theology of the Western World was such that it was not until he was thirty-two that, influenced by Ambrose's preaching, he was baptized and entered the Christian ministry. The conflict in ideals between his ambitious father, still a pagan during Augustine's boyhood, and his saintly Christian mother, Monica, and his own reaction to it are recorded in that most revealing of autobiographies, his *Confessions*. It was the background for that intense sensitiveness which marked his appreciation of religion as a guide to life. He was the greatest of all the controversialists in an age when theology was being hammered into shape and the Church that held the proud title of Catholic or Universal was sorting out the elements in its repository of faith. Controversy was a dominating note in all patristic literature, but no one carried it to such heroic proportions as Augustine. Ambrose, his teacher, was more the churchman, restrained and episcopal; Jerome more scholarly; and Gregory the Great, his pupil, more practical minded. But of the great Fathers of the Church Augustine was the greatest, because he had the most comprehensive view of the vast field of speculation and experience in which the theological discussions ranged and, at the same time, the warmest interest in the human drama. The work in which Augustine embodied most completely his view of this world, what happened to it and why, was the immortal treatise *Civitas Dei,* "The City (or State) of God." Although it is not history—Augustine was not a historian—it furnished by the architecture of its thought the plans according to which history should be written. Others had traced the plans before, as we have seen. Their origins lay already in the Bible itself; and Origen had applied mysticism, Eusebius scholarship, to its development. But it was left for the passionate eloquence of Augustine to build the structure of thought in the form to which subsequent ages looked back. It is a forecast of *Paradise Lost* in power of imaginative conception and of the *Divine Comedy* in richness of detail. But it lacks the high detachment of poetry because its eloquence is after all that of a diatribe, however magnificent in sweep and powerful in utterance. It is an answer to pagans, a defense of the Church such as a pleader makes for a client. This gives it the quality of restless energy as evidence is heaped upon argument, but it carries conviction only to those who view it with the eye of faith.

The City of God was begun in 413 as an answer to those who claimed that the fall of Rome to the Goths and the ravages of the Vandals were due to a disregard of the gods of Rome and a lack of that ancient piety which had marked the great days of the Roman past. The occasion and the plan of the work can best be summarized in Augustine's own words.[1]

> Rome having been stormed and sacked by the Goths under Alaric their king, the worshippers of false gods, or pagans, as we commonly call them, made an attempt to attribute this calamity to the Christian religion, and began to blaspheme the true God with even more than their wonted bitterness and acerbity. It was this which kindled my zeal for the house of God, and prompted me to undertake the defence of the city of God against the charges and misrepresentations of its assailants....
>
> This great undertaking was at last completed in twenty-two books.

---

[1] *De civitate Dei* (tr. Dod), Vol. I, p. vii.

Of these, the first five refute those who fancy that the polytheistic worship is necessary in order to secure worldly prosperity, and that all these overwhelming calamities have befallen us in consequence of its prohibition. In the following five books I address myself to those who admit that such calamities have at all times attended and will at all times attend, the human race.... In these ten books, then, I refute these two opinions, which are as groundless as they are antagonistic to the Christian religion.

But that no one might have occasion to say, that though I had refuted the tenets of other men, I had omitted to establish my own, I devote to this object the second part of this work, which comprises twelve books.... Of these twelve books, the first four contain an account of the origin of these two cities—the city of God and the city of the world. The second four treat of their history or progress; the third and last four, of their deserved destinies. And so, though all these twenty-two books refer to both cities, yet I have named them after the better city, and called them The City of God.

The argument is the familiar one—that the world, under the governance of God, had been the theatre of a continuing conflict between two polities: the one directed by malignant devils, the other based upon the love of God. Beginning with the Creation, he traces the one back to Cain, the other to Abel. The sources to be followed for this scheme of history are the inspired scriptures, which prove their reliability by their agreement. On the other hand, pagan sources are contradictory and are only accepted as they admit the evidence that inspiration supplies. Reduced to their simplest terms, these are the commonplace arguments of the apologists. But here they are massed in encyclopaedic form —so varied and far-drawn, indeed, as to obscure at times the general direction of the thought—because Augustine had ready at hand the antiquarian lore of Varro, Cicero's comprehensive survey of religion and philosophy, the epitome of Livy for Rome's rise, and Sallust's gloomy account of a declining Roman society. The contrast between the way he plundered this material to show the dark side of non-Christian society and his constructive use of the Bible to show the consolations of religion seemed fair enough to the readers of later centuries. But nothing could show more clearly how far the antique world had already lost the sense of secular reality than that this should be the one great book produced by the fall of Rome.

The first ten books are mostly taken up with the calamities suffered by the Romans because of their worship of false gods, for the earthly city, haunt and prey of evil demons, is finally none other than Rome itself. Its most recent affliction at the hands of the barbarians would have been much worse but for the sanctuary offered by the Church. This leads to a treatment of the sack of Rome which has brought upon Augustine the charge of a seeming indifference to the fate of the Eternal City, but it is not the eternal city to him, it is only the last general form of the earthly city, destined in the providence of God to give way to the heavenly. However, one can detect that, underlying the passionate argument, there is a pathetic perception of the historic greatness of the Roman state and of its civilizing mission. It could not have been otherwise for a bishop of the fifth century, sharing as he did in some of the responsibilities of the temporal power. And the alternative to Rome is not that apocalyptic vision of Christ's coming which made the early Christians seem anarchists to the magistracy of their day; it is a new polity which is to succeed the old. The structure of Christian thought is now strong and confident. The powers of evil have wrought their own destruction and one sees the prospect of the City of God, as a Roman thinker was bound to conceive it, a sovereignty dominant and universal, in which all history culminates.

The "City of God" has been termed the greatest work of the greatest of the Church Fathers. But Augustine himself was conscious of its shortcomings from the historical point of view. The arsenal from which it drew its arguments was not so much what men had done as what men had believed, on account of which things had happened to them. It was a philosophy of world history, richly illustrated, the first of a long line of such philosophies. Augustine was using history, not writing it; he had no time left from the arduous work of research and composition to do more. Perhaps, also, he was held back from it by a distaste for the limitations which it imposed; for his mind was not only argumentative but discursive. He ranged through literature for the incident he needed at the time, as an orator enriches his oration with illustration or strengthens the proof with evidence. But he had no feeling for historical continuity. Indeed, this is the chief defect, and a great one, of *The City of God*. Inside the framework of its design, of which we are constantly reminded, it is hard to follow, because it does not trace events as they occurred but as they fit into his scheme. The result is a magnificent manipulation of history, but a manipulation which is all the freer to distort the lesser perspectives because it is indifferent to them.

Fortunately, while Augustine was still in the midst of *The City of God*, Providence placed in his way just the man for the history that should parallel it. This was a young priest from Spain, as yet not quite thirty years of age, but of brilliant promise, Paulus Orosius. Augustine's own description of the youth whose compendium of world history was to dominate in the schools throughout the Middle Ages, is worth quoting. It occurs in his epistle to Jerome (Letter 166):

> Behold, a religious young man has come to me, by name Orosius, who is in the bond of the Catholic peace a brother, in the point of age a son, and in honor a fellow presbyter—a man of quick understanding, ready speech, and burning zeal, desiring to be in the Lord's house a vessel rendering useful service in refuting those false and pernicious doctrines, through which the souls of men in Spain have suffered much more grievous wounds than have been inflicted on their bodies by the sword of the barbarians. For from the remote western coast of Spain he has come with eager haste to us, having been prompted to do this by the report that from me he could learn whatever he wished on the subjects concerning which he desired information.

Orosius' first stay with Augustine lasted only a year or so, and then, in the spring of 415, charged with messages for Jerome, he set out for Palestine. An eager defender of that orthodoxy of which both Augustine and Jerome were then the outstanding champions, he was back again in Africa a year later. But Augustine now had another use for him than controverting heretics. He was just then completing the eleventh book of *The City of God*,

The City of God

the first of the second part of the treatise, that which deals with the origin and rise of the two cities. It would both strengthen the work and relieve the author if Orosius would write the parallel history as a kind of supplement to the whole. So the young disciple set to work and, emulating his master's strenuous energy, presented to him in 418 the finished text, which bore the significant title *Seven Books of Histories against the Pagans*. He himself tells in his Dedication of the work to Augustine just how it came to be written.

You bade me reply to the empty chatter and perversity of those who, aliens to the City of God, are called "pagans" (*pagani*) because they come from the countryside (*ex pagis*) and the crossroads of the rural districts, or "heathen" (*gentiles*) because of their wisdom in earthly matters. Although these people do not seek out the future and moreover either forget or know nothing of the past, nevertheless they charge that the present times are unusually beset with calamities for the sole reason that men believe in Christ and worship God while idols are increasingly neglected. You bade me, therefore, discover from all the available data of histories and annals whatever instances past ages have afforded of the burdens of war, the ravages of disease, the horrors of famine, of terrible earthquakes, extraordinary floods, dreadful eruptions of fire, thunderbolts and hailstorms, and also instances of the cruel miseries caused by parricides and disgusting crimes. I was to set these forth systematically and briefly in the course of my book. It certainly is not right for your reverence to be bothered with so trifling a treatise as this while you are intent on completing the eleventh book of your work against these same pagans. When your ten previous books appeared, they, like a beacon from the watchtower of your high position in the Church, at once flashed their shining rays over all the world.

With becoming modesty, Orosius thus clearly indicates that his manual of antique history is to be taken as a pendant of the greater treatise, and it was likely true that this connection with the great name of Augustine had something to do with its subsequent popularity. It was a history vouched for by unimpeachable authority. Unfortunately that authority was already mediaeval. To Augustine, as to Orosius, the proper purpose of history was one which violated it most. The proof that this was so is supplied in the very next passage of the Dedication, in which Orosius naïvely confesses that it was not until he really put his mind to it that he was able to see history the way he needed to see it if it were to support the Augustinian thesis:

> I started to work and at first went astray, for as I repeatedly turned over these matters in my mind the disasters of my own times seemed to have boiled over and exceeded all usual limits. But now I have discovered that the days of the past were not only as oppressive as those of the present but that they were the more terribly wretched the further they were removed from the consolation of true religion. My investigation has shown, as was proper it should, that death and a thirst for bloodshed prevailed during the time in which the religion that forbids bloodshed was unknown; that as the new faith dawned, the old grew faint; that while the old neared its end, the new was already victorious; that the old beliefs will be dead and gone when the new religion shall reign alone.

And yet, as Orosius planned his world history, he had a sense of something different from an apology for Christianity. The first book begins with a sketch of geography, sufficiently precise for the modern scholar to map it. Then he arranges history in chronological parallels, following the lead which we have traced in preceding chapters. The history of antiquity begins with Ninus. His realm is overthrown by the Medes in the same year in which the history of Rome begins with Procas. From the first year of Ninus' reign until the rebuilding of Babylon by Semiramis there are sixty-four years; the same between the first of Procas and the building of Rome. Eleven hundred and sixty-four years after each city is built it is captured—Babylon by Cyrus, Rome by Alaric; and Cyrus' conquest took place just when Rome became a Republic. But between Babylon and Rome, the empires of East and West, two others of the South and North, Carthage and Macedon, came into the scene as guardians of Rome's youth, "bridging as it were the space of years between an aged father and a little son."

The scheme of the four monarchies was sufficiently familiar to his readers that he did not have to base so rational an arrangement as this one upon the apocalyptic visions of Daniel, which would have been a most unconvincing source for pagans. It is also significant that Orosius refrains from adding the fifth sovereignty, that of Christendom, to this statement of what seemed like plain history. Within a framework readily acceptable, he then detailed the story of war and suffering. As it was his aim to show that the world had improved since the coming of Christ, he used histories written to exalt Roman triumphs to point out the reverse of victory—disaster and ruin. Among his sources—which in the haste of composition (if that was the reason) he used none too accurately—were Justin for the ancient empires of the Near East; Eutropius, whose summary he used almost entire for Roman history to the time of Augustus; Suetonius and Eutropius for the later period, along with material from almost a dozen others. All these were plundered for the story of horrors or for the stage which was the setting of that story, until finally even the Goths and Vandals must shine by contrast with the pagan heroes. Indeed, against the dark background of the past, the history of his own day, that in which the Empire was being overrun by the barbarians, seemed to him to offer nothing to controvert his theory that the City of Man as embodied in the Roman Empire was still capable of regeneration.

After the account of the "warfare among the barbarian nations now being carried on daily in Spain" he sums up the long, tragic, and sordid tale in these words:

> In view of these things I am ready to allow Christian times to be blamed as much as you please, if you can only point to any equally fortunate period from the foundation of the world to the present day. My description, I think, has shown not more by words than by my guiding finger, that countless wars have been stilled, many usurpers destroyed, and the most savage tribes checked, confined, incorporated, or annihilated with little bloodshed, no real struggle, and almost without loss. It remains for our detractors to repent of their endeavors, to blush on seeing the truth, and to believe, to fear, to love, and to follow the one true God, Who can do all things and all of Whose acts (even those that they have thought evil) they have found to be good.

In this note of optimism, with which the book closes, there is no suggestion of the fact that it is the last act of the drama of the antique world which he is watching. The realism of the secular spirit is lacking, but then, there were pagan literary circles in which it was also lacking at the time, and the belief of Orosius that the barbarians would in time become Romanized and Christianized was, after all, closer to the spirit of the time than the pessimism of Salvian, whose work on the *Government of God* (*De gubernatione Dei*) written about a quarter of a century later, presented a picture of depravity and corruption in the Gaul of his day, from which only one conclusion could be drawn, that the old civilization was definitely doomed. As the translator of Orosius has indicated, Orosius' mind still functions in the antique world, that of Salvian in the Middle Ages.

So the City of God found its setting in history. That to the Middle Ages the setting was not unworthy was evidenced by the fact that nearly two hundred manuscripts of Orosius have survived. The freely rendered and abridged translation by King Alfred is one of the monuments of Anglo-Saxon. Thin and inaccurate as it was when judged by either antique or modern standards, it at least preserved some knowledge of the world that lay outside the scriptures for those who sought—not always successfully—to cherish a livelier interest in the world to come and a keener sense of its reality than in mere human affairs. Thus the drama of profane history might edify the faithful, when rewritten by a disciple of Augustine, and yet, like the mystery plays, it never wholly edged its way behind monastic or cathedral doors, where, through continuing wars and tribulations, the City had established its peace.

It is fitting that this chapter should end with the scholar whose text of the Bible is recited yet in every service of the Catholic Church, Jerome (*Hieronymus*). For the Vulgate was, as we have already said, the greatest and most used of all histories in Christendom. Illiterate priests used it stumblingly in their services and Schoolmen stopped their speculations on its sacred frontiers. Neither Luther's text nor the King James version, masterly as they are, can compare with the historic achievement of this greatest of the scholars of the Latin Church. It is not until our own time that the Holy See has ventured to bring out a revision, and, in spite of the competence of the commission in

The City of God

charge, drawn from many lands, the text has taken shape but slowly and is just beginning to appear; that of Jerome still is read in the churches.

We have already seen in "The Formation of the Canon" how Jerome set to work upon this great task, turning aside from the texts which Origen had collected (the *Hexapla*) to Hebrew texts, thinking, mistakenly as it turns out, that they were older than those behind the Septuagint. This meant that his text varied from versions then in use, and he threw back upon the Jewish rabbis, who worked for and with him, the defense of the accuracy of his version. We must leave to biblical criticism, that superlative combination of textual and historical analysis, to trace the varied threads that were woven into the texture of the Bible in the Latin text of Jerome. But that criticism, which is the modern counterpart of Jerome's effort and which belongs with the history of history in our own day, offers no such dramatic episodes as that of Jerome writing from his cell at Bethlehem.

Hieronymus, whom we know as Jerome, was born in a town on the border of Dalmatia about 340. He was therefore slightly older than Augustine, whose tastes for Roman literature he shared to the full. Like Augustine too, he did not turn to the religious life until he was some thirty years old; but his impetuous and ardent nature carried him, not to the episcopate, with all its worldly responsibilities, but to the hermit life as practiced by the monks of Syria in lonely cells, half-starved, with bodies racked with suffering and scorched by the desert sun, but studying or copying the Scriptures in the intervals of their meditation. Jerome became the classic defender of this monastic life, and it is a sufficient commentary on the age in which he lived that he was able to make of such a crude monastic refuge as that in which he lived at Bethlehem an outstanding centre for scholarly research of his day.

Though apparently so isolated from the world, Jerome was, however, kept in touch both with what was going on in the church generally and with the drift of secular events by his correspondence and other writings. His comment on the sack of Rome in 410, in which his disciple and friend, the aged Marcella, had been tortured and killed, had the following poignant note (Preface to the *Commentary on Ezekiel*):

> No doubt all things born are doomed to die, and that which hath grown to maturity must grow old. Every work of man is attacked by decay, and destroyed by age. But who would have believed that Rome, victorious so oft over the universe, would at length crumble in pieces, the mother at once and the grave of her children? She who made slaves of the East has herself become a slave, and nobles once laden with riches come to little Bethlehem to beg. In vain I try to draw myself away from the sight by turning to my books. I am unable to heed them.

It is when one compares this passionate outburst with the calmness of Augustine that one realizes the distance between the outlook of the scholarly monk and the magisterial bishop.

Jerome's interests were more personal than abstract. One of his earlier works (written in 391) was *De viris illustribus sive de scriptoribus ecclesiasticis*, a church history in biographies ending with the life of the author. Taking Suetonius as a model, he covered one hundred and thirty-five biographies from the earliest Christian writers to his own day. It was a compendium designed to show that Christianity had its important scholars and literary men, written by one who had at heart a keen appreciation of their pagan counterparts.

Next in importance, however, to the Vulgate from the standpoint of historiography was the translation of Eusebius' *Chronicle* which he wrote in 380, the year after he was ordained a priest. The research for this work was carried on at Constantinople, where, under the tutelage of the great scholar, Gregory of Nazianzus, he sought to perfect himself in Greek. The substance of this *Chronicle* has been discussed above; our interest in it here is that in it we have the prototype upon which the monastic chronicles of the Middle Ages ultimately aspired to build their lesser narratives. With it, therefore, we pass definitely over to mediaeval historiography; but, in doing so, we are reminded at the end of our long survey of how from early Egypt down, the mathematics of time reckoning underlay any adequate control of the perspectives of the past. It is not without significance that the *Chronicle* was a product of Jerome's stay in Constantinople,

The City of God

the city which became the refuge of scholarship in the Dark Age. But even more significant is the fact, which seems to have escaped attention, that the Byzantine chronographers failed to produce history worthy of their opportunity. Perhaps the conclusion is that Byzantine society, like the Chinese, lost the sense of progress in the maintenance of stilted form and recurrent routine. History, it would seem, flourishes best where history is being made and is the mirror of those things which give life its meaning.

INDEX

INDEX

Absolute, the, of Hegel, 28, 29
Ab urbe condita (Livy), excerpt, 293 ff.
Abydos, lists of royal names, 77
Acceptance, attitude of, 43
Acusilaus of Argos, 155, 175, 257
Adam myth (Babylonian), 91
Aegyptica (supposed work of Hellanicus), 175
Aeneid (Vergil), 264 ff.
Aetiological legend, 49-50
Africanus (Sextus), Julius, 85; *Chronographia*, 349
Against Apion (Josephus), 138n, 148, 153, 154; excerpt, 154-57
Agricola (Tacitus), 302
Album of the Regia, 272
Alexandria, library, 55-56, 87, 245
Alfred, King, translation of Orosius, 374
Allegories of the Sacred Laws, The (Philo), excerpt, 146
Allegory, and the contribution of Origen, 336-46; use by Philo Judaeus, 146; not a creation of Christian historians, 337
Alphabet, 51, 54, 59; objection to, 244; a work of art, 245
Altars and holy places, 113, 119
Ambrose, Saint, 366
Ammianus Marcellinus, 255, 320-21
Amon, temple of, records and inscriptions at, 84
Anabasis (Xenophon), 216
Analogies, use of in anthropology, 39
Ancestral cult of Rome, 270
Ancient Records of Egypt (Breasted), 83
Andronicus, Livius, *see* Livius Andronicus
Animism, 40
Annales (Ennius), 263
Annales (Licinius Macer), 279
Annales (Tacitus), 273, 317, 320, 326; excerpts, 306, 307, 309, 311 n, 312

Annales Maximi, 258, 271 ff.
Annals, 61-62, 130, 283; mediaeval, 11, 353 ff., 362; Egyptian, 78 ff.; Assyrian, 68, 93 ff.; Jewish, 109, 129-30; Roman, 257-58, 271 ff.
Anthropology, 13, 36, 282; comparative method, 38-40, 49 n, 116 n
Antias, Quintus Valerius, 279
Antiochus, 156
Antiochus Epiphanes, 138, 149
Antipater, L. Coelius, 278-80
Antiquarian research, when historical, 8
Antiquarians, Roman, lack historical discipline, 281
Antiquities of the Jews, The (Josephus), 148, 149, 152, 153; excerpt, 151
Antonius, Marcus, 257 ff.
Apion, 148 n
Apocalypse, 331 n
Appian of Alexandria, 249, 318
Aratus of Sicyon, 232
Archaeologia (Dionysius), 248
Archaeology, field of history enlarged by, 36 ff.; reading history from ruins, 74
Aristotle, 9, 22, 161; *Natural History*, 169; *The Constitution of Athens*, 227-29; *Metaphysics*, 228; *Poetics*, 228; regard for documentary sources and emphasis upon fact, 228; influence upon historians, 243
Armageddon, 83
Arminius, Tacitus' reference to, 311 n
Arrangement, in historical writing, 198 n
Arrian of Bithynia, 250, 318
Artaxerxes Mnemon, 100
Arval priests at Rome, 45
Asellio, P. Sempronius, 274 n, 278
Assurbanipal, 94; library of, 53, 55, 94
Ashur-nasir-pal III, 95; curse of, quoted, 95
Assyria, library, 53, 55, 94; astronomy, 67; list of kings, 68; naming of years, 70; records, 93-98

Astrology, 65, 68, 331 n
Astronomical cycle, 71
Astronomy, 65; Babylonian, 67
Astruc, Jean, 141
Atthis (Hellanicus), 175
Attic Nights (Aulus Gellius), 318
Atticus, T. Pomponius, outline of universal history, 283
Augustine, Bishop of Hippo (Saint Augustine), 140, 366; *City of God* (*Civitas Dei*), 23, 282, 361, 364-77; *Confessions*, 133, 366; stirred by story of Dido, 264; ridicule of Varro, 282; conception of church, 361; greatest Father of the Church, 366; shortcomings of *City of God* from historical point of view, 367, 369; its occasion and plan of work, 367; treatment of sack of Rome, 369; quoted, 370
Augustus, 72 n, 149 n, 248, 264, 265, 274, 292, 296
Aulus Gellius, *see* Gellius, Aulus
Aurelius Victor, *see* Victor, Sextus Aurelius
Autobiography (Josephus), 148, 149, 151, 153

Babylon and Babylonia, media for writing, 52; first inscriptions, 60; monograms of names, 60; clear sky, and its effect in aiding astronomy, 66; calendar, 67, 68; Mother of Astronomy, 67; naming of years, 70; records, 88-103; libraries, 88; myths, 89; date-lists, 92
Babylonian King Lists A and B, 92
Babylonica (Berossos), 101; excerpt, 102
Behistun Rock, 98; quotation from inscription, 99
Belshazzar, 98
Bergson, Henri, 17, 33
Berossos, 158; *Babylonica* or *Caldaica*, 101; excerpt, 102
Bible, 107-41; early codices, 57; results of higher criticism, 107, 109, 135; first historical work of genuinely national importance, 107; a collection of books, 109; origin of texts, translations, 139; Jerome's translation, 139, 140, 374; textual criticism, 141; allegorical method of interpretation, 349; *Vulgate*, 374; *see also* New Testament *and* Old Testament
Bibliotheca historica (Diodorus Siculus), 247
Biblos, 54, 55 n
Biography, when historical, 7; from Suetonius to Ammianus Marcellinus, 316-21; concentration upon individuality, to exclusion of social or political view, 316
Board tablets, 53
Boissier, G., 302; quoted, 313 n; on Suetonius' *Lives*, 317
Bolingbroke, H. St. John, Viscount, rationalistic attack upon theology, 25
Books and writing, 51-62; Sophocles' objection to, 244
Books of the Magistrates, 274
Breasted, J. H., 69; *Ancient Records of Egypt*, 11, 83
Brutus, Marcus Junius, 280
Brutus (Cicero), 283
Buckle, H. T., 34; *History of Civilization in England*, 31
Bury, J. B., 214; quoted, 181, 215
Byzantine chronographers, 377

Cadmus of Miletus, 155, 170
Caesar, Augustus (C. Julius Caesar Octavianus), *see* Augustus
Caesar, C. Julius, 219; decree fixing days in year, 71; *Commentaries*, 285
Caldaica (Berossos), 101; excerpt, 102
Calendar, invention of, 63; time divisions, 64; development, 65; lunar, 67; *Fasti* the basis for making, 274
Calendar of Numa, 66
Callias, 156
Callisthenes, 258
Canon of Old Testament, formation of, 136-41
Canon of Ptolemy, 68, 69
Capital (Marx), 32
Carlyle, Thomas, 3, 9, 47
Cassiodorus, preserved classics in *Historia tripartita*, 363
Cassius Dio Coccejanus, *see* Dion Cassius
Cassius Longinus, C., 292
Catiline (Sallust), excerpt, 286
Cato, M. Porcius, 257, 279; real father

Index

Cato, M. Porcius (*Continued*)
of Roman history, 276; *Origines*, 276, 278; neglect of, in Cicero's day, 277, 278; Cicero's defense of, 277
Celsus, challenged sources of Christian tradition and scripture, 327; attack upon Christianity, 342
Censorinus, 69 n
Chaldaean Empire, 97
Charon of Lampsacus, 174
Christ, pagan evidence for life of, 153
Christian epic, 11
Christian Fathers, *see* Fathers of the Church
Christian historian not free to question data as presented, 333
Christian historiography, chief early developments, 335; weakness, 336; Origen's contribution to, 339
Christian history, evolution of material, 347
Christianity, interpretation of history, 22-25; thought underlying apologetic theology, 23; rationalistic attack upon, 25; attitude toward scriptures, 139; and history, 325-77; the new era, 325-35; stimulated little historical investigation, 326; references to, in pagan writers, 326 n; problem of fitting it into Jewish and into Gentile setting, 327; faith the chief intellectual demand, 327; rests essentially on historical basis, 336; relation to Judaism, 336; attempt to harmonize with cults of paganism, 341; paucity of sources for history of, 343
Chronicle, 61, 92 ff., 129-30, 247 n, 347 ff.
Chronicle (St. Jerome), 266
Chronicles, book of, 130, 132
Chronographers, Greek, 247 n
Chronographia (Julius Africanus), 349
Chronology, historical facts part of time, 16; measuring of time, 63-73; calendar, 64; Egyptian, 69 ff., 77 ff.; Biblical, 126, 353 n; absences of exact, a handicap of antique historians, 205; Greek Olympiads, 226, 228; Jewish and Christian history made credible by exhaustive treatment of, 346; and church history, 347-63; Christian, basis of study of, 348;

Chronographia of Julius Africanus, 349
Church Fathers, *see* Fathers of the Church
Church history and chronology, 347-63
Cicero, Marcus Tullius, 57, 215, 223 n, 240, 246, 255, 289; *On the Nature of the Gods*, 21; quoted, 225 n, 259, 270, 271; *On the Orator*, 256; excerpt, 257; on reasons for mediocrity of Roman history writing, 258; on Cato, 277; *Brutus*, 283
City of God, the, or *Civitas Dei* (Augustine), 23, 364-77; ridicule of Varro, 282; occasion and plan of work, 367
Clay, medium for writing, 52, 88
Cnossus, 161, 162, 205
Codex, parchment, 57-58
Codification of documents, 92
Commentaries (Caesar), 285
Commentarii pontificum, 272
Communist manifesto, 32
Confessions (Augustine), 133, 366
Consensus fidelium on scriptures, 138, 139
Constantine, at Council of Nicaea, 351; acts as patron of Eusebius, 351, 356, 360; Christianity triumphs under, 361
Constantine, Life of (Eusebius), 360
Constantinople, refuge of scholarship in Dark Age, 377
Constitution of Athens, The (Aristotle), 227
Controversy, dominating note in all patristic literature, 366
Copernicus, 24
Cornford, F. M., *Thucydides Mythistoricus*, 207 n; excerpt, 209, 210
Crassus, Lucius Licinius, 256-57
Creation, myth of, 89, 115; excerpt, 90; date of, 349 n; line drawn back to, 365
Credulity, 43; faith puts premium upon, 328
Criticism, historical, 3; dawn of, in Greece, 20, 166-70; religion blocks way to, 89, 333; capacity of Herodotus, 189
Cromwell, Oliver, 5
Ctesias of Cnidus, *Persica*, 100
Cuneiform inscriptions, 88, 99

Customs of the Barbarians, The (Hellanicus?), 175
Cycle, 71-73

D (Deuteronomist, the), 119
Darius the Great, 167, 180 ff., 191 n; Behistun inscription, 98; excerpt, 99
Darwin, Charles, 7, 34
Date-lists, Babylonian, 92
David, and the Psalms, 107, 138; story of, 126, 127, 128
Days, 64, 65
De gubernatione Dei (Salvian), 374
Deists, attack upon theology, 25
De rerum natura (Lucretius), 266; excerpts, 268, 269
Deuteronomist, the, 119, 125
Deuteronomy, book of, 119, 120 n
De viris illustribus (St. Jerome), 319, 338, 376
Diaspora, scholars of, use of allegory, 337; their work the basis of study of Christian chronology, 348
Diodorus Siculus, 72 n, 224 n, 247-48
Diogenes Laertius, 228
Dion Cassius, 250, 255, 318
Dionysius of Halicarnassus, 234 n, 248-49
Dionysius of Miletus, 174
Diptych, 53 n
Dispensation, special, 334
Divinity, miracle as mark of, 117
Draco, laws of, 156
Drawings, prehistoric, 38

E (Elohist), 116 n
E (Ephraimistic), 116 n
Eclipses, 276
Economic interpretation of history, 15, 21, 31, 33, 209
Education, gain through entertainment, 221; propagation of knowledge, 221 f.
Egypt, 66; writing materials, 52, 54; libraries, 55; monograms of names, 60; calendar, 69; naming of years, 72; annals, 74-87; royal annals, 75, 77; absence of history, 75; scribes, 75; treasured myth and legend, 76; Hecataeus' interview with priests, 170
Elohim, 116
Elohist account, Old Testament, 116

Elohists, responsibility for ten commandments, 118
Ennius, *Annales*, 263
Entertainment in historical writing, 221
Environment, influences upon society, 30; influence of mind over, 31
Ephorus, 156, 161, 224, 225 n, 229, 258
Epics, 46; *see also* Christian epic, Gilgamesh; Homer; Vergil
Epitomes, 319
Eponym Canon, 93
Era of Enlightenment, 26
Eratosthenes, 73 n; chronology, 73, 247
Esarhaddon, 94
Eumenes II, 56
Eusebius of Caesarea, 85, 101, 102, 347-63; account of Origen, 339; quoted, 344 n, 361; worked out chronology of the world, 350; Father of Church History, 350, 352; influences upon, 351, 352; *Chronicle*, 352 ff.; *Church History (Ecclesiastical History)*, 352, 356 ff.; excerpts, 358, 359; Jerome's translation of *Canons*, 354, 355 n; *Life of Constantine*, 360
Eutropius, 320
Evidence for assigning authorship, 137
Ezekiel, 129 n, 136
Ezra, book of, 131, 132

Fabius, Pictor, Q., 236, 257, 263, 279; first Roman historian, 275
Fabrication, process of, 114
Facts and processes the stuff of history, 34
Faith, the chief intellectual demand of Christianity, 327; an impediment to genuine history, 328
Fasti, basis of calendarmaking, 274
Fasti calendares, 272
Fasti consulares, 272
Father of History (Herodotus), 185
Fathers of the church, formative influence in history of thought, 327; read new meaning into historical data, 334; obliged to work out scheme of chronology, 335; use of allegory and symbolism, 335; influence of Philo upon, 338 n; historiography among Greek Fathers, 362; mightiest army of propaganda ever marshalled, 365; Ambrose, Jerome, Gregory, Augustine, 366

Index

Feuerbach, Ludwig Andreas, historical interpretation, 29, 31
Five Books of Moses, *see* Pentateuch
Flood myth, 91, 115
Folk tales, 48, 49, 50; Homeric poems, 163
Foundation of Miletus, The, 171
From the Foundation of the City, Ab urbe condita (Livy), 293 ff.
Froude, James A., *Henry VIII,* 10

Galba, biographies, 316
Galileo, 24
Gellius, Aulus, quoted, 276; *Attic Nights,* 318
Gemara, the, 143
Genealogies (Hecataeus), 171, 175
Genesis, mythological versions, 41, 90; authorship of biblical, 122; acceptance by western world, 123
Geographers, Herodotus' scorn for, 174; Polybius' distrust of, 238
Geography (Posidonius), 246
Geography (Strabo), 247
Germania (Tacitus), 302, 311
Germanicus, death, 312
German nations, had no interest in antique past, 365
Gibbon, Edward, 10, 26; quoted, 321
Gilgamesh, myth-epic of, 91, 188
Gnosticism, 340
Goethe, Johann Wolfgang von, 47
Gospels, origin of the, 328 n
Government of God (Salvian), 374
Great Rebellion, Jewish, 148
Greece, dawn of critical thought in, 20, 166-70; writing materials, 53; libraries, 55; chronology, 68, 71, 226; naming of years, 72; epochs of history, 73; contact with Jews, 145; influence upon Rome, 261; *see also* Greek history and historians
Greek chronographers, 247 n
Greek history and historians, 161-251; beginnings of history, 8, 20; Homer and the Homeric world, 161; Hesiod, 164; history blocked by poetic material, 165; use of terms, "historia," "inquiry," 168; *logos,* 170; prose beginnings, 170; Hecataeus, founder of historical writing, 171-75; Herodotus, 177-92; use of speeches in historical narrative, 192, 201, 210, 219, 224; Thucydides, 193-213; Xenophon, 214-18; trio of greatest historians, 214; rhetoricians and scholars, 214, 218-29; Polybius, 230-41; later historians, 242-51; their detached position, 242; seek guide to a way of life in history, 251; development of historiography, 257
Greek Old Testament, 140
Greek oratory, 219, 223
Gregory of Nazianzus, 376
Gregory the Great (Pope Gregory I), 366; use of symbolism, 345
Guide to Historical Literature, A, 381

Hadrian, 318
Hagiographa, 137
Hammurabi, 88; code of, 92
Hatshepsut, Queen, 77
Hebrews, *see* Jews
Hebrew scriptures, *see* Bible; Old Testament
Hecataeus of Miletus, 170 n; founder of historical writing among the Greeks, 171-75; attitude of Herodotus toward, 172; interview with Egyptians, 172; faulty generalizations, 174
Hegel, Georg Wilhelm Friedrich, 31, 34; philosophy of, 28
Hellanicus of Lesbos, 156, 175, 205, 226 n, 257
Hellenica (Theopompus), 225
Hellenica (Xenophon), 216, 217
Hellenica Oxyrhynchia, 225 n
Herder, Johann Gottfried von, 48
Herodotus, 4, 10, 11, 57, 85, 147, 150, 156, 170 n, 175, 239, 258, 296, 325; an investigator and explorer, 8; describes the papyrus, 54; composed history for public recitation, 55; his text on papyrus, 56; impressions of Empires of Asia, 100; interest in the origin of human society, 122; use of comparative method, 123; first political historian, 166; extent of inquiries, 169; attitude toward Hecataeus, 172; attitude of critical superiority, 174; wins place for history in arts and sciences, 176; the man and his background, 177; prejudice against Ionians, 177; education and travels, 178; *History,* 179; work of, appraised, 180 ff.; modernity, 182, 185; style, 183, 192; sources, 184, 191; the Father of His-

Herodotus (*Continued*)
  tory, 185; attempt to understand achievement of, 186; researches in Phoenicia illustrate scientific method, 188, 190; critical capacity and reliability, 189; Thucydides, opinion of, 190, 193; religious belief, 192
Heroic legend, 49, 50
Hesiod, 156, 164-65, 168; *Works and Days*, 66, 164
Hexapla (Origen), 140 n
Hexateuch, 113, 124, 136
Hieroglyphs, 37 n, 38, 52, 76
Hieronymus, *see* Jerome
Higher criticism, of Bible, 107, 109, 135; of Talmud, 143
Hissarlik, 161
Historia, term used only of contemporaneous narrative, 274
Historiae (Tacitus), 274, 302, 309, 311, 316, 320
Historiae Philippicae (Pompeius Trogus), 284
Historians, masters of style, 3, 10; Buckle's opinion of, 31; first political, 166; Greek founder of historical writing, 171; "Father of History," 185; Thucydides the greatest of antiquity, 196, 201, 209; trio of greatest Greeks, 214; of antiquity were writers of modern history, 325
Historia tripartita, Cassiodorus preserved classics in, 363
Historia tripartita (Victor), 319
Historical data, Paul's indifference to, 328
Historical Memoirs (Strabo), 247
Historiography, term, 4
History, lack of historians, 3; need of scientific criticism, 3; as a branch of literature, 3, 9; two meanings, 4; in the objective sense, 5; historical attitude toward, 7; dawn of criticism in Greece, 8, 20, 166-70; origin and meaning of term, 8; the art, 9, 11; the science, 10; prescientific origins, 11; interpretations, 14-35; economic, 15, 21, 31, 33, 209; mythological, 17; theological, 22, 33; metaphysical, 27, 33; philosophic, 20, 26, 235, 243-45; materialistic, 29, 33; field enlarged by archaeology, 36 ff.; prehistoric, 36-50; distinction between prehistory and, 37; writing, 37, 38 n, 51-62; earliest books, 54-62; measuring of time, 63-73; annals, Egyptian, 74-87; Babylonian, 88-103; Assyrian, 93-98; Persian, 98-100; Jewish history, 107-58; rearranged by theologians, 126, 134; Greek, 161-251; development hindered by poetry, 165; use of term by Greeks, 168; prose beginnings, 170; insertion of speeches in narrative of, 192, 201, 210, 219, 224; arrangement as argument, 198 n; absence of exact chronology, 205; rhetoric and scholarship, 214, 218-24; entertainment a purpose in, 221; two great creative epochs of civilization, 246; Roman, 255-321; needs an apparatus for investigation, 256; a social product, 256; reflects major interests of society, 277; an aid to statesmen and orators, 259, 260; highest function according to thinkers of antiquity, 314; the epitome, 319; ending of great age of antique historiography, 319; dominated by Christian point of view, 365; *City of God* furnished plans according to which it should be written, 367
History (Herodotus), 179 ff.
History (Posidonius), 246
History of Civilization in England (Buckle), 31
History of the Peloponnesian War (Thucydides), 193-213
History of history, phrase, 3; revolution in, reached culmination in works of Augustine and Jerome, 364
Holy days, 66
Homer, 20, 41, 46, 47; and the Homeric world, 161-64; *Iliad*, 162, 163 n, 164, 168; *Odyssey*, 163 n, 164; myths challenged, 168, 171; influence upon Herodotus, 178; interpreted allegorically, 337
Hours, 64
Humanity, history limited to, 7, 16; the future a reality through, 330
Hume, David, 26, 34
Hyksos, the, 86

Idea, the, of Kant, 27, 28
Idealism, objection to mechanism, 244
Iliad (Homer), 162, 163 n, 164, 168

Index

Immortality, influence of belief in, 329
Impending event, destroys interest in past, 329
Individuality, concentration of interest upon, 316
Industrial Revolution, Marx as interpreter of, 32, 34
Inquiry, use of term by Greeks, 168
Inscriptions, 37; earliest, 60; survival, 74-75; Egyptian, 77 ff.; cuneiform, 88; Babylonian, 88, 92 ff.; Assyrian, 93 ff.; Chaldaean, 97-98; Persian, 98 ff.; used by Greek and Roman historians, 271 n; Cicero's study of, 276
International Bibliography of Historical Sciences, 382
Interpretation of history, 14-35 (see entries under History)
Ionians, originate term "history," 8; dawn of critical thought, 20, 166-70; logographers, 20, 170; Herodotus' prejudice against, 177
Isocrates, 217, 218, 225; influence, 223; school of oratory, 223 n
Israel, story of, an incident in drama of nations, 332

J (Jahvist), 116 n
Jackson, A. V. W., quoted, 98
Jahresberichte der Geschichtswissenschaft, 382
Jahveh, 115 ff., 127
Jahvist, the, 115 ff.
JE, 119
Jerome, Saint, 319, 326, 364, 366; translation of Bible, 139, 140; *Chronicle*, 266; *De viris illustribus*, 319, 338, 376; tribute to Origen from, 338; translations from Eusebius, 354, 355 n; Vulgate edition of Bible, 374; life, 375; comment on sack of Rome from *Commentary on Ezekiel*, 376
Jerusalem, temple at, 119, 122, 127
Jerusalem Talmud, 143
Jesus Christ, pagan evidence for life of, 153
Jews, Josephus' attempt to prove Hyksos were, 86; history of, 107-58; Old Testament, 107-35; royal annals, 130; formation of the canon, 136-41; non-biblical literature, 142-58; Talmud, 142; prophetic literature, 144; under influence of Hellenic civilization, 145; contribution of Philo Judaeus, 145; of Flavius Josephus, 148; Great Rebellion, 148; seek guide to a way of life in history, 251; sacred writings of, the only history of importance to Christians, 331; replace literature of antiquity, 332; story of, an incident in drama of nations, 332; Messianic doctrine, 334; use of allegory, 337; rabbis worked with Jerome, 375
John the Baptist, 153
Josephus, Flavius, 102, 140; fragments of Manetho's work preserved by 85; excerpt, 86; *Against Apion*, 138 n; writings, 148-58; life, 148; one of greatest historians of ancient world, 153; value to Christians in *Testimonium Flavianum*, 153
Joshua, book of, 113, 124
Judaism, references to, in pagan writers, 326 n; relation to Christianity, 336; see also Jews
Judas Maccabaeus, 133
Judges, book of, 125, 126, 127
Judgment Day, 329, 331
Jugurthine War (Sallust), 286; excerpt, 287
Julius Africanus, see Africanus, Julius
Justinus, M. Junianus, 284, 319
Justus of Tiberias, 152, 348

Kant, Immanuel, 26, 28, 34
Karnak, lists of royal names, 77
Kingdom, the, see Messianic kingdom
King lists, 60, 68, 77, 85, 92, 94
Kings, book of, 126, 128

Laqueur, Richard, 152, 153 n
Latin literature, two outstanding figures, 255; history of history in miniature, 259; poetry, 263 ff.; chief aim, exaltation of the state, 264; prose more directly under Greek influence than poetry, 271; decline in, 318
Law (Torah), Jewish, 111, 121 n; canon framed, 138; see also Pentateuch
Leather, medium for writing, 52, 54
Leaves, medium for writing, 52
Legends, a bridge from myth to history, 46; extent and reliability, 48; types, 49; Egyptian, 77; of Old Testament,

Legends (*Continued*)
113, 127; classification, 114 n; Roman, 262
Letters, *see* Alphabet
Libraries, Babylonia-Assyria, 53, 55, 88, 94; Egypt, Greece, Rome, 55; at Alexandria, 55, 245; Pergamum, 56
Libri magistratuum, 274
Libri pontificum, 272
Licinius Macer, C., *Annales*, 279
Lightfoot, John, 349 n
Literature, history as a branch of, 3, 9
Lives (Plutarch), 249
Lives of the Caesars, The (Suetonius), 317
Livius Andronicus, 263
Livy (Titus Livius), 3, 4, 20, 219, 261, 274, 275, 291-300, 319, 325; patriotism, 291, 296, 297, 299; moral attitude, 292; *From the Foundation of the City* (*Ab urbe condita*), 295; excerpt, 293 ff., 296, 298, 299; inaccurate in geography, 297, 299; lacked principles of criticism, 298
Logographers, Ionian, 20, 167-76; Christian, 348
Logos, Greek, 170; Christian emphasis upon, 340
Lucretius, 21, 46, 266; *On the Nature of Things* (*De rerum natura*), 266; excerpts, 268, 269
Lucullus, L. Licinius, 285
Lunar calendar, 67
Lunar year, 70
Luni-solar cycle, 71
Luther, Martin, Hebrew Bible, 140

Macan, R. W., 181
Macaulay, Thomas Babington, *History of England*, 10; quoted, 210
Maccabees, 138, 143; books of, 133
Machiavelli, Niccolo, 34, 300
Malthus, Thomas Robert, 34
Manetho, 157; lists of pharaohs through the centuries, 85-87
Marcus Aurelius, 359
Marius Maximus, 318
Martyrs, Eusebius' feeling for, 361
Marx, Karl, *Misère de la philosophie*, 30; economic theory of history, 31; *Capital*, 32; interpreter of Industrial Revolution, 34

Materialistic interpretation of history, 29, 33
Materials for Research, Joint Committee, 59 n
Mathematics, measurement of time, 64, 65, 68; applied to history, 346
Mechanism, objection of philosophers to, 244; an art creation, 245
Megiddo, 83
Memorabilia (Xenophon), 216
Menes of Memphis, 60
Mensch ist was er isst, Der (Feuerbach), 29
Mesopotamian art of writing, 88
Message sticks, 51, 52
Messianic doctrine, one of most exclusive aspects of Jewish thought, 334, 336, 337 n; discarded by modern critical scholarship, 337
Messianic element in Christianity, 336
Messianic kingdom, 331
Metals, discovery and smelting of, 268
Metaphysical interpretation of history, 27, 33
Metaphysics (Aristotle), 228
Meton, astronomer, 71
Meyer, Eduard, 69, 201
Michelet, Jules, 10
Midrashim, 130 n
Millennium, 331 n
Minos, age of, 161 ff.
Miracle, of myth world, 41; of Bible, 117
Misère de la philosophie (Marx), 30
Mishnah, the, 143
Montanism, 331 n
Months, 64, 65
Monumental inscriptions used by historians, 271
Moon, generally earliest guide toward calendar, 67
Moral conduct, Old Testament, 118; history violated to justify, 134
Moses, 117, 120; "oral" law embodied in Talmud, 143; Greek system borrowed from, 163 n; similarities in Homer and, 164; of greater antiquity than Greek legend, 348
Mother of Astronomy (applied to Babylon) 67
Mystery, myth a realm of, 42; of written word, 136

Myths, defined, 17; role in history, 18; social origin and authorship, 40; term, 40 n; nature of, 41; common themes, 42; divine or supernatural element in, 44; development into legend, 46; Egyptian, 77; Babylonian, 89; of Old Testament, 113; Greek, challenged, 168, 171
Myth of Creation, 89; excerpt, 90

Nabonassar, 68-69, 101
Nabonidus, King, 97
Naevius, C., 263
Name, sacred character, 116
Name lists, ancient, 60, 68, 77, 85, 92, 94
Napoleon I, 15
Naram-Sin, 93
Narrative, earliest development, 61
Natural History (Aristotle), 169
Natural History (Pliny), 281
Natural law, 25, 26
Natural science vs. history, 6, 16
Nebuchadnezzar, 138
Nehemiah, book of, 131, 132
Neoplatonic mysticism, taught by Origen, 331 n
Nepos, Cornelius, 283
New Testament, evidence that apostles failed to study history adequately, 336; allegorical interpretation, 340; see also Bible
Nicholas of Damascus, 149, 248
Niebuhr, B. G., 256, 262 n, 291
Nine Books of Memorable Deeds and Sayings (Valerius Maximus), 260 n
Noah flood myth, 91
Noctes Atticae (Aulus Gellius), 318
Numa, Calendar of, 66
Numbers, mysterious efficacy of, 340
Numerianus, 318

Octaëteris, 71
Odyssey (Homer), 163 n, 164, 263
Old Testament, written on rolls of leather, 54; as history, 107-12; results of higher criticism, 107, 109, 135; style, 108; three main parts, 111; Prophets, 111, 137, 144; Pentateuch, 111, 113-23, 124; Joshua, 113, 124; authorship, 115, 124; Judges, 125, 126, 127; Samuel, 126, 128; Kings, 126, 128; Chronicles, 130, 132; Maccabees, 133; modification halted by sacredness of, 136; formation of the canon, 136-41; divine inspiration the test of inclusion, 137; number of books, 138 n; Septuagint, 140; source material for Josephus, 149; retention of, evidence that apostles studied history, 336; allegorical interpretation of, 337; supplied Christianity with authority of a long antiquity, 341
Olmstead. A. T., quoted, 97
Olympiads, Greek, 73, 226, 228, 355
On the Nature of the Gods (Cicero), 21
On the Nature of Things (Lucretius), 266; excerpts, 268, 269
On the Orator (Cicero), 256; excerpt, 257
Oracles, use by Herodotus, 191
Orators in Cicero's essays, 271
Oratory, Greek, 219, 223; Latin, 255 ff.; see also Speeches
Origen, *Hexapla*, 140; Neoplatonic mysticism taught by, 331 n; allegory and the contribution of, 336-46; greatest master of Christian allegory, 338; St. Jerome's tribute to, 338; modernism of, 340; *Against Celsus*, 342; quoted, 342; influence upon Eusebius, 351
Origin, myth of, see Creation
Origines (Cato), 276, 278
Origin of Species (Darwin), 34
Origins, prehistoric, 11
Orosius, Paulus, 29, 284, 370 ff.; *Seven Books of Histories against the Pagans*, excerpts, 371, 372, 373
Otho, biographies, 316
Outline of History (Wells), 284
Oxyrhynchus Papyri, 225 n

P (Priestly History), 121
Paganism, attempts to harmonize Christianity with cults of, 341
Pagan use of allegory, 337
Palaeography, 59
Palermo stone, 78-84; date, 78; described, 79; excerpt from, 81, 82, 83
Palimpsests, 57
Pamphilus of Caesarea, 351, 361
Panic of the Year 33, 309
Paper, lack of, 51; papyrus, 54; invention and early use, 58
Papyrus, 52, 54, 56, 57; dependence of classic literature upon, 245

Index

Parchment, 54, 56; codex, 57
Paul, Saint, indifference to historical data, 328, 334; the intellectual creator of Christian Theology, 328 n; allegorical interpretation of New Testament, 340
Pauline structure of theology, makes history subservient to religion, 364
Paulus, L. Aemilius, 231
Pelham, H. F., quoted, 299
Peloponnesian war, Thucydides' history of, 193-213; Xenophon's history of, 216
Pentateuch (Five Books of Moses), 111, 113, 124; authorship, 115-23; Philo's commentary on, excerpt, 146
Pergamum, library, 56; parchment from, 56
Persian records, 98-100
Persica, 174, 175
Persica (Ctesias), 100
Phaedrus (Plato), 223 n, 244
Pharaohs, lists of, 77, 85
Pherecydes, 155, 175, 257
Philip of Sides, *Christian History*, 362
Philippica (Theopompus), 225
Philistus of Syracuse, 156, 258, 277
Philo Judaeus, 145-148; *The Allegories of the Sacred Laws*, excerpt, 146; use of allegory, 338; influence upon Christian Fathers, 338 n
Philosophic interpretation of history, ancient, 20-23, 235, 243-45; modern, 26-31
Philosophy of history dominated by Christian point of view, 365
Philostorgius, *Church History*, 362
Phoenicia, writing materials, 54
Photius, 362
Photographing, devices for, 59 n
Photostating, 59 n
Picture writing, 51
Pisistratus, 156, 164
Piso, 257; death, 312
Plato, 216, 218; *Phaedrus*, 223 n, 244; *Republic*, 236; influence upon historians, 243; poetic mind, recoil from mechanism, 244
Plautus, T. Maccius, 275
Pliny the Elder, uncritical character of his *Natural History*, 281
Pliny the Younger, 302; quoted, 293 n

Plutarch, 326; a genuine historian, 249; *Lives*, 249; resemblance of work to that of Tacitus, 316
Poetic legend in Latin, 263 ff.
Poetics (Aristotle), 228
Poetry, Greek history in Homeric and other poems, 161-64; how development of history is hindered by, 165; Latin, 263 ff.
Poets, legends preserved by, 46
Politics, connection with economics, 21; main theme of history in antique world, 255
Polybius, 9, 20, 22, 23, 158, 169, 224, 255, 261, 275, 299, 325; attack upon Timaeus, 226, 237, 240; emergence from obscurity as historian's historian of antiquity, 230; life, 230; history of his world a scientific achievement, 231; analysis and appraisal of, 232 ff.; pragmatic character of work, 234, 241; method, 237; distrust of other scholars, 238; style, 239
Pompey, 285
Pontifex Maximus, 53, 257; annual events kept by, 271, 272
Porphyry, attack upon Origen, 344 n
Posidonius, 246
Prehistoric history, term, 36, 37
Prehistory, 11, 36-50; myth, 17, 40; distinction between history and, 37; legend, 46
Priestcraft and myths, 19
Priestesses of Hera (Hellanicus), 175
Priestly History, of Bible, 121
Priests, Christians as historians, 24; Old Testament, 120, 122
Primitive man, tendency to "animize" his world, 40; imagination, 41
Processes and facts the stuff of history, 34
Prolegomena ad Homerum (Wolf), 163
Propaganda, 221
Prophetic literature implies allegory, 340
Prophetism, 144
Prophets, books of, 111, 137, 144
Prose in history, 170
Psychology, interpretation by, 15
Ptolemy, Canon of, 68, 69
Pythagoras, 155

Quadrigarius, Q. Claudius, 279
Quintilian, 297

Index

Radin, Paul, 43 n
Ramses II, 77
Ranke, Leopold von, *Zeitgeist*, 27 ff., 239
Rationalistic conception of history, 25, 26
Rawlinson, Sir Henry, 99
Regia, 52, 271, 272
Regnal years, 70
Religion, relation to history, 16, 46 n; attitude of acceptance, 43; element in myths, 44; calendar as a cycle of feasts, 65; blocks way to science in ancient world, 89; influence upon history, 326 ff.; falsifies past in eyes of science, 333; *see also* Theology
Republic (Plato), 236
Rerum gestarum libri (Ammianus Marcellinus), 320
Rhetoric and scholarship, Greek, 214, 218-29
Rhetoricians, privilege of, to exceed truth of history, 260 n
Ricardo, David, 34
Ritual, 45
Roman annalists and early historians, 270-80
Roman Antiquities (Varro), 282
Roman history, 255-321; achievement disappointing, 255; groundwork of historical criticism, 262 n; annalists and early historians 270-80; tendency of nobles to exalt their deeds, one of the mainsprings of, 270; Varro, Caesar, and Sallust, 281-90; three best-known historians, 289; Livy, 291-300; Tacitus, 301-15; from Suetonius to Ammianus Marcellinus, 316-21
Roman literature, *see* Latin literature
Roman society in time of Tacitus, 304
Rome, writing materials, 53; libraries, 55; chronology, 71; naming of years, 72; Greek influence upon, 261; legends, 262; sack of, 273, 369; Jerome's comment on sack of, quoted, 376
Rousseau, Jean Jacques, *Social Contract*, 310
Royal name lists, 60, 68, 77, 85, 92, 94

Sacredness, 44
St. John, Henry, Viscount Bolingbroke, *see* Bolingbroke
Sakkara, lists of royal names, 77
Sallust (C. Sallustius Crispus), 286 ff.; *Catiline*, 286; excerpt, 286; *Jugurthine War*, 286; excerpt, 287; style, depiction of character, 289; weaknesses, 289
Salvian, *Government of God* (*De gubernatione Dei*), 374
Samuel, book of, 126, 128
Sargon I, 93
Scaevola, P. Mucius, 257, 273; ended old *Annales Maximi*, and published them, 278
Scholarship and rhetoric, Greek, 214, 218-29
Science, perspectives of, 6; a challenge to theological history, 24
Scientific historical criticism, *see* Criticism
Scientific history, 10
Scipio Aemilianus (P. Cornelius Scipio Aemilianus Africanus Minor), patron of Polybius, 229, 231, 235, 237
Scipio Africanus (P. Cornelius Scipio Africanus Major), friend of Ennius, 263
Scribes, Egyptian, 75
Scriptores historiae Augustae, 318
Scriptures, 137; interpretation by allegory, 340; *see also* Bible
Semites, calendar, 67
Sennacherib, 94
Septuagint, 140, 150
Servius, on pontifical annals, 272; quoted, 274 n
Sesostris I, 74
Seti I, 77
Seven Books of Histories against the Pagans (Orosius), excerpts, 371-73
Severus, Sulpicius, Bible story as it reached the Middle Ages, 345
Shalmaneser, 94
Sisenna, L. Cornelius, 279
Skepticism, historian needs to confine his imagination by, 328
Slaves, 285
Socialism, Marxian, 32
Society, myths created by, 18, 19; in Rome of Tacitus, 304
Socrates, 223 n, 363; "recollections" of Xenophon and Plato, 216; objection to alphabets and books, 244
Solar year, 65, 69

Index

Solomon, history developed at court of, 130
Sozomen, 363
Speeches, insertion into historical narrative, 192, 201, 210, 219, 224
Stesimbrotus, 175
Sticks, message, 51, 52
Stone, medium for writing, 52, 78, 93
Stonehenge, 38
Strabo, 247
Suetonius Tranquillus, C., 153 n, 255; life, 316; relation to Plutarch and Tacitus, 316; *The Lives of the Caesars*, 317
Sulla, Lucius Cornelius, 285
Sumerians, cuneiform inscriptions, 88; king lists, 92; tradition of origin, 101
Supernatural element, in myths, 19, 41, 44
Symbolism, 341; used by theologians, 338
Symbols the earliest writing, 60

Taboos, justified by myths, 19; in primitive worship, 44
Tacitus, Cornelius, 4, 149, 150, 153 n, 249, 255, 301-15, 318, 325, 326; *Annales*, 273, 317, 320, 325, 326; excerpts, 306, 307, 309, 311 n, 312; *Historiae*, (*Histories*), 274, 302, 309, 311, 316, 320; style, 301; *Germania*, 302, 311; *Agricola*, 302; in Asia, 303; effect of social prejudices, 304-5; compares his task with that of Livy, 307; failed adequately to describe Roman Empire, 308; references to business side of politics, 309; never saw his history as a whole, 310; use of oral sources, 311; written sources, 313; takes rank in forefront of world's historians, 314; resemblance of work to that of Plutarch, 316
Taine, Hippolyte, 292
Talmud, 142-44
Temple at Jerusalem, 119, 122, 127
Ten commandments, 118
Tertullian, 359-60
Testimonium Flavianum (Josephus), 153
Thales, 155
Thaneni, inscription on tomb of, 85
Theagenes of Rhegium, 337

Theodoret, 363
Theogony (Hesiod), 164
Theologians, Christian, use of symbolism, 338
Theology, interpretation of history, 22-25, 33; rationalistic attack upon, 25; rearranges history, 126, 134; and faith, 327; Christian, Paul the intellectual creator of, 328 n; creates barrier to investigation, 333; *see also* Religion
Theophanes of Mytilene, 285
Theopompus, 225, 229, 258
Thothmes III, 77; annals on Palermo stone, 83; daily record, 84
Thucydides, 3, 10, 21, 47, 72, 170 n, 171, 175, 180, 218, 239, 250, 256, 258, 259, 325; his history written, 55, 56; opinion of Herodotus, 190, 193; soberness, and consciousness of high theme, 193; *History of the Peloponnesian War*, 193 ff.; life and background, 193; work of appraised, 194 ff.; a modern historian, 195; the greatest historian of antiquity, 196, 201, 209; major shortcomings, 202; method of reckoning time, 205, 206 n; antique spirit, 206, 209, 210, 213; influence, 214; compared with Tacitus, 301, 308
Thutmose, *see* Thothmes
Tiberius, 309; crimes attributed to, 312
Tiglath-Peleser, 93, 94
Timaeus, 156, 226, 259; chronology, 73; Polybius' attack upon, 226, 237, 240
Time, historical facts part of, 7, 16; measuring of, 63-73; calendar, 64; *see also* Chronology
Torah, *see* Law
Travels around the World (Hecataeus), 171, 175
Trogus, Pompeius, *Historiae Philippicae*, 284
Troy, tale of siege, 162
Twelve-hour unit, 64

Universal history, attempt to carry over into Latin the scheme for, 284
Universal History (Nicholas of Damascus), 149 n
Ussher, Archbishop James, chronology, 349 n

Index

Valerius Antias, see Antias. Quintus Valerius
Valerius Maximus, *Nine Books of Memorable Deeds and Sayings*, 260 n
Varro, Marcus Terentius, 281 ff., 316; output, 281; *Roman Antiquities*, 282
Vellum, 57
Vergil (P. Vergilius Maro), 255; *Aeneid*, 264 ff.; religious quality of mind, 264
Vespasian, 148, 149
Victor, Sextus Aurelius, 319
Vita Caesarum, De (Suetonius), 317
Voltaire, François M. A. de, 19, 34; rationalistic attack upon theology, 25, 26

Wars of the Jews, The (Josephus), 148, 149, 150, 152
Wax tablets, 57
Weeks, 64, 72
Wells, H. G., *Outline of History*, 284
Will to believe, 18, 43, 264, 269, 328

Wolf, Friedrich August, *Prolegomena ad Homerum*, 163
Wood, medium for writing, 52
Words, secret value of, 340
Works and Days (Hesiod), 66, 164
Writers, controversy between Christian and pagan, 327
Writing, test for distinction between prehistory and history, 37, 38 n; materials for, 51-59; evolution of, 51, 59-62; cuneiform, 88; Sophocles' objection to, 244
Writings, Old Testament, 111, 137

Xenophanes, 168, 172
Xenophon, 258, 259; ancient and modern opinion of, 214; work of, appraised, 215 ff.; writings, 216-18; birth, 216; a disciple of Socrates, 216

Year, lunar, 70
Year, solar, 65, 69
Years, 64, 65; naming of, 70, 72